This Unholy War

Plowden and Rogers Family Letters
1852 - 1868

Edited by
Jean Lowery Wilson

Charleston, SC
www.PalmettoPublishing.com

This Unholy War

First Edition

Hardcover ISBN: 978-1-68515-052-5
Paperback ISBN: 978-1-68515-053-2

Introduction

Discovered in an antique trunk in an old barn, these three hundred plus letters were written during the Civil War era by Edwin Ruthvin Plowden, II, of Clarendon County, SC, and Harriet Rogers of Bishopville, SC, and by other family members and friends. Ruthvin was living near Brewington, the deep fork of Black River. A respected landowner and farmer, he was left with two young sons after his wife died in 1854. At age 35, he married Harriet, aged 19, in 1859.

Most of the early letters are from Harriet's father, siblings, and friends. With the advent of the war, Ruthvin joined the Wee Nee Volunteers and was stationed at Camp Harlee, and the letters from this period depict some surprising facts of everyday life in the camps. The couple's letters to each other during this time are especially endearing.

Exciting first-hand/eyewitness accounts of the great Charleston fire and the Star of the West are included here, as well as references to Columbia Female College, SC Lunatic Asylum, 1860 Democratic National Convention in Charleston, the Vigilant Society, the Great Awakening, camp meeting at Binnicker's Bridge, Warm Springs, Georgia, the tragic drownings at Boykin's Mill, Negroes being whipped for "frolic," Robert Smalls, Zouaves, Morris Island, and Potter's Raid, among others.

The later letters reflect great tragedy and loss, but also evidence strong faith and total surrender to and dependence upon God throughout all of their trials.

Inspiring and fascinating, these faded epistles transport us back in time for fleeting glimpses of everyday life in rural South Carolina during the "War of Northern Aggression" and its surrounding years. This collection of letters is printed verbatim, to include the spellings and vernacular of the times. Any mistakes regarding companies, battles, and dates of the war in the footnotes are entirely my own.

Dedication

With grateful appreciation to the late Samuel "Edgar" Nelson, III, for his generosity and friendship, and to his ancestors, who preserved these priceless family letters; and to my beloved, patient husband, Tommy, without whose unwavering encouragement and support this book would never have been finished.

Epigram

"Love is patient, love is kind. It does not envy, it does not boast, it is not proud. It does not dishonor others, it is not self-seeking, it is not easily angered, it keeps no record of wrongs. Love does not delight in evil but rejoices with the truth. It always protects, always hopes, always perseveres."

I Corinthians 13:4-7 (NIV)

Table of Contents

The Earlier Years
1852–1860

Bishopville 25 Nov. 1852
My own dear Daughter[1]

Your very welcome letter to your dear mother was rec- last Tuesday, and that of your sister to Charles came the same day. We were much pleased dear Harriet to receive such a good letter from you, and so well written too. It is a great satisfaction to us to have such good daughters as you and Lucy to write to us, and we ought to be very thankful to our heavenly parent that he has given us such children and I hope we are–

I wrote a few lines to dear Lucy last Monday and stated that your Aunt Lucretia had come back from Marion with Daniel. She staid here until yesterday morning and then she and your mother went down to your Uncle Macks and in the Evening your Aunt Mack went with her to -?- and your mother went to your Aunt -?- and returned home last night. She says your Aunt Peggy had a bad chance for talking for Aunt L. kept ahead– your own dear mother is quite well for her, and has not looked better for a long time. Oh how glad it will make us all dear H. when you and your dear sister come home to stay with us.

Well, your aunt says that the Dr. is certainly to marry the widow Elerbe but your mother says she is not (I mean your mother) very willing for the match.

Well dear Harriet I cannot think of any news to write you. To day is a dull, cloudy, rainy day, and I expect my imagination is something like the weather dull like wise but I know that you are both glad to receive letters, though they may only inform you of our welfare. You inquired in your letter who it will be that will go for you and Lucy–Daniel will probably go. I presume he and David will both leave two weeks from next Tuesday, and will reach -?- on Wednesday. Tell your dear sister that I shall hope to receive a letter from her next Friday (tomorrow, and shall again hope to hear that all are well with you.

I might say that our friend W. B. Corbett is going to leave his place and go to Alabama. Wm. T. Kelly is also going and now having

1 Harriet, aged 13

nothing more to say this time I will close. Tell my dear Lucy that I will write to her in a few days and in the mean time we all send you both much love. I remain, my Daughter dear, your affectionate Father & friend

William Rogers

Little Wm.[2] is as lively as a kitten and has improved since you left. You will be amused at his singing. He prides himself on his "Jordans Stream."

All the rest of the folks are well as well as ours. our love to dear Mary etc.

---

2 Harriet's brother, aged 2

Bishopville Apr 12th 1856
My dear Harriet & Amanda[3]

Knowing you are already anxious to hear from us, I will embrace the earliest opportunity of writing to you. We arrived home safely on yesterday. Daniel and Almira met us with the carriage at the depot & you may imagine how glad I was to meet them. We came directly on home, though we called for a few minutes at Uncle Mac's where we found all well. I am happy to say all were well at home also, & all seemed delighted to meet us and very earnest in their inquiries after you both. Mother talks about you so much, has had lots of questions to ask me about you & all are happy to hear that you are coming on so well. On the evening I parted from you at Orangeburg, on getting to Kingsville whom should meet but William on his way to Columbia also. I was so happy to meet with him. almost his first question was after you. he sympathizes with you very much. regrets exceedingly that we were obliged to leave. He will write you very soon. We all went on together to Columbia, had Mr. Tenhet's company also. we arrived in C. a little before sunset, found Sue & her mother out waiting to receive us. we had a very pleasant time there indeed. I have never been more pleased with a lady than I was with Logan her daughter. Mrs. Yongue is also a very sweet lady. We rode out on Thursday morning pretty much all over Columbia, which I enjoyed very much. For the afternoon we visited two very elegant flower gardens. the handsomest I have ever seen. I brought home some cuttings for mother which she was very glad to receive, but it is so late in the season I fear they will not live. Sue is looking for an answer to her letter to you. says you must write to her often. We left very early yesterday morning. We met Bro. & Sister Crook on board the cars.[4] You may tell Annie they were all well, though her father had been sick. She spoke of being in Orangeburg at the time of the qlty[5] meeting. Mr. Munds we hear is not going to Orangeburg, and Mr. Fleming they think will not preach here, & so they have it.

---

3 Harriet is 15 years old, at boarding school in Orangeburg with her sister.

4 railroad cars

5 quarterly

William left home this eve to go to his appointments—will not be back until tomorrow afternoon. The "Smith Family" are expecte here on next Tuesday. they have more performers than they used to have, though Ellen is not with them. She has been married two years and is living in Wadesboro N.C. I hear of nothing else new about Bisopville. I have not seen any one yet scarcely. Oh yes I must tell you that cousin C's Viney[6] had a baby last Tuesday but it only lived two days. They say it was beautifully white. Mother was delighted with the (illegible). they all think it is beautiful. Father would scarcely believe you did it. Mother says she will be glad for you to do anything you wish of the ornamental work, says she knows father will willingly pay for the materials. They received some very pretty bonnets at the store to-day father says & I will go down on morning and select one apiece for you. Daniel still thinks of going about the first of May to see you, though he has not decided what day he will leave. He is very anxious indeed. He seems in very good spirits. Nothing has been heard from (illegible) and May lately. I had almost forgotten to tell you of the death of Rebecca Spann. She died on last Sunday of typhoid fever. I never was more shocked in my life than when I heard it. She died a most triumphant death so it but gain to her. It is growing dark and I must close my hasty letter. Mother and all the children send you their best love. Albert also, and says he will write you very soon. Give my best love to Bro & Sister McCants, Sister D. and the children. kifs[7] Lucy for me. and now dear sisters I remain your devoted sister Lucy.

Mrs. H. is teaching. has a right good school

---

6 presumably a "servant," as they called their help

7 kiss

Bishopville 18 March 1857
My dear sister,

I received your letter of the first and we were all very glad to hear that you and sister Harriet were both well. I am very glad to say that we too are all well. Mother has gotten almost entirely over her cough and but little headache since Sister left. We received a letter last Monday from "Doctor Rogers."[8] He is now at Castleton in Vermont. We also got a letter from Sister[9] last Monday. She says the Baby can sit alone. Sister says that she sent a box to you by Mr. Carnes but has never heard whether you have gotten it or not. Maria has gone to spend the night with Eliza Dixon. I hope she will have a pleasant visit. I had some trouble with the hens and chickens but hope I shall raise a good many. I am not much of a hand at making biscuit yet but I intend to learn more on that subject. You must write to me as often as you can.

I remain your affectionate Sister
Almira W. Rogers

---

8 Brother Daniel is now a dentist.

9 Lucy

My sweet little sister
Dear Girls,

In writing to Daniel you will direct to Castleton Vermont. I will send you his letter and you can send it to Lucy when you write to her. Affectionately W.R.

Bishopville May 12th 1857
My dear Harriet

Once more I take my pen to hold a short conversation with you. We were all truly happy to learn from your last letter that you were well and I am happy to tell you the same good news in return. Mary Jane is still with us. the school commenced on yesterday and she thought she would return until Monday night we succeeded in getting her to stay a few days longer. She will go on Saturday. We have enjoyed ourselves finely and our pleasure would have been complete could you be with us. not a day pafses but we wish for you. I must tell you of the May party we attended at Lynchburg. Mary Jane cousin David Peggy and I all went together. the party was at Mr. Charles Durant's the coronation also. we got there just in time to see Eliza crowned, she looked very pretty indeed though she was frightened a good deal I think. you could not hear a single word any of them said, they spoke so very low. Caleb Bell, whom you of course remember attended the queen and it was amusing to see him. the party was very pleasant indeed with one exception, I was worried a good deal with Squire Commander who made himself exceedingly conspicous that night. we came home Friday morning. Muldrow and Dr. Wilson called on us Saturday evening and we went to ride with them. Muldrow has called on Mary Jane twice since she has been here and took her to ride too. don't you think he must be very much pleased?

Argent Crofwell and the mifes Stuckey,s got home Saturday. the mif Woods came with them, you know they are nieces of mr. John Dixon,s. They were all out at church on Sunday. Argent has improved considerably, she is not going to return, but the other young ladies are. Mif Lizzie Green Eliza and Col Green came to see us on Monday evening. Eliza said to give you her love when I write. Maria went last night to stay with Salina. She took tea here Monday night. I like Salina so much. she is entirely different from her sister Mary. Mary Jane thinks more of her than any girl in school I believe. Cousin Jane is teaching school in Darlington. she boards with mr Andrews. I am very glad she succeeded in getting a school. Amanda is staying with cousin Callie and Lizzie so aunt Peggy and Mary are left all alone. Father and mother expect to leave next Thursday for Graniteville. I know Sister will be delighted to see them.

The funeral sermon of Capt Rembert is to be preached next Sunday by mr Henry Green. Cousin David got a letter from cousin Hugh the other day. he was in Quittman Mifissippi. he said that Jess was married. Tell me in your next letter when you expect to have vacation and how long. I hope it will be very soon. we heard the other day that mr John Dixon was going to give a party this week, but I do not think it is so, as I have heard nothing of it in a day or two.

I was very much in hopes that cousin Annie Jane could come over this May but she could not leave her mother. When you write to Mary Jane do tease her about mr. McLean and Col Green. we tell her she has captivated both.

Martha Frasier is coming to stay with us to night and I hope we will have a pleasant time. Cousin Caroline has gone to see Mrs Dinkins to day. you ought to write to them sometimes. write to us very soon. Mother Maria Almira Wm Mary Jane father cousin David all send a great deal of love to you. M.J. says she will write to you when she goes back to Harmony. Give our best love to Wm.

With much love I remain your affct[10] sister Amanda

(written in margin of letter:)

Mother wanted to send you a birthday present but there is nothing in the store scarcely to send. she however got you a ring there is no other kind in the store but plain gold ones. mother is sorry she could not get a prettier one for you. I send it in this letter.

---

10 affectionate

King Creek, July 7th 1857
Dearest Hattie,

I came to my writing table intending to work a few sums in Algebra, but at the moment I thought you might be pleased to hear from me. I have been thinking of you and my dear Manda, all the evening, and imagining how you were passing the time. Perhaps you are enjoying yourselves so much that you will forget your lonely friend, and allow many weeks to pass away before I can hear from either of you, however I must resist such thoughts and hope to be cheered by letters from both of you very soon.

You have again returned to your dear Parents, not as other vacations to remain a limited time, but to be with then so long as you choose. You and Manda, I suspect, will take all household duties, and thus help that dear mother upon whom these and other duties have been devoking for many long years. With what pride will she think of you if you strive to discharge these duties properly. Think of this my dearest—think of her glad heart at your success; but I need not say more, for I have always kept the first opinion I formed of you, and that was that you were a dutiful, affectionate and confiding daughter. When I commenced speaking of house-keeping I thought how much it used to please my dear Ma to see me interested in such things.

I feel so lonesome without any one to converse with me during these long days, and very very often I have to stop sewing or reading on account of the tears which it appears will fill my eyes. If I am the least sick, it brings fresh thoughts of my dearest Ma, for she first of all always found out, and did every thing in her power to ease my pains. Sometimes I think that she was too careful about me, for then I would not feel her loss so deeply. Oh! Hattie you cannot imagine what a loving, devoted mother she was, and now that sweet forehead which I have so often kissed, is in the cold grave, where I sometimes wish that mine was; but the will of the Lord be done. I must submit to His orders. He has taken our beloved Ma to dwell with Him in glory, until He sees fit to gather us all, one by one to join with her sweet spirit, in praising Him forevermore.

You must always speak of religion in your letters and tell me how you are getting on in this blessed work. I think I have in the last week felt another manifestation of God's great love, and I now tell you as I deem it highly worthy of notice. I hope I am not deceived. Sometimes I have been much troubled in ending my prayers, fearing that I might not ascribe glory enough to both God, and our Lord Jesus Christ. You may not understand me Hattie, so I will make a short explanation. In ending a prayer if I ever said for Christ, our Redeemer's sake, I thought that I was ascribing more glory to Christ than to God, but recently the Lord has enlightened me so that I know it is proper to repeat it as I have said. I have made free with you in telling you my feelings, because I thought I would feel better for some one to know what religion I enjoy. In class meetings I cannot talk as I can write to you, and therefore as a favor you must always answer any questions I ask.

It is very late, and Pa wishes me to put aside my writing on account of my eyes, so I must bid you goodnight. May Angels watch over my dear friend this night.

8th July. Cousin Jane Lawton has been very ill since her arrival, was taken the first day with fever. I went down to see her on last Saturday. She was then barely able to sit up and walk about a little, looks very badly indeed. She has several likenesses of the girls, and in looking over them I was most agreeably surprised to find our dear Miss Wilson's in the number. If cousin Jane will lend it to me a short time, I can have it sent to Savannah, and have one taken for myself. Sallie Timmons' was very good and so was Lillie Jenkins, but I scarcely think the Daguerrean[11] did Sally Wright justice. How many have you and Manda and what girls are they?

Well Hattie after I have finished my letter I feel tempted not to send it, and if it were not for scarcity of time, I would most surely write it over.

My best love to Mrs. Mood and Manda. Tell M. that I shall look for a letter from her very soon.

Your true friend,
Martha R.

Lizzie's examination is over, but I have not heard from her since.

---

11 Daguerrotype—a photograph

King Creek, July 21st/57
Dear Hattie,

I have allowed several weeks to pass away, before replying to your very kind letter. I have not thought any the less of you Hattie, and consequently feel that you will excuse me.

I have been quite busy the past two months, but went through all my duties as if dreaming. It troubles me sometimes to think of the inactivity with which I go to my various callings. I must try to be more uniform, and thus keep myself in a more happy state.

The fruit season is at hand, and all housekeepers are having preserves, pickles, etc. put away. Have you preserved any peaches? I have had two jars filled, and do not think I shall make any more as "Pa" expects to use a number of the preserving cans. Many prefer them in a fresh state, but I think it best to have a few of the old made.

I made tomato ketchup two weeks ago, and had a large decanter to explode. The report was equal to a young pistol. I had an other quantity made today, and hope it will keep well.

I spoke to you of Sallie W. before. I heard yesterday that she cannot speak above a whisper, and is not expected to live. It is uncertain what is the matter. some suppose she has consumption, or is taking it, while the physician thinks it is typhoid fever. If Sallie should die I feel convinced that her spirit will be conveyed to the "mansions not made with hands."

I received a letter from dear Anna a few days after her death. She wrote on the 25th May, and died on 26th.

Em Stephens left this world of sorrow nine days before. How rapidly our schoolmates are being transferred to the next world! Our time must soon come, oh! may the summons prove a welcome messenger.

We had several girls here recently, two young ladies from La. Mary and Martha Davis and Ann Graham were with us more than a week. Ann has grown to be a sweet girl, and very interesting. She is still here, but thinks of leaving in a day or two.

Clara Bowers (Dunbar) was expected at her Aunt (Mrs. Laffitte) last night, and Ann & myself will go late this evening to pay a call. It would surprise me to see Clara, for she has made so many promises, and never fulfilled one.

Ty Lizzie is sick; she was very ill a few days ago. I believe she has billious fever.[12]

It is very warm Hattie, what do you do in such extreme weather? I hope the little boys are coming on finely. Be positive as well as kind and you will receive their heartfelt thanks in after years.

Write soon to your sincere friend Martha

12 Fever associated with jaundice, usually caused by malaria

Clio, S.C. January 15,/58
My dearest Harriet,

I am sure if you knew half the pleasure it gave me to hear from you, you would not have denied the treat, or rather withheld it, such a great while. But you have promised punctuallity in future, that releases you from farther reprimand. Well dear Hattie, I have but two weeks to remain at home now, and enjoy the pleasant society of best friends. If nothing happens I will start to Harmony the first, or second day of February. I mean the first Monday or Tuesday. I feel a great deal more reluctant about going now than when I first went. I have been anticipating a pleasant week with you all Harriet, thought to stay with you the first week in feb, for though school commences then, there is very little accomplished as it is generally a sort of hurly burly with a very few pupils, But when Prof was here he proposed sending to the depot for us on Tuesday, and arrangements were made to that effect, so I suppose I must abide. I intend going to see you though before long without some providential interposition. Harriet why did not some of you accompany Daniel? We would have been so glad if you had. I have not heard of D's arrival yet, I would be very glad indeed to see him. A.J. spent a day with me last week. I asked her if she had responded to your letter. Said she had not, but intended to, in a few days. She said she had just recd a letter from her cousin Hugh, from Georgia. He was well, and taking pictures. I have staid with A.J. a good deal since I came home. She is the same dear girl she always was to me. I expect to go down there next Monday, and if she has not replied to you, I will tell her to do so. Has Maria gone to school anywhere yet? I wish very much she would go to Harmony. Mary Carmichael will return with me. she is a very fine girl. I am very glad indeed to have her share my couch, for of all things I dread an unpleasant chum. I will miss my old favorites Misses Gregg & Cunningham. Eliza Gregg was very much pleased indeed with you, and Amanda hopes she will have the pleasure of again meeting you. We have new neighbors at Clio—cousin James McRae from Montgomery AL Cousin Angus from Little Bede. Clio abounds with McRaes. Cousin Duncan (aspiring scion of the law) is teaching at the academy. They are all very clever people I think. Is Miss Clelia still staying in B? What is Vermeille doing? Does she and cousin David get on pretty well yet? I thought he was coming to Marlboro, and bring some of you girls right away, or I did not think so either, but he said so. Tell him I don't believe all he says, with due respect to his veracity. He has gone to Mississippi. We were all very sorry to see him start. I recd a letter from him a few days since, informing us of his safe arrival amongst his relatives out there, which was a source of sincere gratification to us all. The roads were so bad from the heavy rains about the time he started that I felt very uneasy respecting him.

Oh! A.J. had a beau when I was down there. A young carpenter working on the Parnassian[13] church. I have forgotten his name. I teased about him, and at last pretended that I had cut her out. I will tell A.J. what I have been telling you. I know she will thump my head for it, but she will not hurt.

Well Harriet I can't say anything entertaining or funny anyway so I will close by asking you to keep your promise about writing. Write soon. w. love to your Father, Mother and all,

Your most affectionate friend Mary Jane

---

13 Possibly referring to a church in Parnassus, Marlboro County

Graniteville Jan. 29th '58
My beloved Sister

Today you are to leave the dear home of our childhood, and the loved ones there, for the first time on your own responsibility, and though I have nothing of interest to write, my thoughts are so much with you, that I can not forbear taking up my pen.

I trust my dear Harriet, that the hand of God directs you in this as in every other act of your life, and may He abundantly bless & protect you, grant you health of body, strength of mind. may He give you kind friends, may He make you happy & useful, successful in your duties, and above all may He continually bless you with the outpourings of His Holy Spirit, giving you that peace of mind which passeth all understanding, which the world can neither give or take away. I can never express to you the love, and abiding interest I feel in you as in all my dear brothers & sisters. and oh! if my prayers or the wishes of my heart could avail aught, no trouble or sorrow should ever wound your hearts, but I know not what is best for you, and thank God, the events of your lives are directed by One who loves you far more than I and who does know what is for your good; and I feel well assured that naught will befall you, but what will hereafter make you all the happier.

You are a good girl Harriet, and have always been good. and it has often been a source of pleasure to me to think of how much our Heavenly Father must love you, and of the smiles with which His countenance rested upon you, and then very naturally, it occurs to my mind what a bright angel she will one day make in Heaven, and I wonder then if I shall be so happy as to get there too. I always hope to, but I have such a miserable disposition to contend with that I sometimes fear it is to be my ruin. and I am constrained to wonder that God should grant me ever the light of His countenance, or that He does not cast me off entirely, when I am so unworthy. Pray for me, dear sister, that I may live nearer and nearer to Him every day of my life, and that I may at last obtain a seat at His right hand in Heaven.

We are all quite well, that is Anna and I, and Wm was when he left. He got the Clergy ticket into his hands the other day and could not resist the temptation to pay a flying visit to the folks in Charleston, and he will not be back until tomorrow. Miss Agnes Stroble stayed with me last night and Mary Hurd will stay tonight. I am expecting company to-day also, and that is the reason I am writing this so beautifully. I am anxious to get it done before they come. I tell you I miss dear little Almira now that Wm is away. How much I wish she or Maria were with me. Anna is rosy and fat as ever is very good an does not give me half as much trouble since she was weaned. She has got a crib now and when you come and see her, she can take you in it with her, it is plenty large. I could sleep in it very comfortably, but I assure you I love its room better than its company in day time, for as you may imagine our little room was amply furnished before.

I wish so much I could be with you and Mary awhile now, for she, I know, is like you downspirited but you must cheer each other up, there are brighter times a head for both of you I trust. Do please both of you write me a good long letter very soon for I am all anxiety to hear from you. Tell me all your arrangements anything and everything will be interesting to me. We rec. Mr. G's letter last night. Wm will answer as soon as he comes home thanks for his promptness. Much love to dear Mary I will write her soon, also to Mr. G. and now dear sister I must close remaining your devoted sister

Lucy J Mood [14]

I have just rec. your kind letter dear Harriet, written this week, and many thanks to you for it. I am so happy to hear all are well at home. Hope you succeeded in getting your work done before time to leave. How many dresses did you get made up. I wish I could have been there to help you. I am glad the lancers are getting "cheered up" so David doesn't go does he? I hope not. How did (illegible) enjoy her visit. You did not speak of it, but I must send this to the office write us very soon. love to all. we will write you soon again and as often as we can. Glad you liked your album piece.

Your affet sister L

---

14 Lucy is married to William Wynn Mood, Methodist minister

Bishopville Feb. 3rd 1858
My dear Harriet,

Knowing that you are already anxious to hear from your home I embrace this early opportunity of complying with your wish to write soon. We are all quite well and have been so ever since your absence. Father got back last night from Darlington C.H. He left home on Monday in company with Mr. Wells (Mr. Lyon's friend). He took dinner here last Sunday and we were all very much pleased with him. Cousin Edgar and Mr. Plowden spent Saturday with us and we had quite a pleasant time. They danced as usual last Saturday evening and were so generous as to leave the windows up if we wished to see them. Muldrow brought Martha T. with him and Wm Frasier and Jane Dennis as usual went to ride. We are all so anxious to hear from you as to how your are. Please do tell cousin Mary her mother is with us yet and is quite well. She has done lots of work since she has been here has finished her black basque[15] and nearly done her dress. Mr. Lyon is still better. I went to see him yesterday and thought he looked much better. Dr. Dubose came by to see him yesterday but we have not heard his opinion about him. Mrs. Shaw has a very sick child. it was very low yesterday. we have not heard today. Mr. H. Durant took tea with us last night. He did not stay very long but went over to see them dance. Salina Carnes had gone to Harmony.

We have not heard from Daniel but once. father heard while he was gone he was at Clio. I am getting anxious for him to come home. I have commenced teaching William. he is delighted with Geography studies it very hard. I have not been anywhere since you left. I believe I will stay at home as much as possible. Vermeille and I went to walk Sunday evening and had the pleasure of Mr. Mc— company. He does not have much to say and stammers too. Zimmerman got through weeding and has gone home. Father forgot to give your knife so I will send in this. I will get your ribbon and send it in the next letter written to you. Martha Frasier was very sorry you would not come to see her before you left—said to give you her best love and let her know how you like her friend Dr. Henry. Has Mr.

15 closely fitted bodice or jacket

Skinner returned yet? Write very soon and let us know how many music scholars[16] you have many Mr. G. and cousin Mary have. Aunt Creasy says you and cousin Mary must write soon so she can hear from before she goes home. I had nearly forgotten to tell you that Mrs. Wilson has another daughter. I must close dear sister as it is getting late. Mother father aunt C. and all send much much love to you, cousin Mary and Mr. Garner and accept the same from your affct sister

A. M. Rogers

16 Hattie has moved near Summerton and is teaching music at the Summerton Academy.

Bishopville Feb. 6th 1858
Dear Harriet

With pleasure do I take my pen in hand this morning for conversing with you. I am happy to say that we are all very well. We we(re) glad to learn from your letter that you were all well also and sincerely hope you may continue so. I expect you are quite anxious to hear from Mr. Lyon. I believe he is getting along pretty well now. Oh how much I wish that he could be restored to health once more. Mrs. Shaw has a very sick child now. don't think it will hardly recover. Mother and Amanda went down to see it on yesterday thought it some better. I received a long letter from Bro Wm on Thursday last they were all well said sister had written to you and that he would write soon. He spoke a great deal about Cousin David's going to dancing school we showed it to Cousin David but it did not do any good I believe. On last Wednesday night Daniel came home bringing with him Cousin Mary Jane McCallum we were very much surprised to see her. She was very sorry that you were not here. Cousin Anna J. sent you Amanda and I some beautiful collars she made herself. I will send yours in this letter. we expected Cousin MJ to spend some time with us but were disappointed as she said she was obliged to go to (illegible) Thursday. Daniel carried her over. Tell Cousin Lucy her mother is well and sends much love to her. she has gone over to spend a day or two with Mrs. Dixon. Father left yesterday for Wilmington. Daniel was going down to Lynchburgh on business so Father went with him down to the cars. William went also to see Charlie. They will return tomorrow. The dancing school is still in a flourishing condition. They dance this evening I believe. A good many were out to see them dance last Saturday, I dont know how they were pleased. They want to get the teacher for another term, but I do not know whether they will succeed or not. Well Harriet I believe I have told you every thing I could think off and I want to study my lessons for Monday I must bring this short letter to a close. All join with sending love to you cousins Mary and (illegible) Tell Cousin William I miss him (illegible) deal about hearing (illegible). Hoping that you will answer this letter soon. I will close remaining your very affct Sister

Maria

Milton Fla. Feb. 14th 1858
My dear Cousin.

I am just now returned from my first walk about this very pretty little town. I arrived here on Thursday night about twelve o'clock. Friday and Saturday I was busy consequently could not look about and see what manner of place I was in—I was out this morning and heard a very good sermon, from Luke XIV, 21, 22, & 23. This evening being wearied I took a stroll through the city and returned much pleased with its appearance. The houses are all small but neat. Almost all are newly painted, and have pretty yards, full of flowers even at this season, which gives to them an air of rural quietness scarsely ever found in our more northern vilages. I have a nice operating room, it is fronting on the river of which I have a fine view. I think I must take pictures of two views from my window, and bring them along when I come to Bishopville again. I had the pleasure of attending a wedding near Quincy on the 28th last month. I enjoyed myself finely considering I was a perfect stranger to most persons present. While in that neighborhood I boarded at Mr. Woods (a relation of the Dixons) His mother paid Bishopville a visit last year sometime and thinks there is no place like it. She thinks Capt. Rembert the best Farmer and Mrs. R. the finest lady she has ever met up with. On my arrival here I found another artist in before me, but I thought I would put up any way. The people all like my pictures much better than his. I think I will sell almost all the pictures that are sold here. I will remain a month here and then beat up towards home. I think I will be in Bishopville about the latter part of June. My health I am glad to say is improving. I hope it will continue to do so until I am entirely restored. I have not received a single letter in five weeks consequently I can give you no tidings of "the loved ones at home." The misfortune with me is that when I leave one place I can not tell any friend where to write next. You must write to me as soon as you can for I am anxious to get a letter from B—-.

Tell Aunt Anna that I have written letters of inquiry with regard to Uncle Arch, but have not received any answers owing perhaps to my traveling so much. My letters however will all be forwarded to me so that I will get them sometime or other. I would ask you whether a certain young gentleman had visited Bishopville lately and what progress he was making but I fear you would not like to answer, and especially the last portion of the question. Has Muldrow ever turned over another buggy? Give much love to all -

May the kind hand of Providence ever be over us, and permit us all to meet once more upon earth is the prayer of your afect. cousin

Hu B. McCallum

Bishopville Feb 16th/58
My Dear cousin

According to promice I now seat myself to perform the pleasant task of writing to you. I expect you are thinking hard of me as I promised to write the next week after you left, but I have not been at home much since I spent the whole of last week with Mary Jane. Willie and Lizzie Witherspoon came up to Aunt G—'s last Saturday evening. Sunday night they spent with us and Monday they spent the day up at your house. Lizzie said she enjoyed herself very much indeed. She is the same old Lizzie—no improvement whatever. I never saw Willie as dull in my life. I asked him what in the world was the matter and why was it that he was looking so very blue. he said it was because Miss Harriet was gone. he told me to tell you that he expected (to) visit Sumerton soon. he asked me how to direct a letter to you and said that he was going to send you the prettiest valentine that Manning could afford.

Well Harriet I cannot give you a long letter this morning for it is so cold and I am sitting in hall without any fire. I have not been to Bishopville since you left but I expect to go up one night this week, if nothing happens to prevent. I have not seen Dan— since he came home. I think he might come down and see us and tell us all about Marlborough folks. give my best love to Cousin Mary and Mr. Garner. Aunt Lucretia stayed with us last week. Cousin Drucilla came up Saturday evening and stayed with us untill Sunday evening. Aunt Cretia went home with her. May heaven's richest blessings ever be yours is the prayer of your sincere and affectionate cousin Mag

write soon. you must forgive this short letter and I will try and do better the next time.

(folded & addressed on 1/2 page of letter:)

Bishopville SC
Feby 18th

Mif H C Rogers
Wrights Bluff[17] P O
SC

17 Settlement near Summerton, SC

Graniteville Parsonage Feb 17th '58
Dear Sister

I have just been assisting in putting up a couple of bales cow food (for we have a cow) and coming in finding Lucy writing to Mary. I thought if she would not charge you postage or report me to Uncle Sam I'd enclose in hers a letter to you. Do you believe it—will you believe it. Lucy has quit writing & got my glass & is looking at herself!! We have just awhile ago received your letter and were truly glad to hear from you. glad your health is so good. Hope the number of music scholars will increase.

We are all well. Lucy was complaining of headache yesterday, but got better before night. She has finished a very pretty dress Sister Rembert gave her and she has made her pantalets. Lucy has written however all of this to Mary so I'll not continue on this strain. only I will say to you, and to all the faculty of the Summerton Academy, that there is no telling the comfort & satisfaction there is in having such a little object around you.

We have had some rough weather lately. last Thursday was a lue day that night will be remembered and it was blowing and snowing and frizzing all day Friday. Saturday it continued snowing & frizzing. it ceased blowing. I went through the friz to my first quarterly conf[18] and had the pleasure of meeting my P[19] elder. We had a very pleasant conf- my visit there however has put work upon me—and I am invited to preach every other Sunday morning in Aiken. I hope the arrangement will result in good.

I am much obliged to you for the information given with reference to your mail carrier—whew—has seven (7) children. There are some other inquiries I will make of you—but not now. You will perhaps see in the L Watchman[20] of an accident happening to Asbury[21]—I am glad to say that he is well again. at first it was thought to be a dangerous hurt—had high fever for days.

---

18 conference
19 Presiding
20 Latest Watchman—possibly the Sumter Watchman newspaper
21 William Mood's brother, also a minister

Amanda mentions that William and Lizzie Witherspoon have recently spent a day with her. L says that W is coming down to see you & perhaps I'll accompany him. I attend a wedding in the country tomorrow. Amanda mentions that Daniel was in Winnsboro. Sister Rembert mentioned that Mrs. Martha McLean has married Ephraim Fields.

Remember us very kindly to Mr. Garner and Mary, and accept much love from your Bro

Wm

P S

We are astonished at David's course. If I am not mistaken he'l repent it bitterly in the future.

(written in margin)

Lucy encloses this ribbon for you–I think it is a poor present. if you can't use it send it back-with a long letter by return mail. I forgot to mention that I'll send on for the Home Circle for you. Tell Mr. G. he'l find the LC Ad[22] a far superior paper to the NCCU Ad-

22 Advocate

Harmony, S.C. Feb. 25th 1858
My dear Hattie

There; that's a clever girl, don't wait so long anymore. I was so glad to get your letter, that I will manifest part of the pleasure by replying by first mail. I feel truly glad Harriet, to hear, that you are so well pleased with your new situation, occupation, etc. and hope you will find it pleasant throughout the year. How much real pleasure is derivable from a consciousness of being usefully employed. And I most earnestly wish you may enjoy it, in the fullest extent. I was so sorry Harriet that I could not have the great pleasure of seeing you, when at your home; though I scarcely expected it, as Daniel had told me of your intended departure. I enjoyed the short time I spent there very much, considering the tone of mind just then. I was sorry I could not have appeared more cheerful at least, but I need not tell you, how badly I felt on leaving home, and the thought of leaving made me feel sad enough while there sometimes. oh! it seems a long long time to feel dissatisfied for ten wearysome months and I know I will never feel very well contented till I return. I may go home in May, but it is an uncertainty with me yet. I would have such a short time to stay—only one week at most, and if I would return in time for the commencement of school, I could stay about 3 days, then I would hate so much to come back, that I dont know but it would be as well to remain till the close of the term. I have regretted ever since, that I could not have spent a few days at your fathers, particularly as Daniel was kind enough to bring me over, and you know I wanted to stay a(n)yway, for it would be queer if I had not. I have become acquainted with Mary P, and like her very much, she is such a good girl. She delivered your message, which was as gladly recd. as you could have wished, that introduced us, so we soon became good friends. Poor Mary was very homesick, she would come in my room and sit and cry until she would set me at it too. she was a little sick from cold last Sabbath, and her sister, & cousin, were here at church, so she went home with them, and has not returned yet. I fear she is not well, as she would have been back. I have not heard a word from home since I left, was sure I would get a letter last mail, but was sadly disappointed. I think I will be worse than Mary if I don't soon get news of them. I think I have been here four weeks, though it seems nearer four months. Hattie, I thought I would tell you about the pleasant time A.J., Daniel and I had, while he was over but I have not room to do it justice, so will omit it, any more than to say I enjoyed the time very much indeed. Will leave the detail for Daniel as you will see him soon I recon.

Affectionately
Mary

Bishopville Feb. 25th 1858
My dear Sister,

A letter has just come to hand for you from cousin Hugh, and I will have time to write only a few lines as we wish to send it to the office immediately. Father says to tell you he would have written to you but he has been so very busy and had so many letters to write that it has been impossible for him to get time to write to either you or sister, but he will write to you very soon. We are all well. Have you had much snow in Summerton? We had enough here for sleighing and so I had an opportunity of taking a sleighride. Dr. Wilson came for me yesterday and we had quite a pleasant time. Muldrow and Martha F. rode together. I got thrown out of the sleigh but was not hurt at all. We rec- your letter to day and were happy to hear that you continued well. I must close my short note as Jim is waiting to carry this. All send much love to you cousin Mary and Mr. Garner. Write soon. Your ever affct. sister

A. M. Rogers

Bishopville 28 Feby. 1858
My own darling Harriet,

I fear my beloved daughter that your patience is well nigh exhausted waiting for a letter from "Father." I am length undertaking to write you at least a few lines.

Since you have been gone I have been so constantly engaged at home or away from home that it seemed the only opportunity I could get conveniently was at night at home, and then I would feel too tired or lazy to write. Well dear I am so happy to again be able to say as I have so often done before "we are all well. I am sorry to say though that Mr. Holleyman is sick with pneumonia but I hope he is not dangerously so, Mr Lyon is about as he has been for some time. very little change. John Magee is still confined but is better than he was.

I am sorry to have to inform you of a most distressing accident which occurred at Bishopville last Friday evening—By an accidental discharge of a gun at Mr. Husband's shop. Thads DuBose the Dr's son was shot—the whole round of the gun, from which he was some three feet distance, passing through his arm about 4 inches below the shoulder—Making a hole about 1 1/2 inches in diameter and breaking the bone. Wm Barret was wounded at the same time slightly in the head but the shot glanced and did not go through the bone. Thads was yesterday hawled home on beds in a wagon. The arm may probably be saved but it will take a long time for it to get well if it gets well at all.

John McCallum was here tell Mary night before last and reports all well in Marlborough and all our relatives about there are I think quite well. I wish darling I had time to write you a long letter and after awhile now I hope to have more of leisure. All well at Graniteville a few days ago.

All send their love to you my beloved daughter, and you must remember us kindly to dear Mary and Mr. Garner.

Hoping soon to hear from you agin and with my prayers for your present and everlasting (illegible) I remain most truly and affectionately your Father & friend

William Rogers

Graniteville March 4th (1858)
My dearest Harriett,

Your last kind letter was duly received, and I assure you I was more than happy to get it, to hear of your welfare, etc. You ought to write us often now while you have so much time. I have taken my pen, but I doubt whether I shall be able to write you for really, it is so very cold I can scarcely hold it. We have real old-fashioned winter now haven't we? How do you stand it? I do hope you have good, warm fires, for with all the fire we can have, it is still cold. I find you had snow last week as well as us. Maria wrote me, they had some sleigh-riding again in B. Amanda took one with Dr. Wilson.

We are all enjoying very good health at present. Wm seems unusually well, complains that his clothes are getting too tight, but the rest of us are not able as yet to discover any enlargement. Anna is as usual trotting about, first at one thing then at another, and is just the sweetest, smartest child you ever saw. These freezing days are sore annoyances to her and Lavinia, as they cannot play out-doors. Lavinia contends that "it right warm out in de sun," de wind aint blowin" etc., by way of getting out. I put a quilt in the frame last week, Wm's large-starred one, but the weather has been so cold ever since I have not done much at it as it is up-stairs where there is no fire place. How much I wish I had you & Mary here with me awhile to help me on it. Maum Sarah I find quilts nicely, so she will be of help to me about it. We received a letter from father yesterday, all well at home. how thankful I am to hear that always. Wm Holleyman was quite ill of pneumonia. I hope he is better ere this. A shocking accident occurred there a day or two before he wrote. Calvin Shaw was trying to fix a gun at Mr. Husband's Shop. He was on the outside of the shop by a window and inside were a number of boys. The gun was loaded, and a double barrel, while he was working at it, it went off, and the whole load, wad & all, went through Thomas DuBose's arm making a hole of 1 1/2 inches in diameter and breaking the bone. it also slightly wounded Willie Barrett, but not seriously. It is a great mercy that it was no worse, for it might have caused the death of many. It is bad enough though as it is. There is doubt whether his arm will be saved or not. I sincerely trust it may. I was glad to hear that you (have) the prospect of more music scholars. I have little doubt but you will have several more yet. all the scholars seldom come into a school before spring. Then as they get farther advanced you know they will take up more of your time. I don't think you will find it hang heavily on your hands long. It is I doubt not a pleasant change for you to assist in school sometimes. Dont get low-spirited dear sister at any rate. I was afraid there was a slight tinge of it in your last letter but I thought it was because Mary was sick when you wrote. I know I always feel lonely at such times. How do you like Mrs McKnight these times. Is she still kind? You must practice a great deal too, you can improve yourself much in that way. Where do you give lessons at the Academy or where. Wm has sent for the Home-Circle for you. he says when it comes, be certain to write and tell him whether you got the January & February numbers. if not he wants to get them for you. About your bonnets, I dont know of any particular kind to advise you to get. I think I would just ask them to get "fashionable Summer bonnets lined with white and trimmed with straw-color outside & inside. Tell them to be sure and get them pretty, and be certain to get as many summer dresses as you think you will need. They will do for you after this, if you do not wear them much this summer. We are going out to take supper with Mrs. Powell this evening. I do wish you could know her. I love her so much, that I want all my friends to know, and love her too. Do write me very soon again, my dear sister, and I will promise to do the same. Wm joins me in much love to you, Mary & Mrs. G. and ask one or both of them please to write to us also. Maum S.& Lavinia send howdye to you. You would be surprised to see how much smarter L. is than when we brought her here. I have just called Anna. told her to come and let me kiss her for Aunt Harriett and she came running as hard as she could.

I remain your devoted sister
L J Mood

(written in margin:)

I have been employing myself lately making some linen collars and send you one of them, but dont show it to any one 'till it is done up. I would do it up for you but I could not send it so well in a letter. Good bye my dear. May God ever bless & protect you.

At Home March 5th 1858
Dear Hattie,

I received your letter the very day I got home, it was here waiting for me. I arrived home to day a week ago, and was very glad to get back after such a long visit . I was with Martha nearly three months, and spent the time very pleasantly indeed. I did not intend staying so long when I left home, but when I got down there they would not let me leave until Lizzie left for Spartanburg. She returned there the same time I came home, and expects to be there all this year. She has grown quite stout since she left Orangeburg. She appears to be perfectly delighted with Spartanburg, and says she likes it much better than Orangeburg, but we all told her it was because she was allowed to do too much as she pleased. she denied it and said that they were very strict there. Cuttie Solomons has not returned. it is reported that she is to be married soon. I do not know whether it is so or not, but I rather think it is as she did not return to school. I did not see much of her while I was with Martha, for she did not come to see us though we went to see her several times, but I saw her several times at church. I expect Martha will be very lonesome for she is left by herself, no one there but her father and brother and they are always out of the house attending to business so you see they are not much company for her. Her little brother (Billy) is at school in Cokesbury[23] so you can imagine how lonely she must be, you must write to her often to cheer her in her loneliness. She appreciates a letter from you very much. She speaks a little like visiting me this summer and may be she will come up to see you, but I am afraid she wont come even this far for she says it is very hard for her to leave home. Her Father says he cannot do without her, for she keeps house and sees to a great many things which if she was not there he would have to do himself.

I was very much surprised when I heard that you were giving music lessons, and I hope you will be successful. I would give almost any thing to see you giving a lesson. I hope you are blessed with apt scholars for it must be very tiresome to teach dull ones. I am now

---

23 Once-thriving Methodist college near Greenwood, SC

teaching my little sisters and brother. I like it very well some times, but when I am in a hurry to do anything and I have their lessons to hear it bothers me very much. To day is Saturday and they are delighted, they were asking me this morning if they must say their lessons to day and when I told them know, they were as much pleased as if I had told them they could have a week's vacation. When will your vacation be? You must let me know. I suppose you have had some very cold weather up where you are. We have had some here for the last two or three days. We have had another freeze but not as bad as the one we had a few winters ago.

Mother is quite sick now, she has been in bed for two or three days. we begin to feel very uneasy about her. she has been complaining for some time, but I hope she will be well soon again. She is now taking medicine which I hope will help her.

Mr. Legare's school is now very full, he has ninety-three boarders. The house is so much crowded that he has to put wings on the back, which will make it a very large building when they are put on. You remember Abbie Jenkins room—there are six girls in there now and four in the room I used to stay in so you can imagine how crowded they are.

Mr. Legare has two new teachers, Miss Lee and Miss Birk. Mr. Tay has left. I heard that he was married to Mrs. Reit but do not know whether it is so or not. Miss Mary (the house keeper) has left too but as I have not seen any of the girls lately I do not know whether it is the truth or not. The present house keeper (Mrs. Hall) comes down in the dining room while the girls are at breakfast with her night cap on. Quite different from Miss Mary do you not think so?

I heard Mr. Hamer preach while I was down the country, and like him very much indeed, think him a very excellent man. I also heard Mr. Power the young preacher and liked him very much too. Who have you to preach for you where you are now? We have Mr. Williams and Mr. Ogburn on Orangeburg. I have not heard Mr. Williams yet, but heard Mr. Ogburn last Sunday, liked him very much. He is not any larger than your brother William, and is not near as good looking. He preaches very good sermons, and I think will be liked a great deal more than Mr. Morgan was.

I do wish you could see the baby. she is the most amusing little thing I ever saw. She can sing any thing that she has ever heard enough to learn, and is all the time singing.

As I have written you quite a long letter, I must close.

Write soon. Let no one see this as it is so miserably written.

Believe me as ever your true friend
Jane Sally

Bishopville March 6th 1858
My dear sister

I have been thinking some time of writing to you dear sister but kept putting it off and thus permitted some time to elapse before so doing.

We are all well and we were glad to hear from cousin Mary's letter received on Thursday that you were well also. We were happy to hear that you were succeeding so well with your music class and cousin Mary says you aprest Mr. Garner a gooddeal too. I do hope you may continue pleased. I expect you enjoy your horse back rides very much and I suppose you have become quite expert in managing them.

Cousin Mary Jane is with us now. she came with Daniel. is as lively as ever. Cousins Jane and Mag spent the night with us Thursday night and we had quite a pleasant time.

Poor Mrs. Bell is dead. She died yesterday morning about ten oclock . Mr. Lyon is considered worse to day. I am happy to tell you that William H. is (illegible) owing to his illness we have had no school this week. I am getting anxious to go again. I do not visit as much as I used to. I have staid at home very close considering my propensity to visit. William is learning very fast and is very fond of geography more so than any of his studies. Maria and I are getting on very well with our music and if you do not mind I will learn to sing before you come home. Did you know old Mrs. Greenhill was dead. It is getting late and I must close. Mother father sends love to you cousin Mary and cousin William. do write soon to your affct sister

Almira

Bishopville March 12th 1858
Dear Harriet

Again it is my pleasant task to write you, although Almira has written to you this week still I know you will be glad to hear from us again. We are all quite well. Mother had a very bad sick headache but she is much better now. I received cousin Mary's letter last Thursday and am much obliged to her for it. I was sorry to hear that she had been so unwell but I hope she is well again. I spent a day and night with Anadella last week and as usual had a pleasant time. Lizzie and Pat were there when I got there. They had been spending the day with A-. I know it would amuse you to hear Pat talk. I try to remember what all she says to tell mother and father, but she talks so much and so fast that I remember nothing. They said they saw Dr. Green that morning and he looked like an old widower drooping about. Speaking of Mr. Lyon Pat said she reckoned he would die gradually, she understood the remainder of his family went off that way. Mrs. Mimms has a son four days old. We had a little snow on Monday night but did not cover the ground. Martha Frasier and Belle Kennedey spent that night with me. cousin David and Martha danced some but as I had to play I could not see how they performed. Mr Durant took tea here also but as is generally the case had but little to say. The Frasiers are all going next week or at least they say so. They have sold out everything so I suppose they will go this time. They say they are coming back in June but I do not think they will. Muldrow Dennis called on us last week for the first time since you left. Emma Lackey came up on Tuesday to have her teeth fixed. staid until yesterday noon. Anderson came with her, and as mother was sick the duty of entertaining him devolved upon me. I did my best and said everything I could think of. I told mother it was the hardest days work I had done in a long time.

Jane Dennis has been quite sick but is better now. I went up to see her yesterday evening and found her up. Wm Holleyman is getting well fast, but I am sorry to tell you Mr. Lyon is no better.

We are invited to Mr Wm Dixon's to night. It is Alice birthday and they give her a party. Vermeille and I cousin D. and Daniel are all that are invited besides the little boys and girls. I know we will all enjoy ourselves finely. the dancers meet once a week at Capt Muldrow's to dance. I had an invitation this week but will not accept it. I am going down to cousin Drucilla's next week with Daniels cousin. Jane and Amanda went to see her last week and said they were all well.

Leander comes to see Lizzie very often, though I am inclined to think he got his walking ticket the last time but I have never heard. I got a letter from Annie Jennings a few days since. She says she does not think it is so about Mr. Floyd being married. she says Miss Hahr is to leave very soon for Sweden. I know it will be a sad day there when she leaves. I do not think they will ever get her place filled. Annie said to give you much love; she was sick with the measles when she wrote. And so Belton has been to see you. You see the tables have turned upon you. Instead of my having the pleasure of seeing his pretty teeth, you have had it. I hope you played the agreeable so well as to induce him to repeat his visit. cousin Mary Jane said she heard that Ruthvin and Calvin were coming up, but if they have I have not heard of it. Cousin Charles is now in Charleston. I saw Julia Green at church last Sabbath; she does not look much like she did when she left, is much prettier. I think she has left for Georgia. I heard she was to have gone last Tuesday. I must now close dear sister. do write very soon. Tell cousin Mary I will answer her letter soon. Give much love to her and Mr. G for us and accept the same for yourself. I remain your devoted sister

Amanda Rogers

Excuse bad writing. my pen is miserable.

Graniteville SC March 15th '58
Dear Harriet

I have been owing you a letter some time and propose now to write you a short one hoping that it will find you Mary & bro Garner well. I have nothing of interest to communicate. We are getting along after the old fashon. Lucy is well and is hard at her quilt (mine) the patches were given me when on Sumter Mar' '53. She has put it together with a red cord and is quilting the patches in the shape of a fan. It will be really a beautiful piece of work when finished. Those who have seen it say she quilts beautiful. She quilts certainly very fast. Our dear little Anna Nora is very hearty. Lucy has made her before dinner a sun bonnet. she looks so old in it for it is a complete protection for her head. She is trying now to talk, and says puppy and baby plainly. Tis amusing to see her shut her eyes. She always puts both hands to them before she succeeds in closing them. She is so fond of being in the yard, running at the chickens, and she holds out both hands and says shew!! shew!! A friend has written to us that there are 6 pr of pantalets ready for her. Levinia is well and minds Anna Nora very well. We heard from Bro H. lately and also from Miss Lange! Bro H's college is only 40 miles from Statesville where Miss L. teaches. Bro H has been over to see her & her sister and has engaged Miss L's sister as teacher in music German French. Miss L seems much pleased at it and said she felt very much at home with Bro H in their interview together. The college wants her immediately but Miss L will go up after a while & teach Mary Catharine in music. I think Bro H has done well to get Miss L's sister. Bro H says she speaks English very well, considering she has been in America only 7 months. You may have seen it in the Advocate[24] but I mention any how that Bro. Minick died very suddenly on the 27th Feb. on his mission. He did not have time to say farewell to either wife or child. How sorry I am for her. Surely she needs grace now to sustain her. Dr Betts was sent for in the night but he breathed his last just as he got to his bed side.

24 Southern Christian Advocate, weekly Methodist newspaper first published in Charleston 1837.

I continue my visits every other Sunday morning to Aiken. I have not heard lately how Bro Boone has got. I am fearful he'l not be able to do much hard labor again. I wish much some one could be found to take charge of Aiken sta. You spoke in one of your letters of Asbury's accident. He has entirely recovered and writes very cheerfully to us. He has began a protracted meeting in Greenville. He thought cold & stormy as it was that signs of the time warranted him in making this effort. I am anxious to know how the meeting succeeds. Lucy joins in sending much love to you and also begs to be remembered kindly to Mary, Bro Garner. Write soon again & tell me if you have received the Home Circle[25] and what number it is.

Yours aff-
Wm W M

(written in margin from Lucy)

We are still all well my dear H. I have just rec a letter from father. all well at home. I so hope this will find dear Mary quite well. Much love to her and Mr G and a treble portion for your self. Wm told you a "friend" had written to us; she had 6 pr. of pantalets for Anna it was Mrs Logan. She is now at Spartanburg, but she says they are so strict, she feels homesick. I was very glad to hear that Bro Henry had engaged Miss Lange's sister. He would have engaged her also but says he was afraid to engage two music teachers yet he was quite delighted with them both. And they seem to have been with him also. Aint you sorry for poor Mrs Minick? I do pity her so much. I will write you soon again. Good bye and may God bless you.

(written in another margin)

We have been hard at work to-day using Bed Bug Poison. pleasant business, don't you think? I thought I'd begin in time. Write soon again to us dear H. Be very good to Mary, nurse her all you can. She has done much for us in sickness especially our dear mother. I know your kind heart though. I need not have said this. your devoted sister. L.

---

25 Weekly newspaper published in New York

Bishopville 19 March 1858
My own beloved Harriet

I am about to write to you once more and I hope hereafter I may not find it inconvenient to be to you a more punctual correspondant than I have been since you left home–And now in the first place to make you feel agreeably–I will say that we are quite well. Your other relatives also, Mr Lyon —— is no better–John Muger is improving-Roxaluner since the birth of her son is doing tolerably well. The people generally are quite well. In point of news there is not much in our neighborhood. You have probably heard that Hardy Stuckey and Thomas Fraser are dreadfully out with each other–Mr. S. has sued Mr. Fraser in several cases for slander–Gilbert Crosswell looks on laughing.

Darlington is the place for news. The case of the members of the Vigilant Society[26] is on hand now- there were Sixty three of them took their abode in the jail on Monday last.[27] On Wednesday their case went before the Grand Jury. They are now on trial for their lives. Still in all this there is nothing alarming. None of them can be found Guilty before the Jury though it is possible some may be found Guilty of Manslaughter. This last I do not consider probable. It was necessary for the Grand Jury to find true bill to bring a case for trial at all[28]- After the matter is decided you shall have particulars. Mr. Wilson Stuckey is getting better- will soon it is thought be out of danger- An Irish man living on his place who recd probably small shot, but it is thought he will recover. The Windhams will all get well. You know Freeman and one Wyndham (Ab– or Amos Son of Amos–one Eye) are dead. I mention the name as above so that Mr. Garner may know which one it is–I did not know him-

---

26 Groups of men who patrolled their communities to guard against slave insurrection

27 Shooting occurred concerning a merchant selling liquor to Negroes; the men were found not guilty. The Sun–Baltimore, MD 03/26/1858, Vol. 42, Issue #115, p. 2

28 "Formal declarations...of particular things in writing." Black's Law Dictionary online

Drucilla came up last Wednesday and has been back this morning—all well—but she had sick headache yesterday- She came up to be examined by commission in the case of her mother against Hamilton Executor of his father. We had also commission to examine Mary, but of course could not see her.

I hope my dear that you still continue pleased and well satisfied with your situation and I do hope that Marys health may continue to improve. I was glad, as were all of us, to hear by your letter to your mother that Mary was better.

Charles came up from Charleston last Saturday but we have not yet seen any of the goods brought, shall probably to night.

Business has been about as good as we could expect it since you left.

I will now close. You can let Mary & Mr Garner read this, for I presume they will be glad to see the Darlington news. God bless you—and all your friends

Your affectionate Father
William Rogers

(written on the back of this letter:)

Dear Harriet,

As father had left a blank page I will write you a few lines, though I have nothing new to tell you. Wm and I spent the day at aunt Peggys on Wednesday last. They were all well. Mag had just received your letter and will answer it soon. She spent a few days last week with Emma Croskey and had a very pleasant time. Emma is coming to see her next week and they are all going to walk up here. Vermille took tea with us a few nights ago. She expects five new scholars the first of April, the misses Conners and Virginia Ingram. they think perhaps two misses Plowdens may come. I got a letter from Sallie Roper yesterday. She says they are to have a May party and Carrie (illegible) had been chosen queen and one of the new people Reese crowner. Carrie will make a sweet looking queen. They could not have made a better selection. Tell cousin Mary cousin Drucilla says the reason she had not written to her she had not had paper, but she will write her soon. She had a tooth drawn it did not hurt her any, but she was surprised when she found it was out. Mother says to give Hattie G. her best love and tell her we are all glad to hear she is getting on so well. You must write to me soon.

I remain your ever affct. Sister
A. M. R.

Milton Fla Mar 24th 1858
My dear cousin,

I did not untill recently know that you had gone to Summerton. I wrote a letter to you some several weeks ago and directed it to Bishopville. I presume you have received it ere this, and I suppose answered it. I will not however wait for an answer, but will endeavor to interest you for awhile at least. I received letters from home last week. All were well. Mr. Carson and sister were at Mother,s–Mr. Chamberlin, my step father is going or was going to start to Calafornia about the 10th of this month. I have not heard whether he went or not but presume he did. Mr. Carson is going to remain with mother and take charge of the farm until Mr. C. returns–And what do you think! Jess is going to get married!! Now this is hard on me–or at least would be if I loved her as much as cousin Mary would have it. And I believe you also sided with her, that I did love Jess very much- wonder if she has that famous letter yet. Ask her and tell her to preserve it–it is one of my grandest efforts and I should like to preserve a copy just to see how big a fool I once was- but I had better stop this strain or else you will think that I really did love Jess, particularly at the time I wrote the letter, and that I actually did let her have an opportunity of reading it–which is not the case–So much for this -

Brother James and Dick are coming home this summer. They do not like Texas much–though they are both making money out there.

I have been at this place about six weeks. have sold lots and cards of pictures and am selling them fast yet. I will, however, leave this burg in a few days, I will go to New Orleans, select some stock, see all the wonders of the city, and then come back to Mobile–and go from thence to Quitman Miss. where I will stop for awhile and will I expect meet up with Daniel i.e. if he does not come to this place before I leave here–as he wrote to me some time since that he had a notion of coming south to practice his profession. Should he come it will be the very thing for me. I now get rather lonesome and long for some one with whom I can converse freely, to whom I can pour out my heart without restraint, but I have no such friends about me now–true I have friends–always do have no matter where I go–but then they are only transient friends. They are as the summer cloud that soon passeth away and leaves no trace behind—but the friends I would have about me are as the April showers that diffuses new life into the drooping flowers in the path way.

I have been flying arround among the ladies quite extensively of late, was at a party on last night. There were a good many out. We had a very pleasant time indeed—in fact, I believe I enjoyed myself as well if not better than I ever did at a similar party—I can't say much for the beauty of the Milton ladies, there are a few that may be styled good looking—and one or two pretty ones, though they are all right Eleven girls. And when we come to take a right sober common sence view, we conclude beauty is not much after all, Beauty accompanied with the Christian virtues become more beautiful and when devoid of them is transformed into ugliness. Yes, give me for a companion through life one whose mind is shapen for the sober realities of the world, and whose heart has felt the influence of the religion of Christ, and though she be uncomely, yet I can walk the path of life with her with a buoyant step and a happy heart—But chain me for life to the fairest daughter of eve whose mind is of an unhappy mould and whose disposition is like an angry current dashing over hidden rocks, and I am an unhappy wretch fit for nothing that is noble and praiseworthy—But when Beauty is joined to good mind—pious heart—and a sweet disposition as for instance in the person of Miss ——- (I'm afraid to say lest you would accuse me of being deep in love) with her) then you have a character that the noblest son of Adam might well delight to call his own—

How do you like music teaching? Got any young men in your class? I should like to teach them were I in your place- Does Willie come over to Summerton often now?I guess he does, it is'nt far to where he lives is it? Well Cousin Harriet he is a very fine young man and were I in your place I would say yes, but I expect you have already said that, But you must not be in to great a hurry to call for the aid of the minister. Make W- consent to put off the great day until I come down this summer—but I will stop or you will conclude to blush and say why! cousin Hu you ought to be ashamed to write such nonsense. Nonsensence! did you say—I call it good sense! but never mind. we will drop this subject and get very serious on religious subjects—well—to begin—I have been reading, for the last few days, Mr. Spurgeons last work "The Saint and his Savior" it is a splendid thing—Altogether the best work of the kind it has ever been my good fortune to read—just such a work as he alone is capable of writing—There are fewer Christians and more Unaversalists, etc. here among the young men than any place I have been at in a long time. I have had some very lengthy arguments with some of them—even to night while I have been writing I have been arguing with a young gentleman from Georgia that the Bible is true (So if you see any blunders in the letter you will please excuse them) as one cant well talk an write at the same time but he has gone and I am glad of it) One stumbling block in their way seems to be the unfaithfulness of Christians. Oh! how careful ought we who have (illegible) Christ, to be in our walk before the world—Tell Mr Garner and Mary that they must excuse me for not writing. I know I promised cousin Mary to write to her, but I had forgotten her office and therefore I could not send a letter—Write soon and direct to Quitman Miss—Give my love to Mr. G. and Cousin Mary—

May the sunshine of Heaven ever illume your pathway through life is the prayer of your affect. cousin

Hugh

Bishopville March 28th 58
My dear Sister,

Your kind and very welcome letter was recd sometime since and still remains unanswered, and as I am by myself this afternoon, I will pass away the in writing to you, though I fear my letter will be very uninteresting, as I have no news at all to write you. We are all very well, though Daniel was sick a day or two since with a bad cold but is now up again, and seems pretty well. I spent the night at Aunt Peggys Friday night and Cousin Mag came home with me. Amanda Mag and I made several calls yesterday afternoon. first we went to see Vermeille then Miss Belle and to the store. I think they have very pretty goods in the store now. They have all gone to preaching this morning to Bethlehem. I expect Mr. English will come home with them. Miss Vermeille expects five new scholars sometime next week. Your Miss Connors and Virginia Ingram from Clarendon. We have a much better school house now than when you left. Mrs. Holleyman had to take the old schoolroom for a bed room as all of them were to board there and they had Dr. Holleymans old store fixed up for a schoolroom, and it is certainly a great deal better than the old one. They speak of giving a May party this year but I do not know certain yet whether they will or not. we will not know until the other girls come. I was down to see Mr. Lyon this morning. he still continues about the same, poor man. how much I wish he could get well. we have the measles in our little town now. Robert Dennis came home from Charleston last week and took them a day or two after he got home. none of them have had them either but Muldrow. his mother is very afraid of them. he stays up stairs and no one goes about him atal but Muldrow, so I dont suppose they will spread much. I have never had them but I am not very afraid of them. Muldrow took tea here last night. he comes pretty often here lately I tell you. He walked with Amanda to church last Sunday night and as there is going to be preaching to night I expect he will come again. we heard from Sister last Thursday. they were all very well. Anna was going to have the present of six pair of pantalets sent her by Mrs Logan. the dear little creature. no one knows anxious I am to see her. Father went to Georgetown last Monday got back yesterday morning. was very well. Amanda rec your letter a few days since and will answer it soon. Oh! has Willie been down to see you yet. I would have thought he would have gone long before this time.

It is very warm to day and if it keeps so and dont turn cold again I think we will have plenty of peaches this year. this day four weeks we will have big meeting down to the Presbyterian Church. Mr. Bishop is going to assist Mr. Wilson again this time. as I can think of nothing more to write I will close this letter. all send love to you cousins Mary and William. you must not let cousin Mary or any one see this letter. give my love to Fannie, Dennis and Hattie. write soon to me. I remain as ever your affct. Sister

Maria

Bishopville 29 March 1858

Pardon me my own beloved Harriet for not having sent you the money before as I intended to have done–I forgot to put it in my last letter to you as I fully intended doing–and then I went right of to Georgetown and Marion and was gone from Monday to Saturday last.

We had not the straw ribbon you wanted nor has Mr Carnes, but we have beautiful pink & white summer ribbon that I know will please you, and dear June is hoping to trim two bonnets–one for you and the other for our Amanda. Will send you the bonnet if possible next week–Your mother has been quite gay since I got back. All are pretty well. Mr. Lyon about as usual-

Our love to all–I must close remaining your affectionate Father
William Rogers

Bishopville SC March 31th 58
Dear Harriet

As the mail is just about closing I will drop you a few lines. I have been running about so much of late that I have done no letter writing and even this will be short. In the first place I must inform you that I am going to start for the west and ere this reaches you will be on my way. I leave or expect to day after tomorrow. My destination is Montgomery Ala. I am going to look at the place and people and if pleased will make it my home. I think now I shall remain. When you answer direct to the above place. I think I may be out in July to S.C. There is nothing new about here all are generally well. I have been laid up for a day or two and am suffering much from a cough but hope a change may help me. All friends were well when last heard from. the mail is closing and must stop. I shall write you from Mont

Your Brother
D M Rogers

When other friends are round thee
And other hearts are thine
When other Boys are round thee
More fresh and green than mine -
Then think how sad and lonely
This wretched heart will be
Which while it beats, beats only
Beloved, Hattie, for thee.

April 1st/58

P S Please answer this Soon

Friend etc[29]

---

29 Unknown author

Pine Forest April 1st 1858

Mif Hattie

I cannot forget thee; thy spirit is here
unseen and unheard; thou art still ever near
though long days have passed; since together we met,
thine image still haunts me; I cannot forget

When the soft sighing breeze wafts its melody near,
thy voice; sweetly warbling; in fancy I hear
when bright loveing visions; at eventide gleam
I see thee; before me in glorious dream

On my heart, thy bright image its impress has made;
That imprefs, nor absence; nor distance; shall fade
But here in my soul; will I cherish thee yet
I have Seen Thee; & Loved Thee; I cannot forget

Miss Hattie as this is the first that I have addressed you I think it hardly possible that you will know the author, but If you do please remember me to Miss Amanda & the Family in General. Please ans— this soon as I am all anxiety to hear from one I feel such deep interest in -

Your absent but Sincere Friend[30].............

30 Ruthvin Plowden

Bishopville 14 April 1858
My dear Harriet

I have taken my pen to write to you once more and am happy to say that we are all pretty well and my dear daughter these lines will find you well also. Amanda and myself reached home the day we left you. We got to Dr Dubose's about one oclock and took dinner there and I bought 25 bales cotton of the Dr.

Well dear Harriet poor Albert has left us! He is gone! He died without a struggle groan or sigh about 2 oclock PM on Sunday last. There was hardly any change in him, only he worked lower & lower down until he breathed his last. About five minutes before he breathed his last he took some nourishment in his own hands as usual. Soon after which he drew three breaths at longer intervals than usual, and he was dead. He was buried at the Bishopville church on Monday. Mr Wilson preached from 1st Peter 1st chapter 24 verse- "all flesh is grass" etc. He was buried in a beautiful metalic coffin, as he the night before his death expressed a wish to be sent to his friends north which will be done if his Brothers desire it. He appeared calm and composed on the subject of death and appeared satisfied to give himself up to his God trusting in His mercy—a good many persons attended the funeral. May his death prove a blessing to his friends both north and south. On tomorrow night a Suc,l meeting commences at the Pres. church—Mr Bishop is to be there. May much good be done in the name of the Lord Jesus.

We hear that J J Fleming is to preach at Piedmont next Sabbath. I wish you would give my regards to Mr. Garner, and Mary if she is still at Summerton, and tell him to write Mr Crosswell immediately about the disposition of the funds he gave me. Mr. C. will leave in a few days for Ashville. I dont believe I have any more news of any importance and so will close this letter, and I must try and write to your sister and perhaps Daniel. Mrs Rountree and Lizzy D. started for Georgia yesterday—Daniel is to go on with them.

I notice Dear H. that the most extensive accounts of Religion are passing through our country, such probably as it has never known before. May they cover our own state and wrest from the power of the Evil one thousands of precious souls—It is stated in a paper of ours from New York that 2300 persons made profession of religion in that city in ten days.[31]

My darling child, may God ever watch over and protect you—and may you prove a blessing to many through life- dear girl you have been a blessing to your parents- May Heaven bless you in return -

Your affc. father
William Rogers

My respects to Mr. & Mrs. McKnight & the Miss (illegible) & H. S.

---

31 The Third Great Awakening occurred from around the late 1850's to the early 20th century and was marked by religious activism in America. https://en.wikipedia.org/wiki/Third_Great_Awakening

Graniteville Apr 16th, 58
My dear Harriet

Your highly interesting and very welcome letter was received two days since, and afforded us much pleasure, you may be assured. We are always so glad to know that you are contented and surrounded with friends, passing your time pleasantly. I sincerely hope you may continue to be so where you are at present, and throughout your life. I expect you find it more pleasant teaching part of the time dont you? as you are kept more constantly employed. Poor dear Mary, I know you hated to see her leave. did she go to Mr. Chapel Garner's? May God grant that she may ere long return, in better health than she has known for years past.

I know you had a delightful surprise when father & Amanda went to see you. I thought of you all that day they were with you. I had equally as agreeable a surprise when Daniel came to see us. He arrived here by the midnight train on Friday night. Wm got up to let him in, sat some time talking with him, and then showed him to bed, and I knew nothing of it until next morning, just as I awoke, Wm said "Lucy." If you wish to give any orders about breakfast, Daniel is upstairs. you know I was delighted as well as surprised. He seemed to enjoy his visit very much indeed, was quite pleased with Graniteville. I had more pleasure in his society than I have had for a long time. I felt very sad when I found he was going so far away; and I know dear mother was grieved at parting with him, but I hope it is for the best, and with you dear Harriet, I humbly pray that God may watch over and preserve him from all evil. He left us on Tuesday morning. Mrs. R. & Lizzie met him. He seemed to anticipate much pleasure in going out in company with Lizzie, made me make a beautiful boquet for him to carry to her. I suppose you have ere this, heard of the death of poor Mr. Lyon, he died about two oclock on Sunday last. we were of course prepared to hear of it, for we have been expecting it so long, but as I look back upon all the time that we have known him, and then of his dying away from all his relatives my heart is filled with sadness and my eyes with tears. But oh I am so happy to know, that death to him, was through the mercy of our dear Redeemer disarmed of its terror, that he expressed himself willing to go. Father says he died perfectly easy without a struggle, groan or sigh. Oh may his death be sanctified to our everlasting good, and may all his relatives & friends endeavor to be ready to meet him on high when the master shall call.

Our dear little Anna Nora has not been quite well this week, her bowels have been some what deranged. She has however, been playing about all the time, and is the sweetest, smartest child you every saw. Daniel thought she had improved a great deal since he had seen her. She was very sociable with him, would go to him any time. The rest of us are quite well. Wm is as usual much interested in his garden, and it is now beginning to pay him for his labor. We have raddishes to eat and we had one mess of turnips. The rest of the things are all growing finely also. Graniteville presents a pretty appearance now, there are so many pretty flowers and flower gardens. Our own little yard looks quite pretty. We have some beautiful roses open. I have made a very pretty little shell box lately. It is quite an ornament to our little parlor. Daniel said "it looked distressingly fine." I did not tell you that he came by way of Charleston and also paid a visit to James Island, but I dont think Miss Clelia troubles his mind much. I am glad you and Amanda are so much pleased with your bonnets. I have no doubt but that they are very pretty. Amanda tells me she has a silk dress like yours also. How much I wish you and A. could come to see us here. The folks are so anxious to see you. I wonder who wrote your April fool from Darlington? I can guess who the others were from. Daniel seems to think a great deal of Mr Ruthven Plowden. Says he is very smart.

Have you heard of Sallie Brown's marriage? She was married last month to Mr Charles Smith who lives near Carolina College. I saw it in the Advocate. Mr. M. Kennedy married them.

Wm had a letter not long since from Mr Crook. He says Hennie has been in a very dangerous situation lately. She has been sick for some time. They fear she has an abscess in her side, but I do hope she may get over it. I do feel so sorry for her poor mother & father; her father says though if she was only converted, and had the love of God in her heart he could be resigned either way.

A union prayer meeting has recently been organized in this place, to be held between the Baptists and Methodists two nights in every week and I humbly trust that much good may come of it. Pray dear sister that it may be so. We were very glad to hear you made Mr Gamewell's acquaintance. I think he is one of the best men I ever knew. Mr. Mood joins me in warmest love to you, says he wants to see you very much and will write to you soon. Lavinia is asleep or I know she would have a message to send you.

Do write us again dear Harriet very soon, your letters are a great pleasure to us. Love to Mr. G. and to Mary when he sees or writes to her and remember me to all your friends . And now praying that our Heavenly Father will bless you, and keep you entirely his own, I remain as ever your most affct. Sister,

L. J. Mood

Maum Sarah was mightily pleased with Daniel, says she can tell quality folks, the minute she sees them.

Wm wishes me to ask you if you wish your Home Circle changed from Wright's Bluff to Friendship.

Bishopville April 19th 1858
My dear Harriet,

For the first time since I bade you adieu at Summerton have I taken my pen to write you—a duty I would have performed ere this, but you know the meeting was going on and I did not have time. Father wrote you the particulars of poor Mr Lyon's death, and I know you were rejoiced to know that he was resigned to death. I never saw any one so perfectly sensible to the last as he was. I saw him the morning he died. his brothers wish him to be carried home but I do not know when they intend doing so. I expect you felt very lonely after cousin Mary left but I suppose you are getting accustomed to it. We got to Dr Dubose in good time for dinner the morning we left you. Father had to weigh his cotton so we did not leave until nearly dark. they had eaten supper when we got home. The meeting at the Presbyterian church commenced on last Thursday night. Mr Bishop presiding. I went and was very much pleased with him indeed. I never heard any one I liked more. Mr Bartlett and Mrs Hulette joined on Saturday, no one else has joined since then. The meeting is continued to day it may be protracted longer still. Mr Wilson stated last night that there were several who were serious about their soul's salvation and that the meeting would be continued on their account. I have not heard who they were except Mr Ransom Scarborough. earnestly do I hope that much good may be accomplished and that God may abundantly bless His work in this part of His moral vineyard. Mr R Plowden and Capt. Nelson came up to aunt Peggy's Friday. staid here Saturday night. cousin Mary Jane was also here and we had fine times. Capt. Nelson said to give his best respects to you when we wrote and said he and Willie had been wanting to go down there for a long time but something always prevented, but says they are going now very soon so you may look out for another beau from down there.

Cousin Drucilla came up on Friday. they were all quite well. Mr (illegible) Shaw took tea here last night and I had the pleasure of his company to church. Mr. (illegible) spoke to me on Saturday. I find he is a little more conceited than ever. Mr. Fleming held forth at the Baptist church on yesterday. "The Green" Capt Dubose and Capt Stuckey's family all went to hear him. I was much surprised to hear it.

Dr Green did not go. Daniel wrote to us while he was in Graniteville, says his cough is much better. I found a long letter from cousin Hugh awaiting me when I got home. He says Annie and her husband are to live with his mother while Mr C is gone. Mr English preached for us yesterday, the quarterly meeting commences at St Luke's next Saturday. I nearly forgot to tell you that Laurie Dennis is at home now. I saw him at church yesterday. he looks very well indeed. Mag did not come with him. My paper is out so I must close. Give my love to Wm Mary and Hester James Mrs Gibson and all the others I know. Have you had any more seranades? Does Mr Coulette talk any more? I suppose waffles are as plentiful in Summerton as ever. Muffins also. I have made my silk dress. it fits beautifully. Excuse this bad writing. My pen is miserable. With much love I remain your affct sister

Amanda

Bishopville April 28th 1858
My dear Harriet

Your last letter was received on Thursday last and most gladly welcomed I assure you. we were truly glad to hear that you were well. We too are all well, though mother had a slight attack of headache yesterday but is much better to day. I am sorry to tell you of the death of Capt. Rembert. he died Monday about two oclock and was buried yesterday at Bethlehem. there was an immense crowd present. I never saw a longer funeral procession. Mrs Rembert takes it very hard. his children also, particularly Mrs Barrette. He suffered a great deal before he died. Dr Dubose attended him about a week. I expect Lizzie Durant will regret very much not being at home, though I hardly think she thought she would ever see him again.

We have not heard a word from cousin Mary since she has been in Darlington. Mother intends going to see her as soon as she can. I think cousin Drucilla went last week or at least she expected to go.

There was quarterly meeting at St Luke's last Saturday and Sunday. cousin David and myself went on Sunday and staid Sunday night with aunt Molsey. Perry Carter was there. I rather think he is a beau of cousin Mary Jane's. Anderson Lackey escorted Mag McCallum to the buggy. There were no ministers there but Mr. English and Joe Brown. They are speaking of having a May party at Lynchburg, but I do not know whether they will or not.

I am happy to tell you that Mary Jane McSnead is coming to spend her vacation with us and will be here to morrow. our pleasure would be complete could you share it with us, she too regrets your absence very much. I hope though her visit will be a pleasant one. I will do all in my power to render it so.

I spent last Wednesday night with Martha Frasier. She asked me all about you. said she was certainly going to write you this week and would have done so sooner had she known where to direct your letters. so you may look for a letter from her soon. I expect father and mother will go to Graniteville in the course of two or three weeks. I am so glad they are going, for I know Sister will be delighted to see them.

We received a letter from Daniel on Monday written the day after he reached Montgomery. he was quite well and thought he would like the place very much, had quite a nice time in Georgia and spent several days at Mrs Roundtree's and Mrs. Riley's together. You must be sure and write to him very soon if you have not already done so. he said to give his love to you and tell you to write to him. I believe I wrote you of Laurie Dennis being at home. he left on Wednesday. did not come to see us at all. I went to walk one evening and met him and he came home with me. I asked him all about Mag. he said she was very well.

Mr. Crosswell left today for Ashville. Argent will be at home next Thursday week. I am very glad she will so soon be here. it does not seem as though ten months have passed away since we were there that night does it?

Harriet I am positively ashamed to send this, it is written so horrid, but my pen is bad and I have written hurriedly. Maria came and looked over it just now and says she never saw such writing. Mother father Maria Almira Wm and cousin David all join with me in sending love to you and cousin Wm. Write very soon to your ever affct. sister

Amanda

Bishopville May 1st 58
My dear Sister,

I have waited patiently for an answer to my letter, but not rec- any I have concluded to write to you any way as I expect neary all of your time is pretty much occupied. I will first tell you that ever welcome news all are well. We were glad to see from your letter that you were well. Cousin Mary J. McLucas is with us now, she came Thursday. She and Amanda have gone down to Aunt Peggie's to spend the day. They were looking for Cousin Callie up this week, but I have not heard whether she came or not. Cousin Amanda is going home with her to stay some three or four weeks. I hope she may have a pleasant time while down there.

I suppose ere this you have heard of the death of Capt Rembert, poor old man he is dead. He suffered a great deal before he died but I trust he is now far better off. I feel so sorry for Mrs Rembert. she is left there all alone. she said that house was left desolate. There was a great many at his burial. father said he thought there was some three or four hundred. His funeral was not preached as Mr. English's wife was sick and he could not leave. The schollars from Clarendon have been here for some time now. I am very much indeed with them all. They are indeed lovely girls. Virginia Ingram took tea with me one night, and last night Anna Connors a girl about my size stayed with me and Julia C. with Almira. we spent the time very pleasantly indeed.

We received a letter from Daniel Monday. He was then in Montgomery. He was very well. says he thinks Montgomery a beautiful place. I do well out there. I look forward with a great deal of pleasure to the time when he and Cousin Hugh will be with us again. I do want to see cousin Hugh so bad. Cousin Mary J. is going to spend about two weeks with us. Cousin M. J. is such a nice girl. I love her as much as if she was my own cousin. I get along very well taking music lessons now. I like it a great deal better than I ever thought I would, and I hope I may improve much. I can play post-boy polka with hands now and have take more pieces this session. Ingram gave me a song to learn. I think it is very pretty. the name of it is "Gentle

Annie."[32] Have you ever heard it? Well dear sister I intended to write a long letter but Bishopville is so dull as usual that I can think of nothing else to write. Wm says tell sister Harriet to hurry and come home that he is very anxious to see you. now you must be sure and answer this very soon. All join with me in love to you. Hoping that a kind providence will watch over and protect and permit us to meet once more. I remain as ever your affct. sister

Maria

32 written by Stephen C. Foster

Bishopville May 22nd 1858
My dear Sister,

With great pleasure did I rec your last kind letter and glad to hear that you were well. We are all very well.

Well Harriet we are here by our selves, as father mother and William have gone to Graniteville. They left on Thursday last. I hope they will have a pleasant visit, but I know it can not be otherwise. I know sister will be delighted to see them. Dear little William, how I wish you could have seen him when he found out he was going. I never saw any one more delighted than he was. they expect to come home Tuesday. Cousin Mag came here Wednesday, and went home this morning. Cousin David carried her and cousin Amanda came back with him. She has recently been on a visit down to her sisters. She enjoyed herself very much while there. Have you ever heard that Emma Rogers had a little girl, but it did not live but one day, I am sorry. We heard this week that cousin May had a little girl I am very anxious to see it. When do you have vacation? I expect you are very busy now as Mr. Garner I expect is with cousin Mary now. Virginia Ingram spent the night with me last night. Virginia is a lovely girl. I like her very much.

Next Friday week we will have vacation. I assure I look forward to that time with a great deal of pleasure. I am getting pretty tired of going to school for a while.

Vermeille had measles this week but she has got nearly well agin. I expect I will have them as I have been with her a good deal. A good many of the scholars have stopped school on that account. We had a letter from Daniel Thursday. he was well and still very much pleased with Montgomery. He said he had a letter from cousin Hu said he would be in Bishopville in four or six weeks. oh! how glad I will be to see him. Well Harriet as cousin Manda is here you must excuse this short letter. All join with me in love to you. I remain your affct sister

Maria

At Home May 25 1858
Dear Hattie

I received your kind and affectionate letter more than a month ago, and have delayed replying to it a great deal longer time than I intended; but you must excuse me for this time and I shall try to write sooner here after, before something happens to prevent me as it has done this time.

I was not at home week before last, was staying with Aunt Carrie Moss while Uncle Billie was in Charleston and as I neglected to carry my writing materials I could not answer your letter then and thought I would put it off until I came home. I came home on Sunday the 16th of this month and on Monday the 17th Rosa was taken with scarlet fever. Poor little thing she has been suffering very much ever since, and is very little better now. Isabela was take just one week after Rosa, but she is a little better now. I hope she will not be as sick as Rosa has been and still is. The Dr. comes every day to see them and some times two Drs. come. I do not know wether the rest of of the children will take the fever or not. The Drs. do not think it contagious, but the baby has taken it since Rosa and I would not be surprized if we have more cases of it; however, I hope that it will stop where it is now.

I suppose you have heard of the May party at Orangeburg before this. I attended it but do not think it was half as good a one as we had last year. Carrie Pope was Queen. I think she made a vey good looking one. She was dressed very handsomely and look remarkably well. There was a number of persons at the party almost as many as we have at concerts. The tables, for there was two, were set in Mr. Pays school room. They extended from one end to the other and then all of the guest could not get to them. Some had to stand in between the tables and let things be handed to them.

I wish you could visit the College now to see what a change has taken place since we left. They have nearly all new teachers, and almost an entirely new set of girls, very few are there now that were there with us considering the school is so large. I think Mr. Legare has now about ninety-eight boarders besides the day-scholars.

I expect you have heard that Maner Lawton is to be married soon next Thursday nigh, the 27th she will be come Mrs Dr. Kirkland. I was not much surprized to hear it, but did not think that she would marry so soon, for she was not engaged when I was down there in February. She has only been engaged three months quite a short time I think. When I become engaged I think I shall wait a little longer than three months before I change my name.

I received a letter from Martha not long ago. she had been quite sick but was a little better when she wrote. Lizzie is still at Spartenburg, she send me a little paper the other day, named the "Mountain Echo" and asked me please to get a few subscribers. it is edited by the faculty and pupils of the Spartanburg Female College,[33] and only cost fifty cents per year. it is a monthly paper. I think it is well worth fifty cents. some of the papers contain compositions written by some of the girls, and they are generally very good. If you would like to subscribe for it let me know. If you do subscribe for it send me the change and tell me where to direct it. As I have written you quite a long letter I must close. Please excuse bad writing and all mistakes. Write soon to

Your true friend
Jane B. S.

P.S.

I finished writing this letter this morning. It is now evening and Emma has taken the fever also. I am afraid we will all have it for it seems to be contagous.

---

33 Spartanburg Female Academy, organized 1837; became Spartanburg Female College in 1854. William Gilmore Simms gave the inaugural address.

Harmony College SC[34] May 26/58
My dearest Hattie

Well, I am back at H, again, and have been for more than a week, and positively Harriet, it has appeared longer time than the three, spent at your home. Yes, I staid nearly 3 weeks, and assure you I never spent a more pleasant 3 weeks in all my life. I suppose it would not be very profitable to, anyone, to spend a lifetime in the same way, so we could see but little beneficial effect after, but, then I think a merry day now and then wholesome to the soberest of people. We visited a good deal during the time–indeed it seemed as though we were getting ready to go somewhere every-day and sometimes we went oftener, however, we did not go every day, but to tell the truth, I was so well pleased at home, that I did not care to go any where else, though I was invariably well pleased with all the persons I visited. We wished so often for you and Annie J. If you could have been with us, I don't think there would have been any thing wanting for completion except your kind Mothers good health. She suffered considerably from head ache while I was there. It seems strange indeed, that there is no cure for that head ache. I suppose Amanda gave you a full description of the proceedings and enjoyments of the May party, so I will only tell you that I think I enjoyed the party more than any of the girls there, the 2 weeks not excepted. You should not believe everything Amanda told you, after the affair. I never did meet with as many handsome gentlemen at a party I believe. The greatest objection was, that most of them seemed to have a fancy for the odor of Brandy or some other spirituous stuff. They were not intoxicated or anything like that, but just perfumed their breath I suppose. My oh! if the people knew I was writing such things about them, they would think me audacious indeed. I did not behave extremely well over there, that is, at Bishopville, and have felt a little ashamed at times, since when thinking of it, but I think

34 Harmony Female College, located in Sumter Mineral Springs, also called Bradford Springs, SC. Located in Sumter District, fifteen miles north of Sumter depot, on the very summit of the High Hills of the Santee. (from an online circular of the college, contributed by Presbyterian College)

if all the folks knew half how much I was enjoying it, they would regard my ill behavior as sheer impudence. Your Father has promised to let me go again Peach time, wasn't that clever in him? Hattie, I don't think I ever have seen a family so blessed in Parents as yourse. It seems to me that they are all you could possible wish them to be. Good Parents are indeed, an invaluable blessing, the full truth of which, I have felt, and still feel. But may you long enjoy the kind care, and affection which you do at present.

Harriet can you tell me what has become of Mary Singleton? She has not yet returned. If you see her, tell her, her chair at table is vacant, and should be filled. Also present my regards. Mary is a fine girl I think. I recd a letter from Amanda this week, and have just replied to her. I also had one from A.J. They were all quite well when she wrote. When do you have vacation? I would be perfectly delighted if you would all come to see me when you go home. Maria has almost promised to come, and I hope she will. Maria is a great girl in my estimation. I guess Amanda is pleased to night as she wrote me, she expected her Father & Mother home to night. I wish I could have been company for her during their abscence, though I recon she had equally as pleasant most of the time. I recon cousin David thinks me a right bad girl.I am sorry I teased him so much now, and so foolishly too, but he is a clever boy, and I recon will look over my impertinancies, though it is wiser to not be too presumptious. Well Hattie I guess you are willing to stop with me, so good night. Do write just as soon as you get this, and I will not wait so long next time.

Your very affectionate friend,
Mary Jane[35]

35 Mary Jane McLucas, Marlboro, listed in Class of 1858

Graniteville May 28th, 58
My own dear Sister,

Your affc letter was received on day before yesterday, just in time to cheer me up as I was feeling very sad. Mother, father & Wm having left the morning before. I was almost sorry though it had not come one day sooner, as mother was very anxious to hear from you. I was very happy to hear that you were well, and furthermore that the fare had improved, for it made me right anxious about you. I know that you are happy at the thought that the session is so near its close and of getting home, though I doubt not you will find it hard to part from your many friends there. We were truly rejoiced to hear that dear Mary was coming on so well, and had such a fine little daughter. I trust she is still doing well, and will soon be restored to perfect health. I wrote to her a day or two since. We were glad to get Mr. G's letter. Wm will answer it soon. I need not tell you dear Harriet how happy I was to have our dear parents come and see us, or how much I enjoyed their company while here. I have been looking forward to it so anxiously ever since I have been here. I had such a delightful surprise too in dear little Wm's coming. He made a great many friends while here, every body loved him. Dear mother seemed unusually well for her, and to enjoy her visit very much. She was delighted with the flower gardens, etc. I was only sorry that their visit was so short. I can hardly realize now that they were here. it seems like a delightful dream I have had. We all missed them so much, and were so lonely after they left. I never hated to part with them worse in my life. They seemed to think Anna had grown very much. She was very sociable with them. Mother brought her a beautiful little quilt, and Amanda sent her a beautiful little dress, braided. She is the most fortunate child I ever saw. Everybody is too good to her. I rec. a letter from Daniel this week also. He was quite well but said he was getting nothing to do, much, and thought he would come home and work around during the summer, and return to Mont. in Oct. He thinks he and Hugh will come on together. He had met Bennie Bell and had seen Mr. McDaniel who used to live at Clio. and also our Geography teacher Mr. Tolten has turned up out there. I expect you will all have fine times when you get home together. I would like to be of the number, but that can-not be, so I will try and be contented till fall, when I trust my turn will come. I wish some of you would come and see us. Amanda says she had a good deal of company one night while mother was away. Muldrow, & Dr. W. were the gentlemen. Mother says Muldrow pays his attention to Maria now. I told her she might hope to be rid of him sometime then, as he was pretty near the end of the row. Father, Wm & little Wm went over to Augusta last Saturday, so Wm can say now he has been in a city. But it is getting so late I must close. Do write soon again, dear sister. Your letters are a great comfort to me. Wm joins me in warmest love to you. Give my love to Mr. G.

I remain your devoted sister,
Lucy

Bishopville May 28th 1858
My Dear Sister,

Gladly do I a gain take my pen to write you and earnestly do I hope this will find you well.

We have felt right uneasy about you as it has been nearly three weeks since we have heard a word from you. I trust though our fears may not be realized. we are all well. Mother father and Wm got home safely last Wednesday morning. They left Graniteville on Tuesday and staid with Aunt Molsey Tuesday night. Had a very pleasant visit indeed. all enjoyed themselves finely. Wm was very communicative. He father and bro William went to Augusta and staid one day. Mother says Sister looks better than she ever saw her and that Anna is a very sweet and pretty child. She cannot talk much yet. Mother says her hair curls beautifully. I was never more anxious to see the darling little creature than I am now. We heard from Daniel last week. he was well and sent his love to you. have you written to him yet? He does not write home often only twice since he has been in Montgomery. Mother and father are going over tomorrow to see cousin Mary. We have not heard from her in some time. I got a letter from Mary Jane the other day. she says Mary Carmicheal has returned. I was very glad to hear it as she was so anxious for her to come back. Father told Mary Jane he would send for her again in peach time. I look forward to it with much pleasure. I have been suffering some this week from my face. It has been swollen very much since Monday and does not seem to decrease much yet. It is caused by one of my teeth, the one I had the nerve killed. I expect I will yet have to consent to its being drawn when Daniel comes. Have you heard of the death of Mrs. Porter? the Methodist minister's wife in Sumter. I was truly sorry to hear it. There is a good deal of sickness in Sumter. I believe Bishopville is as healthy a place as can be found now. There is no sickness about here now, scarcely.

Muldrow Dennis is to have an examination next Friday and we have heard that there is to be a picnic but I do not know whether it is so or not. Mrs. Holleyman's school closes next Friday also. They have revived the Singing Society again and meet now every Friday evening. Have the misses James returned yet? I expect you found it quite lonely during their absence.

I have not been to see Argent yet, though I want to go now very soon. The miss Woods are now over in Darlington to see Mrs Harrel. They have produced considerable sensation since they have been here. I have never seen them but once. I met them at the school house one Friday and was introduced to the eldest. The youngest is quite pretty. all the young men have fallen desperately in love with her, cousin David particularly. I presume it will not last long. Mary Connors spent last night and to day with us. she is a nice girl. I like her very much. Mr. McClary has gone home. I expect though he will return next session. It is getting quite late so I must close. Mother father Maria Almira and Wm all join with me in sending you much much love. do write very soon.

Your ever affct. sister
A. M. Rogers

Bishopville 31 May 1858
My darling Harriet

Having with your dear Mother just returned from a visit to Mary, I will write a few lines, that you may know from us that we are all well and that we found Mary very well and the baby quite fair to look upon. Especially for a baby—We hoped when we went over yesterday that we might meet with Mr Garner, but in this we were disappointed.

On returning home I was much pleased to find a letter from my good girl Harriet and so as tomorrow mornings mail will leave I send this ahead by first opportunity.

We had a nice visit to Graniteville, found all very snug and cozy, with Lucy—had a good visit and good (illegible)—Lucy is looking better than for years—little Anna E. is in fine health—William—W.M. about as usual. William A. Rogers was much delighted with his travels—I took him to Augusta—also to the pottery 7 miles from Graniteville.[36]

Your mother stood her trip well, and has been pretty well since we got back.

Well dear Harriet it will not now be long before we hope to have you with us again. before the time comes you must let us know first when to send to Lynchburg for you.

Jenkins Holmes has been frequently sick with chill and fever since he has been here—His wife is good looking and appears clever.

Our garden is doing right well, but all our nice peas and string beans will be gone before you get here, but we shall have potatos, though our crop will be much smaller than it would have been but for the frost.

I suppose Daniel and Hu. B. will be here about the same time that you will return perhaps not quite so soon.

---

36 "Aiken county produces a type of kaolin found nowhere else in the world. Aiken county can boast, too, that the oldest kaolin mine in the nation is located within its borders. It was known as 'The Pottery' during the days of the War Between the States and is still being operated by the Dixie Clay Company." *Ninety Years of Aiken County* by G.L. Toole, II, Chapter XIV

Not having much to communicate in the way of news I will not trouble you with any thing lengthy, but I know you would be glad to hear we are all well and that Mary is so smart. Mrs. Garner is as clever as ever and Mr G. very kind.

Our kind regards to Mr. W.A.G. and all your friends,
Very affectionately Your father & friend
William Rogers

Summerton Ju 2, 1858
Miss Harriet

I suppose you will think that this letter will be a great presumption in me, but I must beg that you will pardon me, for I can not control my heart. I have loved you ever since I first saw you—loved you with all my heart. I endeavored on several occasions while you were in Summerton to express my love for you, but as often have I failed. It was with a sad heart that I saw you leave this little village, without my telling you that all my hopes of earthly happiness were centered in you, and in offering to you my hand and heart, I do it with a trepidation of feeling which no language can describe, since a refusal would plunge me into the very depth of whretchedness and (illegible). And I could not trust myself in your presence untill I knew that there was at least a ray of hope for me. and now, Miss Harriett may I come, my fate is in your hands. And if it is so ordained that I am to be disapointed, God pity me and give me strength to bear it with becoming fortitude.

Your Tru and Devoted lover
W. H. Singleton

Bishopville June 5th 1858
My dear Harriet

We were most happy to hear from you on Monday last as it had been some time since we had the pleasure of hearing from you. I had begun to fear you were sick. We are all well. I am happy to say mother and father went over to see cousin Mary this week and said she was getting on pretty well. Mother says her baby is very pretty. I am anxious to see the little creature. Mother thought perhaps Mr. Garner and carried some thing for you to eat and we were very sorry he was not there. Sister says you wrote her that the fare was very good now. We were truly happy to hear it. I have heard Dr. Green speak of how it was when he was there. he asked me the other day if Mr. McKnight's fare was any better than it used to be.

Mr. Dennis had an examination on Thursday and a dinner also. Mr. Wilson made a short speech after the examination was over. The table was set in the woods—had a nice dinner. I enjoyed myself very much indeed, after dinner they had dancing but I would not stay to see that. Mrs. Rembert spent that day with mother and Mrs. English also—so Vermielle and I came over and spent the evening very pleasantly at home. Mr. and Mrs. English spent the day here on last Monday also. I do love her so much. the miss Barrett's danced, and scarcely five weeks have elapsed since the death of their Grandfather. I felt sorry for Mrs. Rembert but she said it was nothing more than she expected. Vermeille's school closed on yesterday. She had no examination but the girls all read compositions and two dialogues were acted.

I read a letter Mr. Legare wrote to father today and he says he is going to New York in vacation and get our diplomas done up according to his notion. he must be going to have them extra fine, at least I hope so after so long a time. he spoke very kindly and affectionately of us both, called us the "dear girls" all the time. I got a letter from Lou Muldrow the other day and she says Miss Hahr is to leave next week for Sweden. I expect there will be loud lamentations when she bids adieu to Orangeburg and its dear inmates. Lou says there has been an other great revival. she did not tell me how many conversions there had been but says that Maggie Valentine and Cooper (who you know are her roommates) have, are now followers of the "meek and lowly Savior"—I was rejoiced to hear of this. They are to have a public examination this session. Virginia Dennis has been quite sick, but is better now. Mother and I went to see her a few evenings ago and also went to see Mrs. Muldrow. It is the first time I have been there since the evening we went there with Anadella. We heard from Daniel on Thursday. he was well, and he expected cousin Hugh in a few days and they would come on together. I do not know when but think they will be here pretty soon as the attraction for them has returned. Lizzie got home today. I am very glad she has returned. expect I will see her at church tomorrow.

Muldrow Dennis asked me yesterday when you would be at home. said he was anxious to see you. Have you heard that Miss Martha Bradley had presented the Presbyterian Church with a set of lamps. They are very pretty indeed. The misses Woods are not so much talked of now. I do not think I have got acquainted with only one of them. I have to write Daniel yet so I must close. Mother father Maria Almira William and cousin David all send you much love and cousin Wm also. and accept the same from your devoted sister

A. M. Rogers

Graniteville SC June 11th '58
My dear Sister Harriet

There is a letter to Amanda before me began a day or so ago which lies unfinished, and I would finish it now but I have a head ache, and I begin this reluctantly to you fearing it will not interest you, but both of us are desirious that you should hear from us once more before you leave for Sumter. Trust this will find you & bro. Garner well. Give him our kind regards. tell him that I rejoice with him in the "June rain" he had whilst writing his last to me. hope the "June shower" done him as much good as it did us to hear of it—It is very threatening now and the muttering thunder reminds me that rain is not far off—if it comes before this is mailed I'll inform you. You will make this information known immediately if not sooner to bro Garner.

We were glad to hear that Mary & the babe were doing so well. Lucy is well and has been revelling lately in plums. our trees are loaded. She is thinking of preserving some. Our tree is very fine indeed. Anna Nora, the dear child, is now under going her afternoon 'ablution.' she is head & ears in the bason & kicking like five hundred & splashing & tossing the water every where—when Lucy is done with her, & her hair is curled & you could see her I know you'd say she was a sweet child. I don't know who she takes her curly hair after but you—though it does not curl as richly as yours. Did you know that I was a great admirer of <u>your</u> curly hair?

We are knocking on here pretty much at the old rate. I am now busying myself in my missionary collections. I don't find great likability here—though some do their best—As the time advances to the close of your session I know you are anxious to get home—this will be very pleasant for you to meet Father Mother brothers & sisters from whom you have been so long absent. We only wish we could mingle with you in the joyful occasion.

We are to have great times here on the 4th though. I nor Lucy will not enjoy ourselves as we did last July. There is to be given here an extensive barbacue and then seperate arrangements will be made for the children. The stockholders pay for it all and every thing will be on an ample plan.

We are looking for Daniel & Hugh but we expect them when we see them. When you get home tell them all howdy & kiss all for me that want to be kissed & all that don't kiss anyhow. Lucy joins me in sending a great deal of love to you.

Your affect. bro.
Wm

(written in margin:)

Mif Lawton was married by Mr. Hames to Dr N.L. Kirkland family of Barnwell Dist. SC

Do write to us all about your winding up and all that occurred in your getting to Sumter-

We have had a fine rain-

Harmony College SC July 27 1858
My dearest Harriet,

As I have been neglecting to reply to letters for several weeks past, I will respond to you immediately for fear that a few days' delay might insure a (illegible). I scarcely feel like writing, or doing any thing else since my return from B. I met the sad sad news of aunt Peggies death as soon as I got here. and dear Harriet you can better imagine the painful shock than I can describe it. Aunt Peggie was the favourite aunt with all of us, and was always so kind and solicitous about us since our dear mothers death that she seemed little less than a Mother. We will all miss her so much, and not us alone, for I recon few women having died, leaving no children, could be more tenderly lamented. I am sure Kate could never have cherished a deeper, or more devoted love for her own Mother, had she lived, than she always has for Aunt. She wrote me such a very sad letter a few days since. But alas! our love can have no power in averting the fatal stroke, but it falls with the same force on those we most love, as others. Some times I think we should grieve less for friends when we feel assured of their acceptance with God, but I have found that experience, in the loss of many friends, is far from schooling the heart to calm resignation but each new loss is felt the more keenly, as the heart becomes more sensitive. Aunt Peggie expressed her willingness to depart and be with Jesus more than once just before her death. There is an unsurpassable sacredness to me in the contemplation of a Christian's triumph over death and its terrors, through the faithful recognition of the smiles of a reconciled Redeemer. I had just heard, with much sorrow, of Olivias death when I read your letter confirming the fact, as I was slow to believe such sad news. I have since learned that she died very suddenly of congestive fever, was sick but few times so that they did not have a physician at all. This should warn many of us to have our house in order so that we may be ready at any time to obey the sure summons. I rejoice that Olivias friends are not called to mourn as those who have no hope, but with the glorious hope of an eternal reunion in the immediate presence of the God she loved and worshipped on earth. I have no news to tell you Harriet that would entertain you at all. I am very glad indeed to hear that those of you who were sick are improving and trust they may speedily find themselves enjoying good health.

I am so glad Amanda and cousin Hu have gone to Marl.[37] I can sympathize with Cousin Nancy and Annie Jane in their happiness. I never wished so much to go home, as I do now. Sometimes I feel as though I could not stay away any longer. Tell A. she must write to me as soon as she gets home and tell me all about them over there.

Well Harriet I must close, give my love and best regards to all and accept the same for you dear self. I will send cousin David some mefage when I feel more in the humor. My regards to him, and tell him a public concer is in contemplation, to come off when Mr. Smith arrives about 3 weeks hence. I will let him know the exact time when it is appointed, and will be more than happy to see you all out. Now Harriet—do write—as soon as you receive this.

Most sincerely
Mary J.

37 Marlborough County

Parnassus Sept. the 29 1858
My own dearly beloved cousin

Your kind affectionate and thrice welcome letter came to hand last Sunday. it was gladly received by us all you may be sure. I was glad to hear you got home safely and found all well. you had quite a pleasant day for traveling the day you went home. I was glad also to hear that you went to Mrs McLaurin's and enjoyed your visit so much. they are indeed a clever family. Well my cousin I can't find words to tell you what a miserable day I spent at Mr Alford's after you left. it seemed to me I never felt as sorry to part with any one before as you and Daniel. beside that I had a sick head ache. I never had it any worse. we stayed there all day. if you recollect Mr Alford was not at home. He did not come until after dinner. Hu was so anxious to see him he wanted to stay. You may tell Daniel Hu swapt for the horse. drove him home that evening. I was frightened in starting but after starting he seemed to be very gentle. Hu is very much pleased with his trade so far.

Well my cousin I have no news to write. I wish I had something that would interest you. there has been no change since you left only old Mr Lucas is building rite out yonder not far from the gate. I am very sorry for that but cannot help it. I thought them near enough at the old store. I am sorry to tell you I do not expect Kate will go to Harmony the winter. Ellen is there now and has been ever since you left. she has gotten nearly well or quite only she is still weak. she will stay untill Frost and perhaps longer and it is so near the examination now Kate does not like to go. she says they will all be so busy and so much confusion untill after that time. She does not think she could enjoy the visit as much at such a time. I am glad the time is short now that Mary J will be at home. I do not know whether Mc is going for her or not. if he does I expect he will go by Bishopville. if so you will be certain to see him. I am sorry to say I haven't seen a sight of George or Bob since you left but heard from them last week. Susan and Mary spent a day here last week Wednesday I believe. Kate, Ellen and Margaret Ann Alford spent the day here too. Susan and Mary came over on horse back. I wished very much for the pony a little while to take a ride with them.

I heard from Moses the other day. he was still talking about you. I expect you will see him in Bishopville before long. they are going to sing again next Saturday. how I do wish you were here to go. Lizzie Kinnie stayed here Monday night. she sends her best love to you. the Kinnies are indeed clever good people. they think a wonder of you and all of the family that they have seen. they do not think that Daniel's equal is to be found any where. tell Daniel to write to us when he goes off. I wanted to ask him when I told him good bye but I felt like I could not speak to save my life. I trust through the mercy of a Kind Providence we may all be spared to meet again. I hope he will not forget his promise to come next Summer if nothing happens. Hu says he is going over to see you this winter certain if nothing happens to prevent. I never have seen him more anxious to go any where than he is to go to Bishopville but does not know yet what time he will go. I believe I have nothing more to write so I will begin to draw to a close. do write as soon as you get this. what a pleasure it is to get a letter from any of you. O how I do wish we could see each other as often as we can write. Mother talks about you every day. this leave us all as well as common. Hu has nearly recovered form his hurt. he does not limp any now but it hurts him some. more at night than any other time. I hope this may find you all in the enjoyment of good health. Mother and Hu join me in sending our best love to you all. I remain as ever your devoted cousin untill death

Annie F. McCallum
do write very soon my dear.

At Home Orangeburg Oct. 7th 1858
My dear Harriett,

I received your long long looked for letter on the 23rd of last month, and had began to think that you had forgotten me; but am vey glad to see that you have been thinking over your old friends and among them I suppose you thought of Old Dr. John. who will be very glad to hear from you at any time.

I was very very sorry to hear that your Mother and Father and Sister have all been sick, but I am truly glad to hear that they are all better, and am glad that you were with them during their sickness. It must have been a source of great pleasure to you to know that you were there to nurse them.

Since I wrote you last, which was in May, we too have been visited by sickness, yea! even death has entered our dwelling, and has taken from us our dear little Emma. She died on the 12th of last June. It pleased our Heavenly Father to take her out of this sinful wourld when she was only four years and five months old. Dear little creature she suffered a long time before she died. She was sick for eighteen days and had very high fever all the time. She was very patient indeed, did not complain atal until about twenty-seven hours before she died when she commenced groaning, and then every breath was a groan until she drew her last. Dear little thing we all miss her very much. We will never hear her innocent little prattle or her sweet voice any more on earth; but I hope and pray that we may sing with her around God's throne where we shall never have to part again. It has been my constant prayer that God will sanctify her death to the good of our souls. I know she is far better off else I would wish her back. but ah! how could I wish her back in this poor wicked world. I only pray that we may go to her and not for her to come to us.

We all arrived home on last Tuesday from a campmeeting[38] at Binnicaker's Bridge.[39] We tented, and I enjoyed my self very much. I wished for you and Amanda, yes even your whole family. We did not have a very good meeting, though we had very good preaching; but some how or other it seemed as if the people could not be aroused and so they did not get many members. I was very agreeably surprised on our arrival at the campground to find that your Brother William was there. I was indeed very glad to see him, and was much pleased to hear him preach. I truly wish you could have been there on Sunday night to have seen him. It would have done you good to see how happy he got. I could not help looking at him. He was so happy that he could do nothing but walk up and down the alter and exclaim. "I am so happy."

When do you expect to return to Summerton? or do you intend remaining at home? You must not put off writing to me so long any more. I would have written to you befor I received your letter but something always prevented me.

As it is growing late and I have another letter to write to night I must bring this badly written and uninteresting epistle to a close.

---

38 "Camp meeting: a form of Protestant Christian religious service originating in England and Scotland as an evangelical event held for worship, preaching and communion on the frontier during the 2nd Great Awakening of the early 19th century. They gathered in a central location for preaching, hymn-singing, dancing, and fellowship, often staying in wagons or tents over several days. There were few ordained ministers and churches in some areas, so all gathered to hear one preacher after another, all day and into the night. All enjoyed the break from work, and the visiting with friends, family and neighbors." from Wikipedia

39 Binnicker's Bridge, in Orangeburg county, extended from US 301 (Bamberg Hwy.) to the south fork of the Edisto River. It is mentioned in the minutes of the Orange Parish Roads Committee meeting for April 5, 1841, as a committee is named to rebuild the bridge. (Also mentioned is Binnicker's Campground–this is where they held the camp meeting.) Larry Hardy, Dec. 17, 2014, Vintage Orangeburg/Day 41: Binnicker Bridge name goes deep into county history, The Times and Democrat, https:/thetandd.com/news/vintage-orangeburg-day-41-binnicker-bridge

Do write soon. Let no one see this letter. Remember me to all. give much love to Amanda and receive the same for your self from your friend

Jane Sally

Home, Feb. 17th 1859
My dear Hattie,

I had resolved never to write to you again, as I thought that you had ceased corresponding with me but my resolution was suddenly broken this evening by the agreeable surprise—another of your letters. What a good girl you are to tell me of your engagement. I was much surprised to hear that the little soul is to leave home so soon. I humbly trust that you will find in him a kind and affectionate husband. And he is a Presbyterian, that is no objection in my estimation. I was just thinking this morning how much I like the principles of that church. -- There is so much variance in the pronunciation of our sound that I am rather at a loss how to pronounce Mr. P's name. I will receive sufficient instruction, however if you inform me whether or not the v is silent.

I suppose you have been told that Capt. Salley and Becker Pickens were engaged. Becker informed him that she was mistaken in her affections, and broke the engagement. Poor man! I hear that he takes it grievously. Mention this to no one out of the family, as Mrs. Graham is my informant and might not like to have it told. Kate Felder's sister, Anna, is soon to be married to (illegible) Felder, the gentleman, who addressed cousin Jane Lawton. The girls are marrying on every side. Grandma said today, that Miss Lizzie will marry soon. I told her that "Pa" must give me a pretty flower garden, as I am to remain single a long time.

I have been thinking a great deal today of the girls with whom I became acquainted at Orangeburg. How many beloved ones there are in that number! At times I greatly desire to enjoy this society again; but it seems the will of my Heavenly Parent that I am to see very little, if anything of them on earth. May we all meet in Heaven, where we will no more bid each other sad farewells.

I am pleased to hear that you enjoyed your visit to Charleston. I am anticipating a trip to Ch. or Savannah soon. Grandma is undecided as to which city we will go; it makes little difference with me, I am fond of riding either in a boat, or on the cars.

I expect three Orangeburg ladies on tomorrow—Mrs. Graham, Anna Salley, and Kittie Moss. We are all going up to Dr. Erwin's to see Anna (illegible) (Milhous) and Mrs. William Moss.

Hattie, please my dear excuse this poor letter, and receive my heartfelt thanks for your kind initiative to continue correspondence.

My best love to Manda and Mrs. Mood. Write soon, and tell me all about the evening of your marriage.

Your well-wishing friend!
Martha R.
P.S.

I have seen dear, little Anna she is still fleshy, but her face is not so round as before. Jane Salley is to be married the 24th of next month. I will be unable to attend as it is so inconvenient to go so far in a carriage.—Hattie, I daresay this will be little appreciated, being received at such a time. Be sure to write.

Madison Fla Feb 27th 59
My own dear Cousin

Your very welcome letter of Jan 29th came to hand a day or two since, having been forwarded from Albany. You may be sure that I was very glad to receive it and its contents were devoured with eagerness. and now this Sabbath evening while the shades of night are fast veiling the face of nature in darkness, to the music of the pattering rain drops, I will attempt to reply.

I was pleased to hear of the good health of the family, and also that your dear cousin Charlotte was, under the influence of a southern climate, beginning to feel much better. I hope that she will continue to improve untill she is entirely restored to health again.

I was much pleased to learn that Mr. Mood had been appointed on the Lynchburg circuit. It will be so pleasant to have them so near. I know Aunt Anna will be better satisfied at having Lucy so near her. But I imagine Maria made the greatest demonstration of joy at having Annanora so near, in fact, I think Mr. Mood had better keep Anna entirely away from Maria, or at least, permit her to see her but seldom, for if she was permitted to enjoy the pleasure of Miss Annanora's company without stint I am affraid she would eat her entirely up, in one of her most loving moments. Now dont tell Maria this, if you please Cousin Harriet, for if you do I am affraid she will not kiss my picture the next time she looks at it.

I read with pleasure of your trip to Charleston and of your pleasant visits and fine drive to the battery. I have always been sorry that I did not stop longer in Charleston and look over the city more. I missed seeing some fine things. I think if ever I visit the city again I will see more of it. Did you pay Miss Clelia a visit while there? I received letters from home on yesterday. All were well. Sister Mary is at school and Bro Dick writes me that she is learning if possible, faster than ever. I am, I believe, more anxious to see her than any of the family, she is indeed a sweet little girl. I wish you could see her. I have been at this place some over two weeks and will perhaps remain a month longer, as I am doing a pretty fair business. I do not know which way I will conclude to go home, possibly I may go to E Florida, if I do I will return by way of Charleston, and will most likely pay Bishopville a flying visit, though if I come it will be out of my power to remain long, as I must be in Tenn any way by the 1st June and I will not leave this state till May.

It would afford me unbounded pleasure to be present at your wedding, but I will be compelled to forego that pleasure. but, let me congratulate you in advance, and wish you a bright and happy future. May your voyage over the matrimonial sea be one of unbroken success. May no rude gales disturb the even tenor of your way. Let Duty be your polar star, Religion be your sun and may Love strew your pathway with the beautiful flowers of quiet happiness.

I received a letter from cousin David the same time I did yours, it being the first I have had from him since he has been in Balt. It will soon be time for his return I know you all will be delighted to see him. he will be delighted, I know, at being home in time to be present at your nuptials.

As the mail closes in a short time I will bring my letter also to a close. Give my love to all the family, also to Lucy and Mr Mood when you see them. I guess they think I have entirely forgotten them as I have not written in so long, but I intend to supprize them with a letter before long. Accept now dear cousin the best love of

Your affect. Cousin H. B. McCallum

Bishopville 27 March 1859
My dear Children[40]

I will do my self the pleasure this morning to write you a few lines and am happy to say that we are also in usual health. Except Daniel. We have very little in the way of news since you left here a week ago. Daniel after you left continued to improve slowly—and is now able to attend to a little business. He still does not look well though he is a great deal better than when you left.

I had two or three days of severe Rheumatism, but am now almost entirely over it. Mr. Mood sent word last Wednesday—(illegible Tuesday) that he was on his way to Sumter to assist at a meeting there, and begged for Maria to go down and stay awhile at Lynchburg. So Daniel carried her down and she is still there- Yesterday Amanda & myself went over to "Cypress" to attend the funeral service of Hubbard DuBose. We called for dinner with Mr. Robt. J. Huggins- came home before night and heard Mr. Wilson preach last night. Mr. Wilson spoke in reference to Rev. Mr. Bishop and states that he was attacked in the pulpit—became delirious at once, and was carried home to die.[41] Mr. Bishop was present, we hear at the time of the dreadful Bennettsville tragedy—and was with John—and prayed—continued with him until he died- Excitement & Exposure that night it was thought was the cause of his sickness and death—if so there were <u>four</u> instead of three victims. The case of Terrell has been put off until fall court.[42] Drucilla & children came up here last Friday

40 Harriet and Ruthvin were married March 9, 1859, and are living in his family home in the fork of Black River with his two little boys, and sister, Elizabeth.

41 Pierpont E. Bishop collapsed in the pulpit from pneumonia, and died. from A History of Marlboro County, Chapter XXXIII, Presbyterian Churches

42 A Bennettsville merchant was accused of murdering his father and grandfather with poisoned whiskey over a financial/forgery dispute. An employee of the store also died after drinking with them. Source: Library of Congress, Chronicling America, Historic American Newspapers; Edgefield Advertiser; Bennettsville SC Son of Temperance

and they are still here. Drucilla appears rather gloomy but not more so than might be expected. She has a letter from her mother & Mary since the news of Johns death reached them- She thinks they took Johns death very hard—that might have been expected.

I hoped to have sent Jim down to you by this time—but my dear Harriet trust me, and excuse me to the present time—and for some time yet to come. We have so many (illegible) (as well as guano) to get here from the depot—that it seems almost impossible to send down to you—until we get the goods up. If you do get out of patience however you must let us know, and he <u>should</u> <u>go</u> in that case. I think you are already aware that Sacramental meeting comes on here at the Pres. Church—commencing on Thursday two weeks- say 14 April- We shall hope you will be up at that time if not sooner, and stay until the meeting closes. Mr. Bishop was to have been here <u>but</u> <u>his</u> <u>work</u> <u>is</u> <u>done.</u>

I need not say to you for you are fully aware of the fact that it will afford us much pleasure at our earliest convenient opportunity to make you a visit—and we shall hope to be able to do this some time during the Spring. Our dear Harriet must not complain of the <u>time</u> must remember that she has been several times absent from us for months at a time—and now she has the chance of seeing us much more frequently than at former times for now <u>she</u> can come sometimes—and occasionally <u>we</u> hope to <u>go.</u> It is happiness to reflect that all the pain Dear Harriet has (illegible) us was that ocaisioned by her absence from us. But for want of time I must close. I will however say that we shall not only be most happy in seeing you here at any time but also any of your friends. Especially Miss Elizabeth—I have forgotten—if I knew—the office to which I ought to direct this. I will direct to Plowdens Mill, and if not right some of your friends will forward to you.

And now with the love of the whole family—and with my best wishes for your present and eternal happiness—I remain most affectionately and truly your Father and friend.

William Rogers

Lynchburg Apr. 8th, 59
My beloved Sister

I was most happy to hear from you through your brother Wm, who arrived home safely, just in time for dinner, on the day he left you. I was glad to hear that you and the rest of the family were all well, and would have been much pleased had I been able to have joined Mr M in his visit to you, but circumstances would not admit of it. He seems to have enjoyed himself very much, but I was not surprised to hear this, for how could he help it? when he had been with such dear folks. Daniel left us this morning for home, having been down since Tuesday. He seems quite well again. operating does not seem to fatigue him as I thought it would. He left all well at home, though cousin Elisha was up yesterday and says mother was complaining some of headache. I trust however, it was not a severe attack. She and father have promised to come down to-morrow and spend Sunday with us. I am, as you may imagine, looking forward with much pleasure to their visit. Mother you know has not been to see us yet. I feel quite sick (at least in anticipation) just now, father and mother coming this week, and you and brother R. next. It seems almost like an age since I have seen you, and I am growing very anxious to do so. I shall certainly expect you, one week from today, and come to dinner, you can get here easily by that time, and it will give me more time to be with you. I am only sorry that Mr. M. cannot be at home, but thus it is with Methodist ministers, duty often calls, when inclination would lead them to remain. Anna is quite on tiptoe to see "Aunt Harriet's little boys," as she calls them. on finding I am writing to you, she says "tell Aunt H. please bring em up to Lynchburg to see me." She often talks about you and the <u>wedding</u> is indellibly engraven on her mind.

I was very glad to hear that Callie had been able to come up to her mother's, when I last heard from her she thought she was better. the trip did not fatigue her as they feared it would. How much I wish she could get well, but she is in the hands of a merciful Providence, who doeth all things well. Mary Jane was down to see me this week. Lizzie H. came with her to Mr R Durant's. I think L. has improved considerably since I saw her before.

Everett & his company perform at Bishopville to-night, and as usual I presume will prove quite an attraction. Daniel informs us that the "Bartlett House is open for their entertainment, and Mr. Carnes' boarders have also moved there. I believe I have nothing new to tell you of Lynchburg, things are moving on at the same old rate.

Since I wrote you last dear Sister, a most important era in your life has transpired. A new name, new associations and relations, are now yours, and with them come new duties for you to perform. You have started afresh as it were, upon the voyage of life. God grant that your bark though frail, and liable to the buffetings of the tempest-tossed sea, may yet never suffer shipwreck, but ever be guided and upheld by His Hand whom the winds and seas obey. You well know my earnest prayers and wishes for your success and happiness through life. I need not repeat them here, but I commend you to Him who is able to strengthen and direct you in the performance of every duty. You are I feel assurred united to one in every way worthy. Long may you each be happy in each others love, and in the love of all around you. But I must close if I would get this to the mail in time. Much love to brother R, Miss E, & Miss Y. and kisses to the little boys. Thank Miss Eliz— many times for her presents. Good bye my dear. I hope soon very soon to see you. I rem. Your devoted Sister

L. J. Mood

Bishopville April 8, 1859
My dear Harriet,

A letter from Jane reached here on Monday directed to me and as tomorrow is mail day I concluded to write you a short note at least. All are quite well. Mother has recovered from headache. Father has gone to Camden to day in company with Mr. Carnes. He will be back to night I suppose. Emma Rogers and Susan Dubose came and spent the day with me yesterday. Maria went home with Susan and Emma staid with me. Mrs. (illegible) and Miss Barnes were here yesterday evening. Miss B. spoke very affectionately of brother James Perrot. Muldrow has had the academy white washed which has improved the looks of Bishopville considerably. Have you persuaded Fannie to stay longer yet? I do hope she will agree to do so.

Mrs. Bradley had a very sick child. Mother was there to day and she thinks she is some better. Salina Carnes will return home in a week; Maria is writing now to Mary Carmichael and Martha McLeod to ask them to spend their vacation with us. I hope they will come. I haven't time to write longer as Mr. Scarborough will go to the store directly. Give my love to Miss Elizabeth Fannie and kiss my little sweetheart Haynsworth and Ruthvin for me. All the family send much love to you all and particularly to brother Ruthvin and yourself.

I remain your devoted Sister
Amanda

Evergreen April 14th 1859
Dear Hattie

It has been a long time since the reception of your letter and I do feel very much mortified for having neglected writing so long a time, but you must excuse me. You know by experience that people are always very busy before they get married, such was the case with myself. I was quite busy before we were married and since that time I have not felt disposed to write, therefore have delayed replying to your welcome letter to this late period.

I was indeed very much surprised to hear that you were engaged to be married. You are now I presume no more Hattie Rogers but Mrs Plowden. I too have changed my name, and am now at my new home. We were married on the 22d of March, and came right up the next day, have not been down home but once. I am very sorry that I did not have time to write to you before we were married so as to have had you to write to me first. You must write to me soon, tell me all the news, and all about yourself. Tell me how you like married life, and house-keeping. I am very much pleased, have a kind and affectionate husband, and I hope I may make him a "wife" in every sense of the word. It is my desire to be to him all that I can, and I hope I may with Heavenly aid, to make him a good wife.

I think Mr Plowden has in his choice, chosen one whom I think will most assuredly make him a good wife, and a Mother for his little boys. I think you are fully capable of being both an affectionate wife and a good step-mother. When you write tell me the names of your little boys. Have you gone to housekeeping yet? If you have I would like very much to see you engaged in your domestic duties.

I do not know how to direct you letters now, shall direct this one to Amanda and she can hand it to you. You must be sure and tell me, when you write, How and where to direct to you. My direction now is Williston S.C.

As it is getting quite late I must close hoping to hear from you soon. Give my love to Amanda and tell her I expect to hear news about her before long.

Your true friend
Jane B Guignard

Columbia May 4th 1859
My own darling sister,

Gladly do I take my pen to write you a few lines this beautiful afternoon, in reply to your kind letter received more than a week since. I am glad to tell you that this leaves me very well. I had a letter from sister yesterday. father and Amanda were with her. I know they all had a delightful time while together. they were all quite well, except father. He was suffering some from asthma. Well Hattie I guess you are anxious to hear something about our May Party. Well it came off last Tuesday evening; there was no one here except the trustees, and their families & Mr Wightman. we all met together at five o clock and marched from the College down through main St.[43] when we came back, the coronation took place, we had a beautiful throne, and Eliza made a very pretty queen indeed. at eight o clock we had a small very nice supper, an abundance of strawberries & ice cream, which you know was a great treat to us. The cake too was trimmed beautiful. We spent quite a pleasant evening of it though I believe I enjoyed the next day better still. We were all invited out in the country with a Mr Roach who has a large strawberry farm. Uncle Martin, his wife and the teachers went also. Uncle Martin walked with the girls, but the teachers rode. it was nearly four miles we had to walk. They had a delightful place fixed for us in the woods with nice seats. we carried dinner with us, so we had a real pic nic, and oh! the nice strawberries, we had as many as we could eat. I wish I had some of them to day. we came back to the College about four o clock, and went out in town to a concert, "The Swiss Bell Ringers." They too were very interesting, so on the whole we spent quite a pleasant time.

43 "Columbia Female College, chartered in 1854, was part of a general proliferation of denominational schools during that decade. A Methodist institution, the college began classes five years later in a huge Italian-style complex—a four-story structure with a tower nearly 100 feet tall—located on the northern half of the square bounded by Pickens, Plain, Taylor, and Henderson Streets." (Name was changed to Columbia College in 1905) Moore, John Hammond. *Columbia and Richland County: A South Carolina Community* 1740–1990. USC Press, 1992.

They gave us only two days holiday. We are going to commence to (illegible) for the examination next week, the exam time commences the twenty fifth of June, and will close the 28th. oh! isn't delightful to think that in a few more weeks I will be at my dear home. Your old schoolmate Lizzie Edwards is married. She came to see us last week. She married a Dr Whetstone. Tell Willie his sweet-heart Miss Fannie Thomson is here this after noon. she called to see Miss Beaux and Miss Hoyt from Sumter. I saw her and her husband as they were coming in. he is quite a nice looking gentleman.

Well, dear Sister, I will close this badly written letter as some of the girls have come in to see me. give my love to brother Ruthvin Miss Elizabeth and the children. Many thanks to Haynsworth for the sweet little rosebud he sent me. Good bye my dear sister. Write soon to your devoted sister

Maria

King Creek May 14th/59
My dearest Hattie,

Four weeks have passed rapidly over my head since I had the pleasure of reading an other of your letters.

I judge by what you mentioned, you are happily established at your new home. Dearest Hattie, I hope that your married life will always prove pleasant. How strange it is for me to think that my gentle unassuming room-mate is now mistress of a household.

How do you like keeping house? You must tell me all about your garden. Be a smart girl and manage so as to have an abundance of fine vegetables for Mr. Plowden. I would be sorry if I thought that you are as unskilled as I am in raising poultry. As yet I have nothing but a few chickens.

Have you been informed of (illegible) Lizzie's affliction? She caught fire on the 23rd April, and was burnt seriously. She is still confined to her bed, and probably will be for a week or ten days longer.

If this trial would only humble her, and lead her to seek Jesus, it would be such a gratification. I pray for her but my dear Hattie I am so sinful that I feel my petitions very weak and feeble. I am less fervent in serving my Creator than it is my desire to be. Oh! may we all be blessed with more zeal in His service. Sallie Wright wrote to me that she was very much disturbed about her conversion. She doubted and prayed for an assurance of her faith.

Annie Jennings said in her last letter that S. was converted last Sunday three weeks. She also stated that Sallie was looking very badly and doubted if she would live much longer. Do you ever hear anything of Georgie Lyles? She was a (illegible) correspondent, but I have not heard from her since Nov. I would like very much to know whether or not she is living happily etc.

I think Lydia Lucas was at school with you. She is now in Orangeburg, and will remain there until her father has completed the new Court House.

How pleasantly I could spend a few weeks in the College, or even the village. I revert to those days as past never more to return. The lovely faces I beheld every hour will not be seen again until the final day, when I trust all will be gathered into the same mansion.

If you see Manda soon, tell her that I shall write soon. Nothing has prevented my writing before this, but want of time.

Write soon and believe me

Your affectionate friend,
Martha

P. S. Please inform me Mr. P's given name. I am sorry not to direct in his name.

Bishopville May 28th 1859
My dear dear Sister,

A week has elapsed nearly, since we bade you adieu, and as I know you are more than anxious to hear from home, I gladly avail myself of the opportunity of writing you. I am happy to say that all are pretty well, but dear mother has been rather feeble to day. She went down to cousin Drucilla's yesterday and I think it fatigued her riding so far. Sister has got along very well indeed. her breasts have not risen at all and I truly hope they may not again. she has put poplar leaves to them which has done her a great deal of good. The little baby is well. she is the best little thing you ever saw. she is prettier too than when you saw her. they have decided to call her Catharine Amanda.

Aunt Peggy and cousin Jane have just left here. cousin Callie is a little better. the rest are all well. cousin Jane looks very well I think. Cousin David and I went over to Hepzabah to day. Mr. Wilson preached this morning, Mr. Reed this afternoon. We took dinner with Mrs. Robert Mccutchen. Robert Dennis took dinner there also, so we had a short conversation together. Muldrow was here yesterday evening, staid until after tea. he came for me to ride with him but I told him I could not go. he was not near so lively as normal, told me to tell you and brother Ruthvin he regretted very much not being at home while you were there, said he fully intended calling on you but he saw so many persons here on Sunday he gave it out. Said I must be sure and invite brother Ruthvin and yourself up to his examination and picnic. I have not been any where at all since I came home. we have had company nearly every day. I am sorry to tell you that cousin Hugh has not come yet, we have not heard a word from him. I hope though it will not be many days before we have the light of his countenance. I received a letter from Annie Jennings a few days since. She told me that it was thought that Sallie Wright's mind was affected. she doubts her conversion, says she was persuaded to think that her sins were forgiven. Annie says she never saw any one suffer so much mental agony but that she was more tranquil when she wrote. Our Sunday School begins tomorrow. I look forward to it, and particularly our Bible class, with much pleasure. I do not know who is to be our teacher but I expect the Superintendent or the ministers.

Mr Bell has been here several times since you left. tell brother R. he could rank him among cousin Covert's and Theodore's class as being a very dry man. he, Mr. Scarborough and cousin D. went to call on the young ladies at Dr Holleyman's. as usual, the old folks gave them the pleasure of their company. Dr. Harte, of whom you have heard me speak, came over yesterday and took Vermeille out to ride yesterday evening. We have heard that Adeline has given Dr. Blackwell his walking papers and that the old flame between her and Wash is revived, but I do not know whether it is or not.

How is Henry, Haynsworth and Lute. I have thought of you all so many, many times and wished I could be with you. Miss Elizabeth feels like a dear relative to me. I know I love her as much as if she were. I was teasing Anna the other day about Mr. Scarborough, but she told him he wasn't her sweet heart at all—that Lute was. it insults her to tell her of any one else. Have you heard from Fannie yet? I hope very much you have. tell Miss Elizabeth to give my love to her when she writes. We heard from Daniel by Thursday's mail. he was quite well, says he will not be home until the last of June. He has not been troubled any more with boils. I presume Mr. C. Nelson has ere this quit the state of single blessedness.

Cousin Drucilla has been right sick. she has been spitting up blood lately. Mother and Maria found her much better. I feel truly sorry for her. West seems to be very kind to her and was very pleasant indeed. Mr. Wilson and Mr. Reed have given out going down to Brewington Mr. Wilson thinks right hard of brother Ruthvin for not going to see him, says if he were to go down there he would not go to see you at all. There is a good deal of whooping cough about here now. We are afraid that Anna is taking it. she has a very bad cough indeed. it would be bad if the baby were to take it. Brother William left us last Thursday, will be back on Monday or Tuesday. I know he is anxious to get home now. It is getting so late I must close and I am ashamed to send this but I have written so hurriedly so Mr. S. can take it down. with him. you must excuse it however. Do give my warmest love to Bro. Ruthvin, Miss Elizabeth, Henry and kiss Haynsworth and Lute many times for me, though I would much rather do it myself. Father, mother, sister, cousin C—and all send you all a great deal of love. tell H. I hope he is learning as fast as ever- my kind regards to Mr. E. Plowden. I often think of that Sunday evening's conversation. and now praying God's richest blessings to rest upon you all I bid you goodbye—Write soon to your affct. sister

A M Rogers

Georgetown SC May 30th 1859
Dear Harriet,

Your most welcome epistle was received on yesterday more welcome on account of its being so unexpected. I was glad to hear from you as we heard that you were indisposed before I left. Although Father wrote me you were better before I got yours. Amanda wrote me that Sister had given birth to another daughter and was getting on very well. It will be out of my power to go by on my way home as it is some Thirty Miles out of way. So it would be just as well to go from home which I will do as soon as I can. I will be down here this week and perhaps all of week after then I shall go home. I have been very well since I have been here with the exception of boils which have given me a great deal of trouble I have one on my foot at this time which has kept me indoors for some three days. I do hope it is the last for they have been a trouble to me ever since I have been in Georgetown. But with all this I have had a very pleasant time. Have been "sailing" several times recently with "Young Ladies" I heard through someone that they were going to have a "Pic Nic" and present Capt. (illegible) with a cup. which as you say rightly he "justly deserves." I have been enjoying fruit down here. we have plums, "Huckle Berries." I do not know whether this is their proper name or not. There is a nice kind lady here. She has been very kind indeed to me. She is such a good nurse. I do not know what I should have done without her.

If Hugh comes as I suppose he will perhaps he may not be at home if he does not go down to see you before I come It may be I will come then. It is growing late and must close.

My love to Ruthvin and kind regards to friends. Goodbye & God bless you

Your affect Bro
D. M. Rogers

Bishopville June 26th 1859
My own dear sister,

All have retired but father, cousin Drucilla (who is with us tonight) and myself and as they are engaged in reading I will employ a few moments in converse with you. Your letter to Maria has just been received and we were happy to hear from you and to know that all were well. Cousin Callie came up with cousin D this evening to spend the night with us, but had been here but a short time when they sent for her as cousin Covert had come. I am right vexed with him for not coming on himself instead of sending for her. She looks much better and is very lively. Maria has gone home with her. Maria and I went to see Emma this evening for the first time. We all went to the spring which is about half a mile from cousin Albert's. it is splendid water. (as Willie would say) Mother and cousin Hu got home safely Monday evening. Mag came with them, and staid a day and night with us. Father took the cars at Mayesville and went to Sumter. did not get back until last night. Mr. Fraser's case did not come on. they all enjoyed themselves very and were most pleased with their visit to you. Hu says he never had a more pleasant time. I am sorry to tell you that the dear little baby has the whooping cough. She has been coughing very badly for the three last days. The damp weather has been much against her. I earnestly hope the worst is over with. we all feel great anxiety on her account.[44] William and Anna are both better and I hope will soon be well. We are looking forward with so much pleasure to yours and brother Ruthvin's visit. I wish very much Miss Elizabeth and the children would come too. I do not know whether any of us will go to the celebration or not. Daniel will I guess. He is now in Charleston, left home Wednesday evening. will be back next week. Cousin David and Hu are gone over to Marlboro, left Wednesday morning, said they would stay about a week. There is a Sunday school celebration at Cypress church next Saturday. They all want to get home in time to attend it. I went last Saturday to a picnic at Kelley's Mills and I enjoyed myself very

44 The baby, Catharine Amanda, died July 11, 1859, of whooping cough (pertussis).

much indeed. Miss Charlotte Bell, Eliza and Mercy Parrot were there. I also had the pleasure of seeing Miss Nannie Garner, was much pleased with her. Lizzie, Daniel, Jane, David D., cousin D and myself went on in company. I got very well acquainted with Dr Foster and like him a little better than I did at first. Eliza Dixon has come home. She is in very bad health. None of us have seen her since her return. Muldrow is taking on quite extensively about Eliza Bell. he asked Mr. Scarborough to go to Mr. Bells (paper torn) soon. I do not know whether she fancies him (torn) Cousin Mary Jane staid with us last night. She & Aunt Molsey have been up for several days. I do not know when they are going home. Cousin Hu has decided to stay until the 11th of July, so you will see him again. I commenced writing this last night but did not finish it. They are about starting for Maria to come to Sunday school, so I must hasten. I got a letter from Sallie Rogers Wednesday. She says Sallie Wright is lying at the point of death with Typhoid fever. I hope she may be spared to her dear mother, but I have not heard from her since. I wish you would bring my letters with you when you come home. I am making my ottoman and my pattern is among them. Please do not forget it, as I want cousin Hu to help me with it. Mr. Alexander preached for us to day. We were glad to hear that they have (torn) in Manning. All send you brother Ruthvin Miss Elizabeth and the children a great deal of love. You must excuse this disconnected letter. I have written so hurriedly that I do not know what I have said. Tell Belton we will all be glad to see him when he comes, Mag particularly. Sister cannot leave while the children have whooping cough, so we will all be together when you come. I hope you will bring the children with you or one of them at least. Good-bye till we see you which I trust will be soon.

Your ever devoted sister,
Amanda M. Rogers

Parnassus July the 7th 1859
My own dearly beloved Cousin

Some time has elapsed, now, since I received a very kind affectionate and thrice welcome letter from you my cousin. I cannot find words to tell you how very glad I was to receive one more letter from your dear self, my dear cousin. I do feel ashamed of myself for not answering your welcome letter before this time but hope you will pardon my long silence and I will promise ever to do better for the future. Harriet I commenced writing to you two weeks ago this evening. I was at Mcs staying with Kate while Mc was from home. before I finished my letter after supper Hu went after me and O how very glad I was to hear that Cousin Hu and David had come to see us. I cannot find words to tell you how glad I was to see them. They staid with us just one week. The week did not feel as long as too days does since they left. They came Thursday and Wednesday after Uncle Rogers and dear little Willie came and spent one night; well my dear cousin there is no use in trying to tell you what a great source of pleasure it was to us all. I was very sorry your dear Father and Willie did not have longer to stay. Uncle Rogers went up to Floral thursday would have come back here Saturday and stayed untill Monday only that he left Lucys little Baby very sick. I feel very anxious to hear from Lucy and trust when we do hear her dear little Baby has entirely recovered. Oh I would be so glad to see Lucy. it has been a long time since I saw her dear face. how much I do wish and hope she will come and see us some time this year. I think they might come it isnt so far. Cousin David promised to come over again in Aug. When you see him remind him of his promise and tell him he must not break it. How much I wish cousin Hu was coming back with him. Harriet do you recollect uncle Farquhord McRae Mothers Brother He has three cancers on his face and neck poor fellow. He is the most pitiful object I ever looked at. Mother and I went to see him yesterday. I think he is very near the last. I do feel so sorry for his family at home and for my own dear mother. It gives her a great deal of trouble to see and think what he suffers. I am expecting all the time to hear of his death. I am so sorry for mother. She has got so she can hardly hear trouble. any thing that troubles her is almost sure to make her sick. his death would be a dreadful shock to her although she is expecting it.

Harriet how much I wish to go and see you all and stay a long time with you. I know I would enjoy myself so much with you in your own house but if I do not get to go I hope to see you before a great while. any way I hope you will come and bring Mr. Plowden—I am very anxious to see him. I heard Cousin Hu and Daniel speak of him several times while here. Cousin Hu was delighted with his visit to you. he says you are as happy as need be. he told me of a great many nice things he saw down at Harriets. My cousin I could write a great deal more such stuff as this but guess this will satisfy you unless it was more interesting and as it is getting late I must begin to draw to a close. please my dear cousin write very soon. when you write let us know how Callie is getting on as we are all anxious to hear from her. Cousin David thought her a little better when he came over. Give my love to Mr. Plowden. Mother and Hu join me in sending our best love to you. I remain your devoted cousin until death.

Annie J. McCallum

Kate McLeod sends her love to you. little Caty is as smart as ever. she is the most interesting child I ever saw. she speaks of you and Daniel very often. dont forget to write soon

Bishopville July 26th 1859
Dear Harriet

I fully intended writing you on Saturday but I was very busy until late in the evening and when I came to write found there was no paper at the house so I had to wait until I could get some. We are all well and have been so ever since you left. Mother received your letter and we were truly happy to know that you were all well as we felt anxious about you and Maria both, but I trust Belton's cheerful voice has had great affect on M ere this. I know she had enjoyed herself very much. no one could do otherwise with you all. I have missed her a great deal though. You cannot imagine how very lonely I felt after Sister Brother Wm and darling little Anna left. Sister hated to leave very much and you would have shed tears to have seen Anna. She told Almira the day before not to "fy" when she went to Lynchburg. When I was carrying her to the buggy she put her arms around my neck and commenced sobbing. but I am so glad to tell you that she and sister are coming back next Friday. Sister is coming to help me make a dress for mother. I am very busy sewing now. I went down to cousin Caroline's to day and she nearly made a dress for me on the machine. I believe it was before you left that the congregation presented Mr. Wilson with money to travel this Summer to (illegible) his health. he is to leave next Thursday preached his last sermon before leaving last night. preached very well indeed too. he seems very grateful for this mark of kindness from his people. Mr. Alexander preached for us yesterday. Harriet is to be married very soon to Mr. Newberry. I do not know positively how soon it will take place but we heard he had made his last visit before being married. Dorsey Dubose was here to day. he told us that they were looking for Mr. J. Dubose to die all to day. he told us also of the death of Capt. Sinton. None of the family are left now. I saw Martha Fraser at church last night. she told me she was coming to see me next week. I have been to see Vermeille once since her return home. She is delighted with her visit down country, says the people up here seem very amicable after being with those down country. said she found it hard to leave there she fell so much in love with Miss Elizabeth with Haynsworth and Lute also. Muldrow has been here ever since he dismissed school but he and Daniel have just walked down to the store. he is coming back to tea. He escorted Eliza Bell from church last night. The girls have all returned. Tell Maria Almira has commenced Algebra. I believe she likes it very much. I have not seen any of Aunt Peggy's girls since you left. Cousin David says his mother and sister are coming up this week. Father will not come for Maria as Daniel is going down next week. he will come for her some time during the next week. I cannot say exactly when. Has she got homesick yet? We have had several very nice watermelons. I suppose they are very plentiful with you.

I must close dear sister not because I want to but Mr. D. has returned and I will have to go in the parlor. I must not forget to tell you that I dressed Mother,s hair very prettily the other day. It curls like Anna's. all send you Bro R- Maria Miss E- and the children a great deal of love and accept the same from your devoted sister

Amanda

Our love to cousins Joe Lizzie, cousin Covert and cousin Callie.

Charleston 26 July 1859
Mr. E. Ruthvin Plowden
Dear Sir,

Annexed we hand you bill & R. Roade receipt for the articles ordered. Your brother E. N. ordered the same number yards of bagging as you did, vis, 150 Y and to save freight we sent him one roll and you two rolls; but charged each of you 150 1/2 yds so you can let him have the half of one of the rolls sent you, 50 1/2 yds, which will make it right.

We hope your cotton will meet a good market, as prices have advanced since the peace news.[45] good cotton is selling at 12 & 12 1/2 c

Yours truly etc.
Caldwell & Robinson

---

45 France/Austria signed armistice July 11, 1859.

Bishopville 16 Augt 1859
Dear Ruthvin & Harriet

I will write you a few lines this afternoon that you may soon know that your mother and myself expect to leave here on tomorrow—to go as far as Lynchburg, intending to take the cars on Thursday morning. After we leave I will not forget to write to you frequently that you may know how we are getting along. My letters at such time I expect will have to be short but it will be a Satisfaction to you to hear from us no doubt even by short letters. I am happy to say that our white family is tolerably well- though your dear mother has had one of the spells of illness from which she suffers periodically and from which she has not yet recovered. I hope though that she may be better on tomorrow so as to be able to go to Lynchburg, and she probably will.

Linda's youngest two children are not well. Fany is tolerably sick, but I hope neither will be Severe cures—I think they are all three taking whooping cough.[46]

Amanda, Maria and myself went on Saturday last to the Camp meeting and Daniel also. They have a very good meeting and the people all appear to behave well. I suppose the meeting will close on tomorrow—

Willie Witherspoon gave me the package you sent by him, which contained also a letter from my dear Harriet—whose letters as always, so welcome and interesting—always bearing with them such warm tributes of affection. No wonder we all love to see them come. By the way is it not time that my esteemed son in law Ruthvin should also write? Shall we not have letters from both of you while we are north? Your letters you will please direct while we are north to me at New York care of <u>Mefes W G Lane & Co</u>. Harriets request shall be faithfully attended to—in both particulars. You spoke Harriet in your letter of Mr. Laurel Dinkins—Both he and Ty d died on the same day within a few hours of each other, and were buried just about the same hour though in different districts. Poor Mrs. D. is

46 Linda and Fanny are presumed to be servants.

with her family at Charles,s & Mr. Dixon,s. She is a pitiful object and may so give way to her deep grief as almost to take her life.

I must say to Ruthvin that at Boykins we have a very fine crop. the best ever made there. If I live to return home, I hope soon to see you up here and we will look over our little crops. How does Ruthvin's corn and (illegible) Well I hope.

I spoke of "a few lines" in the outset. I have written a good many though not too many if they were of interest. Now I will close. Don't please don't—neglect to write to us, both of you while we are gone. It is a great pleasure to receive letters from our family folks at all times but especially will it be so while we are from home. And now with deep affection—and with love of the whole family for you I will bid you good bye for the present praying that God's choicest blessing may ever attend you my dear ones —

William Rogers

Baltimore 22nd Aug st 1859
My own dearly beloved Daughter

We reached this place this morning at 9 o clock left Washington at 7. Our trek so far has been very pleasant the weather cool—and we have not had a crowd along since we left home. We left Lynchburg at 8 am last Thursday—and reached Washington next day past 2 pm -

Your dear mother has stood the trip finely and both of us are quite well. Dr Powell & Kate were very attentive to us in Wash n We dined and took tea with them yesterday (Sunday) Your mother has seen much to please and interest her and I doubt not will continue to do so. She is now "primping up" while I write. I have just written four other letters—short ones and can make this but short for want of time- Do you and Ruthven write to us to N.Y. care of W. G. Lane & Co—God grant you and all our family may keep well and that we return to a happy meeting in due time. Our warmest love to you and Ruthven and don't forget to remember us affectionately to Miss Eliz. and the rest—Tell Miss E. that I hope to come down again sometime and get another k———

May heaven bless you all is the prayer of your affectionate Father
& Mother
William Rogers

Lynchburg Aug 22/1859
My Dear Harriet,

I owe you many, many thanks for the affectionate letter I rec. from you last week; it afforded me my dear sister, not a little comfort & pleasure. We shall not soon forget the many true sympathizing friends who have been near us in our recent affliction. True the sympathy of friends however sincere, cannot heal our wounded hearts or render us less bereaved, but all who have ever experienced it in time of trial, must testify to its soothing influence. Yes dear Harriet twas a precious treasure that God for a little while consigned to our care; it seemed, only to show us the entire purity and loveliness of Heaven, and to call us thither, then took her to Himself again. I need not speak to you of the fond hopes which have been crushed, and still so hard to be given up, or of the utter loneliness and desolation which at times fills my heart since, but such, may you never know. But still, I do bless & praise my Heavenly Father for the spirit of resignation which has been given me, Amid all. His arm has sustained me, and at times I can even rejoice to think of her as she now is. I know not how many of the rude storms, & temptations, so common to this life our child on earth may have to pass through, but our child in Heaven, is safe forever safe, from all. We were only permitted to see the budding of her life here, but it will bloom all the more perfectly in the genial atmosphere to which she has gone. Oh that we all may meet her there, that we may all be presented spotless before our father's throne.

We are all quite well. Wm has just got home from Graham's C. R.'s. Father & mother stayed with us on Wednesday night last, and left for the north on Thursday morning. I was quite delighted to see dear mother leave so cheerfully. she seemed to be in very good spirits, and both she and father looked as well or better than usual. I went up home in the carriage and Anna and I stayed until Saturday, when Daniel brought us home again. All were well up there, except Linda's two children Fannie & Alice, they had been quite sick, but were better when I left. They all enjoyed the camp meeting very much. I was sorry I did not go, when Wm came home and told me what a glorious meeting they had. There has been a good deal of religious interest manifested here lately. Oh that the Lord would grant us a gracious revival. We have services in our church to-night. We thank you and dear brother Ruthvin, as also miss Elizabeth, for your urgent invitation to visit you. If nothing happens to prevent we hope to have that pleasure soon, as I expect to go with Wm his round of app's. this week, and we hope to reach your place Sunday afternoon. We will preach at New Zion in the afternoon at 3 o-clock, instead of in the morning so as to make it nearer for us. My little sheet is filled so I will defer the rest 'till I see you all. Do give our best love to bro. Ruthvin Miss E and accept a large portion my dear sister for yourself. Kiss the little boys for us. Anna is perfectly delighted at the idea of seeing them.

I remain as ever your devoted sister
L. J. Mood

Bishopville Sept. 1859
Dear Harriet,

As an opportunity offers of writing you, I gladly do so this morning. Mr. Montgomery arrived here safe last night and brought your letter to Almira and we were happy to hear from you and that you were all well but the children. I am sorry they have whooping cough so badly but I hope they will soon be well. You do not know how happy I feel today in anticipation of soon seeing my dear father and mother. Daniel and William are going to start at ten to meet them; they will perhaps get to Lynchburg at one, but father said they may not come until tomorrow. I can scarcely realize that they will so soon be with us. We have all been quite well since Maria wrote you. (I presume you have received her letter.) Cousin Charlotte is pretty much the same. The storm frightened us all nearly out of our wits. It has served Col. Rembert worse than Mrs. Dennis—he is damaged about ten thousand dollars worth. His dwelling house was blown entirely off to the second floor and all his outbuildings but one store were made of brick. It is truly wonderful that no lives were lost but providence ordained that it should be so. What a strong proof of His wisdom and power! It is a strong warning too to us all and God grant that we may profit by it. I cannot describe my feelings when I thought that dear little William was killed. He had just left the house to go to school and I ran to the window to see if I could see him and I saw the trees in the school yard all down. I felt certain that he was crushed beneath some of them. He says he was in the school house until part of it began to fall and they all ran out—a tree fell across the door just as he got out—You would scarcely know Mrs. Dennis' place.

I got a letter from Mary Jane Mc(illegible) Monday, she was quite well and still much pleased. They have almost decided to settle permanently in Ark- Daniel Almira William and I went up to Bethany last Sunday. Mr. Brown had been holding several days meeting up there. Mr. Elijah Alexander calls it a basket camp meeting. I will tell you about the (paper torn) I had up there when I see you. We have got entirely through with Maria's sewing . She got another dress after you left and I have made them all up. Don't you think we have been right smart—I did not put myself in Maria's way last night but he did not say anything to her on the subject of matrimony. I guess (torn) Mr. Bagnal might come to see Vermeille. I still (torn) her about him. We stopped to see Mrs. Mary Jane Kelly (formerly Atkinson) on Sunday. she has a very pretty place and a very pretty baby. Daniel and I named it while we were there. I named it William and he Scott—after Mr. William Scott. They gave us some very nice apples. Harriet Carter and her sister were baptized last Sunday at Mount Moriah. Mr. Scarborough went (illegible) but got too late to see her put under the water—said she was just walking away—he cannot get over it. Charley Stuckey was baptized too. I hope some of his conceit was washed off. Maria keeps at me to go in the parlor and help entertain her beau so I believe I will show him the light of my countenance as brother Wm says. So good bye. all send you a great deal of love and please write us soon. Much love to bro. Ruthin, Miss E— and the children for us. I will ask bro Wm when he preaches at (illegible) and let you know—be sure and come as soon as you can to the wedding.

Your affct sister
Amanda

New York 2nd Sept 1859
Dear Ruthvin

We were very happy this morning in receiving the two good letters from you and dear Harriet. We reached here at 9 o clock last night and now write you but a short letter to let you know of our whereabouts and that we are well. We found all well in Penn. We did not go to Niagara. All worth telling you must hear when we return. May God grant that we may all be sparred to another happy meeting.

We both laughed heartily at your remark about Frind Roy and agree with you. We shall hope soon to see you if we are sparred to return home. May the blessing of Almighty God rest upon you all.

Accept the love and esteem of both your mother and myself to all.

Your affc. father
William Rogers

New York 12 Sept 1859
My own beloved Harriet,

Your last kind letter I have just recd- Many thanks for it- We have also letters from home. all well—thank God for it.

Your dear mother and myself went three times to church yesterday. She sees much to please her. I shall try and go about more for the next day or two with her than I have done. I have had you know to keep very busy. We are pleasantly (illegible) at Mr. P. Mood's and Uncle John Mood is there—as spry as a cricket—very sociable & clever. they all are. this makes it very pleasant. I can't write but little, as it takes time you know and I can't well spare it. We shall hope soon after we reach home to see you and Ruthvin. Our love to him and Miss E & the boys.. and also Lizzy's & Cally's familys.

God Bless you all
fr Wm S A J Rogers

Bishopville Sept 18 1859
My dear sister

Cousin Covert expects to return home tomorrow and as I know you would like to hear from us I will write to you a few lines. We are all well, Amanda Daniel and Almira have gone up to Bethany to day, where Mr. Brown is holding a protracted meeting, so you see Cousin Charlotte and I will be all alone. I went down to see cousin Callie yesterday. she was suffering a great deal with headache. I think she looks worse than when I saw her last. We heard from our dear parents last Thursday, and Oh! how glad we all were to hear that they were well. they attended preaching three times on last Sabbath. Mother was very much pleased with New York. Father said that he expected that they would get home next Wednesday or Friday any way. I look forward to that time with a great deal of pleasure. We had an awful storm here on last Friday—all of Mrs. Dennis' negro houses were blown down, but none of the negroes were killed. her carriage house was blown over and broke her carriage and buggy all to pieces. Mr Gilbert Crosswell's house was torn up entirely. I feel very sorry for him. he is very low-spirited now. we were all very much frightened indeed I assure you, but it was not so bad here as in some other places. the schoolyard looks quite desolate now. all the trees nearly are down and part of the academy.

Sister and Brother Wm are coming up to see us Tuesday. how much I wish you could be here too. give my best love to Brother Ruthvin and all the family. write to us very soon. Cousin Charlotte sends much love.

Your affct Sister
Maria

please excuse this as it was all the paper I had

Bishopville Sept 20th 1859
My dear sister,

I will write you a short note tonight to inform you of the safe arrival of mother and father at home. They got here about one o'clock on last Friday and both look very well. a good many say that mother looks improved but I do not see much difference. she brought me a beautiful party-waist. every one admires it very much. They had their likenesses taken and six photographs which are all very good indeed. They went to Connecticut. Mother is much pleased with her trip but says she is glad to be at home again. but they will tell you all about it when you see them. We have just returned from the Presbyterian church where Mr. Wilson preached the best sermon I have heard him for a long time. Mr. Alaxander preached at the Methodist church this morning. There is a three days meeting here this week commencing on Friday. Mr. W- said perhaps Mr. Hay from Camden will be here. Aunt Peggy came up to see Mother yesterday evening. She says they expect cousin Covert up this week and that cousin Callie would go home with him. I have not seen her since she has been at home. I got a letter from Sallie Roper Thursday night which bore the <u>sad</u> tidings that poor Sallie Wright is no more. No, her freed spirit now mingles with those blest ones around the throne of God. It seems strange that one so young so lovely should be taken but God knows what is best. How I pity her bereaved mother. I think she has only one child, a son left, and he is lying very low with dropsy.[47] Thus one by one of our dear school mates are passing away. how sad to think that so many dear faces we will never again behold them in this world. I or you may be the next called; oh then let us strive to meet those that have gone before in those mansions where we will never again have to say <u>farewell</u>. We expect cousin Hu on Saturday next. I do not think you can read this but do excuse it. it is so late in the night, but I thought you would be anxious to hear from mother and father I would write a few lines any way. do not let any one see this. I am glad the time is so near for you to come home. I wish you would please bring your head dress. I

---

47 Edema, or fluid build-up in the body.

want to borrow it from you next day if you do not want it. all send you much love.

Your affct. sister
Amanda

Columbia Oct. 22nd 1859
My dear Sister.

Knowing you would be glad to hear from me, and as I have a few leisure moments this morning, I will employ them in writing to you. I have just finished a letter to Amanda. I have received two letters from home since I have been here, and I do not think any could be more delighted at receiving letters from home than I am. they were all quite well when I rec the last letter which was sent by Mr. Gamewell, who staid at fathers last friday night. he came to see me on Thursday, and I can assure I was glad to see him knowing he had been home. he told me all about them at home and asked me to go to see them as often as I could, but the girls cannot visit any one except their relatives. his daughter Mary Gamewell is a great friend of mine. she is in my class and is very kind and sociable. I expect you want to know something about how I am pleased, my room mates. I have a very nice room, with two little room mates, Miss Epps and Miss Rapp. they are both quite small though, one fourteen and the other twelve. they seem to be very nice little girls. I like all my teachers very much. take music lessons from miss Craig. she is a very good teacher, I think, and very kind indeed to me. I have taken two walks in the town of Columbia since I have been here, which I enjoyed very much, saw some of the most beautiful flower gardens in the place. the seminary and Asylum.[48] the teachers take some of the girls out to walk every week. I have been so fortunate as to go twice. We enjoyed ourselves a great deal last night, being Friday night, and Dr Smith always will have us to play something, so last night the girls acted several very pretty tablaux which he enjoyed very much.[49] then he had us all to sing "Do they miss me at home" that made me fell very sad I assure you. Several of your schoolmates are here, Miss Lizzie Edwards miss Gersner have both been to see me and seem to be very

48 The South Carolina Lunatic Asylum, later SC State Hospital, was one of the first public mental hospitals in the U.S., admitting its first patient in 1827. https://digital.scetv.org/teachingAmerhistory/lessons/MentalHealth.htm

49 Tablaux: religious scenes, famous paintings, etc., reenacted by people moving or posing

clever. they say I look like you. How has Hayensworth and Lute got of the Hooping cough. kiss them for me, and ask Haynesworth how long is it going to be before he answers my letter. Do Harriet you and brother Ruthvin write to me often, for you know I cant write any time only Saturday, as I to study through the week. I will write to you as often as I can. give my love to miss Elizabeth brother Ruthvin and hoping soon to see a letter from you.

I remain your devoted sister,
Maria

Bishopville 30 Oct. 1859
Dear Harriet

I am happy to say that we are all in usual health. To day your dear Mother myself and Dan'l & Lizzy went over to Cypress Church and heard P. E. Rev. Abel Chritzburg preach—What has become of those Tennesseans? and what has become of our Amanda?

Has she run away with, and married Belton or somebody else, and now afraid to see our faces?

If she has done all this do tell her still to come back over home, and ask pardon and we will forgive her, and tell her she must not do so again -

Well I understand that <u>Benjamin</u> Alexander is to <u>marry</u> next week with the daughter of Mitchel Reynolds.

Edward Spann and Eliza have returned here to stay as I suppose. Eliza arrived at home on yesterday—we begin to want to see you and Ruthvin <u>right</u> <u>badly</u>. When should we look down the road for you? We are now generally quite busy and confined to the store- hope we shall be able to make you a visit though—some time—when did we speak of going—I have forgotten. We have had letters from Maria. She has said she is well. We hear not much news here. Nobody is to be hung in Darlington. Terrill at Bennetsville I hear has been found guilty—no doubt a righteous justice.

Will Ruthvin be at Sumter court? I would gladly meet him there—I shall have to attend I suppose. When will Miss Elizabeth come up to see us? We shall be glad to see her when she comes.

Wm W. Ju. & Lucy were pretty well when last heard from—I only started to write a few lines this time and will close now. Our love to all at your house to Cally Lizzie and all inquiring friends—God bless you all.

Your affec. father
William Rogers

Bishopville Nov 11th 1859
My dear Sister,

Your kind letter received sometime since, which should have been responded to long before this, still remains unanswered but want of time my dear sister has prevented my doing so. And as to night is Friday night, I will occupy a while in the very pleasant task of writing to you. I am glad to tell you that I am quite well, though I had a very bad headache last night, it is the first time I have been at all sick since I have been here. Since I received your last letter, I have had the very great pleasure of seeing Cousin Hu and Mr Marley. I was busy reading a letter from Amanda, just after school on Tuesday, when Dr Smith sent for me to go and see them. I tell you I was not long in getting from the third to first story. They told me all about home their visit to you, A. They spent about half an hour with me and called to see me the next evening. Oh! I must not forget to tell you that I got to go to the fair too on Wednesday. A great many of the girls parents came for them, and as there were so few left, Dr Smith got the teachers to carry the rest of us. You may know we were glad to get to go. I thought perhaps I would meet up with some of my friends from home. Cousin Hu had told me that Mrs. Dennis and Virginia were in town, but I was disappointed in not getting to see them. they called to see me, but I was not here. Miss Hattie Townsend came over to the fair. she came to see Amelia several times, but I did not get to see her. I think cousin Hu was very much pleased when I told him she was here. I saw him paying her attention at the fair. All of them went home to day on the two oclock train to day. I hope they had a pleasant time. I felt very badly after telling cousin Hu good bye. I felt as though I would give any thing if I could only go home with him. I saw Mr Muldrow Dennis at the fair he came and spoke to me. Mother sent me a great many nice things to eat which were very acceptable I assure you, though I cant complain of the fare here for it is very good indeed. but you know anything from home is always so nice. And yesterday when I was going to one of my recitations, Dr Smith told me that a box had come for me. which he had sent up to my room and when I opened it was from you, with a nice <u>letter</u> beside. You can well imagine how glad I felt. I can not find words to thank you for it. there was so much and every thing so nice. My friends and I have nice times eating now, a great many of them say I must tell you they are very much oblige to you indeed for sending such a nice box. Miss Lizzie Edwards and Cornelia Fester were by my room this evening, they asked me to give much love to you for them. Miss Lizzie seems to be such a pious girl. the girls have prayer meetings every Sunday night. she was the first that started it. Hattie I have a great many kind friends here and then the teachers are all so kind. if it were not for this I do not think I could stay contented from home long. How is cousin Callie now? Give my love to her and cousin Covert also to cousin Lizzie and Jo. I received a long letter from Eliza Dixon to day, which I was very glad to get though I cannot reply to it as it is against the rules of the school. You say you expect to go home in December oh! how I wish I could be there then. but I hope the time will pass swiftly and pleasantly away, when we will all meet again at our dear dear home. indeed no one knows what a home is until they are called to leave it. "The dearest spot on earth to me, is home sweet home." Tell brother Ruthvin p l e a s e to write to me. I would be so glad to get a letter from him. give much love to miss Elizabeth for me and kiss the children, and now dear Sister good bye, do not forget to write soon to your devoted sister

Maria

Bishopville Nov. 12th 1859
My ever dear Sister,

I did not think when I parted from you that it would be so long before I wrote you but father had just written you and I had so much to do I have had no opportunity before this. We are all well but dear mother, she has had one of her bad headaches to day but is better now. cousin Charlotte seems rather better I think. Father is not at home. he has been in Sumter since Wednesday he wrote us a note telling us to meet him to day at Col. Rembert's. Mr. Durant was going (illegible) to attend the (illegible), and said he would bring father home with him but he had got back and says he did not come. I hope though he went to Lynchburg and will come home to night. We have just heard of the accident of aunt Peggy but I truly hope that she is entirely recovered ere this. Cousin Hu and Mr. Marley got back from Columbia this evening. they had a pleasant time and enjoyed themselves finely, said they saw Maria every day. she was well and still much pleased. she went to the fair on Thursday. I know she felt badly when they left. Mrs. Dennis, Mrs. Muldrow, Virginia and Muldrow went over and as a matter of course Muldrow came home tight, he drove up and down the streets furiously the night he got home. I thought his mother could keep him straight but it is not so. Mrs Rembert, Mrs McDaniel, Lizzie, cousin H and Mrs M. are going to leave Monday for Charleston. they are all anxious for me to go with them, and if I thought you and bro Ruthvin were going then I think I would have gone. Mother tried to get me to go, but I did not care to stay so long. Cousin Hu and Mr. H. came to Aunt Molsey's last Saturday and attended the singing at St. Luke's to day. they said Buck Scarborough and Emma Lackey were with Mag and Amanda that evening. I am going down to stay with them tomorrow. I spent last night with Martha Fraser. (illegible) speak of going to Florida next week but I do not think they will. Omer has lost her little girl, miss Margaret showed me a dress she had just finished for her. it was the prettiest thing I ever saw. We had a very pleasant time coming home. I had no idea it was so late when we left Dr (illegible) but we drove pretty fast and got to Lynchburg before eight. sister had eaten supper, she was very much surprised to see me. said she thought I had come from home. We came to aunt Molsey's for dinner and then stopped a while at aunt Peggy's so it was pretty late before we got home. I tell you they were all glad to see me particularly Viny. she says she does hope I will hurry down there. then may be I can stay till I get satisfied. The old soul was married to night to Mr Ceasar. she had a small party which is not broken up yet. Revd Wilson married them. When he told Ceasar to salute his bride, Viny vaulted in her room. she is the most bashful bride I have seen for a long time. I fixed her dress and vail for her and Lizzie and I fixed the table. she had every thing mighty nice. Cousin Hu had the pleasure of seeing Miss Hattie Townsend in Columbia. They are going over to Marlboro Sunday week. Sister went with Brother Wm on the circuit this week and left Anna with (illegible). She is the dearest little creature I ever saw. Said she can read her book from one end to the other and knows all of the catechism. Maria says they have weekly prayer meeting among the girls and Elizabeth Edwards superintends them, says she is very pious. Maria and Julia Rembert are great friends. says she is the lovliest girl she ever saw. My paper is out so I must close. all unite with me in much love to Brother Ruthvin Miss E. and the children. You must be sure and bring them with you.

Your affct. Amanda

Kings Creek Nov 18th/59
My dearest Hattie,

It is now ten o'clock but I am alone and feeling rather sleepless, so I concluded to write and have a letter in readiness for that which I hope to receive soon. What has caused you to neglect Martha for such a season? Why you have had me fearing that you were not well, and consequently unable to write. I daresay you have been so well as to

(rest of page too faded to read)

2nd page:

...the dictates of your conscience, where will Martha be in a few years? alas, she will have been forgotten, or looked upon as something altogether connected with past events—I shall not write in this strain any longer, you will not forget me darling even though you will not correspond with me, or know in what country I dwell.

I had the longest spell of illness last Summer that I ever experienced. I was confined to my bed from the (illegible) of September until the 23rd.

(too faded to read)

My Lizzie was taken with (illegible) of the lungs this morning. She went out visiting, and in an hour or two after she left, "Pa" was sent for , and found that she had had quite a severe attack. This is the first, and "Pa" thinks she will be subject to it during life. Afflictions, though they seem severe, are sent in mercy, and I hope and pray this will be the means of opening her eyes to her true state. We will bring her home tomorrow if she is able. Well the "old clock has struck" and I must bid good bye (too faded to read)

(Last page)

Feb. 16th 1860

Well Hattie dear, I little thought that the New Year would come in before receiving your long asked-for reply. It appeared like old times to hear from you once more.

How many changes there have been this winter. Three, perhaps more of my schoolmates have married. Mary Greer's marriage was in last week's paper. Eugenia Moye was married on the 22nd of Dec. to Mr. Dickinson. I hope she has done well, for she is a most lovely (illegible), Anna (too faded to read)

I received a likeness of Kate Felder last week, which she wrote is perfectly

(Here the letter ends; no additional pages were found.)

Bishopvile 23 Nov. 1859
My dear Son,

I am happy to say that we are all in usual health. The time is now here when we expected to make you a visit, which we have looked forward to with pleasure, but I regret to say that business matters are so pressing that it seems to be entirely out of the question for me to leave the store. In fact since I've returned from the north I have not had time to visit at Mrs. McCallums—and of which I feel very much ashamed. I must however beg that you will not allow our failure to make a difference with you and our dear Harriet about coming up to see us. oh no—do come as soon as you can. We should hope to repay you some time by more frequent visits. I was forced to attend court, and now Charles has gone to the RailRoad meeting at Wilmington and as we are in the cotton market we have hands full when both of us are here. Hugh and Mr Marley are with us at present. Washington (illegible) on Thursday (illegible) W. Lee will be up on his way to do the needful tomorrow forenoon. Maria was well by late accounts. Daniel & Lizzie staid last night with Mrs. McCallum.

But I have several letters to write yet and must close—again I urge that you come to see us as soon as you conveniently can. We have never been more anxious to see you both. Cant the little boys come to see us? Oh I forgot to say that Mr Thos. Frasier had an attack of appoplexy Monday morning but he is now better.[50] We remain most affectionately yours -

William Rogers
for self and family

---

50 Apoplexy: stroke

Columbia Dec. 1st 1859
My dear brother,

I received Hattie's kind letter this morning, and was more than glad to hear that you were all well. As I wished to answer her letter, and as it does not seem like you are ever going to write me, I concluded that I would let this be to you, so I expect you to reply to it soon. Brother William came to see me on Monday night. You know I was delighted to see him. I was in my room on the bed busy studying when the servant came and told me my brother wished to see me. I came on up in our fine parlor where we staid together nearly two hours. One of my friends Miss Stephens' father came to see her the same time, so all of us together had a delightful time. But oh how badly I felt when I had to bid them goodbye. I thought that brother William would call to see me as he came on back from Conference but he says he will not have time. I do hope so much he may be returned to Lynchburg. Our good old president went on as he did to Conference. We were very glad too as we got off from some of our recitations. I rec. a letter from Almira yesterday. They were all well at home. Amanda was staying with Sister. brother William said they were going home Friday, I believe and sister will stay until he returns. Harriet told me that you were going home in about two weeks and then all of you will be there but me. oh, how much I would give to be there too. I do not know what I will do now. When I first came here I had Cousin Hu's visit to look forward to, then brother William's and now that they are both over with, I expect I will have the blues right badly sometimes. I have to think now of July, when the time comes for me to go home, and that is a long long ways off. Harriet told me of the nice present you made her and indeed it was a nice one. I know it is a great deal of company for her. She wanted to know the name of some of the pieces I had taken. (next too faded to read)

My teacher says I am getting on very well in music—she is very kind to me. Are you acquainted with Miss Warrington Oliver from Summerton? I think she told me she knew you, she often enquires after you and Harriet. She is going to spend Christmas in Charleston instead of going home. A great many of the girls are going home then, and both of my roommates. Don't you think I will find it lonely? The bell will soon ring for prayers so I must close this. Please write to me very soon. I would be so glad to hear from you. Give my love to all. Write soon to your devoted

Sister Maria

I will direct this to Harriet for fear the teachers will think it is going to a young gentleman and read it.

Wednesday morning (probably Jan. 11) 1860
My dear Harriet

I have not written you in some time and having nothing particularly to engage me, I employ a few moments in writing you. All are well. Mother has not been troubled with headache much since you left. I am troubled a great deal with loneliness since sister and Anna Nora left. We miss them so much. I presume Sister told you I expected Sallie, the day was so bad though she did not come. She is coming though next Friday with Daniel. She will stay a week with me I guess. We look for Almira and William today. we are getting anxious to see them. I was sorry you had such bad weather for your two days meeting. Did you make your dress? I know sister was surprised when she found that father was going to Charleston with her quite agreeably too for she dreaded going about very much. I cannot realize that they are gone so far, it seems as though we must look for them home in a week or two. The morning they left Anna came and put her arms round me and told me that I must think about her when she was gone. I never saw Daniel so disappointed as when he found they had gone. he could not get over it. he had no idea that he would not see them again. he has succeeded in renting a place in Camden. it is a very nice house. has four rooms, a passage between a piazza in front and portico on the back. it is on De Kalb st. Mr. Ransom Scarborough is still alive to the surprise of every one, though he is getting worse. no one entertains any hopes of his recovery at all. he joined the church and Mr. Wilson baptized him Sunday night. He never professed religion though and does not seem willing to die; never speaks of it unless some one asks him. He sent for Mr. Henry Scarborough's father Saturday night. They have not spoken for years before. What a warning not to put off the salvation of our souls until laid upon a bed of death.

I received a letter from Martha Roberds Monday night. She complains of your not writing to her. You must write to her soon. She told me that Anna Rumph was married to Dr. Bollinger. Martha was at a dining party with her and her husband a few days after Christmas. I expect Mr. Banman's heart is almost broken. I had a picture taken in my party dress yesterday. They all say it is very good. Daniel, cousin Hu and Mr. Marly went over to hear Mr. Rogers preach last Sunday. Mr. Boykin wanted cousin Hu to assist him but he did not comply with his request. Last Monday was cousin Hu's birthday and it so happened that Jane Durant spent that day with us. we heard that Anna Howe's engagement is broken off, much to Mr. Marley's delight. He says he must go to Fayetville forthwith. They were both disappointed that Sallie did not come last week. Mr. McCorquedale was to have preached for us last Sunday but he and his wife did not get to Mr. Rembert's until yesterday. She brought her adopted child with her. Cousin Elisha and cousin Mary Alice were up last week. They were here a little while Sabbath morning. She was not very well. Cousin Hu, Mr Marley and I began New Years day to read the bible through. Mr. M. is ahead of us both. You ought to see how much he reads it. I tried to get Mr. Scarborough to begin too but he would not agree. Daniel says he had prayer at Mr. (illegible) one night, but Lizzie says she does not believe him. says he and Mr. Depass are going to lead the choir in the Methodist church. Mrs Bartlette has moved back to her former residence. Mr Higgins still boards with her. Mr. Scarborough says she met him the other night and asked him where he was going. Mr. S told her he was going up to the Methodist church to get a cup of coffee. Dr. Green keeps Bachelor's hall and I do not know what has become of Dr. Wilson. I expect he stays at Mr. Ransom's and he has been sick. We heard that the Reaves were to leave to day. I think I had better ask Mary to stay with him. No doubt she would agree willingly. I know you are tired of this uninteresting scrawl so I will close. Mother sends you all much love and kiss the children for us. Ask Lute if he is not willing to come to Bishopville yet. Give my warmest love to dear bro Ruthvin and miss Elizabeth also to cousin Lizzie and Callie and families. I expect Willie will soon be up again to see Sallie S. I wish you could hear Mrs Vaugn tell about her "surprise party" it would amuse you I know. You must write soon to your affct sister

Amanda Rogers

Columbia Jan 14th 1860
My dear Sister.

Knowing that you would be glad to hear from me, I will gladly avail myself of the opportunity this morning of writing to you. I received a letter from Amanda this week. they were all well that were at home only herself mother and Lizzie. no doubt they all feel quite lonely lonely now. I know you were glad that Sister went by to see you. I received a letter from brother William a few days ago. he was getting very anxious to see sister and Anna. they were to leave for Beaufort on Thursday. I am so sorry they are so far from us, but do hope they will have a pleasant year of it. I know sister was glad father went all the way with her, as I dont think she cared about going alone. Almira and William went home on Wednesday did they not? hope they spent a pleasant time while with you.

We have had quite a nice time this week Hattie. there is a gentleman here who is exhibiting Bunyan's Tableaux[51] and the trustees were anxious that we should see them, and told Dr Smith to invite us all to go and they would pay our way, and you know we were delighted at the idea of getting to go, so on Thursday evening we all got together and started for the Athenian Hall where they were

---

51 "'Moving Panorama of Pilgrim's Progress' consisted of giant painted scrolls depicting scenes from Bunyan's classic book that would slowly unwind spool-to-spool, often to the accompaniment of a narrator and pianist. It is 800 feet long and eight feet tall. These 'motion pictures' were hugely popular as entertainment, and were created in 1851 and toured around the United States to full houses and rave reviews. It had its final showing at the height of the Civil War, when technology rendered it obsolete. In 1877, it was sold to a man whose heirs donated it to the York Institute, now known as the Saco Museum, in Maine. In 1996, the museum director pulled the scroll out of storage in the museum basement, presuming it to be a huge drop cloth, which people had been stepping around and on for years. It is currently (2012) being restored, taking 16 years to accomplish. There are only about twenty of these types of tableaux left in the world." Keyes, B. (2012, June 24). Panoramic View: 'Motion pictures' in Saco. *Portland Press Herald*. https://www.pressherald.com/2012/06/24/p-a-n-o-r-a-m-i-c-v-i-e-w-2012-06-24/

exhibiting. all of us walked together two and two, senior class first then juniors, etc. there were eighty of us all together. Dr Smith was at the head. he seem to feel quite proud of his girls for I never saw him look so pleasing before. We all enjoyed it very much indeed. it represented all the scenes described in Bunyans pilgrims progress. I think I will have to read it soon, as I have never yet done so. was it not kind in the trustees to let us go? at every house we passed we could see heads peeping out at us.

Amelia Townsend is going home on next Saturday to attend her sister's wedding. she is perfectly delighted at the idea she is to be one of the bridesmaids. the wedding is to come off next Tuesday night week. Tell brother Ruthvin I have been looking for a letter from him ever since I came back but in vain. please Hattie write to me as often as you can for you know what a great consolation it is to get letters when away from home. we have to study very hard now as we are preparing for the examination in February, which I dread a great deal, and will glad when it is over with.

We have taken up Geometry now, but I dont find so hard as I expected, but I dont mind anything I have to say to good Mr. Wannamaker. give my love to my relatives in your part of the Country, particularly to "Cousin Covert,, and now dear sister I must close. Mattie sends her love to you, and accept a large portion from your devoted sister

Maria

please excuse this paper as I have written hurriedly.

Bishopville 15 Jan. 1860
My own dear good Harriet

I arrived safely home the Thursday night after I left you—On last Wednesday night I went up to Sumter and Thursday evening Mr. Marly met me at Lynchburg—I am happy to say I found your dear mother looking very well and in fine spirits. Hugh took her picture last Friday—She says she thinks she was prettier than the picture for she says she was dressed "nearly to death."

Oh it was "Spicy" to see Lucy's surprise when some 10 miles below Kingstree she discovered me corresponding with a gentleman two or three seats from her—I bid her good bye as the car left Kingstree jumped into the forward car, and at the Second Stopping went around to the hind part of her car. "Twas rich" just as you will imagine. Found all well in Charleston. Wm & Lucy were to go home last Thursday. Lucy has a new watch- clock- I (illegible). I assume from all I have heard they will be pleasantly situated. we will hope all may be well with them as as also all the rest of us. Mr. Scarborough is still alive—much as when we left, his leg still apparantly dead. he surely must die. I was much pleased with good old Mr. Pierson bless his old soul. I shall be always glad to meet with him. Few men are more full of information on any and all subjects than Mr. Pierson.

The children were delighted with their visit with you. No wonder however at that. They found everything to please them, and I wish we could often visit you all. Mr. Wilson has just called here. he has seen Mr. S. he thinks he can live but little longer. he is now in a kind of stupor. Old Mrs. English is in a bad way. She suddenly lost the use of her limbs It must be something of a paralytic attack. She had gone to see Mr. S. and fell as she got out of the carriage. You must all come to see us as often as possible. We would be so glad to see Miss Lizzy up here. Tell her I won't forget "<u>that</u> <u>kiss.</u>" It seems to me that my dear Harriet should be very happy and I suppose she is—She has many to love her-

But I must close. May kind heaven bless and protect you <u>all</u>. Oh I forgot to tell you that Sweet Sally Roper came home last Friday with Daniel and she went with us to the P. Church to day—I remain your affc. father & friend

William Rogers

Mission Home Jan. 28th 1860
My dear Sister

I really did not think when I parted from you that it would be so long before I wrote to you, but I have been so busy getting things to rights, and "getting ready to live," in our new home, that I found no time for writing. You will excuse me I know, or at any rate I know you would if you had to pass the same ordeal once. This leaves us all very well, and I trust will find you, bro. Ruthvin, Miss Elizabeth, and the children all likewise.

You are aware of the agreeable surprise I had on the day I left you, in finding father aboard the cars, and going to Charleston with me. I never was so completely surprised in my life. I did not find it out, until we had passed two or three stations, and as you may imagine, Anna and I together, made some little noise on the occasion. Wm met us at the depot in C., delighted to see us all. We had quite a pleasant visit there. Bro. John & Sister Mary were there when we got there, but left the day after. I had never seen either of their children before. Their eldest you know is nearly the same age of Anna, a very interesting child. the baby is the fattest thing I ever saw. They seem pleased with Graniteville, and had much to tell us of the folks there. Sister Martha asked after you. said she was much pleased with you, and was very sorry she could not see more of you. she was surprised to hear your age, said she thought you looked entirely too young to get married.

We did not get to see Father's wife after all, as she was on a visit to Georgetown to see her sister when we were there. We left the city on Thursday morning after we got there on Monday and arrived at our destination near 11 o-clock, found our buggy awaiting us, and a cart to convey our baggage, kindly sent by Mr. Rittles, one of our nearest neighbors, to whose hospitable home we went, till we could get our furniture unpacked etc. This family has been very kind to us. His only daughter, Mary, I found had been a schoolmate of yours, and Amanda's at Orangeburg. Do you remember her? She seemed pleased to find I was your Sister, and she has had many questions to ask me about you both, and also of Miss Carnes. (as she calls her.)

After she left C. she went to school to Spartanburg, and was there while Sue was there.

We were disappointed in getting the servant we first expected, but Mr. R- offered us the services of one, until we could get another, which we succeeded in doing in the course of the first week.

We have quite a convenient little house, though plain it is snug & comfortable. It has four rooms and two large closets. The lot, too, and all the outhouses, are well arranged and in good repair. Wm has already been hard at work in the garden. I think you may expect to hear great things of it by-and-by. If he were near enough he thinks he would be tempted to run a race even with Miss Elizabeth, and you know he considers her quite an adept in the art. Our house is in quite a retired little spot, but several summer houses are very near, so after the spring opens I suppose we cannot complain of being lonesome. I percieve no difference in the climate between here and Sumter. we have had very heavy frosts every morning since we came except the first two or three.

Mr. Mood went over last week to see Mr Banks, who lives ten miles below us. He has been on his mission three years, and they have enjoyed perfect health. Mr Mood says he never saw heartier looking children than he has. this is quite encouraging to me. Mr M has now been at almost every point on his mission and seems very well pleased. He has found the planters very kind and sociable, and all seem interested in the mission. He tells me great stories every time he comes home of their elegant residences, and Princely style of living ec. He thinks however he has got pretty well into the good graces of some of them, but I will let him tell you about all this.

So on the whole dear sister I find we are not quite so far out of the world, as it at first seemed. at least we have found friends here as elsewhere, and what is far better the presence of Him from whom cometh every good and perfect gift, the Friend who sticketh closer than a brother. All I mind now is that we are so far off, I fear none of you can get to see us, but I try to think that there are yet many happy meetings in store for us all. I can but think that our appt. here was for some good. God has surely been very gracious to us throughout our past lives and we must not fear to trust Him for the future.

And now dear Sister that my sheet is filled, I find I have been very selfish in writing entirely about our affairs and left no room for you & yours. I would not have done it, but I know you wanted to hear all about our new home. How is our dear bro. Ruthin getting on? He is good as ever I know. Give our best love to him Miss Elizabeth and kiss each of the little boys for us all. Anna often talks about you all. She often asks if it is not almost time for "next Fall" to come so she can go home again. she thinks she is getting large enough to go back. You know they told her she'd be a great big girl when she went back. Do you and bro. R. write to us soon direct to Salkahatchie Bridge S.C. We find this will be nearer to us than Pocotaligo.[52] And now good bye my dear Sister. with all the love a sister's heart can send I remain

Yours devotedly
L. J. Mood

(written in margin @ top:)

Wm wrote you from Charleston did you receive it? I hope so. He is away to day on the mission. Mr. Mouzon our P.E.[53] will return home with him. We look forward to his visit with much pleasure. Give our love to Callie & Lizzie and their families when you see them. When you write tell me how Callie is. We had a letter from Father this week. I was so glad to get it. all were well at home. I find my melodeon[54] a great deal of company for me. I am learning to play on it gradually. Remember our P.O. Salkahatchie Bridge S. Ca.

---

52 Salkahatchie (Indian word for "salt catchers") and Pocotaligo are near Green Pond, SC, and Beaufort, SC.

53 Presiding Elder

54 small reed organ

Bishopville Feb. 3rd 1860
My dear Sister,

Knowing that you are always glad to hear from home I will gladly write you this morning. we are all pretty well but Mother had a sick headache yesterday but is up and much better today. We had company last night, Mr. Weaver, the junior preacher and were very much pleased with him, he is very lively and talkative nothing like Mr. Alston. he made me play a good many pieces and assisted me in singing. Father got a long letter from bro William Monday night. they had got comfortably fixed in their new home and were pretty well pleased, said Anna was busy as a little bee had her hands in everything. Mr. Mood staid with us on Friday night said he intended going to see you next week. we all liked him very much. I think he was in search of his watch that he lost. I hope he will be succesful in getting it = things are going on their usual routine in Bishopville, nothing new transpiring. cousin H is still in Lynchburg. Mr. Harley went there too on Thursday, will bring him home tomorrow. he is going to take Ambrotypes[55] in Camden next. Mr. H. is going up there again on Monday or Tuesday. they have a good excuse to see Sallie now. I have not heard from her since she was here. Daniel will be home tonight I gueſs- There was a union prayer meeting at our church last Sunday afternoon—will be held at the Presbyterian church tomorrow evening. Mr. Wilson preached a sermon on that subject last Sunday night which pleased every one very much. I have not heard whether Mag has got home yet or not. Almira and I intended going down there last night but having company, we could not go. Mary Farmer and her cousin Mr. Parrotte staid with us Monday night. She and her sister Nammie want to get a claſs in embroidery here. she brought with her some bead work she did at floral, it was the prettiest work I ever saw. I do not know whether they will succeed or not in getting a class. Mr. Garner has bought a house & lot in Danceyville. they still have a flourishing school and are going to take boarders this year too. Jane Durant & Jimmie and Jerett Scarborough left on Thursday for Cokesbury, said if they had time they would stop and

55 Photographs on glass; less expensive than daguerrotypes

see Maria. I hope very much they did. Albert Dixon are going to leave on Monday for Mount Pleasant. Mrs. English is much better, or was when we heard from her last. I got a letter from cousin David Thursday night, his examination takes place on the 28th of this month, so it will not be long before he will be at home. Cousin Drucilla has been over in Marlboro. spent two or three weeks, was there when Harriet Townsend was married though not at the wedding, but heard it was a splendid affair said she saw the groom and his attendants pass through Bennetsville. Cousin Annie Jane would have come home with her if she had not been going to the wedding. You must write home as often as you can, we are always glad to hear from you tell bro R. he must answer my letter soon. All send you bro R miss E. and the children much love and accept the same from

Your devoted sister
Amanda

Columbia Feb 18th 1860
My darling sister,

Having some leisure time this morning, I will devote a portion of it in writing to you. Your kind letter received last Saturday was gladly perused by me. glad was I, to hear that you were all well. I was quite sick one or two days last week, but am entirely well now. Mrs Black was very kind to me indeed, Eliza Murchison stayed with me nearly all of the time as she did not have to study until the examination was over. Eliza is a dear good girl and I think a great deal of her. had it not been for her I guess I would have gotten very home sick. she is in the senior class. Well Hattie the examination is over with and you can well imagine how glad I am for it. The examination continued two days, Monday and Tuesday. There was no one here at all though I believe we were as much frightened as if there had been. I was examined in Geometry and Algebra Monday, Nat and moral Philosophy Tuesday. there were some long looking faces when we went to recite morals, as we had to recite it to Dr Smith, but he was very kind so I didnt miss anything at all. Oh Mr Wannamaker was so kind to us too. I never will forget his kindness to me. he is one of the best men I ever saw. I am glad to tell you that I got 9 in every thing I was examined on, which is the highest mark. are you not glad for me? We have got through with Nat and moral Philosophy, Mineralogy, and have taken up Chemistry and Geology. Dr Smith has changed arrangements with reference to teaching. We are kept in school now from nine until two and are then dismissed for the day. We are all pleased with this as we have more time for studying. I received a letter from sister a day or two since. they were all quite well. says little Anna is much more affectionate towards her now as she is away from us. Amanda wrote me this week that Vermeille was to leave next Tuesday for Cokesbury where she is to teach music. I was surprised to hear it. Amanda said perhaps she would stop to see me as she went in. I hope she will as I am always glad to see any one from home. Hattie I got a very pretty Valentine this week, but have no idea who sent it, as I could not make out the post mark. Dr Smith would not let some of the girls have theirs because they had "love poetry" as he calls it in it—but as mine did not have any writing at all in it—he let me have it. I went to walk yesterday evening with Miss Dibble and several of the girls. she took us out into the country. I enjoyed it very much. some of the places reminded me so much of home. I hardly think you can make out this badly written letter, but do it if you can, for I have written very hurriedly, as the mail will soon leave. Give my love to <u>all</u> <u>all</u> and accept a great share from your devoted sister

Maria

Chaston Feby 22 60
Dear Ruthvin

I have bought a wardrobe for Harriet as requested by mother and have ordered it sent to Kingstree where I hope you will find it soon. the freight is paid

Yours
Daniel

Bishopville Feb. 28th 1860
My ever dear Sister

Your thrice welcome letter to Mother was received by last night's mail. we were very fortunate about getting letter, got eleven of them, that is all of us together. I only got two, one from bro Wm and the other from Annie Jennings. she sent much love to you, says Jane Guinyard has a fine son, Miss Anne Salley is married also. We are all well to day. week before last we had quite a time of it, all sick but Lizzie and Mr Marley, mother and I both had headache but soon got well. I forget whether I have written you since Daniel's illness or not. he was very much like he was the week after you were married, was confined to his bed nearly a week. he was recovered sufficiently last week to go to Charleston, made a flying trip of it, only staid one day. he did not go up to Camden until yesterday. Mr. Marley stays considerable of his time up there. he and cousin Hu came home Saturday night, left again yesterday morning. Cousin Hu did not know when he could come again. he is doing a good business in Camden likes the place very much. I expect Daniel and Lizzie will move up next week. we will miss them a great deal. Cousin David will be at home Friday next. Jasper S- has already arrived. City life has not changed him a particle, he does not like denistry much, says there is a great deal more to learn than he thought there was. he reports that cousin David is coming through first or second best in his class. I was pleased to hear it.

You would be amused to read bro Wm letter. he says going to his appointments at one place where he had to cross in a boat. fearing the tide would leave them he went in a half run and with all their haste when they got there, found they could get to the shore only within a certain distance. so he got on a negro mans back and he carried him safe to land. You must not tell him I wrote you about it, though I expect he will do it himself. We had a musical concert in the academy last night. there were two gentlemen and a lady. she played on the melodeon and the gentlemen the violin. they wanted to get a class here but did not succeed. their performance was rather poor. the first two pieces they sung were "old hundred"[56] and "old ship of Zion" Father received a letter from Mr Dalton, the blind man. you remember who was here once with his grandmother. he wants to get a class here also, but I do not think he will. it is the first time I ever saw any writing of the blind. it looks rather strange but you can read very well. Last Thursday was the day appointed by the general Assembly for prayer for the young. Mr Wilson made a short address at night which was very good. Mr Alexander preached for us Sunday and cousin Hu closed for him. he is very graceful in the pulpit. did not seem at all abashed. Mr Brown preaches for us a gain on next Sabbath. We have finished Daniel's quilt. it is pretty too I think. Mother and I did it almost entirely and I was heartily glad when it was finished. It seems as though it has been an age since I saw you all—I do wish you would come up soon. we get right lonely sometimes- I was glad to hear that Fannie anticipated visiting you in the Summer. I know you will all be delighted. You wished to know if cousin Charles was going to New York. they are not going there at all this spring. he has gone to Charleston—left Monday morning. we were sorry we could not get your letter earlier as he could have got your bonnets for you there if you wished him to do so. he said if he had time he would go see sister before he came home. I hope much he may. she would be so delighted. Joanna Rivers is coming home with him perhaps. Mrs Wm Dixon has another daughter one day old. They are having the graveyard at our church fixed up very nicely. it will be quite an improvement. cousin Anna Jane has not come yet. I will not look for her any more. Argent Crosswell teaches for Mrs Holleyman in Vermeille's place, etc. H. was much pleased with Cokesbury says it is the prettiest town he was ever in. Dear cousin Charlotte has not been so well this week but is better to day. she sends much love to you all. mother, brother Wm and Almira also send you, dear bro Ruthvin, Miss E, Haynsworth, Lute and Henry much love. tell Lute he is a brave little fellow to hold on to the carriage so tight. Kiss them all for me. I saw Miss Susan Montgomery at church the other night. she is as large as life still. good night sister

56 Old Hundred, also known as "All People That on Earth Do Dwell"

dear. May guardian angels attend you this night. write soon to your devoted sister

A. M. Rogers

March 1st 1860 Columbia F. College
My much loved Brother,

Gladly do I avail myself of the opportunity this afternoon affords me of writing to you. I am glad to tell you that this leaves me well, and sincerely do I hope that this will find you all well also. Since I last wrote you there has been quite a change in this college, owing to a difficulty that occurred between Dr. Linville and Mr Wannamaker. Oh! I am so sorry to tell you that my dear teacher Mr W. has resigned. Dr. Linville also, they say. Dr. Linville resigned on account of his health. The difficulty took place last Saturday and Mr. Wannamaker and family left early Sunday morning. I tell you this was a sad-looking house Saturday after we heard that our dear teacher was to leave, many many tears were shed about it, for he always was a favorite teacher among all of the girls. Mr Martin is now our president and Dr. Taylor has taken Mr Wannamaker's place as assisting the president. I must confess I am delighted at the change and so are all of the girls, for Mr Martin is so much more kind than Dr Smith ever was, but I don't think I can ever love a teacher as I did Mr Wannamaker. no never, for he was one of the kindest men I ever saw. it was always a pleasure to recite to him. he called the junior class his class, as we recited nearly all of our lessons to him. It was indeed a sad scene when we were all bidding him good bye, he seemed to feel a great deal, oh! I am so sorry he has gone. I don't think Dr Smith was troubled with many of the girls bidding him good bye. I don't like to stay here as much since Mr W left and I feel so lonely now, you must write me a long letter. that would cheer me up I think. To day is the first of March. only four more months and I hope to be in my beloved home again, delightful thought this is to me. we went to walk on Wednesday evening, and Dr Parker, one of the trustees, who keeps the asylum took us there, and carried us all over the building.[57] some of the people came and talked to us, and seemed delighted to see us, told him he must bring us all back again. some of them talked very sensibly. I went into the glass house they have there, and saw some of the most beautiful flowers I ever saw in my life. I received a letter from Brother William a day or two since. they were all quite well. I have not heard from any of you in a week or two but hope to get a letter to morrow. Give much love to Hattie and Miss Elizabeth. kiss the children for me, and now dear brother I must close. write very soon to your devoted sister,

Maria

good bye

57 "Dr. John W. Parker was the superintendent of the asylum. Many Columbia residents used the asylum for a refuge during the burning of the city by Gen. Sherman's forces in Feb. 1865. With dwindling supplies, Parker did the best he could to provide for the destitute citizens and his patients. After the war, the asylum struggled to survive, but Dr. Parker accepted more patients and then used his own funds to provide supplies for all." Craft, S. (1996, May) SC Dept. of Mental Health's *Focus*. www.asylumprojects.org/index.php/South_Carolina_State_Hospital.

Bishopville March 1860
My dear Harriet

I have only time to write you a short letter, but I know it will be more acceptable than none at all. I have been busy all day preparing for Miss Deschamps wedding. I am to leave early in the morning with Mr. Dixon and Alise Emma—cousin Charles is not going as cousin Caroline is sick. she had a little girl on Sunday but it only lived one day. it was a beautiful child. She takes it pretty bad, poor woman I feel truly sorry for her. she thought the baby looked like Rosemary which made her more anxious if possible for her to live. We missed you and dear brother Ruthvin so much after you left. I wish so much you could have staid longer with us. Nothing new has transpired since you left. Cousin Drusilla and Miss Harriet Law came up to see us last Saturday and staid until this evening. I was never in her company before and like her very much indeed. they visited about a good deal I believe we have had no other company since you left. We heard from bro Wm and sister by Mondays mail. they were all well and highly delighted at the idea of having father come and see them. Maria was well also. she says they were going to have a merry party and she thought Eliza Murchison would be queen. she is very fortunate in this respect. I have finished all Marias dresses but one, thought I would not make that until after I came home. I had forgotten so much of Rena[58] that I thought I would read it again and I find it very interesting. hope you found Miss Elizabeth and the children well. dear sister you must excuse this poor and short letter, as you know I generally write pretty long ones and I have no time to write longer tonight. all send you much much love and beg you to write soon. Cousin Charlotte sends love to you all and give a large share for all to Miss Elizabeth and the children and do not forget to write soon to your affct sister

Amanda

---

58 Rena, or The Snow Bird, by Caroline Lee Hentz (1800–1856) published 1851

Bishopville March 10th 1860
My own dear brother

As we can not spend the anniversary of your wedding day with each other I will substitute pen and paper though I would so much rather see you as I am not well gifted in putting my thoughts on paper. Mother had hoped to be able to be with you all to day as she was anxious to go down this week, but cousin Charles was in Charleston and did not return until Thursday night, therefore father could not leave. We are all quite well and were happy to hear through dear Harriet's letter that you too were all well. I was surprised to hear that you had not heard from us in so long as I have written to you very punctually, but I hope you have gotten them 'ere this. Well dear brother Mr. Marley is gone. he left on Thursday morning. it has seemed so lonely since he left we miss him so much. he hated to leave too. Said he never hated leaving home more. he wrote you the day before he left which I suppose you will soon get. Daniel and Lizzie moved this week though Lizzie did not go up until Thursday, I miss her a great deal. I never came as near having the blues as I did Thursday evening after they all left. Harriet told us that you spoke of bringing her up the day she wrote but you could not come, so I took up the notion that you would come yesterday, and I looked for you until after dark. went out to the road to see if I could see the buggy. I never wanted to see you all so much before and I do so much hope you will come up soon. Mother says tell you she and father will come as soon as they possibly can though they cannot appoint the time. cousin David got home this week, he looks very well indeed. he had been up to Camden but returned last night. I received an invitation from Mrs. Deschamps last week, to act as bridesmaid for her on the twenty ninth of this month which I will of course accept. they are to have nine waiters apiece. cousin David and cousin Mary Jane will both wait. it will be cousin D's 17th time. Mother told him this morning she did not want to hear of he and Mr. Scarborough waiting any more. we heard the other day that William Cuttino and Amarinthae were married but as Harriet said nothing about it I presume it is untrue. Tell Miss Elizabeth I would like amazingly well to take a ride with her particularly if Fannie formed one of the party.

Miss Joanna Rivers was expected home with cousin Charles but she had engaged to teach her brother in law's little son and so could not come. She will perhaps come in the Summer. Cousin Charles thought of going to see Sister but did not have time. Eliza Bell spent Wednesday and night with us. after tea she and I, cousin David and Mr. Marley went up to Mrs. Dennis's and spent quite a pleasant time. Muldrow gave Eliza and I quite a pretty boquet of geraniums of various kinds and we both gave them to Mr. Marley to carry to S—-. Muldrow has being doing badly lately. missed school one day on account of being drunk. Tell Harriet that Dr. Green made a public acknowledgement in class meeting last Sunday in reference to his drinking. He did it of his own accord there was no trial or any thing of the kind he spoke beautifully and said that he would <u>never never</u>, God helping him, deviate again from the path of rectitude. every one evinced much sympathy for him. I do humbly hope he may do better for I do believe it is his earnest desire to do right. I suppose Maria has written you of the changes that has recently taken place in the college. she hated very much to give up her favorite teacher Mr. Wannamaker and did not seem to blame him at all but since we have heard what is said to be a correct statement of the affair, and he is entirely to blame. we heard that some of the young ladies wanted to go to the So Ca College library and asked Dr. Smith to let them go with Mr. W. and he refused to let them go, which every one thinks was right. this was what they fell out about—the trustees were called and Mr. W. was asked to resign and Dr. Smith resigned also on account of his increasing ill health. Mr. Martin is now President and Dr. Saylor professor, the girls like Mr. Martin much better than Dr. Smith. he is more lenient with them. Can you not come up soon. we would be so delighted to see you. you must write me very very soon. kiss Harriet and all for us and give them bushels of love. All send you much love. Almira says she would be delighted to have Lizzie Haynsworth go to school with her. The liking was mutual between her and Mr. Haynsworth. I remain your devoted sister

A M Rogers

Mission Home March 10th 1860
Dear brother Ruthvin,

We are anxious to rec. a letter from you, and as I know of no surer way of getting you to write, I have determined to write to you, hoping you will give us a speedy answer. I remember now that this is the anniversary of your wedding-day and before I proceed further, allow me to offer to you and my dear sister Harriet, my warmest congratulations, in this, Mr. Mood heartily joins me, and we pray that you may each enjoy many more happy returns of the same, that the blessings of Heaven may in all things rest upon you. Mr. Mood received Harriet's letter a few days since, and we were more than glad to hear that all were well with you. He sends many thanks for the letter, and also for the buckskin, of which there was an ample supply, and I send thanks to Miss Elizabeth for the receipt. I expect to find it very useful.

We are all quite well, the low-country atmosphere agrees with us finely so far. Anna is as hearty and fat as can be, she has grown so heavy that I cant make a baby of her much longer. Her lively play and prattle does much to enliven and cheer us, separated as we are from all our nearest earthly friends, and where at least at present, we have but little society; but it will not be long now before the summer residents of our little village will begin to flock in and then we will have company in abundance. Mr. Mood has made the acquantance of all the Patrons of his mission and has met a kind reception from each of them. he often comes home and tells me great stories of their Princely style of living. We had last week a very pleasant visit to a family living some twelve miles from here. Anna & I especially enjoyed it very much as it was the first thing of the kind we had had since we came down here. The country was all new and interesting to me, the rice plantations, the neat villages on them, the palmetto & magnolia trees, were all objects of curiosity. Mr. Mood married a couple down here a short time since, I wish you, Miss Elizabeth, and Harriet could hear his description of the wedding, he wrote an account of it to Amanda, when you go up get her to show it to you.

I suppose Fannie will soon be with you now will she not? I know you will all enjoy her being with you, I hope Amanda may get to see her while she is out. I know the folks in Bishopville will all be delighted to see you when you go. Harriet complains that Mr. Marley has not been to see her since I left, but I hope he may be down soon. I really don't like to wound her feelings, but tell her, I fear she may tremble for her claim, now that Sallie Rogers has appeared upon the stage. She will have to devise some plan to keep him away from Camden so much of the time. He & Wm, both seem to be much pleased there. I presume Daniel and Lizzie have got to housekeeping by this time, and I expect are quite happy at being in their own home. I expect David has got home by this time, as we have seen his name announced in the papers in the list of graduates. They have made quite a change lately in the Columbia College. On the whole we are glad of it as we like the present President so much the best. Anna is giving me a great many messages to give to you all especially to Hayenesworth & Lute. She talks a great deal about them. She wants to know "if Aunt Hattie read that pretty piece to them about Julien Ward, that was in the Advocate," if not she must find it and read it to them, it was some three numbers back. The dear little boy lived in Graniteville and was one of Anna's earliest friends.

Mr. Mood joins me in sending our best love to you, Miss Elizabeth and Hattie and tell H. to kiss the little boys for us. I wish much we lived near enough to each other to visit during the year, but this cannot be so we have to look forward the happy meeting which I trust we shall have at the end of this year. Our love to Callie & Lizzie and their families and to all our friends in the "Fork." How is Mr. Witherspoon doing now? any better? And now my dear brother, hoping that you will write very soon, I remain—Yours very affctly—L. J. Mood

March 13th 1860
Dear Uncle

As the roaring wind of "old March" is whistling around the house & a cold rain falling I will embrace the opportunity of writing to you once more.

Fathers family are all well at this time & I believe our relations are well with the exception of Aunt Lizzie Dickey. She has been sick for several weeks but is recovering again.

Dear Uncle I have commenced this letter, but as times are so very dull I am afraid that I cant enterest you much. The farmers are all very busy planting; some are done and others just commencing, that is corn, (hole in paper) not heard of any planting cotton yet but I expect most of the farmers down on Spring Creek have commenced.

Father has had corn up for the last week or two, but I think he will wish that it was in the barn, before March is out. We have had some very warm weather & it has made the trees put on their Spring (illegible), but I think they will look different in a few days.

We hunt but very little now. Father and myself were out last Saturday. The dogs started a cat (hole) it nearly an hour and came on some deer. they ran out by me. I had a fair shot with both barrels, but no meat.

I must close as I wish to take this to Whitney. Dear Uncle. are you never coming out to see us again. I think you might come out once in 4 years as Father goes out nearly every year.

You must excuse this hasty and badly written letter. Father & all the family join me in love to you.

Yours most affectionately, Edgar Plowden

Columbia April 5th 1860
My dear sister,

Your kind letter should have been replied to ere this but I have delayed doing so from day to day, until nearly two weeks have elapsed since I received it. As I am at leisure this afternoon, I will devote awhile to the pleasant occupation of conversing with you though I fear I will fail to interest you. Many thanks for your kind letter. I was truly glad to hear from you but regretted so much to hear that my dear brother had been sick, but sincerely do I trust that ere this he is entirely well. I received a letter from Father a few days since; which was quite a treat; as it was the first I have rec- from him this year. They were all quite well when he wrote. I am so sorry to hear that my dear mother has suffered so much with headache recen'ty, oh! how thankful would I be if she could be entirely relieved from them. I expect Amanda has attended Miss DeChamps wedding ere this. I hope to get a letter from her to morrow, telling me all about it. I received a good long from Sister this morning. They were all very well. she and Brother William are <u>so</u> kind to write to me. one of them write every week nearly. Anna Nora weighs 33 1/2 pounds now. sister says she frequently goes off with her father. darling little creature, how anxious I am to see her. sister sent me a present of a nice collar. What beautiful weather we have now. The large green trees in front of the College look beautiful now. I am writing upon my bed, right by the window, looking out while I am writing at the yard just opposite the College. I wish the yard here was as pretty. I am thinking so <u>much</u> of home this afternoon, oh! how I wish the time was nearer for me to go home, but it will not take three months long to pass away, then can I have that pleasure. I anticipate a great deal of pleasure next Summer if nothing happens. Some of my friends who live in Sumter have promised to visit me then. The election for May Queen took place on last Monday. Eliza Murchison was elected. She is really very fortunate isnt she? we are not allowed to invite any one at all though Uncle Martin says we may just have a party among ourselves. they will give us two or three holydays though, which of course is very pleasing to us. We had a Concert last Friday night. there were a great many visitors here. the girls who played performed very well indeed, and every thing passed very pleasantly away. We are to have another in May. Miss Craig says I will have to play then. it will be quite a trial for me but I will practice hard and try to acquit myself the best I can.

One of the girls here heard yesterday that her brother was dead, she is about crazy. they have not sent for her yet. she heard it through one of her friends. I suppose they will come for her soon. poor girl. she takes it so hard. we could hear her screaming all over the College when she first heard it. I do feel <u>so sorry for her</u>.

Hattie, I expect you are tired of reading this uninteresting letter but you must excuse it, for you know it is a difficult matter to hear news when off at school. much love to <u>all</u>. write soon to your devoted Sister

Maria

Home Apr. 5 1860
My darling Brother.

It has been a long while since I have written to you before, and longer still has it been since you have written to me. Think not though my loved brother, that I blame you for I know your opportunities for writing in Camp are not by any means good. Hattie's letter to mother was received Thursday night, and we were so glad to learn that you were improving. glad too that you did not return to Camp at the time you anticipated.[59] I wish so much you could come to see us before you return though I guess this pleasure will not be afforded us.

I received a letter from brother Wm this morning, in which he said that the last account you had from Sandy he was thought a little better. I hope sincerely he may ere long be entirely restored. Sister is coming home next Monday week, Oh! I am so delighted at the idea of it; I am already counting the days. I believe I never was more anxious to see darling little Anna than I am now. How pleasant it would be if you could all come together. Brother Wm writes that he thinks he can so arrange that my dear Sister Amanda can come too. I do hope she will for I want to see her so badly. When do you think of returning to Georgetown? I know these are happy days to Hattie, in having you at home once more. Tell Amanda when you see her that she must be sure and come home, for the boys in Virginia are expected next week. If they do come, I guess we will have a pleasant time while they are at home, or at least the other girls think so. I cant say though that I do. I will be very glad to see them again, that is some of them. Mary Bradley spent the day with me Wednesday, and Thursday afternoon we rode horseback down to Aunt Peggie's and spent the evening. We had a most delightful time. as we were coming back, we had the pleasure of witnessing a beautiful sunset, and as we each had a rosebud in our hand I told Mary we only lacked one quality of being Martin's Acme of beauty. In his book of Poems he says a beautiful young lady, on horseback with a rosebud in her

59 Unable to find any information about the camp in Georgetown that is referenced here.

hand admiring the sunset was his acme of beauty. as you see we only lacked one thing, that is the beauty. But enough of this foolishness my dear brother to your affc- Sister

Maria

Buncomb SC April 7th 1860
Dear Harriet -

Your clever little letter to me came to hand in good time and we were pleased to hear from you all again though sorry to learn that Ruthven was so sick. He must have contracted a very bad cold. Trust however that this may find him entirely well and able "to go" as usual. You must have enjoyed your trip & visit to Bishopville. It is unquestionably a pleasant place to visit (I mean Fathers). Lucy and I both agree with you in wishing we could have been with you there. but — Have you had any cold? We have had a good deal of it, much to the mortification of our irish men in the garden they hid their faces entirely once on account of Mr Jack Frosts visit, and blushed considerably the second time at his approach.[60] They look only tolerably now. Our peas too have been injured. They are in blossom now. Our cabbage plants are growing very prettily now and when you come to see us we may be able to give you several dishes from our garden.

I am glad to say that we are all pretty well. Lucy is busy (it is Saturday) knocking round with Anna Nora following closely after her. Lucy has been riding with me lately several times to the Post Office which they have moved further from us, making it thereby more inconvenient to get at. Have you (Miss Elizabeth) many chickens? Lucy has two broods & one hen hatching or rather setting. But our finest hen was found dead yesterday. It is dreadful hard living down here. Cant get anything to eat—though on a recent visit to (illegible) in Walterboro he sent the "little Queen" a bag of I. potatoes. was it Ruthvens name I saw in the last Advocate (5th April) as sending 2 doll to that Paper? I am glad he continues it. Have you read the last Advocate and the article headed a "Sabbath on the Mission?" Does it read like any one you know? Tell us how you like it.

I have at last made the acquaintance of all the Planters whose negroes I serve. I am pleased with them all—and have been very kindly received by them. The time is approaching when they will be leaving their beautiful winter quarters for their summer retreats. These are

60 Irish potatoes

lonesome seasons for the missionary. He sees no one there in his visits but the negroes, for even the overseers seek the Pine Lands too. There is but one overseer among all the Plantations I visit who does not remove. And it is well for me that he remains, for I have to stay with him. Is Ruthvin a politician to the distance of leading him to Charleston on the great Convention now soon on hand.[61] Does he have any notion of going to the City there? I had occasion to go to Walterboro the other day. it was my first visit. I cant say I was very favorably impressed. it is a sandy sandy sandy place! Next week is court season here and it will then be decided if Milton Kennedy will keep the handsome property left him by Miss Pic. One of the main witnesses has been decayed off–she is a poor girl. Very strong efforts are made to blow up the will–Milton has engaged very strong council–Miss May Kittles is going to Cokesbury very soon to remain till her brother gets home in July. But I must close. Lucy joins me in love to Ruthven, Miss Elizabeth, and to the little boys -

Yours Affectly,
Wm

P.S.–Heard from Amanda yesterday or day before, all were pretty well. Mrs Lheucers babe lived but a day. Give love to Coverts & your folks tell us how Callie is.

---

61 The 1860 Democratic National Convention met in Charleston on April 23. Stephen A. Douglas failed to get the amount of votes needed to win the nomination. electionof1860.leadr.msu.edu/democratic-convention/

Bishopville April 22nd 1860
My ever dear sister

I received your kind and most welcome letter two or three weeks since and feel ashamed that I have not answered before but I know you will not think hard of me for you know what a task it is for me to write letters.

Father and Amanda expect to leave for Camden next Tuesday. I expect they will get to sisters on Thursday.

Amanda and I went down to aunt Peggies on Friday evening and were very much surprised at seeing Aunt Jo there for we had not heard she was comeing home. she said that Cousin Callie had a little girl. I expect they are all very proud of it. Walice and Jimmie in particular.

I suppose you are learning to ride horse back. it is no use to ask you how you like it for I think I know that already.

The sacramental meeting commences at the Presbyterian church next Friday and we would be so glad to see some of you up at that time. tell brother Ruthvin he must be certain and come for I think cousin Drusilla will be pretty apt to come. Daniel Sister Lizzie and cousin Hu will also be down. Mrs Magee came home with Father Friday evening and staid until Saturday evening. dont you think I ought to tell you some knews? but she did not tell us any thing only about her children and I dont suppose that would interest you much.

Mr Scarborough has gone down the country. he said that if he was any where near to where you lived he would go to see you.

Amanda is going to spend a week with Miss Sallie Rosser when she returns from sisters. says she will write to you as soon as she gets back. You must excuse this badly written letter as I wrote it by candle light.

All join me in sending love to you all. kiss Haynsworth and Lute for me. tell them they must not forget me. I remain as ever your devoted sister

Almira

Bishopville 6 May 1860
My dear children

I am happy to say that Amanda & myself have made our promised visit to Wm & Lucy and found all well and rather pleasantly situated considering the circumstances- we got back or I did last Wednesday—Amanda staid in Camden. We found all well in Camden- and I am happy to say we are well here- Your dear good mother is better off than she has been for some time- Well the time is rapidly approaching when we expect to see you if nothing unforeseen shall occur to prevent us- Next Friday evening seems to be the time when Mr & Mrs Rogers are to visit you and if we start then as we expect to and dont get lost—we may be at your house by 3 or 4 o'clock.

I must now write a horrible tale. Yesterday somewhere below Camden there was a fishing party on a mill pond—by some accident the flat upon which the party were was over-turned—or sunk and some 12 or 15 persons hurried into Eternity-[62] Frank Huggins & Sally were on board but both were saved- but Franks brother Josey Huggins was drowned. It is said he saved one young lady and went back for another, but never reached the shore again alive. The oldest son of poor old Mrs MLeod was among the lost- a brother of the young man killed on the rail road a few weeks since- nor is this all- three daughters of Saml. Young were drowned- and they were Mrs. MLeods grand children- at ten o'clock last night 9 bodies had been found and they were searching for others- as it is time to go to the night meeting at the Pres. church and as we hope so soon to see you and tell you all the news I will now soon close. I forgot to say that I sufferred with asthma nearly all the I was at Mr Moods but am now well again- Maria complains that Brother Ruthvin does not write to her and I hope Brother Ruthvin will be able to respond favorably of himself when I see him-

62 See online article from The Camden Weekly Journal of May 08, 1860

Our love to your Sister Lizzy—the children—and all the McCallum Plowdens and with my best wish is for your present and never ending happiness.

I remain your affectionate Father & friend
William Rogers

Camden Sunday Eve 6th May 1860
Dear Harriet & Ruthvin

I pen you these hasty lines to inform you that we are safe and well but more to inform you of the most sad occurrence that Ever befell a community. On yesterday (Saturday) a Pic Nic party left this place to go by R Road to Boykin Mill about two miles from here. about 4 1/2 o'clock about fifty persons ladies and gentlemen got into a large flat boat on the pond. while out in the pond the boat commenced leaking and sinking. the ladies rushed to one side and this precipitated them into the water. Twenty Six found a watery grave. I thought you might hear of this and not knowing the particulars might be uneasy about us but we were not along. It has cast a gloom over Camden it has made many homes desolate and brought home to many hearts the words "Prepare to meet thy God" come with double force. I have just attended the funeral of ten persons this Evening and write this note in haste for tonights mail. they were all young ladies and gentlemen most of them from "Camden" I will give you a list of those drowned

Lucuis LeGrand and brother, Camden
Miss McKagen and brother, Camden
Miss Nettles, Camden
Miss McCowns, Camden
Miss Howell, Camden
Miss Robinson, Camden
Mr. Oaks, Camden
Miss Crosby, Camden
Mr. Hocot, Camden
2 Miss Youngs and brother, near Camden
Mr. Richburgh, near Camden
Mr. Huggins, Son of Robert Huggins, Darlington
Mr. McLeod, Camden
Miss Jenkins, Camden
Miss Henson, Camden
two Negroes, two or three of them I do not remember

How awful must have been the sight and Oh! how Sad. I will send you paper giving particulars this leaves us all well Amanda is with us now she & Father came from Lucy's Wednesday they were very well she & Lizzie and Hugh send much love. Lizzie is by me and says to tell Carrie & Olivia to go to work. What does she mean by that Write soon

Your affect brother
Daniel

Camden SC May 6th 1860 Sunday dinner time
Dear William & Lucy

We are all well and also pleased to hear through Father and Amanda that you are well. Amanda is with us still. But I have a melancholy recurrance to relate. On yesterday (Saturday) a Pic Nic party left this place to go out by RR to Boykins Mill. quite a large number were present. about 4 1/2 oclocke about fifty ladies and gentlemen entered a large flat boat and were out in the pond when it commenced letting in water. The ladies sprang to one side and (illegible) were precipitated into the water. Twenty-six found a watery grave. As many are known to you I will give the names.

Miss Lizzie McKagin and little brother, Lucius LeGrand and brother about 17 years old, Miss Minnie Alexander daughter of Isaac Alexander, Miss Lu Nettles, sister to Mrs. Mendinghall, Two Miss McCowns of Camden, Miss Howell, Miss Robinson, Mr. John Oaks, Miss Crosby, Mr. Hocot, two daughters and one lad son of Sam Young, Mr. Richburgh, son of the preacher, Mr. Huggins,, son of Robt. Huggins of Darlington, Mr. McLeod, son of old Mr. Fant McLeod, Miss Hinson–Camden, Miss Jenkins–grandaughter of Danl McLeod, 2 negroes–the other 3 I do not know.

Frank Huggins and his wife narrowly escaped being drowned. he swam with her on his back and just succeeded in getting to shore. if he had to have gone five feet more they would have drowned. Hu was invited to attend but did not feel disposed to go. If he had gone he no doubt would have been lost. what a narrow escape. a little son of Mr. Wm Wootman about 12 years old displayed much coolness before he left the flat. he threw off his coat and made for shore. He came in contact with a Mr. LeGrand brother to (illegible) who was drowning and carried him out. The awful accident has cast a gloom over Camden and will throughout the country. On last night sixteen bodies were brought up on the train. four bodies are now lying at the residence of Lucas LeGrand. three other bodies are at another place. the bodies are to be (illegible) this evening at 4 o'clock and I write (paper torn) as you might hear some report and be (torn) until further particulars. Lizzie and myself went down home last week all were well. Mother had been free from headache for two weeks. I have prevailed on her to give up the use of coffee and she says she feels much better. You will soon see full particulars of this sad recurrence in the papers. I will send you the Journal. I would write you much more but as the funeral takes place soon I must stop. Oh what a warning and the words come with double force. "Prepare to meet thy God." Todays sun arose on many Sorrowful hearts, many homes have been made sad and desolate. Father was (illegible) Evening. Lizzie, Amanda & (illegible) send much love also accept much from your Brother

Daniel

I have just returned from the burial of ten persons this evening. Miss Nettles, two Miss McCown were buried in one grave. Miss McKagen and little brother in one grave, the others in separate graves. Oh how sad how sad. Seven belonged to the Methodist congregation, three to the Baptist church, one to be buried tomorrow belonging to the Episcopal. Without a moments warning they were called to appear before their "God." Let us hear from you soon.

Daniel

Bishopville S. C. May 6th/60
My much beloved and Highly Esteemed friends

Not have complyed with your request in the "Spirit, I will, in the "letter", am truly sorrow that I cant have the pleasure of seeing you all again before my return to town, but it must be so. I have spent little over five months in your state, with a people on whom I had no claim, I have formed the acquantance of many, all of whom I have endeavored to cultivate a friendly aquaintance. if I have failed to doo so it has been from ignorance and not from design; but fortunately I know of no instance in which I have incurred the displeasure of any: And I am more than happy to say that the same good feeling beats in my bosom without a discording note. The time has been spent by me as one bright summers day, and will ever be rembered by with the warmest emotions of gratitude and pleasure, and marked upon the brightest pages of my past in glowing capitals: but according to the corse of nature the "best of friends must part" and I suppose its "all rite" But enough of this for the present. (Daniel's "household & kitchen furniture" left for Camden this morning Daniel left yesterday and I will carry Lizzie up on Thursday. Dr. McCallum landed home Sunday evening.I will start down to see him in a few minutes. this leavs all well except your mother, who was attacted this morning with a violent headache. He left here yesterday for Camden. he is doing a good buisiness there and antisapates stoping there some 3 months yet. Oh! how I would like to spend this evning with at Home on Brewington lake with your brother and honored self, but there are pleasures like others that have these their dated hours; and must be numbered with the "things that ware". I will take a sad farewell of Bishopvill Thursday, will stop in Camden a few days and will go by way of Columba, and Agusta, at which place I will take the cars for Knoxville. And now I come to the only unpleasant association connected with my visit, and must bid you all an affectionate (thoug I hope not a final) farewell. remember me kindly to your brother Edger and Joe & Covert Plowden as well as their ladies, and tell them good-by for me; and "last though not least", to yourself and family I bid you all an affectionate farewell. my best wishes for your happiness & prosperity. Please write soon.

Your true friend
Robt F Marley

P.S. Mrs R...says that Mrs. Rogers herself will be down soon. All join me in sending their love.

Mission Home May 8th 1860
My very dear Sister

I received dear brother Ruthvin's very kind letter a few days since, and I appreciate it very highly I assure you, the more so from the fact that it is about the first one I ever rec. that was written before daylight, when I no doubt was lazily slumbering in bed. I have been owing you a letter the longest time tho' and consequently I attempt to reply to yours first.

I was happy to hear that you were all well, bro R- said you and Miss Elizabeth were busily preparing for the May Party at the time he wrote. It has no doubt come off before this time. I hope every thing passed off very pleasantly. You must tell us all about it, when you write again. I know the Queen made a lovely appearance, she is such a sweet-looking child anyway.

We are all quite well. Wm is now going about trying to find a cool place, for we are now having a very warm spell of weather, and the afternoons of such days you know, make us feel kind of "on restless," when they first come on. Anna Nora & Lavinia are playing "lady" in the other rooms, Anna Nora has just been to ask me, "if they can't come in here to see me, as soon as they get their babies made." She continues very hearty, and is mischievous as ever.

You have doubtless heard before this that father and Amanda have been to see us, they left us to day a week ago, having arrived here the Thursday before. It is needless for me to tell you how delighted we were to see them, or how sorry we were to part with them. I think they enjoyed their visit very much, but it would have been far more pleasant if father could have kept well, he had a severe attack of asthma which had not got entirely well when he left us. I was so sorry for this, for it was so kind and good for him to take the trouble to come all the way down here to see us. I wanted him to enjoy it, to the fullest extent. You may be certain I did not let Amanda's tongue rest much while she was here, and after they were gone, I felt as though I had just parted with all of you, talking of you so much made you seem so near me. Wm met them in Charleston and came down with them, then went as far as Charleston with them on their way home. I am sorry it was so Amanda could not be at your May Party. I know she would have enjoyed it so much. Tell bro. R- it would indeed have been pleasant to have gone home with them, were it not for leaving Wm alone, which I dont think I could done unless for so short a time, that it would not pay for the trouble, after a while though, it will not be lonely with us by any means, the folks are all going to move to their summer places next week, so by the time you rec. this, our village will be inhabited. Mr. Mouzon our P.E. visited our mission last week, spent Saturday and Sunday with us. I was fortunate enough to get out on the mission to hear him preach a most excellent sermon on Sunday. There was a pretty large white congregation besides the colored. We stopped to dine at Mr Marvin's near the chapel, and came home in the afternoon. We have one or another of the preachers to visit us pretty often, and we are always glad to see them.

Our garden is looking well now, and we are getting vegetables to eat. our cabbages are heading up very prettily, which is ahead of what we have ever had before at this season. We have also been more fortunate in the poultry line than ever before, but my number will seem so small to you folks that I won't name it.

Mary Kittles has gone to Cokesbury, on a visit, her brother is at school there, she will remain until July—Amanda told me of the birth of Callie's little daughter. I was heartily glad to hear she was doing so well. May it long be spared to them and grow up a blessing to them, and to the church.

Your twenty-first birthday is now near at hand dear sister. Wm and I unite in wishing you many happy returns of the same, and at the close of each, may you find that God has more abundantly blessed you, and drawn you nearer to himself, than the last. May you on this day consecrate yourself, afresh to His service, and may all your influence be to the promotion of His cause. Oh! how near do these days bring my little lost darling to me, The eighteenth of this month will be one year since God gave her to us, and almost a year has passed since He took her to Himself again. Her precious memory is fresh in our hearts as on the day we parted from her, and every day I miss her still, but time passes and I hope ere long to meet her again, and this year that is so fast flying away makes one less, before I hope to be welcome by her at the Heavenly gates. But I must close. Wm joins me in much love to you, bro. Ruthvin Miss Elizabeth, and in kisses to the dear little boys, which you may administer for us. Anna Nora says "tell Aunt Hattie I love her so much, and tell Auntie howdy'e for me, and tell H- and Lute, I'll try and come and see 'em next fall." (I have sent her message just as she delivered it.) Wm says tell you you'll have to guess again as to "Sabbath on the Mission." tho he is glad you were pleased with it. and by-the-way, has Amanda told you that a young gentleman gave her a pair of gold garter buckles—I heard about it while she was down here. a funny present, wasn't it?

Do write us very soon, tell bro. R. his letter shall be answered soon. Our love to Callie and Lizzie and their families when you see them, and to all who inquire after us. And now Good bye my dear sister. May the Lord bless and keep you all, I remain your devoted sister

L J Mood

(written on same page)

Dear Harriet—hope this will find all well. Anna Nora has gone to bed crying with toothache. I feel very sorry for her. We are in usual health thanks to a kind Providence. I presume you have seen from the secular papers an account of the awful calamity in Camden in which 26 persons have been drowned. I cant comment on the terrible affair and only refer you to Daniels letter which we got today which I enclose to you- Truly its a loud call "Prepare to meet thy God," let us hearken to it dear Harriet. Lucy received your kind letter today and we were glad to see you write so cheerfully. Write soon again- Your brother William

Dear Harriet, Wm had carried this to the office to be mailed, when he rec. your last kind letter, and Daniel's also, so he brought it back to add the P.S. What an awful calamity is the one of which D. tells us. I never was more shocked in my life; oh! how grateful I feel to God, that neither Daniel or Lizzie, Amanda or Hu were among the number! Your letter dear H. was eagerly read and I thank you much for it. Love to all. Glad you had such a nice time at the May party.

Yours L.

Camden May 26 1860
Dear Hattie,

It has been some time since we have heard from you though I believe you wrote last but you must excuse me for not being more punctual in writing. I have a great many little things to do that take up my time. We just came home on Saturday from Lucie's we had a very pleasant visit indeed. We first stopped in Charleston and spent several days there went to see the forts and went to church on Sunday the time was spent very pleasantly Anna Nora and little Nora were quite delighted to see each other. Anna has grown some since she was in Bishopville. goes to school and reads very well and can add up little sums on her slate and seems so fond of it. She has a perfect passion for playing tit tat toe. Daniel and I played a good many games with her. Brother William & Lucy were looking very well they live in a very pleasant place their neighborhs are near and are so kind to them. I rode about with Bro. William and saw some of the rice plantations they are very pretty at this season. I know you would enjoy a visit very much down there. when are you going to Bishopville again I would like so much to meet you and Bro. Ruthven when we go down. I expect we will go next week if nothing happens. We are going prepared for Manda to come up with us. Father & Mother were to see us two weeks ago. I am always so glad to see any of them come it adds more to my happiness than anything else to have them from home to visit us. Nora has grown a great deal since you saw her she has two teeth and can get up and stand by a chair. She is not as good quite as she used to be but is a little cross sometimes but it is her gums that make her so. She has not been so well since she began to teethe- you must excuse this scrawl Hattie but I am not very <u>stout</u> and it being so warm it affects my nerves so much that I can scarcely write at all do give much love to Miss Elizabeth Bro. Ruthven and the little boys and accept the same from your affectionate sister,

Lizzie Rogers

(written on same page)

Dear Ruthvin,

I have not time to write a letter. The next visit we make will be to your house which we hope to be able to do in a month or so. I saw while in Charleston a very fine chair for a sick invalid and wanted to get it for Charlotte.[63] I thought it would please her much to have it presented to her by her friends those particularly intimate with her The price was $32.00. She would appreciate this more than anything else. Hu & Jim wish to contribute & the others that I thought would is yourself, Wm Mcd David Mc & myself and Draper. So if you would like to come in to the present send the bill soon don't send over $5. It is the only one in Charleston and want to get it before it is sold.

Affectionately,
Daniel

---

63 Cousin Charlotte, who lives with Harriet's parents in Bishopville.

Home June 21st 1860
My dearest Hattie,

I was much pleased with your dear, kind letter; it reached me yesterday evening just before twilight and the better part of that time, I was thinking of you, and your very agreeable manners all the time I ever knew you.

You made one remark in your letter, which gratified me much, and that was relative to the kindness of your husband. O Hattie darling, how much you are blessed in living with one, who possesses an amiable disposition. It is a great cross, and one which produces much misery to live with those who are very irritable. under such circumstances one can scarcely live happily, fearing all the while harsh words, which are showered down without charity. But what is unkindness and neglect, when our Saviour is near and ever ready to comfort.

I rejoice with you that your sister has become a follower of the Lamb. May God sustain her and cause her to shine forth "brighter and brighter unto the perfect day."—I wish that my sister could experience a change of heart. She has grown fearfully careless, and, at times, intimates her belief that none are lost, then again she mentions some cross that she says may be the means of carrying her to hell. I shall not write more of her, and would like you not to mention it, but pray that I may perform my duty in pleading at the throne of grace in her behalf.

You asked if I ever think of the moment, in which I felt that I could trust God. Yes my dear very often, but I feel, and have felt, for the past year or two that I have never been, as near my blessed Jesus as I should be. My prayer is that I may change and become a more worthy servant. Our junior (illegible) has (illegible) efforts to obtain a better heart and trust that I may receive the blessing. Oh! how happy I would be, dear friend, if I could feel that I "love the Lord with all my mind and heart and strength."

You have promised to have yours and Mr. Plowden's likeness taken for me. I am very much oblige to you for the kind promise, and hope it will be fulfilled. I shall certainly have mine taken first opportunity, it may be soon, perhaps a very long time, as I am uncertain when I can reach a Artist.

I think I told in my last that Ann Bellinger had been to spend three days with me. I desire returning her visit soon and may do so if "Pa" becomes satisfied with his carriage. Our carriage is worn rather too much for travelling but a short distance and he purchased one (illegible) has been (illegible) found to be very defective and a wheel was sent to be refixed. It is now at Mr. Lafitte's shop, and "Pa" seems very unwilling to keep it.

I have not written to Jane Guignard for months, and I do not expect to do so. she always took so long to reply to my letters that I thought I would trouble her no longer.

If I had secrets more than what I have already written you should be made aware of them, for I have all (illegible) have nothing secret relative to my becoming Mrs. Someone. I cannot see so far into the future as to speak or write on that subject. I do not think I can ever marry and leave "Pa" to himself but I should be not surprised to hear that it is to a minister, for the position of a minister's wife I think I would prefer to any other. Now mind this is a secret. Keep it to your own dear self.

May God continue to bless you is the prayer of your
grateful friend,
Martha

Camden June 24th 1860
Dear Hattie,

I am all alone this afternoon and as I have never written to you I will spend a few minutes telling you how we are getting on in Camden. Daniel gets just as much work as he can do. He has been unable to do much for too or three weeks but is getting quite well again. Some time ago he was suffering a great deal with his side. I feel very uneasy about him sometimes he gets so low spirited and says he will have to quit his profession but I am in hopes he will have some rest time before the summer is gone and travel and try some of the springs for his health. he has gone to Liberty Hill and will not return before Tuesday or Wednesday. I feel quite lonely with no one but Hugh with me. I am a little afraid at night alone but I think it best to get used to it for I may have to stay a good deal alone. Father and Mother were up to see us last week. I was very glad to see them for we had no idea they were coming. Ma Matilda and Manda were up this week so I have been in fine spirits for it was the first visit for both Mother and Ma. It always gives me great pleasure to have them come to see us often. We are going to Bishopville Thursday to attend a Pic Nic at the old mill on Marion's crossing they have got to calling it now. they are expecting a great many people there and they are to have a few speeches about the rail road for you don't hear any thing else talked of but that. I would be very glad to meet you there. It has been a long time since I have seen you. Mother told me you were not coming up until July. won't you come to Camden we would be so very glad to see you. Hugh has been talking of paying you a visit this summer but I don't know what time he is going- Mr. Marley spent a few days with us last week on his way from Charleston. he and Hugh went to Bishopville. I wonder how he and Amanda looked when they met. I think he looked better than when here before. He said remember him to all his friends and Hugh sends love to you and your family. I must close dear Hattie it being Sunday I will write but a few lines. I expect Maria will be at home next week. I am very anxious to see her. She has been very much blessed and I know she will be so happy when she gets home- I can't think of her being any better at heart than when I saw her last for Maria was always a very good girl. Give much love to Miss Elizabeth Mr Plowden and kiss the little boys for me and accept your share of love from your very affectionate Sister

Lizzie

Do write soon dear Hattie for we are always so glad to hear from you. give our love to Carrie & Livia when you next meet them.

Pine Forest July 1st 1860
My Dear Hattie

Although only one day has passed since I saw you; yet it appears an age. (that is) to me how is it with you. we all arrived here about 6 o clock & a more jaded set would be hard to find. I had a passable time coming down. I rode with Argent until Dinner then with M. Jane the balance of the way & she was about as communicative as I have ever seen her. we teased the crowd generally, particularly Miss Argent about the Butcher (that is) Theodore Nelson. we told her she is to wait with him, & then when they come out on the floor I am to blow my fist like a horn. she says if I do that she will not be able to face him after that if he understands the joke. I heard to day that they had baked from 150 to 200 Ho Cake at the wedding house if so I presume there will be plenty. when I arrived at home I found the family all well & hope you all are the same. Do you keep your promise for Sunset. I have written this to request you to meet me at the Brick Church[64] at 7 oclock or earlier if you can possibly do so as it is so excessively hot I know from the other day's experience; that if you do not start by 2 oclock in the morning you cannot stand it. I must now close as there is several persons waiting for me to finish writing to attend to other duties. Good bye my own darling & may God watch over guard & protect you is the prayer of your absent & affect husband. Kiss all the dear ones at home for me & give them a portion of my love. Cousin Charlotte a large share.

Yours
Ruthvin

---

64 Salem Black River Church, founded 1759, near Sumter, SC

Mission Home July 9th 1860
My very dear Sister,

Your letter written from home was received on last Saturday and I need not tell you, was heartily welcomed by us. It was the only letter we received last week from any one, which made it the more valuable. I presume that ere this you have all arrived safely at "Woodland Villa" (is that the name?) and I would give not a little to take a peep in upon you all just now, and I flatter myself that some among you would enjoy a sight of my ("illegible") equally as much. I hope you are having it cooler than we are. it seems to me I never experienced such weather. It is said the heat in Charleston last week was greater than it has been since the year 28. We are all quite well however, and are moving pleasantly on. Anna Nora has just taken her afternoon bath, and has gone over to see her little friends, Doria & Julia Copeland. She still keeps very hearty. I told her the other day of your all being up at home, that Aunt Ria was there too etc. She said "never mind I guess it will be my turn to sail up there next fall, and then it'll be, kiss, kiss, howdye, howdye, my beloved little Anna Nora." You see she anticipates a very warm reception. William has just finished a letter to Almira, and is now going about trying to find a cool place. I think he might as well give up. I know his search will be fruitless. He now has an appointment for every Sunday night at our church here, in addition to his regular work. The people were very solicitous for it, and he did not like to refuse. He has stood up to it thus far very well, and I hope may continue to do so. He was down in the City last week for a day or two. he found Sister Martha sitting up, but while he was there she took a relapse, brought on by the exceptionally warm weather. We are still anxious about her. The rest are all well, father is unusually so, Wm says he seems better than he has done, at this season of the year for years past.

We had quite a storm one afternoon last week while Wm was away, and our garden fence fell before it. the result has been that all our fine cabbages, and several other things have been devoured by the hogs. They were kind enough however to leave us, what we wanted most.

Mary Kittles was in to see me a few days since, she was delighted with Cokesbury. Her brother says he promised to go and see David Durant next month, and I think will be at the Sumter C. M.[65]

How sorry I was that dear Maria got home sick. I do hope she may keep well now, take good care of her while she is with you. And you had Mary Jane McG with you also, how much I would like to see her! Well, you, Amanda, Almira, and perhaps some one else have written to us of Lizzie W's marriage; but the important question, "Who is the man? still is unanswered. Tell bro. R. I'll put this business into his hands now, and he must not fail to let us know who he is, and whether she has done well. I hope she has. And Wm tells me to ask bro. R- if he has seen in the "Mercury" the result of (illegible) negroes trial. It seems that I've just begun to write, dear Harriet and my sheet is filled, so I'll have to wait 'till I write again. Give our best love to dear bro. R. Miss E. and the dear little ones also to H, Amanda, Maria, and Mary Jane if they are still with you, and tell them they must all write us an account of their visit- Love to Callie & S & families when you see them.

(written in margin)

My dear Harriet, two more days will bring around the anniversary of the day that my precious baby was taken from our loved embrace to that of her Savior. A strange peace steals over my heart now, and I praise my gracious Father that this new bond exists between us. I often feel that she is my guardian angel. oh, may she ever be, till I meet her where parting is unknown.

---

65 Camp Meeting

Bishopville July 20th 1860
My ever dear Sister,

You see I am fulfilling my promise to write you soon after my return. We got here safely Wednesday night. found all well but father was suffering considerably from a boil on his forehead. it is getting well now. we all enjoyed our visit to cousin Drucilla's very much. Mr. E. made himself as agreeable as possible. Mary Jane was agreeably disappointed in him. she had never seen him before. we stopped a little while at Aunt Peggy. Cousins Lizzie and Callie with their husbands were to leave the next day. Joe looked like he wanted to be at home sadly. Daniel and Lizzie are not coming home this week. we heard from them yesterday through Jim. they were quite well. cousin Hu is in Lancaster. I do not know how long he will stay.

We had another severe storm yesterday evening. It was harder here than it was last year, but did not extend very far. it blew part of our yard and garden fence down. father and cousin Charles are a good deal injured at the store, a good many of the goods got wet. Mr. Cousar is a good deal injured also. The girls at Muldrow's school all run over here and after school before the hardest part he came too. you never heard such screaming as the children had. I thought William would be frightened to death. I do not think the children about here will ever get used to rain now for they never know what is coming. we had no idea yesterday it begun to rain that there was any prospect of a storm.

I suppose you are all enjoying the meeting at Brewington now. I truly hope it may prove a pleasant and profitable one. We have thought of you all and of our pleasant visit so much. I want to see you all now as much as I did before. Tell Fannie Father and Mother says she must be sure and come to see us. I will be so much disappointed if she does not. How are she and Theodore getting on? I guess Mr. Shaw will come pretty often now since he has made a commencement.

Mrs. Holleyman school begun last Monday. she has twenty three scholars. Almira is not going to her, so she will go to Columbia. Well Harriet I know you will be surprised to hear that our long looked-for diplomas have at length made their appearance. they are very pretty, have an excellent engraving of the College on them. I guess Mr. Legare got them when he was in Rochester this Spring. so perhaps we have blamed him unjustly. it has taken quite a load off my mind. I found letters from Martha Roberds and Annie Jennings awaiting me on my return. they were both quite well. Maria also got one from Mr Marley. he is still in Knoxville was quite well. I presume Cousin Callie has told you that Mag was going to the Springs. I told her I hoped she and old Mrs. English will have a pleasant time. she ought to be a great talker when she gets back. The young men from Mt. Pleasant have all got back, but I have not seen them yet. David and Jimmie will be home to day, so the village will be well supplied with young gentlemen for a time. Maria, Mary Jane and myself went to call on Salina Carnes Thursday evening. she has not returned to Harmony yet as she has been quite unwell. had something like dropsy. Jane and Colie Dennis are at home now. Cole is going to Arkansas to buy land. I have not called on her yet. Mother has though. says she looks just the same. has not changed a whit in any respect. Cousin Drucilla says cousin James went to see his mother and sister. they give flattering accounts of him. he and his mother are coming out here in Nov. so they say. I wish very much they would. I am anxious to see him. Cousin Caroline has given out the idea of going North as she expects Mr V, Mrs Greer and Joanna in a week or two. I suppose they will spend the summer. William says to thank you for the nice cake you sent him. he is kissing us as much ever. I told him the other night that you said for me to kiss him for you but I made up my mind not to deliver a similar message soon again. Sister wrote us the other day that Anna Nora had got to be a perfect old Miss Robison. She was playing the lady with her and she came to see her and told her that her homes and plantations were all burned down and she and her negroes were perishing. Sister asked her what did she want. she says just give us anything. we will be glad of anything you can give us. It is amusing to hear how she talks sometimes. Has Mr. Witherspoon recovered yet. his sisters sent directly after we got home to know how he was. we got to cousin Drucilla's the other day ten minutes after twelve long time before dinner. I was sorry I did not send Miss Elizabeth dishes back. but I had no idea we would get there so soon.

Mr. Frierson is paying his distresses to Miss Hattie Laro again and it is thought they will marry. she will do well to get him. he is an excellent young man. I hope bro Ruthvin and the rest all met with good luck hunting after we left. they had pretty warm weather for it. I have missed your nice watermelons since I have been home. I know I will wish I was down there a good many times. There is no fruit here yet scarcely, but I hope there will be. Mr. Alexander preaches for us tomorrow and this reminds me that I have my bible lesson yet to prepare. Maria, Mary Jane and I are all sitting in the long room busy writing. wish you Fannie and Miss Elizabeth were with us. tell Fannie I want to see her "mighty bad" Mary Jane says give you all her heart full of love. All the rest too send their best love. kiss Haynsworth and Lute for us. and now dear sister good bye. May God forever bless you. Your devoted Sister

Amanda

Mother says tell you she would have sent your diploma but father wants to have it framed.

Bishopville July 28th 1860
My own dear darling Sister.

Another week has swiftly fled, and as I know you are ever glad to hear from us, I will attempt this afternoon to write you a short letter, and if I fail to interest you, I will trust to your kind heart to excuse all deficiency. We are all very well to day, for which inestimable blessing we all ought to be very thankful. Dear dear cousin Charlotte is with us now, came over this morning, it fatigued very much, but she seems pretty well this afternoon. Cousin Caroline is expecting Joana and her sister Elisha up in a short time now. Sister Lizzie is at home today. We have not seen her yet; as she only came yesterday. Daniel has gone up to Liberty Hill, but will be back next week. Our good cousin Mary Jane is with us yes—but I am exceedingly sorry to tell you that she will leave on next Monday for Harmony. oh! my! I am so sorry, we will be so lonely without her. I think she is one of the best girls I ever saw. We have been enjoying ourselves a great deal this week. have had a good deal of company, and, we too have been visiting ourselves. on last Monday my friend Eliza Dixon and her mother spent the evening with us and on Tuesday we had quite a crowd to take dinner with us. Mrs. Vaughn, Aunt Molsey, Cousin Amanda and Mary Jane. You know Mrs. Vaughn is a great talker, so she kept us amused all day, the day passed off very pleasantly. I only wish you and your good husband could have been with us. Tuesday night we were all invited out to Mr. Crosswell's (that is) Amanda Cousin Mary J. and myself. Laurie has returned from school, and Jimmie Durant was there, so altogether we had quite a nice time. We had a letter from brother William on Thursday (all very well; he hasn't found out yet who Lizzie H- married. he says this—he & Sister had been greatly "amused" that so many had written of her marriage, and yet had never told who it was she married. Albert Dixon called on us yesterday, he is the same old Albert that he was when he left. Rivers Dixon looks quite badly. he has grown to be very tall, his mother was uneasy about him when I saw her last, says she never saw anyone change as he has, never has scarcely a word to say. Junior DuBose looks badly too. but I believe David looks better than when he left. I have not seen him but once since his return home. Cousin Mary J. and I had Mary harnessed up yesterday to take a ride but just as she got back from her ride (for you know we had to take it one at a time) Albert came so I could not go. we often talk of the pleasant rides we had while at your house. We often wish that we had Miss Elizabeth here to make us laugh, as she did when we were with you. I would give a pretty to see her take off Mr. Pendergrass this evening. Hattie were you not delighted when you heard that your diploma had <u>at last</u> arrived? I tell you I was delighted for you. I had a long letter from Mr. Marly after my return from your house. he writes such good letters. he is a good fellow too. I think a great deal of him. Cousin May is still over in Marlboro at the Springs. they had a letter from her a few days since. she was enjoying herself first rate. How is Miss Fannie coming on? do give my love to her. I know she is a great deal of company for you. Has Lute gotten entirely well. I do sincerely hope he has. kiss them both for us. Cousin Mary J. says to give her best love to you, and says she would give any thing if she could only see you once more before she leaves. I dont know what we will do without her. We have heard nothing from you since we left you. you must write to us next week, and let us know how all are. Mother has just come in and asked to whom I was writing. she says you must kiss brother Ruthvin, Miss Elizabeth—and the children for her, she said this with a smile on her face. Mother is looking very well indeed now. Mr. Scarborough health is improving, he looks much better than he did sometime since. The camp meeting commences next Friday week, which will soon be here. is Miss Fannie going to attend? It has been just one month since I left Columbia, I can scarcely realize it. only two months more to stay at my dear home. I am beginning to think of the time I will have to leave already. Almira is going with me though so that is one consolation. it is late dear Hattie so I must close this. I want to see you and my <u>dear good</u> brother Ruthvin so badly, kiss him for <u>me</u>. mind now you must do it. I guess it will take your best to read this, but make it out if you can for I haven't time to write it over. All join with me in love to brother, Miss E., Miss Fannie and the children, and also to your own dear self. good bye write soon to your devoted Sister

Maria

Hattie I would send the words you wish me to but they have gotten misplaced and I cant find them.

Bishopville Aug 18th 1860
My dear Sister,

I believe no one has written you this week so I will gladly do so this pleasant Saturday morning, though I must tell you at once to please excuse my paper. it is all I can find, and Wm, our errand boy you know, is absent. All are quite well. I had a bad spell of sick headache day before yesterday but have got entirely over it. I was sorry and disappointed that none of you came to camp meeting. I was certain Fannie would be there and looked for her as soon as possible. Olivia J. was there but Carrie did not go. Maria, Almira, Father, cousin Hu, Daniel and myself went early Saturday morning, got there for the eleven o clock sermon. there were eight preachers I think. Messrs Bellinger, Gamewell, Seale, Pegner, Alston, Elliott, Kistler, Weaver. Mr. Kistler did not come until Monday morning, he is one of the best preachers I ever heard and you cannot imagine how much Mr Alston has improved. he preached twice. Father Almira and Daniel came home Sunday evening. Mother and cousin Drucilla came on Monday and Maria came home with her in the evening and as she and father were coming back on Tuesday I staid until Tuesday afternoon. it was such a good meeting. more excitement than I liked but I think much good was done. we have quite an accession to our church. Rivers Dixon, Y. Bannerwear, Joseph and Henry all professed conversion and joined the church. Albert too. Alice joined but was not converted. Mr Wm Dixon also professed religion. they were at the stand all Monday night and were converted about daylight. it would have done your soul good to have seen those young boys. they were the happiest creatures I ever saw. Jane, Susan Sallie and Fannie Dubose all professed religion. there was prayer meeting at Capt Dubose's Thursday night and Albert prayed in public, he is so zealous. oh I hope they may continue so. There were a number of conversions but I do not know how many. oh that I could obtain a deeper work of grace in my heart. I enjoyed the meeting so much. I met Lou Muldrow, miss Susan Montgomery and Bessie McFaddin. Son has improved very much, I think. Joanna was there all the time. she enjoyed the meeting so much. she seemed very much concerned on Wednesday morning when she saw Alice join the church. Said Mr

Kistler talked to her a long time. she and miss Clelia were up here two evenings ago. miss C. looks badly. she has a sweet little baby. Joanna looks pretty much the same. she is a sweet girl. I begin to love her very much. Mr. Greer is not at all good looking. he has gone back to James Island. only staid a week. the others will stay until September. I saw Mr. Gay very often, he is a nice clever man. I think a heap of him. he went with me to the Stand at night once, and I knew he could not see me so I left without letting him know. it troubled him a good deal. said he staid until nearly the last looking for me. he inquired particularly after you said the next time there was Court in Manning he would go and spend a night with you. Jimmie Jessap was there he staid with the preachers all the time. it seemed truly astonishing what a change has been wrought in him, but not so when we consider it is the work of the Almighty. I saw very little of Willie, he seemed uncommonly dull. saw Manning Nelson but he did not speak to me as I only saw him under the stand. Muldrow as usual went there drunk and they came very near sending him to jail. I was right sorry they did not, think it would have done him good. Mrs. Dennis and Jane came here yesterday evening. they are going back to Virginia Tuesday week. Laurie came home yesterday. I do not know how long he will stay. his wife did not come with him. when you write again you must tell us when you are coming home, do please don't let Fannie go home without coming to see us. I wish you could come soon. I am so anxious to see you all. Mr. Kittles, Mary Kittles' brother, is now on a visit to David Durant, he only lives half a mile from sister. he says they are all well. says sister and Anna Nora look very well indeed. he is a handsome little fellow, much better looking than his sister. I have my Sunday lesson to get and good many other things to do so I must stop writing for this time. All unite with me in much love to you bro R miss Elizabeth Fannie and the children. Cousin Charlotte says give you all much love from her. she is much the same. Do write very soon to your affct. sister,

A. M. Rogers

Home August 21st/60
My beloved friend,

Your affectionate and highly prized letter, was received this evening, and I hasten to reply; but cannot promise you that I shall do so again soon, if you delay as long as usual.

It seems a little strange to be writing now. I have felt perfectly averse to communicating anything to my friends the past several weeks. It is because my mind has been closely engaged with seeking after a higher attainment in religion. I wish to hear from them and delight to read their letters, but yet feel a disinclination to writing generally. I hope and trust that I shall have good things to tell you of my poor self soon. I am seeking the love "that casteth out fear," and God is faithful, and surely will not the blessing render me perfectly happy. I am looking constantly for a blessing from on high. Dear Hattie, this lack of love to our Blessed Redeemer was the great cause of much melancholy I may have expressed in my letters. True it is that I had many trials, and those very severe, sufficient to produce melancholy in any excepting the sincere child of God. Now I perceive the hand who sent the chastening in mercy, for it taught me to try and seek comfort from above, as I have but little sympathy here for my aching heart. The evil devices of the adversary make strong and cunning thrusts at my poor soul, but I look to Jesus, and feel that if I can do nothing more, or receive nothing, I shall be willing to perish trying to reach the Heavenly goal. Oh! may it not be long before the song of the redeemed shall be in my mouth.

Aunt Sallie Thomson has been very ill. She was delivered of a daughter on Wednesday night, and had nine or ten convulsions before 10 A.M. We sat up with her several nights, after which she improved gradually, and is now able to notice her infant a little. Hattie Turner, who, I told you, was so ill, is now well. She was in bed twelve months, and now weighs over a hundred and thirty pounds. It appears to my mind that those who are raised almost miraculously from protracted illness, should be so humble and thankful to God, but how many go on not thinking of the merciful kindness he has extended!

Mr. W. Stukes, son of a very good local preacher near Uncle Lawton's, is in quite a difficulty. He is a very wicked man, and troubled the poor free negros very much, a number of whom lived near Mr. L's. One of these was sitting quietly at his fireside when he heard this young man approach the door. On being refused admittance he broke open the house and the negro understanding his character and knowing that his life was endangered fired and wounded Mr. S. in the arm. He has been condemned to be hung but Cousin Jane's half brother, Mr. Joe Lawton and others, say that they shall do all they can to get a reprieve. The difficulty to which I referred is the wounding of free negro girl in such a manner as to cause her death. This, it is supposed, is an inextricable difficulty. the girl was carried to uncle Lawton's where she received all attention possible. I hope she was prepared for a happy change.

Hattie darling, your inference respecting my engagement is mistaken. I remember that I expressed my thoughts of marriage indistinctly, and thought too that you would think just what you have written. My dearest, I am not engaged to our good little preacher, nor do I think that the most distant idea of marrying ever enters his head. I wrote of him because I love to hear him preach, and I love him too, but Mr. Kelly has equally as much of my love. If you only knew both of them, especially Mr. A. you would not wonder at my writing of either.

You must not believe that I am engaged at all, until I write to you of the fact, for I would as soon tell you as any friend in this world. I shall write candidly to you. At present I have no idea of marrying. I believe God has placed me here to be my father's house-keeper, and that my mode of life will not be changed until He sees fit to order the change. May <u>God</u> bless you my dear sweet friend.

Your own
Martha

Bishopville Sept 19th 1860
My darling Sister,

Once again have I commenced a letter to you, and I much fear it will prove quite as uninteresting as the one I last wrote you. nevertheless I will write as I know you are always glad to hear if it is nothing more than how we all are. Well we are all pretty well. We heard from father last Friday through Mr Carnes who arrived home on that day. He wrote that cousin George Rogers spoke of coming home with him, and if he came, he, that is father, would not go to Boston as he intended, as he did not like to detain cousin George who was there in New York, if he did not go to Boston. he said he would be at home sooner than he expected. We have been looking for him yesterday and to day but he has not yet come. He wrote that his health was very good. God grant that he may soon be returned safely to those who love him so sincerely, to his own dear home. How did brother Ruthvin stand his ride home? Has it entirely set him against coming to Bishopville? No doubt he says so but you can get him in the notion again, can you not? We heard through sister that you were all quite well. We were glad indeed to hear this, but you must write soon and give us all the news which may be afloat. William has just come in from school and told us that Miss Sue Greer his old sweetheart was to be married tomorrow night. I do not think it has much affect on him, though when she was here, he really seemed deeply smitten. I suppose though "absence has conquored love." Mother was down to see Amanda last Friday week. She was quite well. Some of brother William's relatives, from Chesterfield were visiting her at that time. Amanda ought never to be lonely. She has so much company. We are looking for her up this week. I hope she may not disappoint us. It has been such a long time since she was to see us. Father and mother do not have the pleasure of receiving visits from their married children often do they? Sirrie Dennis has been quite sick for sometime but is better now. She has had some disease of the heart, at least her heart seemed very much affected. I hear that Bobbie Muldrow and Sue Green are to be married this fall. It seems right strange to think of Bobbie marrying does it not? William is studying very hard this session. he is anxious to go off to school this winter. I expect it will be right hard for us to see him leave, particularly if he goes so far. But it is his desire and for his good. Have you seen sister and brother William recently? sister wrote us that you and Miss Elizabeth spent the day with her sometime ago. I know the visit was quite a treat to them. Brother William was better when she wrote. I hope he is ere this entirely recovered. he has certainly had a time of it. how much he must have suffered. I suppose Miss Benetia Hamit is married. she was married in the church. Brother William and Sister saw them married, did they not? sister told us they were invited. Conference has been put off nearly a month longer. I hope this will cause brother William to come earlier, as sister thought when she was up, that they might wait until after Conference, which of course they will not now do. My dear sister my sheet is nearly filled so I will close this poor letter. Mother with the rest of the family join me in much love to each one of you. Mother says tell you she hopes to get a letter from you tomorrow night. She tells me too to ask you to kiss brother Ruthvin Miss Elizabeth and the children for her. And now dear sister goodbye. with a heartfull of love I am as ever

Your devoted sister
Almira

Bishopville Oct 3rd 1860
My dear Harriet,

It has been but a short time since we parted, but so lonely do I feel this gloomy afternoon that to drive off the blues I have taken my pen to have another talk with my dear sister. We, that is, mother, old Mr Spears and myself are quite well. cousin Charlotte is the same as you left her. I cannot tell you how I hated to part with Maria & Almira. they too took leaving hard, Maria particularly. I think she takes it much harder than Almira. cousin Hu went to the depot with them and has gone again to day for father who will get to Lynchburg this evening at six o clock. we do not much look for them home tonight. Cousin Hu says cousin M. J. is better. The Baptist meeting closed yesterday. I believe they got one more member. I have wished so often that you and bro Ruthvin were coming up this week. You must get him to change his mind about not coming any more until Christmas. Tell Haynesworth if he were here I would be better satisfied. Almira Emma and Virginia went down Monday evening to have their picture taken but did not get a very good one. Virginia is pretty but I have never seen a pretty picture of her yet. Emma took their leaving very hard. I feel sorry for her. I know she feels lonely. to night is our prayer meeting to be held at Capt Dubose's. I am not going as there is no one to go with me.

The misses China came back with cousin Hu. they are at Mr Wm Dixon, expect to stay a week. he found them very lively. You forgot your diploma after all. I was sorry about it but hope it will not be long before we have some chance of sending it. Lizzie went home Monday evening. David went on with the girls. Lizzie told Maria she expected David would court her this time. Said last year he was going to and as he did not do it then, she had better look out. Cousin Drucilla left on Monday morning. she was at the store with Mrs. Bradley and she presented Ella with a very pretty hat.

We did not hear from Sister by Monday mail hope to hear tomorrow. Do you and bro Ruthvin write often to us. Letters will be greater consolation to me now than they have ever been before. <u>I hope</u> very much that bro R is improved. he did not stay long enough. if he had, no doubt he would soon be well again. I have to write several letters this evening, so you must put up with a short one this time. Wm is very busy now gathering hickory nuts. I was trying him last last singing Juanita. he sings it splendidly. Cousin Charlotte mother Wm and Mr Spears too I reckon, write with me in much love to you bro R Miss Elizabeth and the children. Please write soon to your devoted sister

Amanda

Columbia Oct 18 1860
My darling Sister,

I have been wanting to write you, ever since the reception of your kind letter, but want of time has prevented my doing so: I will not let this day pass though without penning a few lines to my dear Sister! We have both been very well since we left home, though we occasionaly have a slight spell of Homesickness. I expect you have returned from your visit to Camden. I have seen you all there in imagination seated around a cheerful fire, the little babe the most attractive one in the group of course. I need not ask if you had a pleasant time for I know it could not have been otherwise. And you passed as near here as Kingsville. now would it not have been delightful if you would have taken Columbia in your route? or at least it would to us. We rec a letter from Amanda Tuesday last. She told us that Col. Bradley had been elected. Well I declare I am glad that he has at last been elected.[66]

It has been more than two weeks since we parted at our dear home, and yet it seems as though it has been two long months since I saw you: the time passes away so very slowly. last Tuesday was my birthday, seventeen years! I cant realize that I am so old as that. I wished many many times that day that I was at home to spend it. We are very comfortably situated here now. We have a room with only three. Anna Loring is our roommate and I find her very pleasant and agreeable. She appears to think a great deal of us both. I am acquainted with both her father and mother, like them very much indeed. All of my friends from Sumter are here again this year; which is of course very pleasant for me. Alice Hayn- did not return until this week. her father did not wish to send her away from home this year, but she was so very anxious to come back that he at last consented. Alice is a dear good girl. I think a great deal of her. She says she passed your house when she was down there a few weeks ago and thinks you live in a charming place. We still have very good fare and both of us too have splendid appetites. We are obliged to walk out in the city twice every week, and this afternoon our plan is

66 Col. Bradley: unable to identify

to walk so I must get ready or it will soon be time to go. Almira joins with me in love to Brother, Miss Elizabeth, and kisses to H. and Lute and accept a great portion for your own dear self. Do write as often as you can to your devoted Sister

Maria

Bishopville 20th Oct 1860
Dearest Harriet

Your very welcome letter to father was received with gladness on Sunday last and we were happy indeed to learn that you were both well and enjoying your visit to Camden so much. I truly hope you found Haynsworth well almost on your return home. You must be sure and write to let us know how he is. tell him he was not more pleased with Bishopville than it was with him. I hope it will not be long before he pays us another visit. Mr. Cousar preached here on Sunday last. I saw Willie at church, he promised to come and see us but did not do it. but I do not blame him as I guess the principle attraction for him has left. I heard they carried Jimmie home with them. Cousin Hu left to day for Camden. I felt as though he were going to Tenn. we will miss him a great deal, you see our family is gradually getting smaller. to day Mr Spears and myself dined together. they were so busy at the store father and Mr Scarborough could not come. Argent, Salina and myself sat up a few nights ago with Adrianna Magee. she is very much the same. she does not think she will live. seems perfectly willing to die and talks calmly about it. says it will be hard to leave her poor mother in her old age but is perfectly reconciled to the will of the Lord. Mrs Magee talks and cries about her all the time nearly. I feel very sorry for her. I got a long letter from bro Wm by last mail and another one from Almira. they were all well. Almira writes very cheerfully, seems to be much pleased. Mr. Alford from Marion called to see us on Monday. he told mother that Uncle Alec McMillan was still living. she had thought him dead. I am very anxious for her to go and see him. Mr A- amused us talking about cousin Sarah McBride, she is the same old sixpence I guess. bro Wm did not say when he thought sister could come home. I suppose you will see Mr Wilson if you attend the Manning meeting. said he was going to stay one night with cousin Joe.

I was amused yesterday at cousin Charlotte being introduced to Mr. Spears. She was sitting up a little while and he happened to come in. I told her I thought they were old acquaintances. The other night Wm was sleeping with him and the wind before daylight beginning to blow pretty hard. he came running to mother's bed as hard as he could . she asked him if he did not think Mr. Spears could keep the wind off him. he said Mr S turned over like he was afraid of the storm too. Your friend Mr Wilson preaches here tomorrow. I never see him but what I think of what Mr Edgar Plowden said the day we were at his home. You must excuse brevity this time. it is very late. all send you their warmest love also bro Ruthvin Miss Elizabeth Haynsworth Lute and Henry—You must write very soon to

Your affct sister
A. M. Rogers

Bishopville 1 Nov 1860
Dear Ruthvin & Harriet

I take pen in hand to write you at least a short letter if no more—though I am as far as I now recollect almost without news. Last Monday we had a letter from W. W. Mood- They were well- a few days since we had a letter from the Columbia girls and they were also well. I am sorry to say that the dear mother is not well to day has a head ache though not severe- Yesterday she and Amanda went to see Adriana—you have heard no doubt that she has been very ill—They found her better and we hope she may get well. You probably heard that David Mc- bought a horse last summer from Walter Mattison—Donalds son- Last week the real owner came for the horse—and he believed before he came here that Walter had stolen her- I have written to his Father and hope he will refund the money that the horse cost.

Mr. William Jennings is sick I hear—he was sick a few weeks ago but had gotten better- but is again sick.

Well, Lucy J. is to be here on next Monday two weeks if nothing prevents- and you will come up <u>wont</u> you and meet with us. Ruthvine- you will be rather at leisure by that time will you not? Do come up for me. I have not had time scarcely to write a letter since I carried off the girls unless at night and then I was (I suppose) too lazy to write, and this must be my excuse for neglecting you so much in the way of writing.

We have during the last month made pretty large sales of goods—have bought a good deal of cotton which is nearly all unsold, but we hope considerable of it will reach its distenation and be sold at some profit.

Mr. Mood was much pleased to visit with his friend Rev. Mr. Pierson—and wrote us respecting it after he returned home. I should be most happy to meet him again sometime at your house.

Old uncle Henry is still knocking along with the house—he will probably get pretty well through with the front part by January -

Well I will close off this uninteresting letter wishing you all health and happiness, now and forever—Give love to all—this includes Miss

Lizzie the little boys and yourselves of course—I remain most truly and affectionately your Father and friend

William Rogers

Salkahatchie SC Nov 1st '60
My dear Harriet

Lucy and the rest of us got home yesterday from Broxtons Bridge[67] cp meeting and were glad to get a letter from you on our return. & to learn that all were well. we had a very pleasant time indeed and enjoyed the meeting very much. on the whole we had an excellent meeting. I enjoyed the company of the Preachers very much. Lucy had it very finely fixed for her comfort particularly at night as she with bro Ino Crooks family the Preacher in charge of this all stayed off the ground every night going to a brothers about 300 yards from the ground after night services & returning in good time in the morning. we all feel a little tired this morning but all are well. Anna Nora has immortalized herself in the singing line. We heard of Miss Martha Roberts through Mr. Kelly who visits her family often. Lucy says I must say to you that she would have written to you but lately she has been so busy that she has not had time. I was sorry indeed I could not see you in my hurried visit to Bishopville. Hope you'l be up when I am there which will include the 2nd Sunday in Dec.—Lucy however will go up before then leaving me down here for awhile. She hopes if nothing happens to be at home in nineteen days from today 1st Nov. She'l be more than glad to see you & Ruthven as soon as you can get there. I'll leave the Monday after the 2nd Sunday in Dec for Conference at Columbia. we have heard from Maria & Almira since they got to C-. M. has been appointed Mistress of the Sr. class. we are alone again in the Pine Land. The waggons of the last family moving have just passed. I'll feel lonely indeed when Lucy leaves which will soon be as she'l spend a few days in the City. we were several times at Mr Stephens tent. Miss Isabella desired to be remembered very kindly to you. she is a nice girl We hope to hear from Bishopville today. So you went to C with the old gentleman! glad you did that you saw Lizzie Daniel & the babe. I thought the babe a <u>very</u> clever child indeed and Lizzie <u>prettier</u> than I ever saw her before. when I was up she called me so sweetly brother William. bless her heart. Daniel I saw but little on the ch ground. I suppose

67 Broxton's Bridge near Ehrhardt, SC

you have heard of the glorious results of the Lynchburg ch meeting. I must close this. Do remember us all very kindly to Ruthven Miss Elizabeth & <u>your two sons</u>. Anna Nora is well—sends love to all & the little boys- The harvesting of the rice is now over- Lucy went to see some of it at the Cays Plantation. she enjoyed it much such times are times of great hilarity—hilarity with the negroes-

Write very soon to your affect Brother
Wm

Bishopville Nov 3rd/60
My dear Sister

Again it is my pleasant privilege to write you a short letter. We are all very well, but cousin Charlotte is suffering more pain than usual this morning. I guess you thought very strange of my not sending the sleeve pattern to you, but I entirely forgot it until two or three days afterward. looking over your letter I saw it. it has worried me a good deal. I am so much afraid you have needed it. I will send it in this letter. I had been spending a week at aunt Molsey's and did not get home until Sunday as I went down early Monday morning to get the trimming and while I was there Mr. Dixon came on. he said would probably go to your house that night. I know you were pleased to see them. I hope the trimming suited you. the dress is very pretty I think. We heard from Maria last mail. they were both well. she had rec-d a long letter from Mrs Loring, which she appreciated very highly—they had been to hear the "Swiss Bell Ringers" and were much pleased. they performed in Camden on Monday and Tuesday night last. Daniel wanted me to go home with him in order to attend, but as I had just got home I could not go. I rec-d a letter from Annie Jennings Thursday night asking me to act as bridesmaid for her. she is to be married the 11th of Dec. I did not think at first of going but father and mother both want me to go so perhaps I will. you must not say anything about it in your letters to Martha R- or any of the girls as Annie told me not to mention it. she is to marry "Col Curtis Faust." I will tell you when I decide with certainty. she is to have only the attendants and her brothers and sisters. Mother and I went over to see Adrianna Magee a few evenings ago and found her a great deal better. I trust she may still continue to improve. she talked a good deal. Mag McCallum went up for Miss Alford yesterday evening to stay until Monday with her. she is the teacher you remember, that they have employed at the Methodist church, quite a nice lady I think. I called on Vermeille Monday. she looks just the same. has not changed a bit. We are looking a little for cousin Hu this evening. he was not well when Daniel and Lizzie were down. every time he preaches he gets worse. Mary Shano's oldest child was buried at the Presbyterian church Tuesday evening. the poor child suffered a long time; had dropsy. I humbly trust that this dispensation of divine Providence may be sanctified to the good of her parents. Cousin Mary Jane and I took a trip over in Darlington last week. went to old Mr. Commander's one night, and spent the day at Mr. James Carter's. I don't know how cousin Jane gets along with Mr. C- I was tired enough while I was there. Perry was there when we arrived which of course pleased cousin M. we drove cousin David's horse. I hope soon to have the pleasure of talking with you instead of writing. When you write you must tell me when you are coming home. I do not know whether we will have any two days meeting at the M. church or not. if we do, it will be the first Sat and Sunday in Dec. You must write us soon. Father, Mother, Cousin C., Wm send you, bro. R, and Miss Elizabeth, Henry, Haynsworth and Lute their warmest love and accept a heart full from your devoted sister

Amanda M. Rogers

Bishopville Nov. 14th 1860
My dear Sister.

As no one has written you this week I will embrace this opportunity of answering your kind letter rec-d a week ago. we were truly happy to hear that you were all well—and I am glad that I too can bear the same good news. mr Scarborough left yesterday to attend the Fair in Columbia. cousin David and Mary Jane, the misses Carter and Perry were going on in company with him. a good many others have gone from this place. I know Maria and Almira will be delighted to see so many "home folks" I hope they may have a pleasant time. I hope this trip will decide matters between Perry and cousin M.J.. We recd a letter from sister on Monday in which she told us that she would get here on Saturday next instead of the Tuesday following. we can scarcely realize that she will so soon be with us. Cousin Hu came down last Sat night and staid until Monday. he is looking better I think, says he is daily expecting his bro James. I am anxious to see him. Cousin Drucilla was up last week. she is looking for her bro James and her mother the last of this month. I doubt very much if they come. We were very sorry to hear of the death of Mrs. Brockington. they are certainly an unfortunate family. Joe told us when he road up that John Bagnal was to be married very soon to a young lady of Florida. Cousin Mary Alice took tea with us last night. she says the people of Lynchburg were delighted with Mr. McDowell and she was particularly so. says she knows his wife must love him. Mr. Weaver preaches his last time for us next Sabbath. Mr. Brown could not be here at his last appt on account of the illness of his wife, so Mr. W. filled his place. We will not have any two days meeting at all this year. Mr. W. is to preach here next Tuesday night for Cousin Charlotte. I too wish I could have been with you all the night you had such fine times. I do not know whether I could have beat Miss Elizabeth laughing or not. I am out of practice in that line. next time I go down we will try together. You must excuse this short letter. I thought or hoped I would see you so soon that I would leave all to tell, do try and come up next week and stay as long as possible. tell bro R he must make us as long a visit as he did Daniel. Daniel Lizzie and the babe were all well when cousin Wm was down. he has an appt at Piedmont Church the second Sabbath in Dec. cousin H. says if I go to Orangeburg he will go with me to Hinesville, which is very kind in him. I expect I will go, expect to hear from Annie Thursday night. Can you bring your Tarleton[68] skirt when you come home, and be so kind as to loan it to me. I will be much obliged. All send you and all your family a great abundance of love. Be sure and come soon as possible.

Your devoted sister
A. M. Rogers

---

68 Tarleton: a fine, open transparent muslin for women's dresses made in Tatar, France. from Chambers 20th Century Dictionary online

Bishopville Nov 19, 1860
My beloved Sister

Another week has swiftly flown, and again it is my privilege to commune for a chat with my absent sister. The date of this letter reminds me that it is dear sister's birthday; God grant that she may be spared to us for many years to come. Father has not returned from N. Ca. yet, but will I presume in a day or two. I hope his time may prove beneficial to him. He promised to send me to see Gertrude as soon as he returns. I had a long letter from her Monday night imploring me to come soon. Well to day or rather last night the Reserves left. Mr Wm Dixon, Draper, and all the men under fifty had to go. Mr Draper Dixon had one of his fits yesterday morning but he went last night anyway. I think though he will be discharged. Mr Wm Dixon came Monday to tell us good by, he seemed quite cheerful indeed, but his poor wife how desolate she must feel now. No doubt she feels more keenly now than ever the death of her noble Rivers. Cousin Charles received a letter from the girls last night. Emma was improving right fast, but Gertrude was sick though she too was much better. Mr Weaver is perhaps a little better for the last two days, but he still looks very feeble indeed. Dr Lucas was here yesterday, and he gave him some encouragement, but I fear he will never be much better. Hu sends love and says to tell you he expects he will not be able to leave here until Conference time. Had a letter from Almira Monday night. she writes me that another one of the girls are to be married. It seems as though people will marry in spite of war times.[69] I meant to call on David's bride last Friday. they seemed quite happy, and David said he and "Tumpie" concluded they could not visit until the war was over. Sister Lizzie says she had no idea of such a thing until after she went home from here, after you left. She says she told them she was ashamed for them. They are staying at Mr Carnes' now. Mr Lifley called the other day to bid us all good by, as he will not be in this section of country again before Conference. He thanked mother and I, a great deal for our kindness to his wife,

69 Though SC had yet to secede, the general sentiment of the people was that war was inevitable after Lincoln's election.

while sick. I know he feels grateful to us. I love him very much, for I believe he is a true Christian. The time is swiftly drawing near for you to come home again. Sister will come next Monday week I guess. wish you could come then too. Mother and sister Lizzie sent off a nice box to Daniel Monday. poor fellow has been living off dry corn bread for some times past. He sent up some pictures taken in uniform and he looks quite thin, though he says he is well. All send much love and receive a large share from

Your affct- sister
Maria

Wm is going to write to Hattie. you will please send it to her by Haynsworth.

King Creek, Decr. 1st/60
My dearest Hattie

According to my notes I wrote the last letter, that was my impression before I referred to them, for I remember looking for a reply, so you have taken three months to answer my letter. Now you must not treat me thus again for a long time.

I have been quite a visitor the past five weeks. I went out to Prince Williams Parish some time since to visit aunt Carrie Bostick, and L. and myself spent a night with Ann Bellinger, alias A. Rumff while out there. She is living in a small house, but things have a comfortable appearance. She is very neat in keeping house, and as quiet as ever. We attended an Association in the village of Robertville last Monday week, and met Minna and Martha McLeod, you remember the latter I suppose. she has not changed. her sister, with whom I went in /54 has grown very handsome. They live on James Island, and I could have heard of our friends of that place and surrounding, but had not time. At these meetings we seldom feel like asking many questions. any way. Rosa Aldrich was there. She is not pretty, but one of the finest looking girls of my acquaintance. I met her mother at Anna Maner's (A. Salley) where I spent the night in company with Miss Kitty Moss of Orangeburg. I found her company very agreeable.—We had the privilege of hearing a few political speeches at the close of the service. The audience stood in front of the church as they objected to speaking within the sanctuary. The speeches were fine, the last by Mr DeBois, whose name, probably, you have often seen in the papers.

Our junior minister left near two weeks ago. He is one of the most innocent, and one of the best men I ever knew. I was much pleased with his preaching this year, and am sorry that the rules will not permit him to return. If I ever marry and have my way, he shall be the minister to perform the ceremony. Do not mention this and destroy this letter through fear that some mischievous eye may glance at these lines. I write what I feel, but I do not do this to but very few.

Mr. Kelly attended Broxton's C. M. and became acquainted with Mr Stephens family. He seems to have taken a great fancy to Isabella, says she is the stamp of one for a Methodist minister's wife. I agree with him. Isabella is indeed a lovely character, and has endeared herself to me almost in a threefold manner the past few months.

I was not only pleased, but delighted to hear that Manda would be a bridesmaid for Annie Jennings, as I am to act in that capacity if not Providentially prevented. I expect to have my tall, black eyed darling, Billie, to accompany me. Annie wished me to go up some days before but on account of "Pa's" absence I shall make as short a visit as possible. I shall have the pleasure of stopping with two friends, Eugenia, my friend of the first session, and Janie Barnes, who lives immediately on the road which leads to Mr. Jennings. Eugenia has a son, sent me a lock of its hair, which is dark for a babe. I shall present the little stranger with a pap spoon on my way up. I wish that I could meet you somewhere. It would be so pleasant. May God bless you my dear Hattie.

Your fond friend,
Martha Roberds

Columbia Dec 1st 1860
My much loved brother

I did not intend, that two long months should pass away, before I had written to you, but it is really so, and to day is the first day of December. But I guess it does not make any difference, as you regarded my letters too insignificant to answer last year. I suppose you will do the same this,—Ah! no. I should not have said that for my dear brother did write me one good long letter; which letter I prize very highly, as it is the first and only one I have ever received from you. We were happy to hear through Hattie's last letter that you were all well. To day if nothing prevented you are at my "sweet sweet home" as Amanda wrote me, that they were expecting you last night. How many many times last night did my thoughts wander to that dear spot, and as many did I wish that we could be there with you all. but Anna of course received a larger share of my thoughts than any one else. Oh, me! I am so anxious to see the darling little creature. There has been quite a panic in the C'ty this week on account of small-pox (as it was supposed to be). The day scholars have not attended school at all this week, as the Trustees advised uncle Martin to use every possible precaution to prevent the disease from reaching the College. The "Board of Health" has reported no new cases at all this week, and the Physicians doubt now whether it is small-pox. You can imagine how badly we felt on hearing that this dreadful epidemic was in the city, but I don't fear any danger at all now, and I really don't think it can be small-pox, for only three persons have had it. they have been sick for only a week and are now very nearly well. The students of the S.C. College left on account of it,—and Oh! let me tell you, we had the honor of a serenad from the Richland Rifle Company; they by some means heard of the students leaving while we were still here pursuing our several school duties, and last Tuesday night they serenaded us.[70] They let uncle Martin

---

70 The Richland Volunteer Rifle Company left Columbia in January 1861 to become Company A of Col. Maxcy Gregg's 1st South Carolina Volunteers (six months volunteers). Field, R. and Smith, R.. *Uniforms of the Civil War: An Ill. Guide for Historians, Collectors, etc.*. The Lyons Press, 2001.

know of their intention, so when they came we were all in the front windows, the College lighted up. they marched up playing most beautifully and gave "three cheers for the "patriotic young ladies of the H- College. they also cheered our flag, for I tell you we have a flag too on our building. uncle Martin thanked them very politely on our behalf for the very pleasant serenade. then "three cheers for the girls we love" after having played a few more tunes they left. I tell you sir, we felt quite fine. I declare I was sorry to see them leave for the music was perfectly charming—But my sheet is nearly filled so I must close; do give much love to all for us. I will be very happy Mr Plowden to receive a letter from you at any time.

With much love from your devoted Sister
Maria

December 16th 1860
Dear Uncle

Your most welcomed letter was received day before yesterday. Belton did not arrive until then. he went by Charleston and Savanna and that detained him. cousin Edward went up to Dovson the Saturday before to meet him but he did not come. I have not seen him only to speak to him. he came here first but I was not at home. I was in hopes you and Hattie would come out when he came but was sadly disappointed. will you never come out to see us again? I know you could (paper torn) would so please come now before (torn) nce another crop. we are very much obliged to you for your invitation to spend Christmas with you. it would afford us much pleasure to do so but would prefer to have you come and spend it with us. if you can't come then come soon after.

Lo Anner and David are married at last. I think it is time, it has been talked about so long. I was surprised to hear that their marriage was so private. I thought they would have had a large wedding. I hope they will be happy.

The Examination in the school at Whitney came off about two weeks ago. the children did very well. the boys spoke at night. we had several original speeches and some of them in favour of Secession. there is a great deal of political excitem(torn) here. I think the majority (torn) -eceding and following old (torn) ample. I read the President's message yesterday. He says very little in favour of secession. I presume that will influence a great many.

Cousin Richard Davis expects to move to Fort gains next week. Cousin Robert McClary is speaking of moving to Whitney.

The times out here are very dull. I have not heard of any Christmas any where. I suppose the times are too hard. I don't expect Belton will enjoy himself much as (rest of letter has been torn off)

2 bushels meal, 1/2 Do Rice, 2 hams, 1 peck wheat flour, 1 quart salt, 1 pint coffee, 1 quart sugar, 1 bushel potatoes, 1 Mattress tick, 1 Blanket, 1 Pillow, 1 Quart Lard[71]

---

71 This list is written on the reverse side of the letter. Could this possibly be Ruthvin's list of supplies to take with him to camp in Georgetown?

Parnassus Dec. 20 1860
My very dear Cousin,

Your very kind and affectionate letter came to hand by last mail. Hattie how much disappointed we all were that your Father Mother and Lucy did not come we looked anxiously for them from Monday untill your letter came Friday but it seemed to me all the time their all coming was too good news to be true but I do hope they will not give up coming at being disappointed once. Have Maria and Almira come home all the girls that went from about here came last week. I haven't seen any of them yet but I suppose the small pox is still raging in Columbia. I hope none of the girls will take it. though some people seem rite uneasy. Mary Jane was here yesterday she is well and is looking very well she some times talks like going to Arkansas this winter. but I do hope she will not go, her Brother has taken a school there for next year and I expect will want her to go as he has to hire a music teacher. Anna Jane Covington spent part of last week with me. she came Thursday and stayed until Sunday Mary J was here a part of the time which made it more pleasant. Hattie did you ever see Emma Spears Edwin Spears wife she was raised in Sumter she is old Mr. Henry Spears niece she is such a nice clever lady I like her very much she is always inquiring after you all I never see her but what she wants to know when I had a letter from Sumter she was here the evening your letter came she said she felt as much disappointed I did she told me some time before that I must send for her as soon as they came they will soon move to their own house Ed is building on the new road from Mc to the spring on this side Hattie do you recollect our going up the hill at the Spring the evening we went with Mc to George Peterkins how you and Mc laughed at me for holding to the dash he is just as lively as ever my cousin it is getting dark and my pen is so poor I dont suppose you can read this at all I must stop mother wants me to set the table please write as soon as you get this Mother and Wm join me in sending much love to you all I remain your devoted cousin

Annie Jane

You must not let any one see this

Pine Forest Dec. 23rd 1860
My dear Hattie

As a few leisure moments present themselves I write you a few hasty lines to inform you that we are enjoying one of God's richest blessings; health; & hope you are enjoying the same. There is but little news down here worth communicating if there is, I have been no where since I returned to get it. Elisabeth went over to see Sister Martha on Tuesday & I am sorry to say she says she looks worse than she ever saw her. she is in bed nearly all the time & I am very fearful she will have a serious time of it soon. Mary Oliver died on last Friday & was buried near Brewington on Sunday evening. Elisabeth said Mr. McDowell made quite a feeling address at the grave; said also she never saw such a crowd at a burial. I have understood that it was thought that Dr. Oliver would have gone crasy before she was buried, but is now more resigned. I have been quite busy since I returned, so much so I have not had time to hunt. Elisabeth had 12 Hogs killed while we were gone, & I killed 13 more the day after I got home. it was 11 o clock at night before we got through. I wish very much for you to see you up to the elbows in grease. But wishing was vain. Hattie you cannot imagine how lonely I feel when I come about the house & you away. You think you cannot come home the first of next week. But no; I will not ask that of you as you are with some of the family you may never see again. If you do not come home Thursday or Friday, perhaps I may come on Saturday, but if I do not, I will try to come the first of the week after. Haynsworth was very much pleased with his visit—had lots of news when he got home. says he wants you at home & so says all the family. I must now close as I have to go to Sister A's to day tell Maria, I will send Edgar to see her my love to the dear girl & all the family. May God watch over & protect you all is the prayer of your devoted husband

Ruthvin

THE WAR YEARS

1861–1865

Bishopville Jan 8 1861
My dear sweet Sister

I feel very very sad, and lonely, this afternoon, and perhaps I can in some measure dispel my sad feelings, by holding a few moments in sweet converse with you. oh! I would that you were with us to day so that we might talk instead of writing. This morning we had to pass through the sad trial of bidding our dear brother, sister and precious little Anna "good by" Ah! is it not indeed sad to say "good by"? Yes! they have left us once more. Oh! that God in His mercy would bless my dear Brother's labours this year and may he be the instrumentality of leading many souls to the blessed Saviour.

We found them all well on our return from your house, and had the pleasure of finding Cousin Hu here. I think he has improved very much, is the handsomest young gent- I have seen recently, though I know your much loved husband will not agree with me here. Cousin Jim was to return to Camden with him but he was quite sick last week so he thought best to wait awhile. he is now entirely well and as lively as ever. Almira and I have one more week to spend at home yet. father had a letter from uncle Martin last Monday saying that he thought it would be perfectly safe for us to return the 15th Did Lizzie Haynsworth leave for Orangeburg to day? Emma went on with sister and brother William. I felt sorry for Emma. she seemed quite sad at the idea of leaving.

Have you seen anything of Argent yet? I hope she had a pleasant visit while down. We heard our junior preacher last Sabbath. he did very well indeed I think for the first. He called to see us a short while this morning, was quite pleasant and sociable. Amanda and Almira attended a party at Mr. Robert English's last Friday night. they had a very pleasant time. they tried very hard to get me to go, but I did not wish to go at all. I believe I know of nothing else to write, so I will close this. Mother, Cousin Jim, and all the children send much love to Brother Miss Elizabeth and Haynsworth, Lute and Henry. Now my dear sister "good by" write us as often when we return to College and let me know where to direct your letters. accept the warmest love a sister's heart can send. from

Your devoted sister
Maria

Jan. 14th 1861 Camp Harlee P. D. Legion[72]
My dear Hattie

I have neglected drill for the purpose of addressing you & dear Sister E. a few lines. I am truly thankful to say I am in pretty good health & humbly do I trust that it may find you enjoying the same rich blessing. I was quite uneasy for several days past for fear I would have inncipetus. there was a blister came on my nose near my mustache, which produced a singular sensation (it came last Saturday morn) & in the eve I got the Dr. (Plain) to give me Nitrate of Silver to put on it. which has turned the place quite black & I still put it on once or twice a day. I write you particularly so that you will not be uneasy if you hear it, as I suppose you will when you see Mr. McDowell. He got here on last Saturday night. We had Prayer Meeting at our tent, & he preached for us three times on Sunday & I think preached as fine sermons as I ever heard. I do not know when I ever saw any one (that was not related to me) that I was so glad to see but was sorry he left so soon, as that was Monday eve. I could not get him to make an appointment to come back. So, dear Hattie & Elisabeth you must pursuade him to come again soon. & tell him I asked you to do it. from what I have heard every person was very much pleased with him. I am in hopes my throat is entirely well. there is some 15 or 20 cases of measles in our company. all getting along pretty well as they are all in their tents & get along better there than they did in the Hospital. When I came back the place looked deserted, but all is life again as 4 companies of infantry and one of cavalry has come in in the last 3 or 4 days & looking for 2 or 3 more tomorrow which will make 11 or 12 companies under Col. Graham's command. We have not yet been mustered in Confederate service but will be as soon as those other companys get here. a few days ago we were ordered to clean up another camp ground some 200 yds from where we are. it is

---

72 Camp Harlee, near Georgetown, SC, was where Ruthvin went via train along with other men who were known as the "Wee Nee Volunteers," on January 4, 1861. These men signed on for a time period of six months, then returned to Kingstree and were reorganized. Their captain was John G. Pressley. Boddie, William W. *History of Williamsburg From 1705–1923*. The State Co., 1923.

a beautiful location high & sandy, far superior to where we are. Col. Graham has ordered 1500 uniforms for his regt. which consists of coats, pants, draws, shirts, shoes & socks which will make our men quite comfortable. Some of the men that has lately come in has itch which I am very sorry for, for I am afraid it will spread through camp. they are put off to themselves & that may stop it. what a change we have had in the weather. for several days it has been disagreeably warm (hot) & yesterday eve a dark cloud rose in the north east & it was soon cold enough to snow & still looks like it this morning. If you killed hogs last week you have had some warm days on it but I hope you will not loose it. we will have to send home for provisions next week & will let you know what to send. Brother E. will write for his waggons to come down & when it goes back I will send you some beautiful shells that came from South Island 14 miles below Georgetown. I cannot give you any news as every thing is quiet here. I thought dear Hattie of you all often last night when the wind was blowing so furiously & then had a dream about you. oh how often do I think about you all & what you are all doing & when our days work is done & the evening shades appear my thoughts wander far, far away to the dear ones at home & the many many happy days we have spent together. When the bright star appears that I named for you what associations cluster around it is impossible for me to describe so will not attempt it. how is the dear children getting on how I would like to see them & you all kiss them for me & tell them not to forget what I told them Good bye darling. May God bless you all & watch over you & protect you & grant a speedy peace & that we may soon meet again is the prayer of your affect husband

Ruthvin

Do write soon as I have not received a letter from you yet.

P. S. Give my love to all the family & let me know if Amanda has come yet. kiss her for me & tell her I will write to her as soon as I hear she is down, & she must write to me soon.

Bishopville Jan 16th 1861
My own dear sister,

It has been some time since I have written you so I will have a talk with you this morning. We received your letter to mother this morning and were happy indeed to hear from you, but sorry to hear that bro Ruthvin was still troubled with pain in his side. it makes me feel very anxious about him. I do so much wish he could be well of it. tell him he had better go through a course of medicine. We are all well. things are again going on in their usual routine. Maria and Almira left on Tuesday morning. they were to have gone to Sumter on Monday but the inclemency of the weather prevented them. father went with them to Sumter on Tuesday, took dinner at Mr Lorings and left on the one oclock train. Mr L went with them, he thinks there is no one like Maria. Cousin Hu came down on Friday to bring David Durant who has left school to volenteer his services to the state. He left Daniel and family in good health. Cousin Jim returned to Camden with cousin Hu. they left the same time M & A did. it is needless to tell you how lonely I felt after they had all gone. I found myself wishing many times that you & bro R would surprise us with a visit. I do so much wish you could come up now—father stopped at Dr Dubose on their way to Sumter for him to examine Almira's throat, which you know has been sore for two months. he said he did not think it anything serious and gave her a preparation for it and I trust it may benefit her. Cousin Drucilla and (illegible) spent Tuesday night with us. she and cousin Jane were speaking of going down to see you all this week. I have not heard whether they would certainly go or not. Cousin D. rec-d a letter from cousin Mary the night she was here. Mr G. has bought the place they live on, have a flourishing school 16 scholars. I hope they may continue to do well. Cousin Mary sent an obituary notice of little Alice written by miss Ward, their assistant last year at nursery good indeed. I was glad to hear that Mr H was pleased with O. I hope Lizzie too may be pleased. Cousin Charles too was much pleased with Mr. S. I am glad Lizzie and Emma got acquainted so quick. The family have not heard from Emma yet I think. Mr Banks opened his school here on Monday, he has twenty scholars and will have a good many more I expect. William likes him very well so far. Mrs Hollyman's school will be small I guess as Mr Banks has several girls. Cousin Charles does not send any as Mrs Dennis does not. Cousin Drucilla gave me the news of Eliza Murchison's wedding, it was quite a fashionable affair. the guests assembled at nine, they were married at eleven. and supper at twelve. the company dispersed immediately after supper. there was no enjoyment scarcely. Amelia Townsend was one of the bridesmaids, Carrie and Olivia both waited. Eliza had her dress made in Baltimore. it was plain white silk with illusion, said it did not make much show. we have heard from bro Wm and sister once since they left. sister was in Charleston, bro Wm had not left for his mission. sister did not intend leaving until yesterday, they were all well. found Mrs Mood's health much improved. sister and bro Wm were in the City when the "Star of the West" was fired into.[73] said there was great excitement. We have heard nothing new of much consequence for several days. we have a daily mail here now which enables us to get the latest news very soon. Willie told us that bro R had volunteered. I have patriotism enough to be glad that he has offered his services to his country, but do most earnestly hope there will be no need for them. I think it is the opinion of a good many now, that it is doubtful if there will be any or at least much fighting done. This has always been Mr. Spear's opinion and I put more faith in his opinion than any one else. almost twenty-one from here have volunteered. Mr. Scarborough is third sergeant. I humbly pray that He who over rules the destinies of nations may avert civil war and yet restore peace and happiness to us. Mother and I are just finishing the dress you gave her it makes up very pretty. You cannot imagine how much I miss cousin Jim. I expect it will be some time before he comes down. he hated to leave right badly I think. Maria and I

---

73 The Star of the West, a civilian merchant ship, was hired by the Buchanan administration to carry troops and supplies to reinforce Fort Sumter. Newspaper reporters published the pending voyage, and in the early morning of January 9, 1861, South Carolina's batteries opened fire on the ship as it approached the harbor. The unarmed Star of the West suffered minor damage, and turned back to New York after receiving no assistance from Fort Sumter. https://www.history.com/this-day-in-history/star-of-the-west-is-fired-upon

went visiting last week. staid all night with Eliza Dixon and spent the day with Anadella. Sallie Stuckey was staying with her. Willie and Argent came in the evening, so we had fine times. Mr Hodges the new preacher called to see us a short while when he was here. Mr Smith will preach next Sunday. I suppose you have heard of Mrs Brown's death. she died before his return from conference. Dear sister you must write me often now. You know we are always happy to hear from you. Give much love to dear bro Ruthven Miss Elisabeth Henry Haynsworth Lute for us all and accept a large share for your own dear self.

Humbly imploring Heaven's divine protection over you all that we may all be spared to meet again- I remain your ever devoted sister

A. M. Rogers

Mission Home Jan. 18th 1861
My beloved sister

It seems like a long time since our sad parting with you all on that gloomy December morning, and I have wished much that I could hear from you. I would have written to you before, but thought I had better wait until I could tell you I was safe at our low-country home again, and I feel grateful to our kind Heavenly Father that I am able to tell you that we are here in health and safety, and already pretty comfortably fixed. We left home just one week after we parted form you, left all well, except that Almira's throat was still ulcerated some. It seems to me I felt worse at parting with you all this time than ever, but every year it seems so, it is a trial I cannot get accustomed to. We arrived in Charleston on Tuesday night (8th Jan.) having parted with Emma and Cousin Charles at Orangeburg. We were all much disappointed at not meeting with Lizzie H. and her father. I suppose they must have gone on the morning train. I hope the girls will be pleased there. Wm left Emma & I in Charleston then and came on down, and had everything got in readiness for my coming. So you see, everything has been moved away, and moved back again, and I have steered clear of all the trouble of it. I cannot help congratulating myself that it is so, for I cannot say I am particularly fond of that sort of fun. We had a very pleasant visit in Charleston. Sister Martha has recovered her health again, and is the same good creature she has always been. She made particular inquiries after you, and your family, and would be glad to see you again. The excitement about political matters is still very great there. I am afraid matters are not to be settled without bloodshed. We were there at the time the "Star of the West" was fired into and run back, and the whole city was in a perfect state of excitement. the morning before we left (last Wednesday) we all walked down to the battery, saw the big guns arranged there, and by the aid of a telescope had a good view of the Forts. I could but feel bad as I saw steamboat after steamboat laden with troops sailing for Forts Morris & Moultrie, for I thought how many a poor mother and sister's heart may yet be brought to bleed for the loss of those so dear to them. Asbury was down at the city while we were there, his nose and tongue are both as long as ever, but he is a clever fellow notwithstanding. We left C- yesterday morning at nine oclock, and arrived here between one & two. Beck our cook was glad to see us, had things in nice order, and dinner ready for us. We have already had ample testimony that our friends around here were glad to see us back in the shape of fresh pork, sausage, fresh butter & c. How kind and thoughtful they are. I feel that God will repay them though we never can.—We both realize fully now that another year has opened upon us, with its duties and responsibilities. would that we might be as faithful to the Master we try to serve as He has been merciful to us.

Anna keeps well, she wants you & uncle Ruthvin to know that she got her tea-set home without breaking any, and that her aunt B- in C— gave her a pretty book. She says you must kiss auntie, and Lute & Haynesworth for her. and then by way of consolation I suppose she adds "and tell 'em never mind, I'll be along there again next fall." We got a letter from Maria yesterday, all well at home she said. she expected to leave this week for Columbia. said David Durant had come home to see them before going with his company to Charleston. I know it will be hard for them to see him go, if he has to leave. Wm joins me in warmest love to you, to our dear brother Ruthvin, to Miss Elizabeth and the little boys. He says he will write to one or the other of you soon. Do write us dear Hattie very soon and as often as you can, and tell bro. Ruthvin please to do the same. Give our love to all our friends down there.

And now Good bye, may Heaven's richest blessings ever rest upon you all. I remain as ever your devoted Sister

L. J. Mood

Remember our P. O. Salkahatchie Colleton Dist. So. Ca.

Bishopville Jan 28th 1861
Dear Brother,

I have just finished writing some letters, not to my sweet heart, though, and having a little more time before dark thought I would write to my dear brother. We are all pretty well, and do hope you can tell us the same good news when you write, if that will ever be. trust the pain in your side is entirely well ere this. Daniel & Lizzie came down on Friday. Mr Hopkins from Baltimore came with them. he left yesterday evening, took the cars this morning for B- we all liked him very much. he was very pleasant. reminded me very much of Mr. Costar who visited Daniel three years ago and died soon after his return to Baltimore. Daniel and Lizzie returned to Camden this evening. they have had several pictures taken of the baby which are very good indeed. We have heard from sister and bro Wm last week. they were all well. we have heard the roar of Cannons to day. Mr. Bradley says Louisiana is out. I rec-d a letter from M. J. McLucas Sat. she has had a negro girl fourteen years old burned to death. It was a sad affair. I feel truly sorry for her. she has been so unfortunate. she has given out the idea of going West unless her brother persuades her to go after he comes. Aunt Peggy and cousin Drucilla made quite a visit in your country. we heard to day they did not get back until Saturday. I went with Albert and Eliza Dixon over to Darlington to see Eliza Bell. We staid two days and a night, had a very pleasant time indeed. I expect Eliza over some time this week. Did you ever see such weather as we had the past week. I was glad indeed to see the sunshine once more. Mr. Hopkins went to see Maria and Almira in Col. said he found it hard work to get to see them but he kept staying until Mr Martin sent for them. they were very well. Almira throat was better, she has been following Dr. Dubose's directions since her return to C. I wish very much you and Harriet would come up to B- soon. a visit from you would do us a <u>heap</u> of good, for it is right lonely sometimes. I expect cousins Hu and Jim will come down the last of this week. Mr Marley has gone to Texas again. cousin Dick went with him. I think cousin Jim wanted to go back too when he heard of it. Is Lizzie Haynsworth pleased with Orangeburg? She and Emma are rooming together. hope they may have a pleasant time. Emma is very much pleased she entered the junior class. Have you heard from Fannie recently? I suppose she is not married yet.

Willie came to see us the last time he was up. Charlie began school to day. Mr Banks has thirty scholars. Tell Harriet that Harriet Alexander is married to Mr Tiller. she kept it a great secret. no one knew it until after they were married a day or two. did not have any wedding.

You must write to us often and Harriet must too. Mother Father Wm send much love to Hattie Miss Elizabeth the children and yourself. kiss Haynesworth Lute and Harriet for me, and my dear bro accept a sister's warmest love, from

Amanda

Camden SC Feby 4th 1861
Dear Ruthvin

I have been promising to write you time and again but have been slow in doing so and even now you cannot hardly claim this as a letter as I may have to stop short soon and then it is in some business. I am glad to say we are all well. our babe has been a little restless for a day or two but am in hopes it is getting over it. we are getting on in the same old way. times are pretty quiet here now. I had a friend from Balt. to visit me last week. he spent several days with me. it was Mr Hopkins. he went down to Bishopville with us. all seemed to like him very much. I saw aunt Peggy two days after his return and was glad to hear that you were all well. she said you still complained of your side. perhaps it may be neuralgia. if so just take a few doses of quinine and this will stop it. I think now it was neuralgia that was the matter with me last winter. Old Mr. Spears has not finished the house. Jim and Hugh are both with us. they are doing a goode business just now. we would like very much to visit you soon but we will have to wait until warm weather on account of the baby. we had a very good picture taken of her. it is a sweet little thing. Ruthvin I wish you to try and get the money on the enclosed a/c. Frank Brown paid a part of his. the bal. is $5. the a/c of Mrs Hodge I left in the hands of Coogler to collect. see him and if he has not got the money try and get it for me. the other on Robt MLeod also a note on Bilton. he sent me word he was ready to pay it so you can tell him you have it. you can receipt the a/c DMR per yourself. take no denial in the a/c as the money I must have. If Belton is not ready to pay the note you can wait on him. You can send the money by first opportunity or by letter. We hope you are all getting on well. Write soon you or Harriet one. Love to dear Harriet and Miss Lizzie and the boys. God bless and be with you.

Affectly
Daniel

Charge interest on note prior 1st May 59

Charleston 13 Feb 1861
Mr E. Ruthvin Plowden
Plowden's Mill
Dear Sir

In compliance with your request of the 11th inst we have sent you to Kingstree the Salt you write for as per Bill & RR Receipt enclosed, which we hope will reach you safely.

We will look out for you 7 bales cotton and take charge of them as soon as they arrive & will endeavor to give you satisfaction with our sale.

Respectfully yrs
Reeder & DeSaussure

30 Sacks Salt @85c	$25/50	
Freight to Kingstree	10/50	
Draying	2/25	$38/25

Salkahatchie SC Feb. 14th '61
My dear Sister -

I ought to have written last night as I intended to do then it could have gone toward you tomorrow but I got reading & the time passed away. Any how I write to you now- and remember it is valentines day (night). Hope this will find you well with Ruthvin and Miss E in good health. remember me to them and also to the two sons. Lucy received your last. I think she has however written in answer to it. I am not certain however. We are all well thanks to a kind Providence which has ever watched over us and getting on at about the usual rate. We have had crowds of rain and a regular April shower has just passed over with considerable thunder. The air is balmy and the moon shines very mildly upon the earth. She is peeping in the window at me now. I wish very much we could have some pretty weather- the roads about here are horrid indeed. Several Sundays past have been rainy but I have gone to my appts. I wish you could see what Lucy is sewing on. I dont suppose you could guess if you were to try until the sun rose. It is a wonderful affair in good many respects. There is involved in her work a garment of mine which I miss very much. Wonder if you have any idea what it is. lets hear of some of your guesses in your next. If you guess <u>right</u> I'll make you present next Christmas. Now let's hear from you. I have made some changes in my miss. work as I have the miss. alone. I have thought best to take a little more work upon myself and what I formerly done in 4 I now do in three weeks. The patrons appear very well satisfied I believe. I have taken up a new preaching place and will go to it for the first time sunday night. a sail of 3/4 of an hour from my afternoon appt brings me to the landing place. And if want to indulge in a sail sometimes go with me to that point. This gentleman has a steamboat in miniature which he uses in going & returning from Beaufort. it is very complete in every respect. He made it himself. I had a hard time last saturday it rained so much. But when I did get to my resting place I was fixed. Had a grand oyster supper at about 11 at night. They have at this place just gotten through the pear crop and the trees were then loaded with luscious oranges—really these low country sea island homes are great places. The ladies gave me some fine music while I was there and Sunday morning they were present at services. I administered the sacrament to the servants in which the family united. really it was an interesting sight to see owners & servants all engaged in this solemn ordinance. Those people who dont like to sit upon the same floor with Negroes ought to see such sights as these. But I must close this. Lucy sends much love to you, Ruthvin Miss E and to the little boys- Anna Nora sends howdy to you & to all the rest. Write very soon to your affect brother -

William

Columbia Feb 16 1861
My very dear Sister

Your very welcome letter of the 8th was gladly received on last Wednesday, and again were we cheered by that ever-welcome news that all were well. How thankful do I feel to my Heavenly Father that he has blessed us so much in this respect. I regretted so much to learn of the sad accident that occurred at Mrs. McCoy's. have they any idea who could have done it? I do hope who ever it might have been will be found out yet. I received a letter from Hattie this week, the first I have had from her since we returned. they were all very well. I know she will be delighted to see you and Cousin Jim. hope you will have a delightful time while there. I have no doubt though but what you will, all the folks down there are so lively. I guess mother and father will find it quite lonely while you are away, the family will be small indeed then. We were so delighted to receive dear father's letter last week. what a great pleasure it is to receive his letters. how much I wish he had time for writing oftener. Dr. Talley has been to see Almira this week, and prescribed for her throat. he says it may be sometime yet before it is well, but does not think it anything dangerous. sometimes it looks considerably better, and then again it will be very much inflamed. The doctor says she needs a great deal of exercise, out doors. Aunt Martin has her to walk every evening, but you must not feel at all uneasy about her, for I will be certain to write if it gets any worse. Aunt Martin told Dr T- to write to father and tell him all about it, which he said he would do, though I do not know whether he has done so or not. She seems perfectly well all the time, and has an excellent appetite too. I do sincerely trust that her throat may soon be entirely well. Tell mother not to feel at all uneasy about her. Well the first half session closed thursday. only four months and a half now before we will go home. how delightful to think of: my office as monitress has closed, now Miss (illegible) was appointed in my stead. Uncle Martin made quite a speech to those of us who had been in that office for the last session, expressed his gratitude to us for the very faithful manner in which we had discharged our duty. we of course were much obliged to him. Mary Gamewell spent the evening with me yesterday. she is as lovely as ever. she told me to write to father for permission to visit her so she wants Mamie Stephens and myself to spend the day with her very soon. I know father has no objection but Uncle Martin cant let us go unless we have a special permission from our parents, so please tell him that next time any of you write to send a note to Uncle Martin permitting me to visit her, and I will hand it to him. he gave me permission in a letter last year, but I have not it here now. Almira and Anna both send love <u>all</u> <u>all</u> of you. I had a very sweet letter from Anna's mother this week. she has quite a high opinion of me and my "gentle sister Almira" as she calls her. kiss dear little William for me.

Your devoted sister
Maria

Bishopville 17 Feby 1861
My beloved Daughter

State mail has but so little news from the place where Mary lives and your dear mother was so anxious to know the news from there that we took the liberty of opening it although it was your special property.

We found it to be from W. A. Garner. If it is so that his letters to you do not reach you, perhaps you had better advise him to direct to this office especially in making you a remittance of what he owes you. If he will send you check on some bank either in New York or Charleston. it will be the safest way for you to get what he owes you. They seem to be coming on very well and I am glad to hear it for I hold Mary in high estimation. Oh- I forgot entirely to send Ruthvin money on act of the corn when James & Amanda were down. I regret it for he may need it. If any one is coming up this way tell Ruthvin to ask them to call on me and I will endeavor to make payment.

We rather expected James back by this time, but he has not come as yet but we hope that all are well your way. He will probably be here in a day or two. I am glad to say that we are all quite well here. Your dear mother has done extremely well since Amanda left. hope she may continue to keep as well as she now is. It would be a great blessing. Tell Amanda that Tommy has got well. I returned from Wilmington on last Wednesday night. Your aunt Molsey has been here.They were all well. Druscilla is now here—came this evening.

I am sorry to say that Mrs. Ambrose has been very ill for some time. She was not expected to live—but she is getting better. Mr. Ambrose was not at home. was in Charleston. It was an attack of some kind of which she has suffered some what before.

There is still nothing new about the firm. Mr. McKay is now I think as well fixed as before the fine.

Your dear mother says to tell "Harriet & Amanda that we are coming on first rate." Dear Charlotte is with us now. She is about as usual.

When shall we see you and Ruthvin this way again? Tell Ruthvin we were very sorry to hear of the loss of his horse but trust he will have better luck next time.

There is no news from the "Seat of war lately" nor from Washington. We here do not think that we shall have war–still it may come.

The night before last William had Bobby Camy with him. They were busily engaged in making up and directing Valentines–Making use of the Dictionary of love" as an assistant to their labors.

Well dear one I must close. Our love–our united love to you all. We all want to see you all very badly, but we can't go down soon and I fear to urge you as your up here w us the last visit. but do tell Ruthvin to come if he well can.

Most affectionately your father & friend-
William Rogers

Columbia Mar 15th 1861
My own sweet sister,

It has been so long since I have written to you, till I am really ashamed to write now, but then I know you will excuse me, for I am kept right busy here even on Saturdays, for then I wash my handkercheifs and collars and write a composition every other Saturday. I have just come up from a concert it was just one among the girls, there was a piece of poetry recited between every piece of music. Maria recited a piece of poetry and she did it very well too, the piece was "Tell me ye winged winds"[74] dont you recollect the night father had you all reading that piece, to see which would read it the best. oh! let me tell you something, we had a marriage in the college the other night, guess who it was. oh I know you will never guess so I may as well tell you. well it was Miss Flora Preston to Mr. Philip Anthun, but mind they were both servants. Well Hattie my throat has not gotten well yet though it is a great deal better, but what do you think the Dr has gone and given me cod liver oil to take. I declare it made me right vexed when they brought it to me. with it he sent me two bottles of ale, and because I felt in a very lively humor this afternoon Maria and Anna accused me of having taken too much ale. dont you think they are bad girls.

We received a letter from Amanda the other day, said you were with them at the time. I hope you and brother Ruthven both enjoyed yourselves very much. Amanda was perfectly delighted with her visit. The bell has rung for us to retire so I must bid you good night. I hope you will have a good nights rest, and many pleasant dreams.

Morning has again dawned, and I must proceed to finish my letter. Anna and I had fine times in here last night. we slept in here all alone. Maria slept with some of her friends next door. she came in so early this morning, knocking at the door and woke Anna and I both up so that we could not get to sleep any more.

Hattie I must close this letter as I wish to write to sister this morning. Please you and brother Ruthvin write to us some-times, we never get letters from any of you.

---

74 Tell Me, Ye Winged Winds is a poem by Charles Mackay (1814—1889)

Kiss Haynsworth and Lute for us, and give our best love to Miss Elizabeth and brother Ruthvin, and accept a great portion my dear sister from your devoted sister,

Almira

Bishopville 30 March 1861
Dear Ruthvin & Harriet

I wish I had time to write you a long letter but it is late and I cannot well do it. We left Charleston on yesterday morning and last night staid with your Aunt Molsey last night. Your dear mother staid with Lucy six days and I staid three. Wm Lucy & Anna Nora came with your mother to Charleston last Wednesday but went back next morning as it was said there was Scarlet fever in Charleston. They were all very well. Anna is a great reader and will read by the hour when she can get a chance and they try to restrain her. I bought a pretty fair stock of all kinds of goods as usual. we sent you a carpet—or Rugg—and centre table to Kingstree which please send and get. the expense on the table is paid, and I think on the carpet also. We hope they will please you both. I suppose the articles are at Kings Tree now.

A bundle is just handed me from my Harriet for Amanda—I dont know the contents—will carry it to her now.

We have letters from the girls at Columbia. they appear to be doing well. Almiras throat is getting better they say. All are well about here. We want to see you all badly enough—Hope we may be able to do so in a few weeks.

God bless, and preserve you—love from all and to all most truly and affectionately your father and friend -

William Rogers

Bishopville April 14th 1861
Dear Harriet

Your letter to Almira was received more than a week ago. we were happy to hear from you again to hear that all were well. I presume you have seen Aunt Peggy ere this and heard from us through her. She seemed to dread leaving home a good deal. Mother and I were to see her the evening before she left and Manda, Mag and myself went and called on Mrs. Lottie spent a very pleasant time with her, but when we got back to Aunt Peggy's she and mother wanted to know if Lottie was not at home said they did not think we had time to get there. You wrote me to tell you all about the wedding, it had been so long perhaps you have heard before this. Well I went with Mr. Dixon, Alice and Emma. We were going to meet James W. Rembert for dinner, but we met him and his wife coming over here so we went on to Sumter and got dinner at the Hotel staid there until four o'clock and then went on to Mr China's about four miles from Sumter in a very pretty place. When I got there none of the waiters had arrived but cousin Mary Jane. She had just got there. Mrs. D. had five attendants. Cousin M.J., Mr Tommie Durant, Mr Wm Spencer, Miss Rebecca Fraser, Dr Dennis, Miss Julia Deschamps, Cousin David, Miss Bessie China and Mr McDonald and myself. Mrs. D. Was very pretty. She wore a colored silk with white illusion cape and her veil hung entirely round her touching on the floor. Mr. Durant (illegible) well on the occasion but he laughed during the ceremony said he thought of something John Fullerton said. I believe I saw all the gentlemen I knew but Mr. Guy, he was not there, but Mr Graham, Mr Pool and Mr. White were, also Mr. Wilder Miss Fannie Thompson's intended husband, they are to be married soon I hear. We left next morning early after breakfast, came by the camp ground. it looked very lonely I assure you Almira Alice and I went into all the tents and over all the ground. Father, William and I went up to quarterly meeting at Bethany last Sunday. There were a great many there. Mr Gamewell preach he preached an excellent sermon and then spoke so beautifully at the communion table. Mr. Brown looks very feeble indeed. I am afraid he will not last long. I got Maria's things done last week, so Mr. Gamewell took charge of the trunk from Sumter to Columbia. Father has been in Sumter all the week attending court. He and Muldrow went together. They are both on the jury. Mr Fraser's and Stuckey's case was thrown out of court and decided by arbitration. I believe it is settled now—we will hear all about it when Father comes, which will be tonight. Mother has been quite well since we wrote you last—the rest of us also. We heard from Maria by last mail. She was quite well. She says they are not allowed to write as much to their (next several lines illegible/stained)... Sister and bro Wm were quite well when we heard from them. I got a letter from Martha Fraser last week. She writes a beautiful letter. sent much love to you. She does not think her father will ever be well again. Omera had a little boy and has named him Thomas Fraser Thomas. strange name. Our Sabbath School begins tomorrow. It was organized last Sunday. have but nine scholars as yet. our whole class is small too. Mr Weaver preaches tomorrow. The reason cousin Annie Jane has not come her mother was sick. She had her trunk and all ready to start out but she could not leave her mother. She says she is going to see you whenever she does come. her uncle she does not think will live much longer. I am getting ready now to go with Father down the country. We are going week after next. I wish so much you would go. I could enjoy it so much more. Do write as soon as possible and tell me if you want father to get yours and Miss Elizabeth's bonnets, if you do he will take great pleasure in getting them. Daniel and Lizzie came down yesterday. Lizzie is up at home though. we have not seen her yet. Daniel and William are gone down to Dr. Gregg's, where he had some work to do. Cousin David staid with us a night this week. he said he was going down the country yesterday. was poor Terrel's day to be hung.[75] I could not keep it out of my mind all day, poor man. I pray that he was prepared to meet his sad fate. Mrs McCorquedale leaves Monday for Shelby. She and Mrs. Rembert spent yesterday with us. Mrs. R. looks much better, but she is so low spirited. She is going to spend the summer with

---

75 John C. Terrel of Bennettsville, who poisoned his father, grandfather, & clerk with tainted whiskey.

Mrs. Mc at the springs near Shelby.[76] will leave in May. I hope it may be of benefit to her. but I must close. Love much very much love to bro. Ruthvin Miss E. the children for us all. Tell the servants howdye for me.

Your ever devoted sister,
A. M. Rogers

76 Lithia Springs, GA, was a very popular resort whose mineral springs supposedly possessed healing properties.

Bishopville 24, April 1861
My own beloved Daughter

We had the pleasure by last mail to receive your dear letter. We were glad to hear again that you were all well, and I again have the pleasure to say that we too are all well.

I notice what you say about the war, but this morning every thing looks rather bright and cheering to me. Virginia has moved and is now with us, and General Scott has it seems certainly resigned his commission—all this is greatly in our favor- Maryland too is said to be united against the coercive policy of the U. S. Government. Pres. Davis is pressing the War toward Washington and my opinion is that the "Ides of May" will show him in possession of Washington. This may cost some lives, but so energetic are the movements of our troops that even Washington may fall into our hands without a large loss of blood. But we must of course expect trouble and trials in this Great Cause but we trust we are right, and "The Lord of Hosts will be with us." The God of Jacob will be our refuge. The fall of Ft. Sumter, and the removal from Charleston of the U.S.Vessels of War leads us to believe with all the Preshure now upon Lincolns Gov. that our enemies whom we saw in Charleston we shall see them no more forever—that the war in S.C. is for the present at any rate closed.

I am glad to hear that you recd Mr Garners letter safely, and it was right to sell the draft as you did. I mentioned that we could give the money for it here, thinking you might not readily sell it at home. Mr Garner overpaid a little what he owed the store and I think I wrote him so but I cannot now find what the amount was. do let me know what it is if he wrote you what it was. I think we have it somewhere but I cannot find it readily. We will pay it to you. The other matter you mentioned—please do not speak of more (the acct.)—it is all set right by me, and just as I would have it—and no other way.

To Ruthven—I may say my man Smith is through planting cotton and is plowing corn and putting guano to it.

We shall try and make a good crop of corn should the season be favorable.

Our business is very good in the store—sales pretty large.

We miss Henry—and he was a good fellow. but we get along tolerable well. In case of another call for Soldiers—I expect we shall lose Albert.

Mr. John O Durant saw the girls in Col. and he is (illegible) lately. He says they both look well, and Maria is pretty well over her excitement about the times- I rejoice at this. I have not lost an hours sleep on account of the difficulties myself—being determined to take things as I find them—not to anticipate difficulties that may never be realized.

If Ruthven should be called off I hope and trust that my own Harriet will keep up a stout heart—that Ruthven will not have to say to you as Paul said at a certain time to his friends, "What mean you to weep and break my heart?" and But that he may say I am ready—not only to suffer but to die in the cause of my country. But after all he may not be called away. Still we should expect it and be prepared for the occasion should it come.

Mr Durant says that all are well at Daniels—that Daniel expects to come down there on next week.

And now I will soon close. Do write very soon—tell Ruthven he must write. Give my love to Miss Eliz. and tell her I will come for another K_ _ _ soon but I cant now set the time—perhaps during the month of May—love to the boys—Yes love from all to all—and may blessing of Almighty God be and abide with you all—now and forever—

Your Affectionate father
William Rogers

Columbia May 27 1861
My Brother dear.

I have long been wishing to write you, and as I have a leisure hour now, I will gladly devote it to this pleasant task; though I shall have to beg you to excuse (torn) letter, for it is so very warm, that (torn) scarcely feel like doing anything at all. Would that it were my privilege to talk with you, dear Ruthvin, instead of writing, and happy indeed am I, that the time is near at hand when this exquisite pleasure will be mine, oh! sweet indeed is the hope of meeting those we love once more.

We have had letters from home quite recently, and were cheered again by that ever welcome news, "all well. I was agreeably surprised to hear that mother and father had decided to pay a visit to Marlboro, hope they will have a most delightful time, and I know they will if mother can keep clear of headache.

We had quite a pleasure excursion on Friday afternoon last, there are about 12000 Soldiers camping, seven miles from the City, and we were all quite anxious to visit their camp see them parade (torn), and we prevailed on our kind President to take us. But the most pleasant part of it was, that we went on the Cars. we all enjoyed this ride very much—passed by Barhamville which is quite a pretty place but do not like it so well as this dear old College. The train leaves at five and returns at seven, which rendered it much more pleasant, now dont you <u>know</u> we had a nice time. Almira received letters from Emma and Lizzie last week, they were both well; they wrote such sweet letters.

Brother Ruthvin I am glad to tell you that I have finished my <u>Valedictory</u>, only four weeks from next Wednesday, I will have to undergo the trial of delivering it. Cannot you and Hattie attend our Commencement? We would be more than delighted to have (torn) here. Judge Longstreet will preach (torn) Commencement sermon which I guess will be good. But the dinner bell will ring in a few moments so as I want to mail this when I go down, I will close. do write soon. Almira joins me in love to you & every one. You must give my love to that favorite Cousin of mine. you know who it is I guess, so I will not tell his name. good by my own dear brother.

Your devoted sister
Maria

Bishopville 5 June 1861
My beloved Daughter

On last Friday week your dear mother and myself left home to visit Marlboro and N.C. We made visits and calls at Mr. Davids, Mr. Thomas' to see Eliza, Mr. Bishops, S. Thomas's, your aunt Nancys, Sarah McBrides and then on to lunch Alex 2 McMillans place. The good old man we found had been dead about two weeks—This was sad news. We went to Mrs McKays and over to the College—and back by Clio to your aunt Nancys again. Called on Mrs. Haney and Julian and round to Mr Weatherlys & Davids then on home last Saturday night. We found all pretty well except Nancy McBride and your cousin Alex McMillan—but both of them were able to be about. On last Sunday morning Daniel and Harris Hopkins came here. All well in Camden. Yesterday Amanda went with them to Camden so we are "thined out to a stand." We all keep pretty well.

Well dear Harriet what can I say about a visit to you—until we heard of the illness of uncle Alex sr Mc- we expected to have seen you before this time—and now between Amandas absence and going after the girls how can we make the visit to you. I am so sorry and we will go as soon as we well can. I dare not ask you and Ruthvin to come and see us again before we go to see you. I do wish though that I <u>was</u> bold enough for perhaps you <u>might</u> then come. This is all I can venture to say.

Charlie and Caroline talk of going down, and I hope they will—as I have been gone some time I think it is his turn- But don't dispair of us. I think it will not be very long before some of us come- We have letters from the girls—all well. Albert is a volunteer and he may soon be called off. No news lately from Henry.

If Albert goes there will be no one left with us but Draper but it is all right and proper that we should also make some sacrifices as well as those who leave their homes.

Mrs. Rembert is home not very well. She suffered with Rheumatism in Ala. and now with love from all to you and Ruthvin Miss Eliz. the boys and <u>all</u> I remain your affectionate father

William Rogers

Salkahatchie SC June 13th '61
My dear sister -

Lucy is writing sitting on the front doorsteps and it is raining at the same time but anyhow with the likelihood of drops falling on this I have taken my seat to scribble a few lines to you. I have just wished for a good pen & Lucy has said I dont want you to write to me with such pen as <u>that</u> for I know I cant read it. Now what am I to do I cant write well with the steel pens and I have no gooses about to get feathers to make quill ones with. So what am I to do. But I am inclined to think Lucy is mistaken in what she has just said and that if I was away from her she'd not inquire much about the material used in doing the writing nor quarrel much if she had to study as hard as you <u>will</u> to make this out. Today is fast day and I tried to preach to a large & serious congregation from 122 Psal. 6.7.8. and 9 vs—I suppose the day has been observed in your parts by all. It should be and I trust that the many prayers offerred up to day will be heard by the great God and that this days humiliation may tell upon the present struggle. I have no fears of the issue and only desire to make a personal showing in the defence of the honor and liberties of my beloved country. There have been many greater ones no doubt preached today in every part of these confederate States. A remarkably appropriate text was used today in Charleston by Dr Backman of the Lutheran church Obadiah 1 chat 7 & 8 vs'—look at it. I suppose you have been aware of the battle of Bethel church Doubtless we'l soon hear of one grand effort. I trust a spirit of mercy will be exercised by our men even while they are doing the legitimate work of war. I suppose you have heard of the capture of the Privateer Savannah of Charleston.[77] One of the officers that little vessel is a Harleston very respectably connected. Wo be to Abe's men if any of that crew are here—It will be blood for blood then in a terrible recompense. the vessel a slaver captured some time ago the Echo of which you have read is now in Charleston harbor she is a fine brig. her name has been changed to Jeff Davis. she is a remarkable

---

77 The "Savannah" was the first Charleston privateer to take a prize in the war—the Union brig "Joseph."

fast sailor. She is now being fitted out as a Privateer. Has some 5 guns one a pivot gun & is manned with 80 men. every one of whom have declared that they'l never be taken by the Linconites. They will strike for one of the Aspinwall steamers & try to get some of the shining dust.[78] Wish she could have been out before this & taken the Northern light with its villins—that would have been a fite!! I hope to hear of brave & valorous acts from this name (Jeff Davis). You have heard me speak of Septimus Ackio whom Father adopted.[79] He has been aboard the school ship & had 14 months to serve at this time but he has escaped with 6 others & gone Obd. It was his watch on deck the night they cut out. Wonder if we'l ever hear of him again? Poor Boy—Mother alone could manage him & when her eyes closed in death he lost his best friend—Poor Boy—my prayers go with him.

14th I must hasten to close this as I have an opportunity of mailing directly. I went to the city Monday to see Cousin Sarah Andrew—she has been in SoCa- since the fall. I was glad to see her and had the pleasure of meeting Brett and Mary Catharine there- I suppose you have heard from Bishopville since the folks got back. Am very sorry that they missed the main object of their visit- They had an agreable time and revived many old recollections. The girls will soon be at home. wish you could attend their commencement. but I suppose you cant. Hope dear Sister that this will find you with Ruthvin & the children in good health. Lucy joins me in kind regards to them & to Miss Elizabeth. Let us hear from you very soon. tell us all the news. Lucy is busy sending off by Lavinia some fine cabbage to our neighbors this morning—and Nora as usual is gone ahead to the school House. I wish you could hear her read in the Bible. She reads any

---

78 Aspinwall steamer ships sailed down the east coast, around Cape Horn, then through the Isthmus of Panama and up to the west coast. Originally carrying mail for the postal service, they were also used, beginning in 1849, to transport gold from the California gold mines back to banks in the East.

79 William W. Mood's father adopted Septimus Ackio, who apparently lived aboard the "school ship." The "Charleston Marine School" was begun in 1859 by Rev. William B. Yates and the Port Society to help poor boys and at-risk youths. It sailed SC waters. www.correctionhistory.org

where very readily and is on the whole a pretty clever child. Tell Miss Elizabeth I wish I could live near her or you at least so that we might go into partnership in the garden line.

I hear the continual falling of trees. their incessant falling reminds me of the bombardment of Ft. Sumter. The cause of it is that a large force are now at work near us working on the Port royal rail road. It begins near us with the C & Savannah rail road -

remember us very kindly to all of the relatives. But I must really quit now—God bless you dear Harriett and all connected with you is the humble prayer of

Your Brother
William

Amanda was in Camden when we heard last. Mrs. Rembert has gotten home.

Home, June 21st 1861
My dearest Hattie,

Your affectionate and much prized letter, reached me the same evening that I sent mine to the office, hence my delay; I thought probably you might reply, but I perceive that my little "deary" means that I must attend to this business.

It is late, after ten, but I am thinking so much of you to night, that I felt constrained to enjoy the pleasure of addressing you. If "Pa" knew my intention he would have me to bed in a hurry, but I shall be easy so as not to disturb him.

I have been quite a delinquent the past two months occasioned by the unusual tax on my fingers etc. I believe I gave you a sketch of these duties, the most of which I have completed, and now am feeling rather free. You know dear Hattie, that we are under less restraint while doing for ourselves than for others.

I never dream't that I would live to see such times. sometimes I feel a little uneasy, but expressing myself generally, I can well say that "fear never troubles." The privilege of looking to a dear Saviour is the source from which my peace springs. oh! may our faith increase, for it is a blessed state to live trusting in Jesus. Jesus, how much of sweetness, comfort and peace in that word!

Just about this time, a year ago, I commenced to intercede for a nearer relation to the Saviour, and He has heard my prayer for I do know more of Him. I do love Him more, but not yet have I received the witness of His holy spirit. If I forfeit not the grace already given it will be mine. Oh yes! dear Hattie, as soon as He sees best to bestow the blessing. The longer I live, the more I desire that my dearly beloved friends should make their election sure, and another desire which fore dominates, is that they should all be farther advanced in the divine life than myself.

I suppose Manda may mention the plan of the insurrection, which was providentially disclosed. It is true that the Negros said they would reserve the young ladies for their wives, and the manner of their contemplated treatment is too horrible to be communicated. What a time for the trial of faith! God grant that we may come forth a more worthy people.

I appreciate Mr. Plowden's compliment of my merits and looks but let him know the true pictures of appearance and qualities. It makes me happy to be assured that I have such friends as to prepossess others in my favor.

Do you remember uncle James Roberts likeness, which was kept on the table in our room? We received intelligence of his death a short time ago, which took place in Washington City, his residence for the last year. I have full assurance of his acceptance; was more earnest about leading a holy life than any Baptist I ever have met. I intend no reflection on that sect by my remark, for I love the church and desire its prosperity. L. is looking very healthy, and enjoys good health.

May the blessings of God attend your household is my prayer.

Ever your loving friend,

Martha

Hampton Legion Columbia
Camp Hampton June 29 1861
Dear Ruthvin

Will you be so kind as to notice about when you are hunting cattle and if you see any of mine please drive them up and mark them for me and if you see any that is fit to sell and it will not be you to too much trouble you will please sell them for what ever you think they are worth and I will try and return the favor by kiling Yankies. I have been very busy to day washing my cloth to start off Monday. I am very well please with camp life except eating we enugh plain crackers and bacon sometime beef but we have to eat it stewed and you know I am not much on a stew. we have all enjoyed fine health ecept colds. we are getting on finely drilling. Our officers are not very good but they are learning fast. Those is some of the company that understand the miltary tacticks better than the officers. you must excuse bad writing and spelling as there is no accommidation here for such. you must write to me and let know how you are getting on. give my respects to Capt Eggar and tell him I wish he was along with us and you also.[80]

Direct your letter to WVW—Capt Manning Company Hampton Legion Richmond VA

give love to all remain your well wisher
Willie V Witherspoon

---

80 Edgar Plowden, Ruthvin's brother

Camp Manning Richmon Va July the 15 1861
Dear Cousin

I have riten you a few lines to Inform you how I am getting on dear Cousin I must tell you some thing a bout camp life it is the hardest life that I have ever lived we have the strictest laws that you ever saw we cant leave the camp without a written permit from the Captain. Cousin I wod like to be in the fork now very much to have a hunt with you all. I no that you are giving the game Soot. well lute I have no news to tell you our company does fine and we ar well driled our men behave very well the legion is to be presented with a flag by President Davis this evening our company has bin selected to carry hit well Cousin I must close I am so tired I have been Drilling all day I heard a great a bout prety girls but have not seen none so prety as miss Ann well Cousin I must close give my resects to all you must rite to me soon Direct your letter the Care of Capt B Manning Hamptons Legion Richmon Virginnia you must excuse this badly riten leter and Rite soon till Cousin Edgar that he must rite soon to me I remain your afectionate Cousin

G M Plowden

Bishopville 20 July 1861
Dear Ruthvin

We have re_d Amandas letter. The drive is for next week and consequently we now suppose you will not be here at that time. Mr. Campbell has entirely recovered from the measles and none of the family have any symptoms of their continuing in the family. The Vols are off for Virginia except Rivers. He came home very unwell–had fever–He is better–hope he will soon be well. Mrs. Adeline Seale is dead–was buried last Wednesday at Saint Lukes Church. Jack left Sunday for Va. Zeus Dixon is in a very critical situation–is more comfortable to day, but I fear very much he will not recover. The people generally are well in the neighborhood our own family as much as usual. Startling news for the last few days there is probably much fighting going on near and at Manassas–Letter day before yesterday from Henry Scarboro to Charles–He was well. Had met up with young Rawlins Rivers.

Mr. S. F. Cousar left this morning for Va. R. M. English went last Wednesday with the rest of the boys -

Several of the girls about here went with them to Florence. Before the Regt. left Florence the most of them sang "Dixie" but our boys sang "I'm going home to die no more."[81] It must have been very moblising.

How shall we get Amanda home?

There is to be a camp meeting at Sumter Camp Ground. Thursday week (illegible). I must close to send this to Lynchburg. Love to all all. I remain most truly and affectionately yours

William Rogers

(written on back of letter:)

write immediately

My corn in Darlington is flourishing

---

81 I'm Going Home to Die No More was written by William Hunter in 1838, and expresses the assurance of the Christian for a home in the Father's house where there are many mansions. https://hymnary.org/media/fetch/113766

Bishopville Aug 2nd 1861
My own darling sister

As Jim is going to meet Amanda tomorrow morning or rather to-night, I thought I would write you a few lines, as I knew you would be glad to hear from home. I am so glad Amanda is coming home, it is really lonesome here without her. though I am always very glad to have her stay with you, as I know she is just as much company for you as for us. We were very sorry to hear that dear brother Ruthvin intended leaving so soon for Virginia. we would be so glad to see him before he left. Father says to tell you he cannot disapprove of his going . says you must be a brave soldier at home, he and mother will try and go down next week so that they can see brother Ruthvin before he leaves. I did not think when I told him goodbye the night he was leaving here that it would be the last farewell, before he went to war. Sincerely do I hope that he may before very long, be permitted to return to his dear home.

We received a letter from cousin Hu this evening, he said they were all pretty well. Daniel was not at home but expected to return to day. They are all coming down next week. I am very glad to hear it, for I am so anxious to see the dear little babe. William wrote a letter to Henry a few days since, has he received it yet? Tell him William will be very glad to receive one from him soon. Is Lizzie Haynsworth with you yet? Amanda wrote that she had come home with you. give my love to her.

Hattie if you could just peep in here now you would be amused. Maria and Lucy are both fast asleep, and Lucy is snoring considerably. I am the only one up in the house, and it is time I was beginning to prepare for bed, dont you think so? Well my dear sister I must now bid you good-night, All join me in sending their very best love to all the family, and we each send a farewell kiss to our dear brother. Oh! God grant that we may soon see him again. Again I bid you all good night.

Your devoted and loving sister
Almira

Camp Pettus, Aug. 2, 1861[82]
Dear Lute.[83]

As I have not written to you since I have reached Virginia. I will take this opportunity of doing so. I have not received but one letter since I left home and have been very anxious to hear from my native state. It have been very wet and unpleasant for several days the land is all clay which makes it so much worse. I suppose that you have all heard the particulars about the last great victory of of the Manassus junction.[84] It have encouraged our armies greatly to see how many more of the enemy than we had and then to give them such a complete defeating. they are still bringing in prisoners four days ago there was brought to Manassas fifty Yankees taken that was concieled in and old church in the neighborhood of the battle field the most of them was wounded. and on yesterday there was one taken here making his way to Washington. he had laid in the woods since the battle he was nearly exhausted with hunger. he claimed the Alabama as his Reg but he could not come it over us so he confefed all. he says that if they would let him go that he can stop six Reg from fighting against us. but this you know wont be done. his race is too slippery to trust. I tell you Lute the Regulations here are very ridged but no more so than should of be for men require such. I would not complain if they were even more so if possible. I have not been put on extra duty for negligence since I have been here and do not intend to be. though I have to push at roll call some mornings when I sleep too late I rise running. this thing of sleeping you know is one of my favorite luxuries. our Reg had a very hard march on last sunday evening from Manassas to this place Seven miles we started at two ocl the sun was very hot and then we had to take on our backs all of the clothes blankets cartridges musket and a canteen of water, which in all was a heavy load with provisions. it commence to rain on us in two miles of this and continued till dark it was damp

82 Camp Pettus, located in Fairfax County, VA

83 "Lute" was apparently a nickname for Ruthvin, and his second son, Edwin Ruthvin Plowden, III, was also called Lute, or Lutie.

84 First battle of Manassas, or Bull Run, was a victory for the Confederates. It was the first major battle of the Civil War.

sleeping that night. the fare here is not as good as it was in Carolina. we get coffee flour and meat enough but sugar and rice we do without about four days out of seven. I will learn to live cheap here in the sugar line. as long as I get enough it makes little difference what it is. the enemy has evacuated Alexandria and gone to the Arlington hights and chain bridge there I think will be the next bloody fight it is thought that there will be a great many lost at that place. but there is no telling it was thought that we would be destroyed at Manassas and see how it was we have it is said and I believe over twenty five hundred prisoners and killed over fifteen thousand of their men. I have seen a great many my self. there was very heavy canon fireing yesterday in the direction of Washington for what purpose we cannot tell. it is current here that old Scott is dead.[85] such report here are passed unnotice. Some of our pickets took three more prisoners last night near Vienna. I have just heard. We have a nice young man for our chaplain from Lancaster his name is Craig a presbiterean. I have seen Calvin Manning, Bill W. Neal Burgess Gee McLaurin they are all quite well. Calvin looks better than when he left home. I am glad to inform you that all the soldiers here are temperate there has been no liquor in camp for two weeks nor none allowed to be brought in by any one. we expect to leave here today going on to fair fax there are hear four SC Reg and four at Viena. we are gradually marching on to the arlington hights. I am still in good spirits and hope to meet my friends and relations at home please remember me to cousins Hattie & Elizabeth & some one else particularly and accept the best wishes of your cousin,

Theodore

85 Winfield Scott, though a Virginian, was commander of the Union army. From an article about him in the Anderson Intelligencer dated May 02, 1861: "This life-long distinguished general has at last thrown off the mask, donned the habiliments of treason, and covered himself all over with as much of infamy as could be raked up from the cess-pools of earth, and the purlieus of pandemonium." http://chroniclingamerica.loc.gov (Chronicling America, Historic American Newspapers, Library of Congress)

Bishopville August 6th 1861
My dear brother

I see that it is needless waiting any longer for you to write to me, so I will not indulge in any formality but try and write you a short letter tonight. I have just returned from Mrs. Rembert's where I went with cousin Caroline to see Miss Anna Howe, a niece of Mrs. McCorquodale's. she is quite sick with measles. they spent last Monday with us and the next day they broke out on her. she is not aware of any opportunity she had had of taking them but I expect it was on the cars. We got home just in time to escape the rain. it is now pouring down, has been raining nearly all the afternoon. Maria and Daniel got home safe on Wednesday night. they took dinner with sister who had just left us that morning. Cousin Mary J. and Aunt Molsey were there also.

Father has had a very bad attack of asthma. he took it on last Thursday week and is not entirely clear of it yet. he was very bad on Tuesday and Wednesday but has been getting better since then and I truly hope will be entirely well in a short time. The rest of the family are all well. Mrs. Dinkins is now at cousin Charles' she came home with them from the funeral. she will not return to Camden. I do not think I ever felt more for any one than I do for her. she seems to be utterly cast down, does not get any more composed, talks about him and cries all the time. she takes trouble so hard and his death was so unexpected to her. he had talked a great deal with his little daughter Sarra Ella, told her that he would not live long, but that she must not grieve, for he was going home to Heaven, told her too not to tell her mother until he was gone as it would grieve her so. she is an extra ordinary child, converses with her mother and tries to console her. her father told her that she and her mother had been the means of his conversion.

Cousin Charlotte came back to day. she is not as well as when you saw her last. Miss Mary Spann and her brother James spent last Sabbath evening with us, staid until after tea. he promised to bring his sister to see us while father and mother were gone. Vermeille Virginia and Mr. Pool from Sumter took tea with us last Tuesday night. He is quite a nice young gentleman I think V. likes Mr. Bagnal very much. I expect he will soon be up to see her. I was surprised to hear that Belton was clerking in Manning. it was impossible for him to leave Miss Santes. Which is to gain the victory, he or Mr. Nelson? I heard a few days ago of the marriage of one of our school mates which surprised me much. The young lady is Miss Emma Wannamaker. She married a Dr. Pond and they had to runaway. her father was very much opposed to it and thought that she had given it up when she asked him to let her go with some of her relatives to the Springs. he very readily gave his consent and two stations from Orangeburg Dr Pond got on board and they went on to Columbia, where they were married. I do not know whether her father had forgiven her or not. I received a letter from cousin Hu last week. he speaks as though he will come back in September. I hope very much he will.

We were sorry to hear of the illness of Mr. Plowden and Mr. Haynsworth but I trust they are entirely well ere this. I wish I could be with you to get watermelons. I have not had near as much fruit as I want this summer but you know it takes considerable to satisfy me.

Father's being sick prevented our going to Camden this week but if nothing prevents we will go on Monday. Mr. Reed is expected to preach at the Presbyterian church tomorrow. Mr. Alston preaches for us in the afternoon. Harriet work is much admired that she sent home. it is as pretty as any I have seen. Maria talks a great deal about you all. she enjoyed her visit very much, fell very much in love with Haynsworth and Lute, but no one could help that they are such good children. AnnaAdella Dixon and Eliza came to see me last week. E. looks much better than when she got home. Tell Harriet her old friend Mr. Jaefer is engaged to be married to Miss Connor, daughter of the President of the Cokesbury College. He is teaching now at Sanrensville, but Eliza says he visits her very often, says he holds a pretty high head too. It is getting late all have retired but Almira and myself and she is asleep in the rocking chair as usual, so I believe I will stop. I am getting a little sleepy too, so you must excuse bad writing and letter in general. All join me in love to Harriet Miss Elizabeth and yourself. Kiss the children for us. Our love to Cousins Covert and Callie also Cousins Joe and Lizzie. Please write very soon if you deem it worthy a reply. tell Harriet to write too. And now praying that Heaven's choicest blessings may ever rest upon you and yours I bid you good night.

Your devoted sister
Amanda

Bishopville Sept 20th 1861
My darling sister,

As I promised before I left you that I would write to you often, I thought I might as well begin this morning. Sister and Amanda left for Campmeeting this morning. I hope though that you may see them there before you get this. Sister Lizzie has also gone. she left the baby with us. I am very much pleased at this arrangement I can assure you. I am going to take Anna Nora and little Nora visiting this evening. Tell Haynsworth and Lute I would be very glad indeed if they were here to go with us. And Haynsworth has commenced going to school has he? I expect he will like that better than learning at home. He will have a nice time with Miss Anna now wont he? Tell him he must kiss her for me if she will let him. Maria has not returned from Sumter yet but will sometime next week I expect. Oh! Hattie such a very sad accident happened up here night before last. Mr Robert McCutcheon was found dead in the woods. He left home in the afternoon to go to a plantation of his, and that night the horse came home without him, which frightened the family very much I expect. They commenced hunting for him right away and that night about ten 10 o clock they found him. They all think the horse must have thrown him. Mr Wilson preached his funeral sermon yesterday evening. there were a great many people there. Dont you pity his poor family? You know he has two sons in Virginia. Givens Dixon left last night. he is going on in company with Mr Lawrence Scarborough. Mother received your letter on Thursday night. we were all very happy to learn that you were all well. You said in your letter that Mrs. Croskey wished to know what we must carry for our rooms. tell her two pair of sheets and about four or five towels will be a plenty for her to carry. Give my love to Mary when you see her. It is nearly time to send this so I must close. All join me in our very warmest love to Miss Elisabeth brother Ruthvin and Henry. kiss Haynsworth and Lute many times for us.

I remain dear sister as ever your devoted sister
Almira

Jane has just told me to tell Miss Hattie howdey for her.

Camp Connor Sept 30/61
My Dear Friend

I have taken my seat this morning to answer your truly welcome letter which came to hand sometime since & which I would have answered before this but circumstances were such that I could not. the day after I got your letter, we received marching order & left the same day for this camp. we are now encamped on the banks of the Potomac & since we have been here we have been so busy preparing for a Battle that I have not had time to write. on last Sunday week we commenced building a Batterie on Freestone Point a point of land which extends into the Potomac River about twenty miles below Washington & five miles above Dumfries. we finished our Batterie on Monday & was to commence a fire on the Enemies vessels on Tuesday morning at day light but the order was countermanded before day on Tuesday & during the day the Enemy found out our Batterie & on Wednesday morning they commenced firing on us. some of our party were down near the River gathering crabs, when the guns commenced booming & the way those fellows left that place was astonishing. the firing was kept up for three or four hours, when the enemy drawed off out of reach with one large Steamer struck in three places (which has sunk since that time) it was so badly damaged that it had to be draged of down the River by another vessel. there was one more that is so badly damaged that it never will be of any use to them. there was two more vessels that is slightly damaged, the firing was commenced again on Thursday & kept up by our Battery of & on during the day but the enemy did not return the fire during Thursday. they would not venture up near enough. the first shell the Enemy fired on Tuesday fell quite near to Col Hampton.[86] it threw

86 Wade Hampton, 1818-1902, was born in Charleston, SC, to a wealthy plantation-owning family. Known in his youth as an avid bear hunter, he killed as many as 80 bears.He was trained for the law, but never practiced. Though enlisting as a private in the war, the governor of SC insisted he accept a colonel's commission, though he had no military experience at all.He distinguished himself throughout the war, was promoted to lieutenant general, served as governor of SC after the war, and then as a two-term senator before his death in 1902. https://www.battlefields.org

the dirt over him, it was a fight of Artilery. we were kept there ready to defend the Battery if the Yankees had of landed, but they thought prudence the better part of vallor & did not land. we had to ly on the bank of the Potomac four nights to defend our Battery, the object in building this Battery at this point was to attract the Steamers from Dumfries where they were building a Battery for twenty guns which will command the River as it is not more than one & a half miles wide at that point. there was no one hurt on our side in this fight :& we do not know that there was any of the Enemy hurt, but our Pickets took five of the Yankees Prisoners on Friday night. they told us about the vessels which we know is true. I will not say anything about the fight at Manassus as no doubt you have heard all about it long before this time. I cant tell you how many of the Yankees I killed from the fact that it is impossible for one to say how many he killed when a whole Legion is fireing at the same time but I must say that I done my best & I know I killed several who were standing or squating of to themselves fireing at us. those were the Zouaves.[87] that is the way they done the most of their fighting. I shot several several of those that I saw fall. I am truly glad to hear that the men of our gallant little District has turned out so well for the defence of our state. for I am fearfull that the Enemy will try to give our state a brush before this war is over. if ever they do you may look for us for I don't think Col Hampton will remain here if that is the case, we will want to come.

You have no idea dear friend how glad I was to get a letter from you. I have written three letters to Cousin Edgar but I have not heard from him yet. tell him I will be glad to hear from him. there is still a good deal of sickness in our Legion but not as much as their was a week or two since. there was frost here this morning & it is getting very cold, it has been cold enough for frost here for several days. I

87 Zouaves: This name was first given to some regiments of the French army in North Africa, and their uniforms, consisting of baggy pants, short jackets, sashes, etc., were adopted by some regiments during the war. Zouaves "utilized light infantry tactics that emphasized open-order formation, with several feet between soldiers, rather than the customary class order, with its characteristic 'touch of elbows.' To fire, they sometimes rose on one knee..." https://en.wikipedia.org/wiki/Zouave

hope the cold weather will stop the fevor. Jos. D. Strange,, a son of Mr James Strange, died on Saturday night last. John N Hodge has been very ill but he is now improving fast. he will be home soon on furlow. we have lost some fine young men out of our company since we left home. Belton Plowden left here a few days since on furlow on account of bad health. I hope he will soon recover. he will be very much mist. we have just received inteligence of the capture of three thousand five hundred of the enemy in Missouri. I hope it is true. My own health is very good much better than it was when I left. & I hope it will continue to improve as I want to serve my country all I can during this war. I expect we will cross over into Meraland in a few days as Gen Beauregard is concentrating all of his forces here on the Potomac.[88] if we stay here much longer we can cross over the River on the ice. I hope dear Ruthvin you will write to me as often as you can. I will answer all your letters. I hope this letter will find you & your dear family all in good health. remember me kindly to cousin Elizabeth & cousin Hattie. tell them I would be more than glad to see them now. & also to cousin Edgar. there is no news in the camp worth your attention. You are all better posted on the war than we are for we hardly ever see a news paper. I would like to be with you hunting now if the war was over. I must close. accept the best wishes of your friend

W C Nelson

(in margin:) one of the yankeys we caught on Friday night was hid in a box in a ladies house who beged for him, but the Pickets made the fellow role out in a hurry.[89]

---

88 General P.G.T. Beauregard, 1818–1893, ordered the firing of the first shots of the war, with batteries manned by Citadel cadets, upon Fort Sumter. Hickman, Kennedy. "Civil War: Battle of Fort Sumter." ThoughtCo, Feb. 16, 2021, thought.com/battle-of-fort-sumter-2360941

89 Picket is a soldier or group of soldiers on a line forward of the position to warn of enemy attack. In *Wikipedia*.

Home, Sept. 30th/61
My dearest Hattie,

I received your kind and highly appreciated letter soon before I had bilious fever.[90] It proved a very beneficial letter, and when I got able I had it brought to read over again. Oh! it is a good thing to have friends to write in a pious strain, and to feel that they are sincere in their expressions. How often does it console the weary pilgrim, and refresh him for more arduous duties!

After recovering from the fever we had a quarterly meeting at our church, which was protracted several days. It was a good thing to be there. The revival was in all hearts, yet there seemed to be no undue excitement. Some afternoons the whole congregation was bathed in tears, and when dismissed would press hands without uttering a word. Oh! it was such a sweet time. I was in bed several days at its close, and after getting up spent the most of the time in reading hymns, the Scriptures, and prayer to our blessed Father, until three weeks ago, I returned to my customary duties.

I have had a great deal of company of late, and have had much waiting on the sick to do. Our best house servant was ill, and having company I was compelled to take up several of her duties, such as making bread etc. had also to prepare to leave to-day for my brother's in Lowndes Co. so that all duties crowding upon me at once gave me chill and fever. The exercise was too much for one in my present state of health. I had fever yesterday until night, but am up today. Have given out the idea of leaving at present as Bro. did not receive my letter, and consequently had not his wife and little daughter at home, and is also absent being stationed near La. I was not disappointed as "Pa" has to leave so soon, and I shall have a better opportunity for preparing for his departure.—I dare say you think me strange to invite persons to see us at such an unsuitable time, but I did not do this. They were four in number, and all City relatives. two requested that "Pa" should send for them a week sooner, but he had six negros so low that he said it would be best to delay until last

90 Bilious fever was marked by fever with nausea and vomiting. In *Wikipedia*.

week, and although the sickness continued he concluded to send for them at once. The last went this morning; are girls twelve and fourteen from Augusta. The older is as much like Manda as possible, talks just like her, but not so sober, diligent, etc.

I have not heard from Manda in a long while, and feel uneasy about her, for she is always so punctual. Oh! how I do wish to see you both. I was telling the girls about you both last night, what good girls you were, how kind to each other, and to me. I never shall forget those happy days—never.

There will be an other quarterly meeting the second Sabbath in the month. I hope to attend this meeting and trust that we shall experience a mighty out-pouring of the Spirit of God. I hope always to live in the service of my Creator, and it has been my prayer that if I shall ever desire to do anything against his will that He may cause me to suffer until I submit. I write in haste. Write soon to your devoted friend

Martha

Lynchburg SC Oct. 15th 1861
Dear Harriet & Lucy

With a sad heart I have sit down to write you. Our Jimmie is no more.[91] and I am down here to meet Pa in the morning with his remains. Pa left on Friday morning and telegraphed to me after he got there stating that he found him alive but sinking rapidly. he also knew him. I brought the dispatch down to Ma. on Tuesday I received another bearing the sad intelligence that he was dead. he was at Charlottesville Hospital.[92] We will take his remains up home in the morning. We are in deep affliction. the first out of so large a family and a few weeks ago he was in the bloom of health. Dr. Rembert the Col son was in attendance upon him in the hospital. Pray for us that we may have grace to bear it. "The Lord gave the Lord hath taken away bless be the name of the Lord." God grant that his end was triumphant. then can we shout farewell Brother we will meet thee yes meet thee again. It is hard to bear but Lord we would not murmur. May the Lord be with us all and grant unto us an abundant entrance into thy kingdom in heaven

Your affect brother
Daniel

---

91 Jimmie was James Asbury DuRant, son of John O. DuRant, born March 18, 1843, and died October 14, 1861, aged 18, of typhoid fever in the Charlottesville Hospital in Virginia. https://www.findagrave.com/memorial

92 "In a September 3, 1861, letter, thirty-four patients in a Confederate hospital in Charlottesville, Virginia, petition 'his Excellency Jefferson Davis' for his help in dealing with incompetent medical care. 'We have lost 10 times as many men by sickness as by warfare...We humbly protest that three fourths of the surgeons of the army are wholly unfit for their positions...especially those who were all appointed for political reasons and not with a view to their qualifications.' They warned that typhoid fever was 'fast becoming the scourge and dread of the army.'" http.//www.encyclopediavirginia.org

Columbia Oct. 19th 1861
My own darling sister,

Once more I find myself engaged in the more than pleasant task of writing to my dear sister. I received your kind and most welcome letter about a week since, and I assure you I was delighted to receive it. Is it not a great pleasure to receive letters from those we love, and who are far away from us? I think it is indeed. I received one from brother William also last night, he was quite well when he wrote, had just returned from another campmeeting, said they had a very good meeting indeed. The campmeeting at Brewington comes off very soon, does it not? Uncle Gamewell intends going if he has not already gone. Do you intend going? Hattie have you heard of the death of Jimmie Durant. I expect you have ere this though. oh! isn't it a sad thing, how awful his poor family must feel. I do not know any of the particulars of his death as I have not heard from home since his death. Anna received a letter from her mother telling her about it. I am so anxious to hear all about it. Cousin Hu was to see me on last Saturday, he told me about Jimmie being sick, and said his father was going after him. I do not know whether he got there before he died or not. but I sincerely hope he did. I expect sister has been to see you ere this, has she not? Cousin Hu told me she intended going some time the first of the week. I suppose Anna Nora went with her. Maria wrote me about Anna's going to act in one of the tableaux. You know in the peice called the old Grandmother. Maria is going to act it as she did before, only she is going to have Anna Nora with her. I would like so much to see it, but I suppose that is impossible. You reccollect where we were the night of the other concert dont you? I do not think I can ever forget. I have just been relating the story to one of the girls. Mary is now writing to Lizzie. she received a letter from her not long since. I want to write to her to day as I am owing her a letter. I would be so glad if Lizzie could be here with us.

Hattie ask brother Ruthvin for me, if he has caught anymuch fish since I was there. I have a composition to write to day and as I want to write it before dinner, I will have to hurry with my letter, for it is not very long to dinner now. We will have a minister from Richmond to preach for us to morrow, I am anxious to hear him.

hope we will hear a very fine sermon. I expect you have heard that Mary is rooming with Anna and myself. I am very glad of it too. she seemed to hate the idea of going to room with any one whom she was not well acquainted with. So Julia Hook the girl who had written to room with us, said she would room with one of the other girls and let Mary stay with us.

I must now close this.

Give my best love to all. Kiss Haynsworth and Lute both for me. Anna and Mary send love. Good-bye.

Your ever devoted sister
Almira

Pine Land—Nov 1st 1861
My dear Sister Harriet -

Your very affectionate letter reached me some days ago and this is the first time I have had the chance of writing to you—I presume you have had a pleasant visit from dear Lucy & Anna Nora—that you returned home with them & have now returned home again to your own happy home. I greatly prefer my dear Sister talking all this to you, but now I cannot. I earnestly trust that the cough Lucy writes to me about in her last (28th Oct.) is decididly better. Do be careful with yourself and do something for it. Hope this may find Miss E with Ruthvin & the children well. remember me very kindly to them. I was rejoiced to hear to day from my precious Lucy Jane, Anna Nora & the rest of the dear ones. It had been so long since I had heard that my anxieties were being aroused. And so Jimmie Durant is no more—but dear Harriet how consoling my heart throbs with grateful emotions when I reflect that our loss is his Eternal gain. I'd not bring him back, no! if a word would do it. And so we are passing away—who will be next? My mind has dwelt much on death lately. I trust the good Lord is weaning me from this world. oh! how my soul longs for perfect rest from sin. for "there let the wildest storms arise. Let tempest mingle earth and skies—no foes no violence I fear, but all my treasure with me bear."—I have had dear Harriet much of the presence of the Lord with me of late. My heart has rejoiced in God my Savior—I have been able by faith to take a view of my Home above and my prospect of Home in Heaven has made me forget lifes anxieties and cares. I have sung with buoyant hopes the lines "O what are all my sufferings here?" I trust my dear dear Sister that your soul still enjoys communion with God & that in the discharge of your Christian duties your soul is fed as with marrow and fatness, remember the promise is "Be thou faithful unto death and I will give thee a crown of life." oh that our common Saviour may so guide us in this life as to bring us off from this more than conquerors through Him who hath loved us & given Himself for us.

I continue well and am trying to be patient 'till the time comes for me to go to my dear family. It is (this separation) certainly a great trial to me—but the promise is. The trial of your faith is much more precious than <u>Gold</u> which perisheth. I think Lucy writes cheerfully which rejoices me very much. wish the time was <u>nigh</u> when I was to see her, but I cant say now when I can go up—Sunday is Nora's birthday. I have heretofore been with her on that day. the dear child I want to see her so badly. The little frost we have had has caused a stir among the folks. several of the famalies have moved down. some go tomorrow & by Wednesday next, I dont presume any will be left up here. I'll be lost when they all go & will feel my isolated condition more than ever—We have had quite a storm all day. and I have been thinking a good deal of the Yankee ships on the coast—But I must close this. Do write very soon to your affectionate Brother.

William

You had better direct to us in Charleston care Dr Jas R. Mood—Give much love to all inquiring friends and tell Lute & Haynsworth to be good boys. tell Henry howdy too -

Columbia Nov 9th 1861
My darling sister,

I do not know a more pleasant way of passing off a few moments this beautiful Saturday morning than in answering your kind letter which I received two or three days since. I thank you dear sister very much for it.

You guessed right when you thought I would spend the greater part of my birthday studying, for I did, or rather I was reciting my lessons from nine o'clock until two. I was very sorry to hear of the death of Mrs. Hampton Plowden, but was truly glad to hear that she was so willing to die, this is indeed a great consolation. to have the hope of again meeting her in a far happier world than this. Hattie are we not having serious times on our coast, a good many lives have been lost there already. stil I do hope we may be as successful now as we have hitherto been. and I firmly believe that we will be victorious in the end, for I think we have every reason to believe that God is with us, and if He is with us, who can be against us. There are two hundred and fifty prisoners in Columbia now. they came on las Saturday and passed right by the College. A company from Virginia came on with them to guard them, the captain of which was Patrick Henry's grandson.[93] I believe I have written to you that the measles were in school. there are several cases now, but they do not seem to make the girls very sick. I have not taken them yet. perhaps I may not, as I did not take them when they had them at home. I am very glad you were so much pleased with the concert, I would have liked very much to have been there. tell brother Ruthvin he ought to have gone to see the tableaux if nothing else. Mary is by me writing. she sends a great deal of love to Miss Elizabeth and yourself and her respects to brother Ruthvin. Mary is a sweet girl. I love her very much. I must now close this. Give my warmest love to Miss Elizabeth, brother Ruthvin and kiss Haynsworth and Lute for me. And now good bye my own darling sister. May God bless you. I remain your true and devoted sister.

Almira

---

93 Col. William R. Aylett, b. May 14, 1833, d. Aug. 8, 1900, was with the 53rd VA Infantry Regiment and was the great-grandson of Patrick Henry. https://www.findagrave.com/memorial

Camden SC Nov 21st 1861
Dear Ruthvin,

I have a little spare time just now and I will drop you a few lines. I hear you are a member of your brother's company, and why I write to you now is that if your company has not attached to any regiment as yet, I would be glad if you would join Col. Chestnut's now forming it is for Special Service in this state.[94] I expect to go into this regiment and would be very glad if your company would come in with us. I heard you were about to join Gen. Cunigham in Charleston. I hope this is not so as I never should go under such a man. If you have not joined any regiment come with us. we are all well. Maria is with us now. Hu left this morning for his regiment near Beaufort. He was not in the fight at Port Royal he was on a visit to town at the time. He got back last Saturday and brought his sister Mary with him. She is now down at Fathers. Have you any beef cattle for sale a gentleman asked me if I knew where he could get any. I did not unless in your county. If you have or know of any write me and also the price. The company I have joined is Manning Browns. It is not yet made up but we hope to succeed. He will make a good Capt. having served through the Mexican war. I hope you are getting on smoothly and all keep well. William passed here on last Friday on his way from Beaufort to Bishopville. I understand he has gone back to try and get his things away. I am working hard to get through what business I have on hand and then shall close up. Please answer soon. Col. Chestnut is the present member to Congress. He will make a capitol Col. Give a heap of love to Harriett and Miss Lizzie. Haynsworth & Lute. We expect Ann to have measles soon as she has had a chance to take them.

Affectionately Your Brother
Daniel

94 James Chesnut, Jr. (1815–1885) was born near Camden, SC, and served as a lawyer, then senator, and was a senior officer of the Confederacy. His wife, Mary Boykin Chesnut, was the author of A Diary From Dixie. https://www.scencyclopedia.org/sce/entries/chesnut-james-jr/

Bishopville Nov 23rd 1861
My dear dear Sister

It has not been long since I wrote you but knowing you will be glad to get a letter and thinking perhaps it may cheer you up I will gladly write you. We heard through Mr Barrette that dear bro Ruthvin was gone or was to go last week and deeply did we sympathize with you and dear Miss Elizabeth, and often have we all wished that we could be with you. We were so sorry too that we could not see bro Ruthvin before he left. This is the hard part, telling the dear ones good bye. I am glad they were sent to Georgetown as we hope there will be no immediate danger, the enemy will scarcely ever attempt to land there. Do not be low spirited my dear sister look on the bright side and put your trust fully in our Heavenly Father. May He in mercy grant that this dreadful war may soon cease and then may dear bro Ruthvin and all our relatives and friends be permitted to return in safety to their homes. We feel his departure keenly though we are not with him. And I have ever looked upon him as a dear brother and loved him as such. I know that he will let you hear from him as often as possible. Did he and Mr Plowden write in my album before he left. I am so much afraid they did not. Did Isaac Montgomery go with them. Do write us as soon as possible. we are so anxious to hear from you all. Mag told me that cousin Lizzie was coming to stay with them after awhile. I am glad she is, it will be so much company for them. We are all quite well but bro Wm is complaining a good deal of pain in his side. he got home on Sat night, succeeded in getting his things off safely—He with Sister and Anna have gone up to Mrs Rembert's to spend the night. Aunt Molsey and cousin Mary Jane spent last week in Bishopville. they went home yesterday. They have heard from cousin David two or three times since he left, his company were sent to Long Island, which is near James Island. said they were encamped in a grove of Palmetto trees, he was quite well and handling camp life very well. Cousin Hu has not written to us since his departure. Miss Roxy and Anadella spent to day with us—they are very anxious to hear from Johnie since the battle at Pensacola. I truly hope he was not among the number killed -

I suppose Lizzie Haynsworth is at home ere this. we heard the school had broken up, and that his relations from the low country were boarding with him. I guess it will be some time before the school will open again. Mr Haynsworth did not go in Mr Plowden's company did He? I was in Sumter when the troop left and heard that Mr Dinkin's son was in it so Mary's brother has gone at last. Maria is still in Camden—Mother rec-d a note from her one Monday night saying that Nora had the measles but was not sick much. She said they would come down as soon as she got well. they have two cases now at Mr Durants- Almira has not taken them yet—they did not spread at all—only had two cases—she was quite well when she wrote. Anna Loring has not gone back yet. Cousin Mary Jane does not think she will return—Mother Father William Cousin Charlotte and Mary write with me in warmest love to you Miss Elizabeth and the children—Write soon to your affct Sister

A M Rogers

(written on back of the last page:)

My own beloved Harriet
Amanda has written you a good long letter but I know that you will gladly have me to fill out this page. I know dear Harriet that it comes very hard upon you that Dear Ruthvin should leave you to go to the war, but my dear daughter, it is <u>his</u> <u>country</u>—<u>your</u> country—<u>my</u> country—<u>that</u> <u>calls</u> and he has gone because <u>duty</u> to that common country has <u>called</u> <u>upon</u> <u>him</u> <u>to</u> <u>go</u>, and hard as it is to part with our dear friends thus, I cannot say to any of them—dont go—Cruel—cruel war! War between people of the same race of same blood—oh how <u>unnatural</u> but so it is—May God grant that this unholy war may soon close that peace may soon be proclaimed throuout the land—and that we of the South may be free and independent—Dear Harriet—can you not come and stay with us awhile? Can dear good Miss Elizabeth spare you to come? If so we will send when you say you can come and bring you up. Write—Love to <u>all</u> <u>all</u> Heaven bless you.

Your affectionate Father
William Rogers

Camp Harley Nov. 23rd 1861
My dear Hattie,

I write you a few lines informing you of our arrival here today at 10 o'clock. We soon had a place secured, & brought in our men, but at first they appeared so much dissatisfied, fearing they would be mustered in for the war, that the company came very near breaking up; that is a part of them. But now it is 7 oclock & all appear more reconciled but say they will not remain longer than 12 months. I was very fearful I would have to volunteer as a private in some other company, as a good many others would have done the same, & we may have to do it yet. There is about 800 men at this camp & about 1100 camped 2 miles from us there is still 4 companies lacking in this Reg. & we may be here for some time. The men I am acquainted with is in fine spirits plenty to eat but course & do not make much calculation that there will be much more fighting, which I truly hope may be the case. Dear Hattie I have never had to address you under such circumstances before. I am inadequate to the task to picture my feelings since I left & I know it is the case with yourself. But we must not give up to gloom & despondency. our cause is a righteous one & I fear not the machinations of our enemies; for I firmly believe that God is with us, therefore we need not have no fear. I must close as there is Preaching here to night & they are waiting for me. Give my love to <u>all</u> tell H. & Lute howdy for me & kiss them Tell Elizabeth her bucket lasted until to day Love much Love to her. <u>Direct to Georgetown</u> <u>Harleys</u> Legion care Capt. Plowden now darling good night & may God bless you is the prayer of your devoted husband

Ruthvin <u>Write</u> <u>Soon</u>

Pine Forest Nov. 25th 1861
My ever beloved husband,

It was with pleasure that I re'cd your dear kind letter, for I was so anxious to hear from you, and knowing that you would like to hear from your own dear home, I have taken this early opportunity of writing to you, but oh! how I wish it was so that we could converse with each other face to face instead of writing, but this great great pleasure is now denied me, and I now do so through the medium of pen and paper.

Sampson got here about dinner-time to-day and you can imagine how quickly I ran out to see him, and how many many questions I had to ask him, I was so thankful to hear that you were all well. Norrell brought my letter and it was with eagerness I perused it I can assure you, and many many thanks to you for it, and in being so good too in writing to me so soon after you got there. It is useless for me to tell you my dear dear husband how greatly we have missed you since you left, for I presume you can well imagine our feelings, Yes! indeed it was the greatest trial I have ever had, in parting with one near, and dear to me as you are, but I pray that our heavenly Father may enable me to bear this trial, for my trust is all in Him, and humbly do I pray dearest that soon if God's will, that he may bring you safely back to us again in health, for it is in the hands of God my dearest husband that I have given you, and I know that He alone is able to protect and defend you wherever you are, and put your whole trust in Him alone, and ever strive dear Ruthvin to let your faith be ever firm in Christ the blessed Savior, and oh! that He may enable you to live nearer and nearer to Him each day, and that you may (torn) enjoy His love and presence wherever you (torn) and that He may spare your precious life to return safely home to us, is the humble prayer of your ever devoted wife. I was thankful to hear that you all arrived at your place of destination safely, and you must all try and take (torn) good care of yourselves; I do hope that you are comfortably situated in every way, and in your next letter you must write me every thing you can think of, however trivial for all that you can tell me will be of interest to me. I am happy to say that we are all well, and dear little Lute was complaining a little when you left, but he soon got perfectly well again, and the fever left him entirely by next morning after you left. The dear little children have both been very good, and Haynsworth went to school this morning, and it is now nearly time for him to come home. I asked him what I must tell father for him, when I wrote to you today, and he said to "give you his love, and to tell you that he would try to remember to pray for you in his prayers," and Lute says I must "give you his love also, and a kiss to uncle Edgar for him too."

Dear sister Ann and Mary Emily came and spent the day with us (torn) I was so glad to see them, it seems (torn) me I never was as glad to see them before, but they left this afternoon, and I am now all alone in the parlor writing to you, my darling husband, who is nearer and dearer to me than all other beings on earth, but oh how happy would I be if you were only in here with me. Do dear Ruthvin write to me very often for you know my anxiety to hear from you. Dear sister Elizabeth sends a great deal of love to you all, oh! I do not know what I would do without her, for she is such a great comfort to me. You must not be uneasy about us, but remember my dear Ruthvin that God ever watches over and protects us all. and you know if anything was to happen we would let you know, but I trust that your own dear self and that all of us may keep in the enjoyment of good health, and I sincerely hope this may find you perfectly well. Haynsworth (torn) came and has just been in here with me and he says I must tell you that, he never got any bad mark to-day, and that you must write to him. Dear Ruthvin do tell me in your next letter if your company is in for the war or for twelve months, and if you have had to go in some other company or still remain in the same, I agree with you dear Ruthvin in truly hoping that it may be the case in there not being much more fighting, and oh! how I wish that we could now have peace without any more war or fighting, and humbly do I hope and trust that it may be the will of a kind Providence to grant it unto us, oh! how highly would we all prize it, for we little knew how to appreciate peace, when once we possessed it.

Friday evening after you left aunt Rachel came to see us and stayed until Sunday morning, Sister Elizabeth and myself did not go to preaching yesterday. I am glad to know that you have preaching where you are, and I hope that you may all enjoy it. Uncle Gabriel and Sam took dinner with us yesterday on their way from church, and how much I missed you, and not only then but all the time, for I am thinking about you nearly all the whole time. Uncle G. said that Bilton would leave this morning. Did I tell you about the socks and gloves that Mary Dinkins knit for Theodore, she sent them over to Sister Elizabeth Saturday evening to send to Belton for him to carry to Theodore for her. if he knows who the giver is I know he will prize them very highly. She did not want Belton to know that she sent the bundle, and wanted sister E. to send it as though she sent it herself. I do'nt know, but I think that Mary is quite smitten with Theodore, but enough of this.

Dear Ruthvin I hav'nt forgotten your dogs once since you left, and I guess it would amuse you to see me throwing the bread to them, but I flatter myself that I am already quite an expert hand, and they have got so, that as soon as I open the door they all run to me. at first I could even let them take the bread out of my hand, but I am rather too timid for that, for I should not like for them to take a bite at my hand, but I do'nt think they will ever do that; oh! Ruthvin it makes me feel sad to see them, and particularly when they bark; they miss you I know, but I hope we will be able to take good care of them for you. I hope I may get a letter form home tomorrow, and I have to write home to-night myself, as I hav'nt written right lately. Haynsworth says they are all well at bro' Edgars. Do you not think that you can come home sometime to see us? oh! you well know how delighted we would be to see you. I do hope you all have warm and comfortable tents. we have had very cold weather lately, and while it was raining Friday night you do not know how I thought of you, but Sampson told me you all kept dry, which I was glad to hear.

Dear Ruthvin as I want to write home to-night, I must begin to close, and do write to us very often, for I will be so anxious to hear from you. Sister Elizabeth and the dear children join me in our best and warmest love, and I send many many kisses to you, also give our best love to Dear brother Edgar and all of our relatians with you, and tell them all to write to us. I hope my dear Ruthvin you will have a sweet nights rest to-night, and during all the time, and I now bid you a sweet good-night, and hope that pleasant dreams may be yours. I had a dream about you last night, and I thought of seeing you so plainly. and oh, that I could have one about you to-night. I expect dear Ruthvin you are tired of this uninteresting letter, but it seems to me I have so much that I can write you, but I must close now and oh! that Heaven's richest blessings may ever rest upon you all my dearest husband, is the prayer of your ever devoted and loving wife.

Hattie C. Plowden

Mary Emily has sent you a little Palmetto tree to put on your hat, which I will enclose in this letter. how I wish I could be with you to sew it on for you.

Hattie

(written in margin:)

Dear Ruthvin do if you please excuse this blotted letter, I never did until after I finished writing, and I am sorry to send it in this way but I hav'nt time to write it over, for if I did I would do so but I know you will excuse it and you must try and not look at these big blots. Write Soon

Camp Harlee Nov 26th 1861
My dear Hattie

As a few liesure moments present themselves I will write you a few lines. I am truly thankful to say we are all well & humbly trust this may find you all the same. We have a poor chance for news here in Camps, all we hear here is false It was reported yesterday that Beauregard & Johnston had McClelland Surrounded & had Sent to him to Surrender, but I fear it is only a hoax. News current this morn from Fort Pickens that Brag has given the enemy off with some damage to their Fleet I believe this is all I have heard of any consequence We are now encamped only 300 yards from Georgetown. I have paid two visits on business & one to Preaching & that on Sunday morn. We had quite a fine sermon from a Methodist Minister by name of Prichard on the same night attended Prayer meeting in camp, Major Mung conducted the meeting and heard some as good prayers as I ever heard. We were singing at our fire and were invited over to the Prayer meeting. I stopped at Brewington Church & got Elisabeths Hymn Book & one of my note books & I expect when we are not too tired we will sing pretty often & I hope will soon establish a prayer meeting among ourselves. The promise I made you dear Hattie of our Spirits holding Sweet Converse at Sunset, is hard to attend to on account of that being the hour of Dress Parade. But I hope it is not the case with you. although rest assured my dear Wife if I do not meet you then often very often my thoughts are wandering to the Loved ones at home (Sweet Home) yes when nature is hushed in quiet repose & the mantle of night is thrown over Slumbering millions then it is my thoughts keep watch around thee, & my dear Sisters & Children & oh let me beg you both to point them early to the Lamb that taketh away the Sins of the world. We are tolerably well situated here as well as we could wish under the circumstances. Our provisions still hold out pretty well. They are very high here Coffee 75 cts per # Salt 3 Dols a peck I must now close as I am expecting very soon to go on drill & So much to write to you about Tell Elisabeth I write to her in a few days. I know you are still uneasy about my tongue It is quite well again & I hope will continue so. Dear Hattie I must now bid you good bye & may God watch over

& protect you all is the prayer of your devoted Husband. Brother E. & J. Plowden begs to be remembered to you all. tell all the negroes howdy for me. do write soon & often.

Yours truly
E. Ruthvin Plowden

(written in margin:)
You must direct your letters to E R Plowden Georgetown So. Ca. Pee Dee Legion

To Care Capt Plowden
Pine Forest Nov. 28th/61
My very, dear husband.

Thinking of you so much I feel as though I cannot refrain from taking up my pen this afternoon in order to write you a few lines. although I have nothing of interest in the way of news to communicate, yet notwithstanding that I know it affords you great satisfaction to hear from us. but how I wish my dear Ruthvin I could see you, oh! I could not describe the great pleasure it would afford me to behold your dear familiar face. I hope you may get my letter safely that I wrote by last mail, as I well know you are getting anxious to hear from home. I truly hope that I may get a letter from you again very soon for you know my dear husband how anxious I am ever to hear from you and I know that you will write to one just as often as you can conveniently. Dear Ruthvin I do not think I could ever be able to describe my feelings the morning I parted from you, yes! they are indescribable, but oh! humbly do I pray and trust that God may spare your precious life to come safely back to us all again in health, and let us endeavor more and more to find our whole dependence and trust in Him. I am glad to say that we are all well, and I sincerely hope this may find you brother Edgar and all of you in the enjoyment of good health. Sister Elizabeth said I must ask you if there is anything you want from home. do let us know if you do, and tell me if you have a plenty of cover. how glad we would be to send you anything you want, and do always let us know. I don't stay from dear sister Elizabeth much now, but I stay with her at whatever she is doing nearly all the time. oh! Ruthvin, what a great source of comfort she is to me now. it seems to me I never realized how much I did love dear Sister Elizabeth before, until now. The children are coming on firstrate, and they are so much company for us. the other night at the supper table I could not help but feel very much amused at what Lute asked his auntie. he said "well auntie who was it that first told the tale that the cows kneel down and pray the night before Christmas," but I told him I hardly thought he would ever be informed as to who was the first that told that tale. They are both just as I told you in my letter before such dear good children. Haynsworth if he were here I know would have some message to send you, but he has not come yet as it is not time. Dear little Lute has just been in here with me and he says I must tell you howdye for him give you his love, and he kissed me and says I must tell you that was for him. he also says that I must tell you to kiss uncle Edgar for him, and then he must kiss you. Dear Ruthvin you recollect what you said about our thinking of each other at sunset. my dear Ruthvin you are scarcely ever out of my mind, but then I feel that I know we are thinking of each other at the same time and oh! how sad I felt when first I tried to play on the piano at that time, and knowing that Juanita was a favorite song of yours I tried to play that, but it was only to sing a line or two and then burst into tears, yes! dear Ruthvin it always makes me feel sad to play now, for it seems as though you ought to be here with me, and as I told sister Elizabeth it appears as though I can almost see you ride up on Rena, and hear you call Hamlet, and you know that it would be very often just about that time when you would come home.

But during the sweet hour of twilight when all is hushed in stillness, we ever find it a pleasant time for reflection, and it is then too my dearest husband that I not only remember you in thought but in prayers. my petitions though they are weak, yet my dear husband you are always assured that you are ever remembered by me at a throne of grace. Dear Ruthvin how I wish you were here with me this evening but such a wish I know is in vain, but I hope I may hear from you very soon again, and my dearest husband don't you think you can come home to see us soon? oh! you well know what great delight it would afford me and all of us. I hav'nt heard from home since you left but hope I may to-morrow. I trust tho' they are all well. Mr Windham was here yesterday. he said that the negroes were all coming on pretty well. for the last day or two they have been hauling rails. Dear Ruthvin I wish I was a good hand to give you an ac'ct of everything about your farm but you know I am a very inexperienced hand. Haynsworth has come from school and he says they are all well at brother Edgars. he says I must give you his love and you must write to him. oh how much I could talk to you if you were only here and how I wish you were here. All join me in our best and warmest love to you, dear brother Edgar & Cousin Joe and Isaac. Write very soon to your own dear

Hattie

Bishopville, Nov. 30th 1861
My own dear brother,

Knowing that you are now far away from your dear home this evening and that you will be glad to hear from any one almost I will gladly write a few comments in conversing with you. I cannot tell you my dear brother our feelings of heartfelt sadness as we heard that you were gone. How much I wish we could have seen you before you left. that I could have made one more of our old boring talks together; it did not take us much by surprise when we heard that you were going forth in defense of your Country. God grant that you may be permitted to return in safety to your dear family—oh that it may be His will that this dreadful war may soon cease that we may triumph over and drive back the invaders of our soil! We received a letter from dear Harriet Thursday night—how much I feel for her, Miss Elizabeth and all who have had to bid adieu to loved ones. I know it almost broke her heart to part with you. She writes so sadly. but says she has given you into the hands of your heavenly Father. This is our only comfort, what a privilege to have such a friend to go to in our times of trouble and sorrow. Yes, we can only put our trust in Him, feeling assured that He alone knoweth what is best for us and doeth what is good in His sight—we are all quite well, father has just returned from Camden and brought Maria home with him. She has been staying with Lizzie more than two weeks. Spent some of her time with her schoolmate Sarah Lizzie Gamewell. Daniel has not gone yet—he is in Mr. Manning Brown's company and it is not full yet—, they will go in Col. Chesnut's regiment. It will be a hard trial to see him go—but we are willing knowing that it is his duty. Cousin Hu left here more than a week ago, he only staid a short time, came by on his return from Tenn—he brought his little sister with him to stay until times got a little lef excitable in east Tenn. His company is stationed near Hardeville Beaufort Dist- Cousin Daniel is on Long Island near James Island. His mother and sister spent last week up here and they had heard from him several times. (Illegible) he was well—said they were encamped in a beautiful grove of palmetto. How do you stand camp life. Do write us very soon and let us know how you are getting on I hope it may improve you. Give my love to Cousin Joe, and Mr. Edgar Plowden I know it must be lonely times in the "Fork" now since you have all left—Bro Wm is with us now—he has not been very well but is better now. he will leave for Conference next Monday week—I am anxious to know where they will be sent another year. Anna Nora has just come in and she says "Tell Uncle Ruthvin I wish I could see him and that he must come soon," and winds up by sending her best love. Mother Father Sister bro. Wm Maria Wm and cousin Charlotte all join in sending their best love to you, we often think and speak of you. you are very dear to us all, and I have ever felt a sisters love for you since you became a member of our family—earnestly do I hope that many happy meetings are yet in store for us. It is now after tea, and what do you think I laid by my pen so long for—well, for the great pleasure of welcoming dear Harriet—it was quite a joyful surprise to us. I hope her visit may cheer her up a little. Haynsworth is with her. Harriet says she will write you some to night in this, as I will close as she can tell you more that you want to hear than I can. May God bless and keep you under His Protecting hand and bring you safe to us again. Goodbye my dear brother. Write as soon as you can to your devoted sister

Amanda Rogers

(on same page)

Sunday evening Dec. 1st 1861

Doubtless dear Ruthvin you will be surprised to hear of my being home so soon again, but I recd a letter from Amanda Friday evening saying perhaps that our dear brother too would have to leave soon, so I felt anxious to come home and see him before he left, and Maria just came home from Daniels yesterday evening and she said she thought he would be down Tuesday or Wednesday. Oh! dear Ruthvin what a hard hard trial it is for us to part with those so near and dear unto us, but humbly do I pray and trust that God may bring you all safely home to us again in health, and my dear brother too. Daniel wrote to you before I left, and I thought I would just forward the letter in to you. Oh! my dear husband how many times I have wished you were here with us, yes! I have talked about you so much, and wished for you, and then would get to crying too, but oh! dear Ruthvin I hope that erelong it may be that you can come home to see us. last night Amanda and I were talking of you until we went to sleep, and I believe she got to crying too as well as myself. Dear little Haynsworth came home with me and he was so much company, and they were all perfectly delighted to see us I was glad to find them all well, and I left all the dear ones at home well. Haynsworth has been a dear good child all the time. if nothing happens I guess we will go home Wednesday and if Daniel does not come until then perhaps I may stay until Thursday, sister Elizabeth told me if I wished I could stay until then, so I know she will not be uneasy anyway. My dearest husband how much I could write you if I had time, but it is getting so late, and I must close, I thought as Amanda left a space I would finish it out. Haynsworth seemed perfectly delighted to come with me, and to see Wm and all were so glad to see the little fellow here again, he has just been in here with me, and says I must give you his love, and you must write to him next week anyhow" and now with my best and warmest love I remain as ever your devoted wife.

Hattie

(written in margin:)

We went to the Methodist church to day heard Mr. Elliott. I presume you recalled him. I do hope I will hear from you by next mail, do write to me often, I am anxious to hear from you again. I had to write this Sunday evening as Amanda wished to send the letter to the office to night.

December 1st 1861
My dear Uncle

Although I have not received an answer to my last letter, I have concluded to write to you again hoping that you will respond to this and let us hear from you soon.

You have doubtless heard throug fathers letter to aunt Elisabeth of our deep affliction in the loss of my very dear brother, it has been a very severe trial to all of us to give him up and I can scarcely realize yet that he is dead, if he had only been at home when he died I could have been so much better satisfyed, but alas! none of us were permitted to be near in his dieing hours, but I should be satisfyed as it is, as it was God's will for him to die there on the Aleganies far from those that were dear and he orders all things for the best, but we are so prone to do evil that it is very difficult for us to think so particularly where we are called on to suffer a great deal. You have no idea what a dear good brother he was to me, I had cherished fond hopes that his life would be spared and that he might some day return to us, but hopes anticipations and all has been blasted, it has been a source of great consolation to us to know that he was resigned to die, it is another tie to bind us nearer to Heaven, he is far happier there than he could ever be in this world of sin and sorrow, he is now freed from all its temptations & I trust is with those that are dear in Heaven, I hope that this affliction may be the means of bringing us nearer to God and that we may feel more our dependence on him and that at last we may all meet around the throne of God there to join in singing his praises forever. It was a great satisfaction to us to know that he had such kind friends to him during his sickness, I know dear uncle that all of you sympathize with us in this our sad bereavement for I believe he was love'd by all that knew him, I am very glad that he went to see you on his way to Virginia for it was the last time on this earth, but I trust that we shall all meet at last in a happier & brighter world above.

I wish you could see Tilla my little sister she is a very interesting child and is so much company for me, she has proved a great blessing to us already in keeping our thoughts from dwelling too much on the dear one which we have lost, we are now realizing the sad effects of this War in our once peaceful land yet we have our great source of comfort. I believe our cause is a just one and the hand of Providence is clearly to be seen in our favour and if God is for us who can be against us?

I was very sorry to hear that the Federalist had invaded your state and taken Port Royal and that the planters on the Coast had to sacrifice so much of their property, I hope it will be the last place on the Coast or any where else in the Confederacy that they will get possession of, but it is thought by several that they will take Savannah before the end of winter but I hope not. Where is cousin Edgar & cousin Isaac? aunt E. mentioned in one of her letters that they had left, but did'nt say at what place they were stationed tell me in your next. I wrote to Lizzie Haynesworth several months ago & she has never replyed tell her to please write to me soon, I hear from all of you so seldom now please answer this very soon and not treat it in silence as you have done some of my others, I hope I will hear from you by Grandfather we expect him home Wednesday. Give my love to Hattie aunt Elisabeth the children & my other dear aunts and uncle Edgar. Tell Hattie & aunt E- to please write to me soon and please dear uncle answer this immediately. I remain as ever your devoted niece

Fannie

(undated—pg. 2 of a letter?)

we are so anxious to hear from you all. Has Mr. Edgar Plowden's company been called? Mr Carnes is getting up another company here. Bishopville will soon be deserted almost and we are very much afraid the militia will soon be called out. bro. Wm came home last Friday night much to our surprise. we did not know he was any where about until he walked in the room. he came in his buggy, but he had to go right back Monday to see if he could possibly get his things off. Sister does not know when to look for him. Sister rec'd a letter from Mr Asbury Mood on Monday night. he was called off and was to go into camps on Tuesday, said he plead his calling in vain, but he was willing enough to go. I think it will be hard for bro Wm to resist the temptation of going now. he told us perhaps he could not resist going when we got to Charleston, but I know he will not go without coming first. Cousin Hu got back from Tenn last Sunday and brought his little sister Mary with him. said it was such dreadful excitement up there he was afraid to leave her. She is a pretty child and very good. Cousin Hu left yesterday. Do Harriet if you see any any possible chance send me my album. I am so sorry Daniel cannot write in it and cousin David has never written in it either but he wrote a piece for me which I prize very much. Perhaps you will have an opportunity of sending it yet before Daniel goes. We hear from Almira right often. she is well. I saw Anna Loring in Sumter. she came home to have measles, but as her father is gone I doubt she goes back. She says Mary Coskrey was the most home sick creature she ever saw at first but was very well satisfied now—said she and Almira used to try and console her but they would both get to crying too. Mother sister Wm Anna Cousin Charlotte join me in warmest love to dear brother Ruthvin Miss Elizabeth the children and your own dear self. Write us very soon—tell them all I would give a world to see them to night. May God bless you all is the earnest prayer of

Your devoted sister
Amanda R.

Disember 1
My Dear Brother

I riceived your welcome letter to day. & was so thankful to hear from you all & that your tongue had got well we are all well Amanda rote to Hatty last Frid to go up & see Doc Rogers he was going to leave as soon as the company could leave, he also rote to you to go up & join the same company it is from Camden I think Preacher Brown is the Captain, Hatty went up Saterday Haynsworth went with her they will come back Wednesday & Mariah is coming with her, tell Joe howdy for us & Covert was hear yesterday & said lizy was quite well and all the rest tell Edgar Lillias is well & all of the children I herd from them to day the neighbours have all been to see us we have not been a day with out company & tomorrow Susa & Liza & Mr. Richburg is to spend the day but my Dear Brother all of them cannot fill your plaice, but I trust God will take care of both of you & bring you home to us again you rote some nuse in your letter but I red every thing in the murcury[95] this evening but their was no nuse only the yankeys is prepairing more fleets to seed on, they are going it sink some ships near our arbours so as to blockade them General Lee has given orders for Six more regiments from Southcaroliner he says their must be no time lost in making up these regiments you must rite me particular word when I must send you another box for I will send it whenever you want it Hatty never forgets you at ever meal she wishes you had some of what we have & you are the mose she talks about Hue M has brough his Sister from Tenesse she is living at Mr Rogers a family has moved from James iland to Mr. Spencers I think their name is Rivers.

George says he cleaned out all the stables one day raked one & maid the gravyard fence & wheet patch fence listed one day in (illegible) & planted wheat Saterday the men has been splitting rails he says the hogs is doing very well but 2 of the fatning hogs died he gives them a pec basket of corn every night he is going to give out allowance of corn to the negroes in the morning, tell Isick howdy

95 The Charleston Mercury, a daily newspaper published from 1825–1868 https://www.loc.gov/item/sn83045168/

for us & his Mother come over & paid Joe 7 dollars for 3 days & a half work but he did no have iron to make the last plough he said if he have had it he would not made it for he had worked till 12, do you & Edgar wright to us very often Luty says I must tell you he wants to see you so bad he send howdy to you & Edgar I hope God will bless both of you

(unsigned, from R's sister Elisabeth)

(written in margin:)

I was so glad to see you expected to commince a prayer meeting I pray that God will be with you all & a gra deal of good will come from it. Your dogs is fat & harty, I don't expect you can read this it is rote so bad do burn it

Sunday Evening Dec. 1st 1861 Camp Harlee P. D. Legion
My Own Dear Wife,

You cannot imagine, how, how much I thank you my darling little wife, for your kind consideration of me in writing me two such long letters. I have also written you 2 & this is the third & one to dear Elisabeth one to your father & one to Brother Edward so you see I have spent nearly the whole of my Leisure moments in writing. But my dear wife, it is a greater pleasure to write to you than all the rest put together. it seems more like old times than any other way I can substitute. I am thankful to state that this leaves me now quite well when I last wrote I had a severe cold from exposure I presume & I humbly trust in God this may find you all enjoying the same rich blessing. The health of our company is pretty good only two on the sick list this morn. the same that has been reported ever since our arrival. one has sore leg & the other White swelling I am afraid.[96] Do when you write say all of our families are well (that is if they are) for Brother E & J. P. always enquire how all are & be certain & write how Brother E's family are for you know Lillis has a bad chance to write. You requested me to give full particulars of every thing so in the first place in the morn 1/2 past 6 oclock Drum beat & all called up to roll call. It would amuse you to see some run out to answer to their names. Some in their shirts & pants, some bare headed, some bare footed. then at 7 we eat Breakfast. at 8 go on drill & drill until a few minutes of 9. at 10 drum beats we go back & drill untill a few minutes of 11 then drum beats & we the officers go back & drill one hour which makes it 12 oclock. between 12 & one oclock we eat Dinner at 1/2 past 2 we go back on drill & drill untill near 4 then 1/2 past 4 we go on Dress Parade. at that time we all appear in full uniform. every evening since we have been here there has been from 6 to 12 ladies at dress parade but we do not like to see them for it reminds us too much of the dear ones at home. not that we do not like to think of you but because you cannot be here. also, Sunday eve as it is, in the course of a few minutes we will have to go on dress parade, & I am truly thankful that is the only duty we have to perform on this holy day, except those that have to stand guard that

96 White swelling: tuberculosis

you know the officers is clear of except when they are officers of the guard. I fortunately have missed, I have thus far but I am afraid I will have it to do this week as all the others have been in this week. If I do come in I will have to be up nearly all night. I forgot to mention we had supper about sunset & cannot go to bed untill drum beat which is at 9 oclock. our Prayer meeting takes place every night 1/2 7 oclock. for the first time last night I had to pray in public & my dear wife & sister pray for me that I may discharge my duty faithfully to my God & to my country. I attended church again this morn (Methodist) Mr. Prichard preached a splendid sermon. I could not refrain from tears when I thought of you all & where you were. We enjoyed a great priviledge there—for Soldiers there was Communion & little did I think I would be allowed that priviledge. while in camp there was 3 connected themselves with the church. we had to stop at the General Quarters on our way to church, therefore did not get there untill after Preaching commenced. there was quite a crowd out. I expect we will be mustered in Confederate service in a short time for 12 months. report has reached here that it is reported in Clarendon that our company is about to be broken up. But it is not so. Tell George take good care of the horses & hogs & especially Rena. I have just been appointed one of the officers of the guard from 9 oclock in the morn untill 9 next. I cannot tell you when I can come home. I wrote to Bishopville I would try to come the last of this month, but I doubt it. (do not expect it) My dear dear wife I must close. tell H. & Lutie be good Boys & not forget their prayers. give H & Lutie a kiss for me & let them kiss you my dear for me & may God watch over & protect you all is the Prayer of your devoted husband Tell all howdy for me & much love to you all good bye darling pleasant dreams

Your Ruthvin

(written in margin:)

Do write soon & often all particulars Good night darling

Yours
ERP

Camp Harlee P. D. Legion Monday morn Dec. 2nd 1861
My own dear wife,

As I have a few moments, I will continue my letter from yesterday. I am now officer of the guard, & will have leisure from this time which is after 10 & untill 3 oclock this eve. I will then be on duty untill 9 to night sleep untill 3 in the morn & on duty untill from 9 tomorrow when I will be clear of duty untill 1/2 past 4. I will have to go on dress parade but that only last about half an hour so you see there is no rest for the Soldier or but little from one day to the next. I am truly glad to state that I have not been tired since I have been here. My feet has been a little sore, but I am in hopes they will soon be all right. I was just saying last night "if you could be at our table you would be afraid we would not have enough," but thank God we have plenty. We have rice & beef coffee & potatoes for nearly every meal so you see we are getting along as well as we could wish. Lieut. Chandler we have made the head of our family so he always asks the blessing. you also stated in your last we must send word if we needed anything. so far we are well provided for both as it regards something to eat & plenty of covering & as well satisfied as we can be from the dear dear ones at home. If we can get all of our company in Confederate local service (that means for the State) for 12 months I will be still better satisfied & I think they will all be willing for that as they will get more pay more rations all will be uniformed & be better provided for every way. My dear wife, it was quite late last night before I got to sleep. Memory was on the wing. It carried me back to the first time I saw you, & oh what pleasure to look on the past. how many pleasant hours we have spent in each others society & may God grant many many more to us. I thought how many times at the close of day when all nature was hushed in calm repose the sweet converse we had in the end of the piazza in the dear old arm chair with you in my lap. I know it will make you sad to read this, but the reflection of the past will be sweet to you as well as I, many many sweet reflections I am in hopes is in store for me to night, as I will have to be up a good portion of it. But my dear Wife, you & my dear sister E must not give yourselves unnecessary fears about me for my trust is in Him above who is able to save. You cannot imagine how sorry at times I am after I have written to you how many things I have neglected to write. But if you were only here one day & see how much we are bothered while writing you would be surprised. Nearly every moment some one calls in on some business & it makes it very hard to keep the connection. But all this I know you will excuse matters not how many mistakes I may make. General Harlee told us if we went in Confederate service there would be a chance for us to return home next summer for the enemy would hardly remain on our coast during the summer months but would have to return or fill out our unexpired time in the winter if required. I hope that will not be the case. In your next write me if you have killed any hogs & tell George to tell you how many pigs there is & what kind of work they are doing & if he or Mr. Wyndham has any trouble with the negroes. tell them all howdye for me & that I think of them very often & tell George I say I can never forget him. he has been so good to me & mine & that God will reward him for it. give my respects to Mr. Wyndham & that I will soon write to him. kiss the dear children for me & them you for me. Good bye, my darling, & also may God watch over you all is the prayer of your devoted husband

Ruthvin

(written in margin:)

Write soon dear Hattie & you must not look for a letter in a week as I will have many letters to write to others of the family. give my love to all friends. Mr & Mrs McDowell next Sunday

Yours
Ruth

Bishopville 4 Dec 1861
Dear Ruthvin

Your highly esteemed favor came duly to hand and before I recd it I had seen a letter written by dear Harriet to Amanda stating that you had left home for Georgetown with your company and that the boy Sampson had returned leaving you well. Poor Harriet—her letter was written in Sadness—it made us all feel sad. Still she looked up on high for support, and felt that it was all right—and most thankful she was that in this time of her affliction She had a dear sister in Miss Elizabeth to lean upon. Daniel too expects soon to leave and to day with his family he leaves Camden for home preparatory to his going into the army.

Well, my Dear Harriet came up here last Saturday in order to see Daniel before he should leave. as well as to see the rest of us. As Daniel does not come down until today Harriet has delayed in order to see him, and tomorrow she returns home. Dear Harriet seems very much composed and I trust she will bear up like a philosopher. These are indeed times of trouble, but under the circumstances I think you have acted right. I could not have advised you to any different course from the one you have pursued and the same applies also to Daniel.

I am indeed very sorry that we could not see you before you left and if you can come up about the time of Christmas and can inform us in time, we will some of us try to go down and see you. I think Maria will go down on tomorrow with Harriet to stay awhile. We are all tolerably well. Wm Lucy and Anna are with us, next week he goes to conference.

We hear that there has been a fire in Georgetown—hope the damage is not large for our people can ill spare anything unless compelled.[97] Some of us dear Ruthvin will write you often and I will not trouble you with a long letter now as I have but little time this evening to write—may Heaven protect and bless you—may the time not be long ere you can return—and then may we all know a Glorious and lasting peace. With love from all—I remain dear Ruthvin most affectionately and truly yours -

William Rogers

---

97 "The alarm of fire was sounded in this town on Friday morning about half-past 2 o'clock. It originated in or about the warehouse of S. S. Fraser, and so rapid was the progress of the flames that scarcely was time given to the gentleman who had the keys of the office and safe, to save Mr. Fraser's books and papers. The warehouses, offices, wharves, with some 3,500 barrels of Naval Stores, the buildings on the same range owned by Wm. Cain and H. J. P. Ellis and occupied by their families, were consumed, as were also two dwelling houses, a cooper's shop, and a storehouse and contents on the opposite side of the street. Two houses on the southside were torn down, which with the assistance of the engines, prevented the further extension of the fire." The Richmond Daily Dispatch, Dec. 6, 1861, by Cowardin & Hammersley

Camp Harlee P D Legion Dec 6th 1861
My darling Wife,

I have just seated myself to say good night to you & dear Sister & manny many thanks for the Box & Jug of Brindies milk for only a few days ago we were talking if we only had some how it would help out our meals You can imagine how thankful we all ought to be for having such considerate wifes & Sisters. Sister Martha sent us a Box, also so you see we are quite independant. Although we have a good supply on hand that we brought with us, we got out of sugar & had to buy 2 Dols worth. our Wheat Flour is just as it was when we came here, & I think it is likely to remain so. I am truly thankful to hear you are all well & I am also thankful this leaves us the same. What for a visit did you have to Bishopville how I would have liked to have been with you but God has ordered it otherwise & I humbly trust he will enable me to do his will without one murmer. It is now 1/2 past 4 oclock Saty morn. I had to stop my letter last night after 9 as we have to out our Lights. I have been awake some time & got to thinking about you all, so sleep is driven far away. but this is often the case dear Hattie, once I ever wake it is long before I get to sleep. You did not say in Amanda's letter if you had received more than one letter & this is the 4th to you & the 3rd I have written since yesterday morning. One to Amanda & one to Sister. Mr. Isaac Montgomery got a letter from Edgar yesterday stating that there has been improvement in his health & I hope it may continue. Do when you write give full particulars of every thing going on about home. If you have killed any hogs & how many. For several days past it has been a fine time for it as it has been very cold & one severe night of Rain & as luck would have it that night I was officer of the Guard, but about 9 oclock the Colonel issued orders for the guard to come in & it was good news to all. You cannot imagine how glad we all were to see those men from Manning &, such reports as they brought from Clarendon Georgetown burnt & all of us taken by the Yankees & many others of the same kind. Dear Hattie I must close, as the waggon is soon to start & Brother E. has to write. Tell Hayns & Lute I will write to them next. Goodby darling, all of you May God bless you all

Yours
Ruthvin

Pine Forest Dec. 8th 1861
My very dear, dear husband. (each word is underlined 6 times!)

I cannot find words to express to you my thanks, for being so good, in writing to me, and such dear good long letters too, oh! you do not know how I prize them, and I perused them again and again, I have re'ed four letters from you. I came home Thursday evening last and dear Maria came with me, and she is so much company for me, for you know how funny she is some times; I had a very pleasant visit at home, but oh! dear Ruthvin you can't imagine how greatly I missed you; it would seem to me that if you were only with me, how glad I would be; I could not tell you the questions that were asked me about you, for you well know that you are one that my own dear family all love so much, and it seems to me that there is no conversation now that I enjoy more than in talking about my dear Ruthvin, and when at home, sometimes when speaking of you to the dear ones, I could not refrain myself from bursting into tears, and dear sister it seems as though I can hear her sweet voice now saying, don't cry Hattie, and dear cousin Charlotte would say, I think he will come back again; oh! dear Ruthvin how grateful do I feel when I think of how many many loved ones you have that love you so dearly, and to pray for you oh! yes! humbly do I pray and trust in God that ere long my dearest Ruthvin may be permitted to return safely home to me, oh you little know how much I think of you, and if you were only here with us now. Maria and I are now out in the piazza, at the platform where you and I have so often been, writing to you, and it seems as though I can almost see you here too with your head in my lap, and what a great great source of pleasure would it be, could such only be so this evening, but I hope it may not be long before this pleasure may be granted me again; you must excuse our writing Sunday evening, but we have an opportunity of sending our letters to-morrow and do this on that ac'ct, and Ruthvin what do you think Maria and I have been trying to see which could have the most underscores, in the beginning of our letters, but I do not think she is ahead of me. I have re'ed letters from father and Amanda since I came home which they wrote before I went home, after I had written to them about your going off. It appeared that they both tried to cheer me up, father said in his letter that if sister Elizabeth could spare me I must go and stay at home some with them, and that he would send down for me and carry me home, but I went before I got his letter; father re'ed your letter while I was at home and I was delighted to hear from you, and always am you know, and on my return home I found three awaiting me, and with what eagerness did I get them and read them, and this morning before I went to church I said to Maria oh! if I could only get a letter from dear Ruthvin to day, so my wish was granted, for I had not been there very long before I did get one, and was so thankful to hear that you were well, and that you had re'ed the things sent you, and did you also get the potatoes and corn & flour? and sister E sent you a few lines with the things also, which I hope you got safely. I am so glad that she had the opportunity of sending you a box. I would have been glad to have been here to have helped her in fixing the things as it was to you, but I had not then returned home. You must write if you re'cd all the things I have mentioned. We all had the pleasure of hearing Mr McDowell preach again to day and a very good sermon it was, from 3rd chap. of Habakuk 17th 18th & 19th verses,[98] and oh my dearest how vacant your seat looked; and how I missed your dear sweet voice in the choir, but I presume you can picture to yourself, what my feelings of sadness were being there without you, and my thoughts were wandering towards you, but I miss you wherever I go and at the table how sad it seems not to see you there. In your letter to father you stated that you would try and be home the last week in Dec. or 1st Jan, and you can't imagine how delighted I was to hear it, and it was the first thing I thought of when I awoke in the morning, but in your letter to me you say that I must not expect it, but oh! Dear Ruthvin can't you come? oh! what feelings of joy would fill my heart for you to come and see us. do try and do so if you possibly can.

98 Hab. 3: 17-19 "Although the fig tree shall not blossom, neither shall fruit be in the vines, the labour of the olive shall fail, and the fields shall yield no meat; the flock shall be cut off from the fold, and there shall be no herd in the stalls: Yet I will rejoice in the Lord, I will joy in the God of my salvation. The Lord God is my strength, and he will make my feet like hinds' feet, and he will make me to walk upon mine high places." KJV

Maria and sister E unite with me in sending our best and warmest love to you, brother Edgar, and cousin Joe also give my love to Isaac and ask him if he knew that his little sweetheart Mary C has had the measles but I presume she is well of them ere this. Now with many many kisses and praying that God may ever watch over and protect you all and that we may all be permitted soon to meet again in health is the prayer of your ever devoted wife

Hattie

(written in margin:)

Maria said she would give you twice the number of kisses, but I told her ten thousand million but she changed it, said she would not put that many, but you know my number would be far greater than hers. oh darling how much I could write you, and I do hope I may be able to write a more interesting letter than this next time.

Pine Forest Dec. 8th 1861
My darling precious brother

It is Sabbeth afternoon; but I feel it will be nothing amiss for me to devote a few of its minutes in writing to you my dear Soldier Brother. Yes, another Sabbath with all its sweet enjoyments is soon to be numbered with the things that are past. And as I look at yonder setting sun (for Hattie and I are both in the piazza where we can behold it) withdrawing his presence from us arrayed in all his pomp and glory, my mind wanders to you in your tented field and again and again I wish that you could be with us this Holy evening. Oh! how I love the Sabbath eve, yes at its close I love to examine myself if I have spent it as I should have—I improved its precious fleeting moments as it was my duty to have done; ah! no! no! How very merciful kind and good has my Heavenly Father been to me, notwithstanding I have lived so far from him and have so often trampled his holy law under my feet—yet, still he has blessed me with so many blessings. Oh! my dear brother pray that I may improve the precious moments as they glide along, and strive to live nearer to Him every day of my life, so that in the end I may receive a crown of glory. As you know, Hattie went up to see us a week ago and I returned with her, and never no never my precious brother can I describe my feelings when I arrived here. yes in spite of myself a tear would bedim my eye and I would sigh for my absent Brother. Oh! how much I miss you I can never find words to tell. But such is life! truly this is a world of sorrow and disappointment. Those Old Yankees see how much trouble they have caused us; yes tis them who have called us to pass through the trying ordeal of parting with those who are so near and dear unto us. Truly our national horizon is now covered with dark dark clouds but sincerely do I trust that ere long peace sweet peace will shine upon us. Happy day will that be indeed. We attended preaching this morning at Brewington, heard a most excellent sermon from that good man Mr McDowell. How changed did everything appear there; yes your melodious voice was not to be heard. But we must not complain. you are engaged in a noble! noble! cause, and into the hands of God dear dear brother Ruthvin do we commit and commend you feeling assured that "all things work together for good to them that love the Lord. It is getting late so I must conclude, Hattie says if you were here she would give you ten thousand kisses and I would give you twice that number. How I wish you could be at home now while I am here. I dream of you every night and last night I was made very happy by your coming to pay us a visit—May God meet with you all in your prayer meeting to night—and that your own soul may be abundantly blessed is the prayer of your devoted sister

Maria

Remember me to Mr. Plowden & Joe. Haynsworth says to tell father to write to him and that he intends to send you word until you do. good by

Camp Harlee P D Legion Dec. 11th 1861
My dear Harriett

With feelings of pleasure I address you a few lines in answer to your Long Looked for but welcome Oh! how welcome was your kind letter I had written two & no answer I had begun to think the mails was in fault but just as I had concluded I would not get one before Tuesday (that very night, Lieut. Montgomery handed me one in quite a crowd I broke it open to devour the good news, but my feelings compelled me to seek seclusion I was truly thankfull to see that a Mercifull Providence is still taking care of you my own Sweet Wife & All the rest of the family & well do I know that he will continue to do so if we will put our trust in him for in Him alone do we receive every good & perfect gift This leaves us all well & I humbly trust it will leave you all enjoying the same rich blessing Dear Hattie I write so often & news so scarce I am afraid my Letters will not be very interesting in that particular but otherwise I know full well it will Dear Hattie, how I would have enjoyed that sweet; sweet converse on last Sunday Eve with you all, but God has disposed it otherwise, but I hope the time is not far distant when we will meet again, but the particular time; it is impossible for me now to say, you have no idea my Dear Hattie how constantly employed the officers are kept there, therefore the chance for me to get home before the middle or last of January will be a bad one. I expect Joe Plowden will be at home in the course of 8 or 10 days & I wish it was so I could come with him He says tell Cousin Lizzie if she will send for him he will come at that time, but of that he has already informed her. he also sends his love to you & dear sister E. & the rest of the family. I got permission to day to visit the Islands south of Georgetown, distant about 12 or 14 miles, but was disappointed on account of the abscence of the Gentleman that issues the permits, but I want to try & get off tomorrow if it is a good day. I hope it is not as warm at home, as it is here if so I am fearful you will be apt to lose more or less pork. It is so warm here nearly every one is without his coat Our Regt. was presented yesterday evening at Dress Parade with Basket containing Palmetto wreaths also Palmetto tree with Cotton & Rice worked on them The Servant that brought the Basket brought it to some 3 or

4 of us there was a note in it stating that it was from Miss Waterman we sent a committee to thank her for her kind consideration She came out to where we were standing on her way to Georgetown. She was dressed neat but not gaudy; tolerable good looking The Ladies Dresses bodices quite short skirt very long (very much against my taste) I have not seen but two ladies since I came here that I was acquainted with & did not speak to them. I fear I will almost forget how to behave in their company if I stay much longer. Dear Hattie I would be so delighted if you were only here seated by me in our Parlor what a strange appearance it would be to you just imagine a Pine Straw Carpet on one side and Bedding on the other that composed of the same material of the carpet & the checked counterpane neatly spread on it just the appearance would give comfort to one wearied from a days Drill, but dear dear Hattie I am seldom if ever tired, & oh thankful I ought to be for when our camps are hushed in quiet repose, then it is dearest my thoughts are hovering around thee & all the dear ones at Home Sweet Home. It appears to me as soon as my eyes are open I begin to think about you all & sleep bids me a final adieu Tell the dear Young Gal I write to her soon & she must write soon & so must all of you Good night, darling May God watch over & bless you all is the prayer of your devoted husband kiss the children for me & tell be good boys & mind what I told them in their letter Love to all good night Ruthvin is yours only

Pine Forest Dec. 14th 1861
My own precious Ruthvin,

Yours of the 11th ins't came safely to hand yesterday evening. I wished I do not know how many times yesterday that I might get a letter from you so when Haynsworth came from school, Maria and I went very quickly to the gate to meet him, and to my great satisfaction he handed me a letter from your own dear self, and oh! with what eagerness did I open it, and peruse the precious contents it contained, for I always thank you so much dear Ruthvin for your kind and affectionate letters, and in being so very good in writing to me as often as you do, and I full well know that you can ever imagine what a great great source of pleasure it always affords me to hear from you; truly grateful do I feel to our heavenly Father to hear too the good news that you are all well, and humbly do I pray and trust that such may continue to be the case, and in reply I am happy to say that we too are all quite well, and trust this may find you all in the enjoyment of perfect health. I was glad that you recd my letter, and I presume you got Maria,s with mine. it is one of my most pleasant employments now in your absence from me, to be engaged in writing to you. I was sorry that the time seemed so long to you before hearing from me again, for I do wish it was so dearest that we (torn) hear from each other every day, but I hope the time will not seem so long now (torn) you hear from me again, and you know dear Ruthvin what a source of pleasure it is for me to write to you during our absence. I wish I had some thing to write, that would in some way render my letter interesting to you, but you know that conversations mostly now are about the war, oh! my dear husband how I wish that peace sweet peace we could have; (and how little did we know how to prize and appreciate that word peace when once we possessed it) and that my own dear husband and all the poor soldiers could be safely returned to their homes, but we must all only look to God and trust in Him alone, for we know that He is willing and able to shield and protect us wherever we are, or in whatever circumstance we may be placed, and oh! how thankful do I feel dear Ruthvin to know that it is in God you put your trust, and dependence, yes! it is to Him alone we must all fly for refuge. My dear Ruthvin in parting with you (as I have previously told you) and in being seperated from you is one of the hardest and greatest trials that I have ever experienced in all my life, but then I hope and trust that this severe trial has been the means of enabling me to look more and more to a merciful Providence, and of bringing me nearer to our blessed Savior, and I trust that it has too had this effect upon you. I fear and know that I have been living too cold, too indifferent, and too far from our precious Savior that dear Friend from whence all blessings come, but as I have so many times told you before my beloved companion, oh! let us pray earnestly to our Heavenly Father that He would help us, to strive and endeavor to live nearer and nearer to Him each succeeding hour of our lives, for without his help we know that within ourselves we can do nothing. and oh! that God may very soon restore our beloved country to peace, and that peace and prosperity may soon everywhere prevail, and that my own dear husband with all the beloved ones, may be returned safely and in health to us all again is my humble prayer, and we know that if God is for us no one can be against us. When I was at home Mrs Rembert and her cousin Miss Maggie (torn) spent a day at fathers, and Mrs R. inquired of me very particularly after you, as to how you were and where you were stationed etc, and she told me to tell you that she liked you better now than she ever did before. I think too you would be pleased with her to get well acquainted, as she is such a lively talkative lady. Dear cousin Charlotte said I must tell you that she often thought of you, and that she remembered you in her prayers. Wednesday last cousins Hu and Fannie came and spent a day and night with us, and cousin Lizzie came awhile that morning, but returned to cousin Callie's before dinner, the same day. also uncle Gabriel stopped and took dinner with us on his way home from James Plowden,s. I was very glad to see them all, so you can tell cousin Joe and brother Edgar that all are quite well. You cant imagine Ruthvin how very much delighted we were all made the other evening, when Haynsworth came from school and told us that Andrew Burgess said that you would probably be home before Christmas; I tell you it made me feel happy to think of it, but in your letter to me you say you do not think you can come before the middle or last of Jan. I wish it was so you could come sooner, but my dearest Ruthvin do come home to see us as soon as you can, and as often, oh! what my feelings of delight would be to see, and embrace my beloved Ruthvin, and I presume you can well imagine them, but I pray and trust that soon our kind heavenly Father may bring you (torn), safely and in health to us all again. Maria too with the rest of us (torn) to hear you were coming home, and she was so in hopes that you might come before she went home, but you know dearest when it suits you the best, and do try and come just as soon as you possibly can. I presume you would like to hear something as to what the negroes are doing; they have two days been listing up cotton ground, and yesterday being such a good day for killing hogs, Mr Windham had 21 killed, one of which (torn) weighed 150 lbs, was sent to the gentleman you spoke of in your letter. I (torn) this is fine weather for the business as it is very cold today. yester(torn) sister Elizabeth and myself were very busy in the grease line, when (torn) ould drive up but Mrs Leanert and two of her granddaughters, but they did not stay very long after dinner, and they went from here to Dr Durant,s. I thought miss Cornelia Boyd quite a pretty young lady, and was pleased with her for so short an acquaintance. When sister E. and myself got through with the sausages etc I told her how I did wish that Ruthvin was here now, but Jimmie Burgess has just came this morning to inform us that Andrew is going to return tomorrow, and wants to know if we wish to send a box to you, so I am very glad we have (torn)tunity of sending one to you. I wish I just knew what all you would like for us to send you; it would be a great pleasure for us to do all that we could that would in any way add to your pleasure and comfort. Fannie has written to you, so I will enclose it in this. what a good letter she writes, and Daniel wrote to you also after you left & which I forgot to send and as I havnt space to write what he has written I thought I would enclose it also. I gave Daniel his notes back. Tell Sandy howdye for me, and tell him not to forget what I told him when I bade him good-bye which was to take good care of you, and not to forget to pray, pray.

(written in margins:)

The dogs are all in splendid order. I have just come in from giving them some bread from the dinner table. how I wish my own darling you could be here to dine with us also. Ruthvin you are aware I am right forgetful, but rest assured the dogs are one thing it seems that I never forget. Sister Elizabeth says I must tell you that what salt she gets in brushing off the meat she thinks she will have enough to salt at least twelve more hogs, those that were killed yesterday were indeed very fine ones. Last night after reading your letter to the dear children they both very readily got up and gave me a sweet kiss, and Haynsworth says I must tell you that he had not got a bad mark this week. I told him that he had been a smart boy. Henry came over this morning as it is Saturday. I am always so glad to see him come.

Do give our love to dear brother Edgar and tell him I want to write to him next, and that he must all join me in sending our very best and warmest love to you my precious husband also to Joe, and my best love to Isaac. Write very soon dearest, to your own dear Hattie.

Brewington Dec. 14th, 1861
Dear Ruthvin

Your very acceptable letter came to hand a few days ago also the one written to your sister. we were very much pleased to hear that you were all well. we have heard from you several times within the last ten days. I saw one of the men belonging to a company from Manning at Gourdins Depot a few days ago and he informed me that your company had been mustered into the service of the confederate states. if so there will be no opportunity for any of your men, should they be so disposed, to back out. You requested me to find out when Hal got home. I understand that he passed Mrs. Montgomery about ten oclock on the second day after he left the camp (very good time for a sick man). I have not seen him since he came back. I attended the funeral of Mr. Thomas Tobias on last Monday. Mr. McDowal preached. there was a good many persons there. Mr. McDowell visited him a few days before his death and had a conversation with him. from what he said to him he thought that the old man was prepared.

I left home for Charleston on Tuesday night about 9 oclock arrived there the next day about 10. about 9 oclock on Wednesday night the alarm of fire was given and as the House where it originated was not more than three hundred yards from the Charleston Hotel I was one of the first that arrived at it.[99] I hope it will never be my sad lot to witness such another. The wind got up very high soon after the fire commenced and it was impossible to do any thing with it. It commenced at a sash and blind shop in the northestern part of the City and burnt a course through the city in a southwestern

99 "At about 8:30 p.m., a fire broke out in a sash and blind factory on Hasell Street in Charleston and quickly spread thanks to a strong north-west wind. By the time it burned itself out it had destroyed 575 structures and scorched 540 acres, around a third of the city. Among the buildings completely destroyed were St. Andrew's Hall on Broad , where the Secession Convention had met, and the Institute Hall nearby, where the Ordinance of Secession had been signed. Recovery was long and slow during the war years." Osborne, John, Frazier, Walter J., *Charleston! Charleston!: The History of a Southern City* (Columbia, SC: University of South Carolina Press, 1991), 253-255.

direction to Asly River. I left there on Thursday about 12 oclock and the fire was still raging. it had not at that time burnt through to the Ashly River but I have learned since, that it was stoped about 1 oclock. There was an immense amount of property distroyed nearly equal to the fire of thirty eight.[100] My business to the city was to get salt but I did not succeed. Caldwell and Robinson was both of them in the country and their clerk could not let us have any money, in fact they doubted if we could get it from Caldwell if he had been there. they say that they have refused every application for money for some time, that they have no money by them and could not furnish it to their customers without borrowing from the bank. His clerk said if we would send down a few bales of cotton he thought it could be sold at 8 cents and he would get the salt for us. I found no salt in Charleston but at two stores. at one of them they would sell but two sacks to any one man. the other had only ten sacks. one of them sold at $12. and the other at $13. I called on them the next morning and they had sold every sack they had. They say that the salt they had was sent to them from Savannah. that they have been selling on commission, that they may or may not receive more, that they could not tell. I am at a loss to know what to do. if I send the cotton there is some doubt if we could get the salt in Charleston. I think that it would be better to borrow the money up here if I can get it. I will make the effort and if I do not succeed I see no other alternative but to sell the cotton at what it will bring, and get the salt if I have to go to North Carolina for it. I wish you to write to me and let me know if I must send your cotton, if I should send mine before I hear from you I expect to send yours also.

We have just heard the sad news that Arthur Burgess has committed suicide—that he blew his brains out with his musket.

---

100 General Robert E. Lee was staying at the Mills House Hotel the night of Dec. 11, 1861, and was hustled away to safety and taken to the Edmonston-Alston House on East Battery. The cost in property was estimated to be between $5 million and $8 million. Photos taken of Charleston in 1865 show a ruined city, and some would assume the destruction was caused by the Union army, but most of the damage was caused by the fire. https://lowcountrywalkingtours.com/charleston-stories/the-great-charleston-fire-of-1861

So many of us have been loosing Hogs on this side of the Swamp that we concluded to make a search for them. this morning we found in Wm Coskreys negroes pens thirteen hogs with the marks changed. six of them I am satisfied is Edgars. the ear with the (torn) has not been changed but the other has been croped off with one half of it with the old half crop and the other not yet quite healed up. we saw at one of the pens where one hog was killed last night. Mr. Richburg says he saw it in the pen yesterday. that it was a sutty sow in the same near 12 of the six that I think is Edgars. I let Mr. Johnson know it and told him to take Henry and Gadson over there and they would know them if they were his.

Yours affectionately
R. P. Haynsworth[101]

---

101 This may be Richard Peter Haynsworth, 1816–1877.

Camp Harllee P. D. Legion Dec. 17th 1861
My dear dear Wife,

It was with the greatest pleasure I read your welcome letter & learned that you all enjoyed the same good health. It found me quite well except sore throat & I am thankful that is better this morning. My dear Hattie you cannot imagine how much disappointed I am that I could not come home with those men. I had made my calculations to come this morn, & take you all by surprise; but we formed a new company yesterday & had to have another election of officers & I am sorry to say that Mr. Chandler got cut out of his office. Butler beat him badly. Mr. Logan from Manning opposed me but my friends stuck up to me. I got four times the number of votes he did which you know was gratifying & I know will be to you all. It makes me sorry for Chandler for he is a very fine man. he was to stay & I was to go home but after being cut out I am compelled to stay. I will now be kept busy all the time as I am the only officer left in the company. I was Lt. of Guard last night untill 9 oclock & had to get up this morn at 3 oclock. So you see I only slept 4 hours, but I humbly trust God will enable me to perform all my duties faithfully. I do not know if it will be in my power to come home when those men return, but be sure if it is in my power I will be certain to come. I can only write a few moments longer as I have to be at the guard house. There was one death in the hospital at 9 oclock Sunday night the poor man exhorted all that was around him to prepare for death. he a wife, & one child. how sorry I am for her he was very wicked untill 3 days before his death. he became quite penitent. I feel very much obliged to you & Sister E. for the many good things you have sent me. I know you had a busy day when you killed so many hogs & I hope you will not loose any of it as it is very cold here. You must write to me soon & let me hear from you all & let me know if Maria is with you as I wish to answer her letter. Dear Hattie you cannot imagine how often I think of you all particularly at night. if I awake the first thoughts is of you all & sleep takes its flight. Good bye darling May God bless you all. Sandy sends howdye to you Dear Sister

E. & S-.[102] tell all the negroes howdye for me. kiss E., H., Lutie for me & now receive my warmest love to you & all & may God watch over & protect you all is the prayer of yours devotedly

Ruthvin

102 "Sandy" appears to be one of Ruthvin's servants who attended him in camp.

Pine Forest Dec. 21st 1861
My own beloved Ruthvin

Now while all is hushed in stillness, I feel as though I could not spend a portion of my time more pleasantly than in writing to you, although it is at quite a late hour of the night, but thinking of you so much, and having not the delightful privilege of conversing with you face to face, I cannot refrain from taking up my pen, and writing to you, but in reading your letter this evening to sister Elizabeth, informing us of your having sore throat, makes me feel so anxious about you, and oh how sorry I was to hear it, and how I wish my dear Ruthvin you were at home with us so that we could do something for it, but humbly do I pray and trust that you may soon be entirely well of it, and restored to perfect health. do try and take the best of care of yourself, and I hope what you do for it may be of great benefit to you; oh! that I could only be with you to do all that I could for your throat, but I sincerely hope 'ere this it is entirely cured. Joe Plowden got here last Tuesday night, but it being so late he did not stop at the house, and gave your letter to me, to one of the negroes which was brought to me next morning, and I send you many thanks for it, but oh! how glad would I have been if you could have only come yourself, what great pleasure would it afford us, and I am sorry you could not come, but I trust it may be so that you can come home to see us, when brother Edgar returns, and it appears that I can't help but look forward to your coming then, (as I told sister E yesterday) for I am so much in hopes it may be so that you can at that time. I have had the pleasure of seeing bro' Edgar. Maria and myself went over to the examination Wednesday last (Sister Elizabeth wanted to stay with sister Lillis so she did not attend) and after the examination was over we came to bro' E,s and stayed until next morning, he was not at home when we first got there, so when he did come I met him at the door and gave him a kiss, and the first thing I thought of you may be assured, was to begin to ask questions about you; Maria and I were out in the piazza, and I told him to come and tell me all that he could about Ruthvin; he told me he thought I would have the pleasure of seeing you in a few days which you know was good news to me; I think brother Edgar looks as well as he did when he left home, it seemed so natural to be with him again and what a pleasure it was to me too, but far far greater would the pleasure have been could my dear Ruthvin only be with us, but I must stop writing for to-night dear Ruthvin, as it has struck twelve o'clock, but Calvin Nelson's wife and Eliza came this evening to see us, and spend the night, and we all sat up quite late, Lizzie Haynsworth is on a visit to us at this time also, she came over Thursday afternoon, and sister E is over at bro' E,s, so they and Maria are all sleeping up stairs and I am in sister E's room writing to you and dear little Haynsworth and Lute in the bed fast asleep, and oh! how I wish dearest you were here too, last night Lizzie and Maria slept in here with us also, they in one bed and the children and myself in the other, and this morning long before daylight, the dear children and myself awoke, and they joined me in talking about you my dear Ruthvin, for it seemed to me as soon as I opened my eyes I began thinking about you, but I must now bid you goodnight dearest, and pleasant dreams, and a sweet nights rest be yours, and I trust that our Heavenly Father may watch over and protect us all, to behold the light of another Holy Sabbath day and many many more to come on earth and this is my prayer if consistent with His will.

Dec. 24th

I began this Saturday night thinking perhaps I might have an opportunity of sending it by Mondays mail from Kingstree, for I was afraid the time would seem so long before you hear from us, but after sister Elizabeth came from brother Edgar,s Sunday she told me she thought you would get this just as soon to send it to-morrow as to send it by mail, so I have postponed awhile on that ac'ct, and therefore my dearest I hope you will not think at all hard of me, but oh! no I know that you would not do that, for you well know what a great pleasure it is to me to write to you while you are away from us. Oh! my dear Ruthvin I am looking forward with the greatest pleasure imaginable to your coming home, for I am so much in hopes it may be so that you can come, and humbly do I pray and trust that a merciful Providence may soon bring my dear husband safely home to us all again in health, oh you ca'nt imagine my feelings of delight at the idea of seeing you; this morning I was awake long long before daylight, thinking about you, and how glad (torn) would be when you came home. Do be certain to come if you can You (torn) can't imagine darling how bad bad I want to see you, Anna Haynsworth and Martha Agnes are with us now, and tonight at the supper table we were talking about you coming home, and dear Maria is so delighted at the idea too as well as all the rest of us. Sister E & Lute went back to bro' Edgar's this evening & Lizzie H. went with her, so you may know we feel quite lonely now, dear sister E told me when you come I must send right after her. I will be very glad when sister L gets well enough for her to come back home to stay for I do miss her so much when she leaves me. Sister L is getting on tho' now very well, and I hope she will again soon be entirely restored to health, she has the largest baby I ever saw for its age, I would have been glad to have been with brother Edgar more, but he had to go to Columbia and be away so much from home that he has not had the opportunity of coming to see us. That was indeed good news which our last Mercury contained in England and France's going to recognise us,[103] which I hope there will be a chance for peace soon,

103 England nor France ever formally endorsed the Confederacy.

oh what indescribable happiness would it afford us could we only have peace and have you my dearest with all the other beloved ones safely at your own dear homes again, but to God alone we must look for help and place our entire trust in Him alone. The appointments of the So Ca conference came out in the last Mercury and you can well imagine my feeling of delight on seeing that bro Wm and sister were sent to Manning district for how much it will afford me a great source of pleasure in having them so near us, and I know they are all glad at home that they are sent so near them. Father wanted to come down and see you when you came home so I am in hopes it may so that he and mother can come. 15 more hogs were killed Monday it is indeed fine weather for them and I believe sister E said she will still have salt enough to kill twelve more when we will then be through I believe. Ruthvin you must try to make out to read this scrawl if you can but I have written at night and I hope you will excuse it. It is now Christmas eve Tuesday night Oh how I wish you were only at home with us too, oh! how happy would I be, but I hope and trust we may all be permitted to meet again soon. Maria rec'd a letter from Amanda by last Friday's mail in which she stated that she "had rec'd a dear good sweet letter from dear brother Ruthvin" and that she had written a long letter to you and brother Edgar. Mr. Haynsworth wants Amanda to teach at the school down here next year, and as she is acquainted down here, and being so anxious to get a situation, I hope she will comply with their wishes, so I will then have the pleasure of seeing her often too. I am very glad at the idea of her being so near me.

Cloe and Charlotte says I must tell you howdye for them. Sometime ago in one of your letters you spoke of how often you thought of the pleasant times when I would be in your lap in the corner of the piazza and very vivid in my mind are those pleasant times too dearest and I hope soon I may again have the great pleasure of sitting in your lap again, oh! how happy happy will I then be. Maria says I must tell you that she wishes you a happy Christmas, and that hers would be far happier if you were only here to cheer us with your pleasant smile and heartily my beloved Ruthvin do I join her in saying this, but I guess Christmas will be dull every where this year, and you know it can't be otherwise with me when you are away from me but oh the thought of so soon being with you, dear Ruthvin you can't imagine my ecstacies.

I must now close this dear Ruthvin and Mariah Anna and dear little Haynsworth all join me in sending you our very best and warmest love and oh! that Heaven's choicest and richest blessings may ever rest upon you my own dear husband, is the humble prayer of your ever loving and devoted wife,

Hattie Plowden

Pine Forest Jan. 11th 1862
My dearest Ruthvin.

To-day is Saturday, and as I have not written to you since you returned, I will most gladly avail myself of the opportunity of doing so this morning, and would have written by Fridays mail, only I thought that Sandy was coming home, and I could just send you a letter by him. Mr. Mixon got here (I think it was between 8 and 9 oclock) Wednesday night. he gave me your letter which met with a warm reception, I can assure you, and I was thankful to hear that your throat still continued better, and I sincerely hope and trust that 'ere this it is entirely well. Mr M. spent the night, and sister Elizabeth let him have Kirkpatrick to go as far as John Harvin's next morning, he said that he would send him from there home. I was glad to hear you found everything so quiet on your return to Georgetown. oh, I pray and trust that you may all keep well, and that 'ere long you with all the beloved ones may be protected to come safely home to us all. It is needless dear Ruthvin for me to try to tell you how greatly I have missed, and my sadness of feelings since you left me, but all this I presume you can well imagine. I stayed at sister Ann's until Tuesday morning. sister E. did not go down, so I came to prayer meeting with Mary Emily, met sister E and the children there and came home with them. how sad and lonely were my feelings on entering the house, for my thoughts were about you, indeed, this is a hard seperation, but in a Just God we must place our entire trust, and humbly do I pray that soon we may all meet again. Mr. McDowell had a small congregation at prayer meeting, and there were only five to recite the bible lesson. I made out to study mine at sister Ann's, but I tell you I found it quite difficult to place my mind upon it, for you well know in what direction my mind was wandering, yes! my thoughts were about my loved and absent Ruthvin. Have you heard or read an acc't. of any of the proceedings of the firing going on this week, I guess it is at Port Royal.[104] I am anxious to see some late paper, but I presume we shall get one very soon now. The negroes heard the firing going on. We heard yesterday tho' that

104 Battle of Port Royal was a Union victory.

the Yankees had certainly landed, and as the firing continued two or three days, I fear it was a pretty severe battle, but I hope and trust we gained the victory, oh! how sad to think of such times, as our country is now passing through, but oh! that a merciful God may be with us, and that this unholy war may soon cease, and peace sweet peace and quietness may everywhere reign, and that you my dear husband with my dear brothers, and all those so near, and dear, may be brought safely to your beloved homes, is my humble prayer. I am happy to say that we are all well. Sister E's cold and cough I think is getting better, and Henry was over Thursday and all were coming on firstrate at brother Edgar,s, he said his mother was getting on very well, and I hope now she will soon be restored to her usual health. I trust this too may find you all in the enjoyment of good health. There was a very nice young lady here (with her brother also) yesterday afternoon, one with whom I have spent many pleasant moments, and who I think became very much enamored with you on so short an acquaintance, so I want you to guess who it is, doubtless your curiosity will be a little excited, but I just want to see what for a hand you are at guessing, I heard when I was at home how greatly she was taken with you, but I forgot to tell you, of course I feel very glad to know that such a nice young lady as she should fall so desperately in love with you. she told me two or three times to give you her best respects, and that she came to see you but you were not at home, and I think she told me to let her know next time you came so she could come to see you, said she thought you were very lively and also very handsome. she wanted to see your ambrotype so I tell you she took a good look at that. now on the whole do you not think she was quite taken with you. she asked me for both of the children, and H. and Lute both came in to see her. Sister E says I must tell you she wonders that one who should be so much taken with you, and think so much of you, and you never do mention the young lady to her, so now you must guess who it is. they only spent the afternoon, and I was sorry they could not have stayed longer. it was sister or Amanda that told me how much she fell in love with you. Tell Isaac I say that, as this young lady was so much taken with you, but as you are a married man, perhaps she would take a still greater fancy to him, and that he had better try his hand. that is, if he does not love

Mary C. too deeply, but I guess his mind is too far set upon her to think of any other. but enough in this strain, so I must proceed with my letter. I have not heard from home since you left, only that my dear brother had left home, as I know how hard it was for my dear mother father as well as with all the rest of us to part with him, but then I know dear Ruthvin that our Heavenly Father is just as able to shield and protect you all tho' exposed to the dangers that you all are, as he is in the bosom of your families, and soon if His will I pray that He may bring us all together to many many happy meetings on earth safely and in health and to remain with us all at your dear homes. Monday last Sister E had six hogs killed, and she says if some one does not come for the others soon she will have the others killed next cold spell. Uncle Gabriel dined with us last Tuesday, and said he had made the fires to kill three times but would put it off, so I think it was Wednesday he killed anyway, and I fear he chose rather a bad time after all, as it has been quite warm since. Do write us very soon again and very often as I am so anxious to hear from you. the children says I must tell you howdye for them. they have both been very good little boys. All write with me in sending our best and warmest love to dear brother Edgar, Isaac, and accept the same dearest from your ever devoted

Hattie

(written in margin:)

Henry has just come over, and says all are well at bro' Edgars.

Plowden's Mills So Ca January 20th 1862
To Lieu't. E. R. Plowden
Dear Sir,

I take this opportunity of writing you a few lines which will inform you that I am not well by no means. I never got home from Mr. Keelse's until the 19th inst. I am still very low, though I hope to be able to be there in the course of three weeks from this. Though the Dr. says that I must not turn out under a month in the fix that I am in. I have a very bad cold as yet. an another thing I came home and found seven in Bed with measles at one time. My Father Mother two sisters one brother and two Negroes. And there is not one soul on the place to do any thing but myself and one Negro woman. I say in such a case as that, if I was well I could not leave home. I know that you would not do it, But if I am not there when you muster into service you can answer for me. That is if They will let me still hang on to my little office, and if I don't keep office my name must stay nutral until I come. For you know that I had hard work to raise to that night in the Company, though you need not say any thing about the above. You can tell the Capt. my situation and oblige your friends. I will be there as quick as possible. give R.J.W[105]—–, R. F. Felder and Capt. Plowden my respects. F. B. Brown also. write soon and give me all the best news, I will be proud when I go back there again to drill though I had much rather stay at home.` But this is no time to stay home when the foe is upon our soil. There is no true patriotic man that would stay at home in a time like this if it was a possible thing that he could go. I know that I can't for one. If there are any letters in the Post Office for me please send them to this office. I have no news at present to give you more than what I have related in the above about measles. write soon. nothing more but remain yours as ever

J N Hodge

P S

Excuse bad writing as I am not able to write as I would wish to do. I think that I will be able some of these days.

---

105 R. J. Witherspoon, 25th Regular Volunteers?

Camp Harlee Jan 23rd 1862
My dear Hattie,

I seat myself to answer your welcome, yes, thrice welcome, letter which I received (from the mattress) this morn; & see how punctual to ans. it I am; as it is not Dinner; & oh what a nice dinner it will be; for I can hear the nice things (complaining in the pan) from where I am writing; many many thanks to you & dear E for your kindness; I tell you I was glad to see the Boys & waggon for we were running quite short, so much so we had to borrow some rice two days ago; I had to turn in on a shoulder of meat; and you know I did not relish that much as I do not eat it at home (Sweet home) & may God bless you all my own sweet little wife, & may we all soon meet in peace & prosperity is the sincere desire of my heart. I am truly thankful to state I never was in better health as far as I can judge, & all of my relations enjoy the same rich blessing & the health of the camp have improved very much. every one that have not had measles except one has had them & are now up & doing pretty well, but I am fearful that some of them will be down again as this one of the most inclement days we have had this winter. It has been raining all day & it is almost cold enough to freeze but I am in hopes there will soon be a change; for it is dreadful to stand about in the rain & smoke. You cannot imagine how sadly disappointed I was when Norrel told me he had no Letter for me & it was about 2 hours before I found the one you wrote, but I knew there was one Somewhere. You have Sent me more than I think is requisite but will try & take the best care of it I can, but as some of the things got a little damp I am fearful they will spoil; but I believe I was as glad to see the mattress as anything you sent, as our straw mattresses get so hard & now by putting both together will make quite a comfortable bed. The officer that is to muster us in confederate service came yesterday & we were to be mustered in this morning, but it will have to be put off untill tomorrow owing to the weather & there is some of the men that will not be mustered in Oly Hemming is one of them & I think there will be some 4 or 5 more but the Col swears that they shall not return home & we are all rejoiced at it. Tell dear Sister Lucy that I wrote to her this week & directed to Manning & that she must answer it soon &

that I would have been delighted at the idea of seeing her before I Left, but an alwise Providence directed it otherwise. So give her & (torn) my love & a kiss for me. I also wrote to your Father a few days ago, but have not heard from Bishopville since my return; Tell dear Elisabeth I will write to her next Letter which will be about next Tuesday. My dear Hattie, you spoke of watching your namesake the other eve & from what you wrote I expect I was watching it at the same time & was thinking you were doing the same thing as it had been cloudy for several eve's & did not make its appearance. I must stop as we are just called out to be mustered in & I am so glad of it. I will tell you the names of those that are not mustered in. We are now in the service for 12 months & glad to say every man came in, if you only knew the anxiety that I,ve felt about the men not going in you would not be surprised that I am so glad about it. I must now close dear Hattie much much Love to you the dear Children and Elisabeth & kiss each one for me; (do write very soon) May God watch over & protect you all is the prayer of your devoted husband

Ruthven Plowden

January 25 (1862)
My Dear Brother

I will wright you a few lines to let you now that we are all quite well Lillias & all of the children are well the baby has got a slight cold Henry says I must tel you the negros is listing up in the fork path field & cleaning out the stables this week, George says he has finished listing up the old house field & ridged it up & is now plowing in torment field. they have been 3 days piling manure in the lot & what time they could work but it rained so much that they could not do much at it. Mr Windom let 4 of the women spin one day he stopt 4 of them 3 days to spin the plow lines but I don't think he will have inough. Hatty says I must tell you we maid some bread yesterday & I told her I would name the two loves & the one that rose the best yours or hers that one love the hardest & hers beet yours a long ways. she says I must tell you howdy for her & try & come up to see her soon she is very bussy knitting little sox the foot is not longer than my finger & she is now cutting up an old dress. Mrs. & Mr. Mood went to Maning yesterday she has got better she was quite sick last week. Marther went to see W Croskey when he was at home & she had a very sick time with the measles last week. M Agnes was at Mary Haynesworth & caught fire & burnt all most all of her close of her but only her back & arm was badly burnt but it is getting better tell Isack his Mother is well Elenor is still mending but the baby has the colick every night. Margret comences her school Monday & Mander is coming down friday to comence next Monday. we went to church to day & Mr McDowel preached a very fine sermon from I Samuel 30 chapter & 6 verse.[106] oh how thankful I would have been to had my Dear Brothers their but my sincere prayer is that My God will bring you back to us better Christians. My Dear Brothers read your Bibles & I trust God will Bless you & your familys forever. since all of the ships has left port royal it is general believed up hear that their next attempt will be at Georgetown, but I trust that all of their wicked

106 I Samuel 30:6 "And David was greatly distressed; for the people spake of stoning him, because the soul of all the people was grieved, every man for his sons and for his daughters; but David encouraged himself in the Lord his God." KJV

plans will be destroyed. the man come Wednesday for us to pay him for the tobacco & I told him I could not & he said he would leave the box til he come in march & if you wanted it you could keep it if not you could pay him for what you had used. he said you had not used much of it. Haynesworth & Lute sends you two pipes. I did not now that they had got Caroliner to get them till they brought them in. they never forget you.

Saterday night

Norel has not got back yet I told him if flander went he must come back but I reckon he wanted to see you too.[107]

107 This letter, though unsigned, is written by Ruthvin's sister, Elizabeth. Hattie's letter of the 27th confirms this.

Pine Forest Jan. 27th 1862
My <u>own</u> <u>dearest</u> <u>Ruthvin</u>,

Sister Elizabeth wrote to you Saturday night last, but as I have an opportunity of sending a letter by Sam Plowden to-morrow, you know as a <u>matter</u> <u>of</u> <u>course</u> I could not refrain from taking up my pen to write you a few lines anyway, and in the first place I send you my <u>sincere</u> <u>thanks</u> for your kind and affectionate letter, which you sent me by Norrel, and oh how delighted was I to hear that you were all well, and so <u>thankful</u> too to hear of your <u>good</u> <u>health</u>, and I humbly pray my <u>dear</u> <u>husband</u> that you may continue to enjoy this <u>great</u> and <u>rich</u> <u>blessing</u>. It was I presume about two o'clock Sunday when Norrel got home, and I tell you I had begun to feel very anxious, as I did not know why he did not come home. Henry told me tho' he thought you had him hauling wood, which was a pretty good guess. I heard from you tho' before he got here. Sunday morning as we were going to church, we met a gentleman by the name of Fleming, and sister E inquired if he was from Georgetown, and as he replied in the affirmative, we had several questions to ask about you, and when he informed us that you were all well, I assure you it was with a <u>thankful</u> <u>heart</u> that I then went to church, and I felt as though that this should learn me to place my trust more and more, in our heavenly Father and to have <u>firm</u> faith in <u>Him</u>, and oh! that He would grant unto us all more faith more religion and enable us to live more and more zealous each day of our lives, is my prayer.

I am glad that I can inform you the same good news that all are well, and hope this may still find you <u>all</u> <u>well</u>. how our hearts should be filled with gratitude to God for these great mercies and blessings, for all the <u>praise</u> and <u>glory</u> be ascribed unto His most <u>great</u> and <u>Holy</u> <u>name</u>. Mary Emily and Samie came over this morning. Mary E. is going to spend the week with us, for which I am very <u>glad</u>. we have just come in a short time ago from the piazza, and she says I must tell you that we have been taking a look at the lovely bright star, and talking about you, and also sends howdye to you, Isaac and bro' Edgar. I wish very much you could have all been here to attend the Sacramental meeting at Brewington. Mr McDowell had no assistant, but the meeting was quite interesting notwithstanding, that is the sermons were very good no one connected themselves with the church. Although you were absent yet rest assured dear Ruthvin my thoughts were about you, and when we were all seated around the table of our blessed Lord there too were you remembered by me. Brother Wm and sister went to Manning Friday. I missed them a great deal after they left. I am glad to say that sister was much better when she left, tho' still quite weak. she was not sick in the way that she was last summer. you recollect I told you, she was very fearful she was threatened in the same way that she then was. I feel very thankful that such was not the case. I have not heard from them since they went to Manning, but hope I may very soon, as I am anxious to hear from sister. I hope tho' ere' this she is entirely well. I am looking for Amanda next Friday, and I expect father will come with her. I look forward with great pleasure to seeing them, but I know it will be hard for my dear mother to see Amanda leave home. Perhaps I shall go home with father, tho' I am not altogether certain of it yet. I do not know how long I shall stay, but if I go do write to me very often, for you know how anxious and glad I am always to hear from you. I was glad to hear that you had written to sister. I am getting anxious to hear from Daniel, have not rec'd a letter from him since he left but I sincerely hope that he is well. Sister told me when she was here that cousin Charles and Mrs Dennis were very anxious indeed for Amanda to teach their children. they offered her three hundred dollars to do so, but mother did not like the idea much of her teaching there anyway, as she thought it would look selfish, just to teach for those two families, and I agree with her, and Amanda did not want to take it for them anyway. but for a wonder Mrs Dennis is now going to send to Mrs Holleyman really I was surprised at it, for I have heard Mrs D talk about Mrs H, and as you might suppose cousin Charles is going to send Lucy Spencer of course. Cousin Charles was very anxious for Amanda to give Emma and Gertrude music lessons again, and I suppose to teach other branches too, but as she declined he has got Maria to give them music (torn). Can't you tell (torn) when you have an idea of coming home again? you (torn) tell me in your next letter. I hope tho' it may not be very long before you can come, as we are all getting very anxious to see you, but you well know that I am that all the time. oh! dear Ruthvin you can't imagine how much I thought of you during the weather we had last week. one night I could scarcely sleep any at all, for I was thinking about you so much, but I am glad that you kept well, but I remarked at the time of it that perhaps the Almighty had sent that weather for our good, as the Burnside expedition then I know had great things in view, but from the last Charleston paper we re'cd, I presume the Yankees were quite disappointed.[108] I saw it stated where there were seven hundred troops aboard all supposed to be last. I suppose we will be apt to hear a good deal with reference to the gale last week. It certainly seems as tho' we have great evidence to believe that God is with us. I rec'd a letter from dear Almira last week, she was well. I know you were glad to hear from bro' Edward, I was truly thankful to hear that he was better, and I trust now, he may soon be entirely restored to health. I felt almost afraid to inquire how he was when sister E told me who it was from, and we should feel very grateful that he is as well as he is. Tell bro.' E. I saw sister Lillis at church yesterday. she looked almost as well as ever. I knit a pair of little socks for sister L's baby the other day, but they were so small that sister Elizabeth said she did not think they would last any longer than the meeting. Sister laughed at them considerably when I showed them to her, but of course I thought they would be large enough. I only wish I had some cruel to crochet a pair for him, and make them fancy, as I learned to do when at Orangeburg. those were for Anna Nora, and they were very pretty if I did make them. but I must now close as sister E wishes to write some too, and do my dear Ruthvin write to me very very soon. Haynsworth started to school to-day and has been getting his night lesson to-night. Sister Elizabeth & Mary E have just been laughing at me saying they know that every line was something about darling beloved but I answered in the negative. but I

108 The Burnside Expedition was a series of engagements fought along the North Carolina coast between Jan. and June 1862, and was aimed at closing blockade-running ports inside the Outer Banks. "Severe weather hampered progress so much at times it seemed as if the whole mission would have to be scrapped." Wikipedia online

must stop now as it is going on eleven o'clock at night, and now wishing you a pleasant nights rest and (torn) dreams, I must now bid you good night. All join me in our best and warmest love, and accept of the greatest portion from your ever ever devoted Hattie.

I was right amused yesterday Mary E asked me how old Susan Nelson was and I told her I thought about your age, and she then inquired how old you were but I understood her to say Mr Richbourgh, so I replied very earnestly saying about forty-five or fifty, and I knew by sister E's breaking out in such a laugh that I had made one of my mistakes, so when she told me I could not think of it all day without laughing. really I must pay better attention for I know you would dislike it very much for me to be telling that you are that age, but of course you know I corrected myself and told her right. Please excuse this scramble but try and make it out if you can. you must give our best love to bro' Edgar and Isaac. I was sorry to hear some of the things sent got damp, but I hope that very little got so. oh! how I wish my darling you were here sitting by me now and I was talking to you instead of writing, but I must say good bye now until I write again. Write soon to me again, and very often.

Hattie

(written in margin of 1st pg:)

It is again morning, and I take my pen to tell you that the way I did dream about you last night but havn't time to relate as we are now looking for the Nelsons Mr & Mrs Richbourgh to come and spend the day with us and how I do wish you and bro' E could be here too. I wonder if Mrs R will be as affable as she was when I last saw her. Father sent his waggan down last week to bring bro' Wms things to Manning, and what do you think Viney came all the way down here with Jim to see me. I was right glad to see the old soul. she said "she wanted to come and see how I was getting on without you." she went to see her brother at Rob Felders but she was not at all pleased with the looks of the place said "it was the nowhereist place she had ever came across" I suppose she got this word from her own vocabulary but is it not a shame she said that Lizzie had gone to Manning and left her with brother Jimmie with the negroes and that he just slept with them at the negro house, poor child I feel sorry for him how she can do so I can't tell.

I thank you very much for the shells you sent us.

Plowdens Mills Jan. 28 '62
Dear Friend,

As you seem to complain of me for not writing to you sooner I have concluded not to delay it any longer you must not think that it was because I do not think of you but it has been that old habit of putting of that has kept me you know I always was a slow hand to write. I feel that if I was with you I could sit and talk with you all night but when it comes to writing I am out. Myself and family are quite well at present with all of our relatives and friends except Lawrence Nelson he is quite sick again. I saw his father this evening. he is fearful he has pneumonia. I was at your house this eve. all are well there and in good spirits. Capt. Hainsworth was at your house all so cousins Ann daughter Emily. they said all was well and that all were well at Edgars. I was glad to hear that your health was so good. I do hope it may continue and also that of the company. Joe is still quite unwell with that rising worse off than he was last week he had began to improve a good deal but the Doctor thinks that lump may yet give him a good deal of pain. we received a letter from Georgia yesterday which I am glad to say stated that cousin Edward was mending very fast. Whitfield has gone to your house to take a hunt in the morning. we were out yestoday trailed all the morning but did not start it was the first hunt I have taken since I hunted with you. Whitfield speaks of going back to Virginia with Dr. Allen Huggins when he goes but I don't know whether he will or not as his head is no nearer well now than it was a month ago we have heard from Sumter today of a battle in Missouri where we gained a complete victory the whole army haveing been killed and taken prisoners.[109] I only hope this may be so. yo have heard so I have been told of the great to do your negroes had some 10 days a go. it turns out as I said from the first to be a very small affair nothing more than what they might have seen you at when you were a widower only playing old Sister Jibby and so on. I was very sorry to hear that some one had written to you about it knowing that hearing the tale you heard that it would make

109 Battle of Roan's Tan Yard, Missouri, on January 8, 1862, resulted in a Union victory. Unable to confirm any other battles in Missouri in January of 1862. Wikipedia online

you uneasy. I think who ever wrote to you about it had very little to do. I hope there is still enough of us here yet to attend matters of that sort with out troubling you about it. your affairs seem to be getting on finely in the way of farming. Spencer seems to be nearly ready to plant. when I go down to your house and see how things are going on it scares me. I never have done as little before in the way of getting ready to plant since I have been planting. The times are duller than I ever knew them. There is no news at all and every body gone makes it so lonesome that when not engaged I am at a loss what to do as there is no body to visit. I want to see you very bad do remember me to cous Edgar. tell him I would be more than glad to get a letter from him. and now dear friend I will close fearing that it will try your patience to read what I have written. you must write soon. Callie and the children join me in love to you take care of your self and may God bless and protect you is the sincere prayer of your sincere F.

J C Plowden[110]

110 John Covert Plowden, born 1825 in Alcolu, SC, and died 3 May, 1865, in the Elmira prison camp in New York. His wife, Caroline (Callie), sent money over a period of time to have a marble marker placed on his grave. https://www.findagrave.com/memorial

Jany 28–1862 Clarendon Dist. So. Ca. Lieut. E. R. Plowden
Dear Cousin

I have been for some time expecting to drop you a line and haveing an opportunity of doing so by Saml. Plowden I will proceed to tell you that your fammily as well as the rest of your frends are all in good health. Haveing seen them all at church last sunday. Nero received your letter on yesterday. we were glad to heare from N that you wear in good health and that the health of our soldiers weare improveing. I hope that for the future that you all may Enjoy good health now that they have got through with measels. I am glad to heare that you have so fine a cumpany and are mustered in the confederate service. This is as it should be now that our state is invaded and our enemy beseting us on Every side. With its over whelming numbers let us be prepaired to meet the scoundrels and drive them back from our shores. If they land at George Town I hope that our Brave men will give a good account of them. The last letters I got from Calvin and Theodore they were all in good health and wrote as if they intended to Inlist for two years or during the war. I expect letters from them today when I will be shure heare that they have Inlisted. They wrote to me for my advice on the subject and last mail I sent is our young men ought and would not stay at home, as long as the war continued. And our state invaded. for one thing is certain we either must conquor a peace or we are a doomed people.—But I need not say any thing to you on the war or on politicks as every man is posted on the subject and his fealing. Inlisted in the cause of liberty and the fredom of his cuntry—and heare I will dismiss the subject and will proceed to give you all the domestick nuse that I am in posession of. In the first place—The assesors for the war tax are now takeing return of all the taxable property under the late act Belton Bagnal or say Clarendon will take four 4 hundred dollars as a Basis to vallue negroes upon. Bluff Lands will Impound us three dollars and 25 cents per acre pine land two and one dollar per acre agreeable to quality. I suppose this tax will superceed the cotten lone which I have herd nothing of lately. I see from your letter that some person has written you a letter about a meeting of the negroes two saturday nights a neare your fathers olde place. I am sorry that it was done no good could result from your knowing it. but the contrary. It would cause you and Edgar some uneasiness and the question would at once arise with you (what are the men at home adoing that they would send for us to keep things straight when our duty lay in the armey. But I will give you a true statement of the hole affair as I got it from Mr. Evans on last Sunday night weak I got a message from Mr. Evans that the negroes had had a large muster, your negroes, Edgars Haynsworths Croskreys and Dr T Burgess. and if I would come over he could tell me who the captain was. so on Monday morning Lawrence and myself roade over to Mr. Evans to heare the particulars of the meetings. Mr. Evans said that one of his negroes had come in his house after supper and told him that the above negroes weare to have a muster in the swamp that night and had persuaded him to join them. But he would not do so after heareing this Mr. Evans collected three men and went over to the place pointed out by his Boy and at a late hour found the negroes jus about braking up from their frollick. two or three of yours and two women of Cap Hainsworth stood their ground some of them ran off when John More fired of his gun. Spencer went and eamined their stomping ground and says that they had trod down the grass all around the fire in a large circle around the fire, as if they had been a playing. And which I suppose was all. The day that Lawrence went to see Mr Evans finding that none of our negroes weare at the meeting we advised him to go up that evening and let Capt. Hainsworth know all about it as we thought him the propper person to see in to the matter. which Mr Evans did do. I saw Hainsworth on Sunday at church But the subject was not mentioned and I concluded that as they weare all fammily negroes, that there was no harme ment. The worste feature I see in the case was their rebuilding the foot logs after Edgar and your self ordering not to be done. This was impudence and a disregard of his orders and your own. But to be candid I do not think that any mischief was intended by them, but we will try and prevent any more sutch meetings—or gathering of the negroes now that their masters ar at so grate a distance from their. Nead has just tolde me that Spencer will investigate the matter today or tomorow after which Nead says that he will answer your letter. I hope that you nor Edgar wont give your selves any uneasiness about this matter for be ashured that your neighbors up heare will try to keep the negroes under good disiplin. And do what we can to keep order on this part of the cuntry. I will close my dul letter by reaquesting you to give my kind regards to Capt. Edgar and all other of my frend and please accept the Best wishes from your frend truly

J. J. Nelson

P S

my fammily desires to be affectionately remembered to you, Edgar and the rest of frend

J. J. N.

January 30 1862
My dear Brothers

I received you most welcome letter by Mr F I was so thankful to hear you was getting on so well. I trust you both will be bless with health & put your trust in God & he will bless you in all you have to do. you said I must tell you all about this affair with the negroes. 8 men met hear today & they could not find out a single thing from them only just about what I rote to you in H letter. Nero says he was not no captain neither was theim any oficers they were call by them names in the play their fifes was 8 blowing canes they said if they had nown it would have maid a fus they would not have done such a thing they said tell you had the old house puled down they used to meet their & dance, the men give them all a little whipping & I was sorry for it for I bellieve the negroes did not mean any thing by it. some of them said if you & E had been hear you would not have let them been whiped for old Aims lies the way she come to tell on them she wanted Prince & some more of them to go to her house to sing & they would not go & then she went & told this big lie, dont you believe any thing you hear about it for I have heard about 20 difrent storrys if any thing hapens that is rong I will wright to you, I am sorry you herd such a thing for we did not pay any attention to it. Mr H said he would wright to you about it. Haynes commenced school Monday he says I must tell you he is going to try his very best for he want that saddle. I was sorry it was so you could not spare Henry to go to Mander. Mr Lagree say she has a splendid education & says their is few ladies that understands arithmetick as she does, but I trust it wont be long before we will have piece & then when you all get home oh what a glorious & happy time we will have then, I herd from your home by H this evening they are all well, all well at Anna M., Agnes back is still very sore we are all well, I hope God will take care of both of you & bless yoou & soon bring you back to us.

S E P[111]

Hatty sends her best love to both of you H & Luty says I must tell you howdy for them H says he is head in one class & studing gramer.

---

111 Ruthvin's sister, Elizabeth

Manning So. Ca. Jany 29th '62
Dear Ruthven -

It has been in my heart to write to you long before this but really so many matters have called my attention that today is the first time I have had the chance of writing letters. I have written several already to other friends. I trust this will find you and your associates all well. and those who are sick getting on very well. We felt for you and all the rest in the recent dreadfully inclement weather we have had. We could not however realize how bad it was nicely esconced and snugly put away in your comfortable home. With the fine oak fires all these had we could not tell much about it. We only form some idea of it from the papers which reach us telling us of its effects upon the Piratical Fleet.[112] I presume more of the "particulars" will reach us tomorrow, our regular mail day. We left all well at Bishopville. Brother John O. DuRant who has been ill was improving. Had not heard from Daniel since he got to "Lightwood Knot Springs." [113] Hope we'l hear soon. We had a pleasant day to come down to your home. got there last Thursday was a week. remained till last Friday when we got here. Lucy was quite sick a while at Harriets but she is pretty well again. Mrs. Rena Chandler spent a night there. and Joe Lizzie and Covert with Jane & Amanda McCallum all were to see us there. Capt. Haynesworth dined one day also.

We of course have had a heap of fixing to do since we got here and having had kind ones near us we have had it more easily done. We are now fairly upon a new year and I trust I may spend a pleasant and useful one among my people. I have been around my work and find a hearty welcome. We are living in Mr. Calvin Nelson's house. It is snug and neat and has a great many rats & mice (illegible) it on the adage "the more, the merrier." But I must not give you all the "items" for I may thereby steal some of Lucy Janes thunder. She is now writing to you—Do write to us Ruthvin when you can. I don't know but that I may come down and see you one of these days. I

112 Referring to the "Burnside Expedition"

113 Lightwood Knot Springs was a camp established on the Columbia and Charlotte Railroad, south of present-day Blythewood. www.history-sites.com/cgi-bin/bbs62x/sscwmb/webbbs

want to see Bro. John also—I presume Amanda will be at your house Friday—Farewell—Peace be with you is the prayer of yours affectly

Wm W. Mood
Manning, So. Ca.

Manning Jan 29th 1862
My dear brother Ruthvin

Your very kind and thrice welcome letter was received last Friday evening, and I need not say we were rejoiced to hear from you. It has been a matter of much regret with me that I have not been able to write you before, but as Wm has doubtless told you, I have not been very well lately, until within the last few days, and they have been spent in getting things to rights in our new home. I spent a whole week with Hattie & Miss Elizabeth, and a very pleasant one it was notwithstanding I was not well some of the time. The little boys too & Anna had fine times; they seemed more fond of each other than ever before. You may be assurred dear brother, your name was often upon our lips, and oftener still in our hearts. During the dreadful weather we had, it made our hearts sick to think of what you and the other poor soldiers might have to suffer. we have not heard from you since, but I do hope you got along better than we imagined.

Amanda is not down yet, but I hope she will be this week, and that she & Hattie may come to see me on Saturday, as father pastly promised they should do in case he came down with Amanda. I am very well pleased our new home. I like the location better than any other in the town it is so much more retired. we have found here, as elsewhere we have been, kind friends who seem willing to anything in their power to make us comfortable. Mr. Mood seems pleased with the cl= and I trust he may be very useful among this kind people. Another year has dawned upon us with new duties & responsibilities, and in looking back upon the past, how much do we see to call forth our gratitude to the gracious Providence that has been over us. Oh may His goodness lead us nearer to Him, and to live for the future "with an eye single to His glory." The sentiments of friendship ripened into affection so warmly expressed in your letter my dear brother were truly appreciated, and I assure you are warmly reciprocated. Yes, from the time I first met you I was <u>your true friend</u>, but you must not thank me for it but yourself. The true, & noble character which I so soon discovered to be yours could not call up any other feeling; and from that time until the present I have only felt <u>more</u> & <u>more willing</u> to call you by the sacred name of brother. Like you I do sincerely wish you could be with us this year but God has ordered it otherwise and we must submit.

With kind regards to you brother I rem-
Your affct= sister L. J. Mood

Do write again soon.

Camp Harllee Feb. 1st 1862
My dear Hattie

Although a few days have elapsed since I wrote to you, yet I will avail myself of the present opportunity & write you that this leaves me still in the enjoyment of good health & I assure you that I am most truly thankful to God for this great & rich blessing. & oh how thankful I am when I receive a letter from you to hear that you all enjoy the same blessing. I think I have felt my dependence on Him who is the dispenser of every good & perfect gift more since I have been in camp than I even did before & I humbly trust that my entire trust is placed in Him as I full well know that he alone is able to save.

Dear Hattie I have no news of any importance as you are as well posted politically as I am. My opinion of this unholy war is that it will not terminate as speedily as I once thought it would for the signs of the times indicate (to me) that it may last for one or two years more, although others think differently dear Elisabeth said in her Last Letter (& just here) give her many thanks for me, for it, & tell her please write again (soon) that it was the opinion of some up there that the Burnside fleet was destined for this place, but as yet it has not made its appearance but if it does make its appearance & will give us a chance, I think we will give them a warm reception. Elisabeth wrote me that Mrs. Nelson had bought the hogs, which was good news to me; as it has some what relieved my anxiety about you both. as it will allow you both to get some clothing & other necessarys which I know you both need. You must not keep back one cent for me; as I have no use for it & you are quite welcome to it & I only wish you had three times the quantity. I hardly know where to direct this as you expected to go back with your father when he brought Amanda down. so please, write soon & let me know how long you will be gone. Tell Haynsworth I heard good news from him this morn by J. Burgess. says Miss Margaret says he is a smart boy. tell him he must study hard to get the saddle & not let Isabella beat him. tell Lute he must learn fast & if I live I will make him a present also. tell dear Amanda to write soon & give her my best wishes for her future welfare & much love to her, to dear E & the dear Boys & much very much to you dear Hattie. Tell George & Maum Elsa &

all the Negroes howdy for me & that I was glad to hear that Scrape was no worse than it was.

P. S. Good bye, dear Hattie & may God watch over & protect you all is the prayer of your devoted husband. Give my respects to Spencer & tell him do write me how he is getting on.

Yours
Ruthvin

Home Feb 2nd 1862
My darling brother

I have been a very naughty girl for allowing so long a time to elapse without having written to you; I confess I should not have done so, and would ask your pardon and beg you not to retaliate but return "good for evil." Your kind letter to father was duly received and very gladly welcomed and perused by all of us. We were glad to learn that your regiment had again been made up in so short a time. I am anxious to learn who your field officers will be. hope the election will result to your gratification. Oh! my dear brother I am so lonely now for my precious darling Sister Amanda has left me; yes she went down Friday last. father went down with her and will be back to morrow and I am so glad Hattie is coming with him. she will be so much company for us. I only hope she may spend several weeks with us. You can somewhat imagine how I miss Amanda for you know she is a great treasure in my sight. I know not how to be grateful enough to her for she has ever been so kind and good to me. I feel assured though that a rich reward awaits her in the Heavenly land. I am looking forward now with pleasant anticipation to seeing one of the Soldiers. guess who it is? why Mr Scarborough. he has been at his father's in Darlington now for a week and I suppose will be here the early part of this. It will seem so natural to see him here again. Every one was delighted when they heard he had come and I heard that a certain young lady almost took a "duck fit" as the saying is. So you see the young gent is quite popular. It dont look like my poor sweetheart is ever coming back from their. Don't you pity me? why I have not seen him since he went off at all. but never mind. I can live in hopes.

Mr Spears will commence teaching in the academy soon. he wrote father that he would be here to morrow. I expect he will board here. Sister Lizzie and Nora are with us now and dear little Nora is so much company for me. But I must close. Do my dear Bro write to me very soon. all send love and be sure to accept a heart-full from your affect. Sister

Maria

Live Oak Lawn Feb. 4th 1862 To Leut E Ruthvin Plowden
Dear Cousin

I am now seated to answer your very welcome letter received last week. It is always a pleasure to receive letters from absent friends. I would have answered your letter last Friday but for unavoidable difficulties. I knew your relations that is your family had written you all that you wish to know from me. Capt. Hainsworth Pa & Mr. James Evans John Mr. Pendegrass & Mr. Windham met at your place on last Wednesday and had all off your young Negros up but could not prove any thing of a serious nature against them. It seems as if they meet to play at or near where those footlogs comes out at the old mill. I do not think you need give your self any uneasiness as regards your Negros for I do not think they had any bad intention in view in the meeting. They give them a light whipping. They were very humble. I will try & be more strict in patroling in future. Mr. Windham has had those footlogs cut therefore the communication is broke up. I will write about something else. Mr. McDowell has had his communion at Brewington church last Sunday was a week we had a very pleasant meeting. I do not believe there was any additions to the church.We did not have any help he only preach one sermon on Saturday & pray meeting in the evening & bible class. Mr. McDowell & his lady spent a night with us last week. he was on a visit to his congregation on this side of the water. I hope you have not had as much rain down about Georgetown as we have up with us. our Negros are doing what Mr. Hodge said once his was doing do nothing one day & pile it the next. I think that I have succeeded in getting up all of your sheep. I have been hunting up pas & found five 5 head of yours & assisted Henry to carry them hom on Saturday evening. I do not know how your hogs are fearing. I can hear of a sertain individual hunting every once an a while. I have offered to send Cisero to help get them up but have not been called on yet to sent. they may be up in the field for what I know. I think they would be saft if in the pasture. I suppose you have heard that our forces under Zolicoffer was whip & he kild. we lost most of our bagage &

several cannon.[114] a dispach has come on now stating that Johnson went with reinforcements and they turned in & whip them & took all the bagage we had lost & all of theres an killed 1700 men. I do hope this report may be true. Dear Cousin there is no news in this neighborhood at this time every person that is at home now is trying to prepare for planting as much as the rain will admit. Mr. Rodgers came down on last Saturday & brought Miss Amanda her school will commence Monday so I hear Cousin (torn) is going back with her father. but I suppose you will get a letter from the family by Mr. Freeman. We got letters from the boys last Tuesday they were all quite well at that time. They had reinlisted for the war then but I expect they have by this time. I saw Burgess Plowden Sunday he had got better & was up again but looked badly. I was glad to hear the health of your company is improving. I hope they may enjoy better health now. I heard that one of your men that is at home a Mr. William Evans died Saturday from measles or the effect of them. He was buried at Brewington church. Dear cousin I must now close this. I hope to receive a letter from you soon. You must give best respects to Cousin Edgar & say to him I will write to him soon. You must look over all errors in spelling & writing & believe me as ever your affectionat

Cousin
Samuel E. Nelson

P S I sent Cisero down to hunt hogs for you to day with Mr. Windham I believe they got some yours to.

Ned

114 The Battle of Mill Springs (Battle of Fishing Creek per Confederates) in Kentucky on January 19, 1862, resulted in the first significant Union victory. Confederate Brig. Gen. Felix Zollicoffer, amid fog and dim early light, lost his life not knowing he approached a Union, not Confederate, officer. https://nps.gov/misp/battle-of-mill-springs.htm

Bishopville 5 Feby. 1862
Dear Ruthven

Harriets letter this evening will inform you that that dear child is here on a visit, having come up with me on my return from carrying down Amanda—I was glad to find all well.

To night we have company with us. Mr Scarborough and Mr Perry Carter are here from Virginia. The consequence is I have but little time to write. I would postpone writing until another day, but tomorrow is mail day, and I want you to do a favor for our concern. We hear that <u>rice</u> is very <u>cheap</u> in Georgetown, and beg you to see at what price we can buy some 2500 #s—or at what price by the bushel it can be had. We have heard of some at $1.00 or $1.25 per bushel. If there is an inducement, we will send down our wagon. You can inform us when the rice can be bought when you write so that if you are away there need not be a lost trip. Please write soon—all send much love. May kind Providence ever protect you.

Yours Most Affectionately.
William Rogers

All well at Capt Haynsworths

Brewington So Carolina Thursday Eve February 6th 1862
Dear Uncle Ruthvin,

As I wrote to Uncle Edgar last, I will attempt to write a short letter to you this time. I hope you will excuse my long silence. I expect you are surprised to see from the heading of my letter that I am still in Brewington & I thought that I would have been on my way to Orangeburg, but sickness has prevented me. Father expected to take me to Sumter today but both of us have been sick and are not well yet. I took sick first with a pain in my shoulder and before I got well of that, something very much like measuls broke out on us and father is quite sick with it today. Mother and Mattie have had it and we think brother is taking it. Several of the negroes have had it. Uncle William Coskrey brought it with him when he came to visit his family and they have all had it there.

Mander Rogers came down last Saturday as far as your house and spent Sunday with Mr. Mood in Manning. Mr. Rogers brought her here Sunday evening. Aunt Hattie went back with Mr. Rogers to spend three weeks. Mander commenced school Monday morning and seems to like it very much. The children are all delighted with her. I dont believe she is quite as strict as Miss Mary. We heard from Miss Mary last week. She was quite well and enjoying herself finely.

I heard from auntie yesterday. She was at aunt Anns. They were all well at both places. When I heard from aunt Lillis last they were all quite well. Although this is a short letter I must close for I have written all the news. Please ask uncle Edgar to write soon & I would be very glad to hear from you. We all join in love to you all. We are all well except measuls.

Your sincere niece
Lizzie

Feb. 6th 1862
Dear Ruthvin

I will write a few lines which leaves us all tolerable well and I hope this may find you enjoying the same blessing. I expect you would like to hear something from home how we are getting along we have the old field below the avenue listed and broke up and torment broke up and the field up at the mill listed and the cotton patch ground broke up and the ploughs will go up to the mill to day to cover the list The hands will finish to day listing the potato ground at Edwards old yard and the guinea corn patch we would have been further on listing but the hogs were spoiling the list we had made so much we had to stop and fix the fence. We are also done splitting rails. we have not got manure enough hauled to say any thing about but if you could see how much we have in the lot you would think we ought to have been hauling a month ago. I see from the letter you wrote to me that your feelings were very much roused about your negros but I do not think the negros meant any harm or any thing but to have a play and I think that if the brave men of SC can keep the Yankies from hurting the women and children that there is any danger of the negros doing any harm. the negros are doing very well and working and getting along without much trouble. you must give my love to your brother Edgar and all your brother officers and except the same for yourself.

Yours truly
T O Windham

Sunday eve Feb. 9th 1862
My dear Hattie,

Many many thanks dear Hattie for your long & thrice welcome letter, which I recd this morn, & oh! how thankful I am to God for his watchful care of you all & ourselves also. we have been truly blessed in every particular as regards this world's goods & oh! how we ought to strive for that inheritance that cannot be taken from us." Let us strive my dear wife to lead such lives as not to bring a reproach upon ourselves or the cause of Christ. many & numerous trials assail us in camp. sin in every form meet us at every step & oh! dear Hattie pray that God will give me grace to support me & enable me to discharge my duty faithfully to Him, & to my country. This leaves me well with the exception of cold & sore mouth. Brother E has been quite unwell for several days with cold & slight fever but I hope he will be all right in a few days. the health of the company is much improved. only 10 reported on the sick list this morn. The last man in the camp is now down with measles. The Col. has appointed a committee of 5 to go in the morning to hunt another camp ground about 4 miles from this place. it is owing to the sickness in the regt. so I am fearfull that our chance for Florence is a bad one. It was thought we would be sent there, so if our services were needed we could be sent to any point that is expected to be attacked. I was sorry to see from your letter that you had not recd my last. before you left for Bishopville I wrote by Jimmie Burgess & you ought to have recd it last Sunday or Monday. but from your letter you did not return home from Manning but from there to Sumter. I would like it very much if it was so I could be with you & be with all the dear ones at home but that may be some time yet. but if I can do so I want to try & go home about the 15th of March & hope I will have the pleasure of meeting all the family there. I wrote to Maria a few days ago that I expected to be at home at that time & to Elisabeth two days ago, the same. I recd a letter form Elizabeth last night telling me you were gone & that she was quite lonely & that all were well. I have been fortunate this week. I recd 8 letters the past week, & only hope I may recd as many this. I had begun to think something was rong as it has been a week since I recd one from you but concluded you had gone up home & would write from there just as you did & please do so again as soon as you receive this & let me know all the news & when you are going home. Tell your father I recd his letter which I am very thankfull for & that I will attend to his request early in the morning & will let him hear from me by the evenings mail if I have time, if not will by the next. We are not our own masters here & have to be governed by circumstance. Tell him rice is worth 1.25 cts pr bushel or 2$ pr 100 lbs but I will give him particulars as soon as possible. I attended church this morn & heard a fine sermon from 11 chap Matthew 6 verse.[115] there was not as many out as usual owing to the state of the weather, which is very wet & disagreeable so much so dear Hattie I've not seen your namesake for days & days but be sure if my life is spared, when it does appear, I will fulfill my promise. I thought of you often often in church to day & could hardly refrain from tears for I thought your petition was also asscending to a throne of grace in my behalf. I must close Good bye dear Hattie much much love to you & all the family & dear cousin Charlotte. May God's blessing rest and abide with you all is the prayer of your ever devoted

Ruthvin

P. S. Give my kind regards to Mr. Spencer & family Mr. Scarborough & their friends.

115 Matt. 11:6 "And blessed is he, whosoever shall not be offended in me." KJV

Manning So Ca Feby 10th 1862
Dear Uncle,

I was at your house on 31st Januay and saw your family and all were well. I went down to get your returns for war tax but Capt R P Haynesworth had returned to B. Bagnal which was all right. While I was there I saw Nero making plough stocks. I asked Aunt Elizabeth if he knew how to make them and we went to shop and I shewed him the tule and I noticed nero looking singular and on our return to house Aunt told me that he had been whiped the day before by the neighbors for having a gathering on swamp by footway. he with ten others was whiped a little. when I left and got over to muster ground nero caught up with me and appeared very much excited and asked me if I did not want to talk with him very much excited he then told me all about the affair and appeared to hate it very much. I talked to him some time and finally became convinced that it was only a gathering for amusement. nero said he would rather take two hundred lashes than to of had such a name after. I am satisfied that there was nothing wrong in the affair. And write you thinking you might be uneasy probably having not heard only of the affair. Write to me and let me know how you are getting on and all the news. We are all well and trying to get ready to plant but very there being so much rain.

Yours very Truly
D. E. Hodge

Febuary 12 1862
My Dear Brothers

I will write you a few lines to tell you that we are all well but Sely & Judy. I am afraid Judy will lose her eyes. she says it come from pain in her hedd it is as read as a lump of blood. I am a fraid it is from her old disease Scrofoler.[116] she says the flax seed & shugar of lead has helpt it more than any thing else.[117] I did not now any thing was the mater with her eye till Saterday & she said it had been hurting her 3 weeks. I was over at church last Sunday. Mr McD preached a very fine serment from 14, Hosea, 1, 2, 3 verses.[118] oh how thankful I would have been if my Dear Brothers could have been there with us but I trust in God we all will meet together again to praise his glorious nam for thousand of his rich blessings that he is bestowing on us. I expect you have herd of the deaths that was over at midway last week Mrs Ivans old Mrs Polly Ivans Miss M, McFadden Mrs William McFadd she left an infant 3 days old, down at the other church Mr. Barfeel & two Welches. we have had the greatest fawls of rain that we have had for years. yours & E beef cattle is all out of the swamp. I saw 2 fine yerlings that was not marked. one was your & the other was with a dulap cow. Covert told me yesterday he seen 3 unmarked ones on the roe hill that was yours & E. I sent Sam with Haynsworth to shoot but when he come last night the weter had run half way the saddle skirts. I sent him this morning & begeg Lillis to keep him till Friday. Sam brought old pat back. you must not scold me about the

---

116 Scrofula, an infection caused by the tuberculosis bacillus, typically results in a mass in the neck, but can also cause sore eyes, among other things. https://en.wikipedia.org/wiki/scrofula

117 Sugar of lead, or lead acetate, has a sweet flavor, and is toxic in large quantities. https://www.thoughtco.com/sugar-of-lead-3976065

118 Hosea 14:1-3 "O Israel, return to the Lord your God, For you have stumbled because of your iniquity; take words with you, and return to the Lord. Say to Him, 'Take away all iniquity; receive us graciously, for we will offer the sacrifices of our lips. Assyria shall not save us, we will not ride on horses, nor will we say anymore to the work of our hands, 'You are our gods.' For in You the fatherless finds mercy." KJV

nice partriges. I thought as you & E was not hear to shoot them you would not care if we cought them. their is another flock at the shop about 20. you must make Sandy fry them. I have also sent you a fresh ham to fry & turkey. do whenever you want any thing let us now it. I was very much oblige to you for your kind ofer in giving Hatty & myself that mony but we will not use no more of it than we can help. H caried 6 with her to pay for the carriage. it got broke when she was up before. she has not rote me word when I must send for her. I expect she will write by Friday mail. I miss her a gradeal. George says he is hauling manure in the cotten field but they cannot put in a half load the wagon cuts gown. the rest is howing up (illegible) at the graveyard. Spencer has not let them spen a day since you left only 4 spun 3 days (torn) plow lines. I think he will make (torn) of manure. I did not now John was going to send down till to night. Luty says he sent you the birds. he says I must tell you he is getting good lessons & howdy for him—also E & Isac. I trust God will protect & bless you all is my sincere prayer good night my Dear Brothers

SEP

Mr H family all have french measles. Samma is staying their to have them. Lillias is well. some of the children have colds. she was at church & had all of the girls. Anna family is well.

Bishopville Feb. 12th 1862
My own dear husband

Again have I taken my pen to write you a few lines, and humbly do I hope and trust that this may find you with all the rest well. I could not tell you dear Ruthvin how many times I have wished I could get a letter from you I thought perhaps I would get one Monday night last but I was disappointed but however I do hope I may receive one from you by to-morrow nights mail. I expect perhaps you have written home to me, and that I had left before it got there. I have heard from sister E and the dear children once since I came home through a letter that sister wrote to mother. Mr. & Mrs. McDowell had been to see them, after being at the prayer meeting and they informed her that they were all well, which I was glad to hear. I am getting anxious to see them. I have just written to Sister E when to send for me, father is going to send me as far as the Brick Church and I wrote to Sister E to send to meet me there to-morrow week which will be on Thursday. and oh how I wish dearest you could only be there too, oh! I do miss you so much, and I want to see you so bad. Mother asked me if I could not stay longer, but I told her I would like to do so, only that it seemed to me I heard from you so much oftener being at home, as someone is frequently passing from Georgetown to Clarendon, and besides I get so many of your dear good letters, you can't imagine how very anxious I am to hear from you, as I have not heard from you since I came home, so my dear Ruthvin you must write to me very soon, and I do sincerely hope I may be so fortunate as to get a letter form you to-morrow night; after you get this I guess you had best direct your next letter to me at home, as I presume I will be there by to-morrow week if nothing prevents. Oh! how I do wish this war would close, and that we could have sweet peace again, and that you could all be returned in safety to your homes, and if consistent with God's will I humbly pray and trust that soon He may grant all this unto us. You little know dearest how much I think about you. Maria has gone this evening to pay a visit to Salina Carnes, but will be home after a while. Lizzie and Nora are with us now. Nora is very pretty and a dear sweet little thing. We all make a great deal of her. she is now sitting very near me eating.

Lizzie speaks of going home to-morrow. She and father went up and spent a short time with Mr. Rembert this afternoon, but have returned. Mr Weaver commenced his school Monday I presume. he will make an excellent teacher. Wm has also began going to school again, he seems to be very busy at night, and in the morning, studying and ciphering. I expect perhaps he will commence Latin this session. Sister wrote to mother that the folks about Manning were very kind to them. I hope they may have a very pleasant year there. Mr and Mrs McDowell she said, expressed themselves as desiring that they might all be very sociable with each other. I know they will be pleased with them, as I do not think anyone could be otherwise with Mr & Mrs McD., who are well acquainted with them. We have not rec'd a letter from Amanda yet, but expect we will to-morrow, we heard from her tho' through sister's letter. I want to see dear little Lute and Haynsworth very much, also dear sister Elizabeth. I hope H. gets on well with his lessons. When I was at home he would take his seat by my side and learn his night lesson until he knew it, by my asking it to him. one night he came home, and he said, "Mother I am getting on very well with my lessons now." said it so sweetly too. I sincerely hope they may both be smart good boys, for this is what I want them to be, and my prayer for them, as it is for all the rest of us, is that we may all all be true and devoted followers of Christ. I hope darling you will excuse a short letter this time as I want to send this by Wm directly to the store. I attended preaching with the dear ones at home at the Methodist church last Sabbath, and heard a very good sermon by Mr Sifly the junior preacher on this circuit this year. I hope you will have the pleasure of attending church often. Lizzie heard from Daniel last Sunday he was well, she thinks he will be at home on a visit the last of this week, but I doubt if he comes this week; father rec'd a letter from Almira Monday she was well also. I do hope dear Ruthven it may be so you can come home to see us very soon after I get there, oh I do not know what I would give to see you, and to have you here with us. the other day I was in Cousin Charlotte's room, sitting at the foot of the bed when oh how I did wish you were there by me, she laughed and said she did too, but do you not remember how we asked to be in her room, and have such long talks, I believe she looks better than she did when I saw her before. Mr Scarborough and Perry Carter stayed here the other night, I think Mr S looks older than when he left somewhat, tho' he is looking very well. I tell you Perry is an amusing fellow, and is a great talker, I guess cousin M. J. would have been right glad to see him, they expect to return to VA before very long. My dear mother and all unite with me in sending our best and warmest love to you my own dear darling husband, and now praying that God may protect you and enable you to live as one of his devoted followers, and soon bring you back to us all again in health and in safety, this my dearest is the prayer of your ever devoted wife,

Hattie

Feb. 13th 1862
My dear brother,

I have been intending writing you for some time but some how, I have not been able to accomplish it, but will gladly embrace this opportunity of doing so. I am writing at the school house and it seems strange to me yet to be here day after day—away from my dear home. It was a hard hard trial to leave them all, and I felt almost unequal to the task but overcame these feelings after a desperate effort. I felt almost like backing out. I felt that it was an untried path I was about entering and did not know what awaited me. I told Hattie to tell mother she must not expect me to leave home again, that I had now quite made up my mind to continue in "single blessedness." I could not help though soon feeling at home at Mr. Haynsworth,s. they are all so good and kind and I love them so much. I like teaching too very well. the children are all obedient and easily controlled. I heard from home last night for the first time since I left and oh I was so overjoyed when Mrs. Haynsworth told me there was a letter for me. All were quite well. they had just heard from Daniel and he had improved some. Maria said they were expecting Mr. Scarborough to dinner the day she wrote. We heard he had come home before I left and was anxious for him to come then, and regret so much that I cannot see him. Mr. Weaver came two days after I left too and a young gentleman from Cheraw had spent a night with them, so you see I have missed a good deal. You cannot imagine brother Ruthvin how much I missed you when I was at your house. You know it is the first time I have been there since you were away. I have thought of you all so much being exposed the dreadful weather we have had. it must have been very hard for you. Bro Wm was to leave home to day to preach for the soldiers on James Island next Sunday. Sister wants me to go and stay with her Friday and Sat nights. Bro Wm came for me last Friday evening and I staid until Monday morning. they are all quite well. Lizzie left yesterday morning for Orangeburg. I miss her very much. she hated to go right badly. Emma Spencer is not going back at all or at least until the "times" get better. I have not seen Miss Elizabeth since I was there—wish she would come over. I hope Hattie will have a pleasant time at home. I have written to Daniel to day, for the first time since he left, as I did not know where to direct his letter until last night. Maria wrote me to direct to Charleston, Capt DeKalps Company. I hope Bro Wm may see him while he is gone. How long before you will be home again. I trust it may not be a very great while. Mr. McDowell expects to go down to James Island soon I hear. I believe his appt is Sunday week. I have recd a letter from Mary McLucas since I have been here. She has had a brother sick in Virginia but he was getting better. I trust we have met with our last reverse in this dreadful war. It makes me so sad to hear of any misfortunes attending our brave armies. God grant they may soon regain all they have lost. I guess the arrival of Beauregard in the west will inspire them with new courage. but I know we must not look too much to the efforts of man, but to the ruler of the universe for deliverance, and may He speedily make us an independent and prosperous nation. It is almost time for school so I must close, I have been writing all intermission. Do please my dear brother write me very soon. I prize your letters so highly. Remember me kindly to Mr. Plowden. Good bye. May Heaven bless you.

Yours affectly.
Amanda M. Rogers

Home Feb. 15th 1862
My dear brother,

Thursday night last brought three letters from you, one of which was for myself, and I thank you much very much for it. I am always so glad to receive your letters, they are so interesting and always so much in them by which I may be profited. I wish you could have seen Hattie when William came in with your letter, she seemed so perfectly delighted to get it. She was sitting at the piano playing for Mr. Weaver (who is extremely fond of music and thinks Hattie sings alto so beautifully) but when your letter came I tell you she bounced up in a hurry, and eagerly devoured its contents. Now don't you think I have been rich in letters this week? Why I received five Monday night and three Thursday night. it will take me some time to reply to them all. We had a long good letter from that darling child Amanda this week. She was homesick some when she first went down, but now that she has gone regularly to work and surrounded by such kind friends, I feel confident that her time will be spent very happy. Have we not had some beautiful weather this week—why it had been raining so much recently that the sight of "Old Sol" was a perfect treat to me. But to day the sky is all obscured by clouds and I fear we are going to have another long spell of gloomy weather. We have been hearing bad news this week for the Yankees have taken Roanoke, and some of our good men prisoners.[119] oh: is it not sad to think of their being in the hands of such cruel enemies. The times indeed seem to be growing darker and darker, but I try to console myself by thinking that brighter times are yet ahead of us, yes that "There is a silver lining to every cloud." We can only rely upon the arms of a Blessed Father, and I hope and pray that he may yet bring us out conquerors. Dear Hattie is still with us, and is now sitting beside me writing to you. she has written to Miss Elizabeth to send to meet her next Thursday. I really think she might have stayed with us a longer time than that—only two weeks. I do hope my dear Brother that it may be so, that you can go home at the time

119 The Battle of Roanoke Island, North Carolina, Feb. 8-9, 1862, was a decisive Union victory. https://www.history.com/this-day-in-history/battle-of-roanoke-island

of which you spoke, for it is such a pleasure for dear Hattie I know. I only wish you could come to see us too, but suppose you cannot be absent long enough for that. Oh! if peace could only be made by the 15th—and you could return home for good, what exquisite happiness would that be. Mr. Scarborough has spent one night with us since his return home. he had been in the hospital three weeks before he left—but was looking well when he came here. his furlough will be out the 22nd of this month,—but he promised to call again before he left. You are mistaken about my having a "tender" feeling for that young gent—no, I like all the Soldiers. We are looking for Daniel to come and spend a few days home now—Sister Lizzie went down to meet him Thursday, but he did not come. he wrote however that he might not get there until to day and not to be uneasy if he did not come. hope though he will be here to day. Father says Mr. Ambroze will go down to Georgetown Monday so we will send these letters by him. I hope that this will find your brother quite well again, do present my kind regards to him. I guess you are weary reading this very poor letter so I will conclude, as I know Hattie will tell you every thing any way. All send a great deal of love to you and accept—my darling Brother—bushels of love from your devoted Sister Maria
Heaven bless and keep thee.

Bishopville Feb. 15th 1862
My ever beloved husband.

You just cannot imagine how delighted I was to receive your dear kind and affectionate letter by Thursday nights mail, for I was so anxious to hear from you, but I saw from your letter that you had written to me at home, but had left before it came. Maria and father also re'cd theirs. Maria is now by me replying to your letter, and dear mother is very near us sewing. Father informed us the other night that Mr. Ambrose was going down to Georgetown Monday, and that we could write as many letters as we pleased, so we wish to send ours by him. I was sorry to see from yours that you had sore throat and mouth, and that bro Edgar was not so well, but I sincerely hope and trust that 'ere this you are both well again. you wrote me you would try and come home the 15th of next month, and you can imagine how glad I was to hear it but I was very much in hopes that you would come sooner than that time, but if it is so that you can'not come before then, I pray and trust that it may be the will of our kind heavenly Father, to permit you to come safely home to us at the time you wrote. I am so very anxious to behold your dear familiar face, and to be with you how I wish you could only be here with us now, and that you could be at home when I return, for oh! dear Ruthvin I miss you so much and am so very lonely without you, but ever rest assured that my prayers ever ascend on high to our Gracious Father in behalf of my dear dear Ruthvin, and for all of us. I did not know before you had any idea of coming up to Florence. I believe I wrote to you the other day asking if you were not in the service not to go out of the state, but I expect you forgot to inform me, so you must do so in your next. I am sorry that I have no news to write you that would in some way interest you, but Bishopville is quite a dull place at this time. nothing of importance seldom ever transpires here now. I went with Maria to the society the other afternoon, but they only weighed out some wool, and divided amongst them. they are going to have it wove for the Soldiers.

Maria and myself spent yesterday at aunt Peggies they were all well. they were looking for Coverts family and cousin Jane up; cousin J. has been down there two or three weeks, but they had not come when we left. I was in hopes that they would come before we left, as I wanted to hear from home. I have spent a very pleasant time with the beloved ones at home, and could your own dear self only be here with us the pleasure would be complete. but you know that I can't enjoy myself much, when you are far absent form me, for my thoughts are ever wandering about you. I felt very much relieved after receiving your precious letter the other night. cousin Charlotte asked me if I told you about the cry I took, but that was Monday night when I did not get a letter from you, but she would tell me that she knew you were well, which I hope was true. Mr Weaver told Lizzie he thought if I did not get a letter from you soon, they would all have to sit up with me. I told Lizzie to tell him well they all must prepare to sit up Thursday night provided I did not get one, so Thursday evening about dark I was playing on the piano when William came running in with a letter for me from you, and I tell you it was with eagerness that I took it from him, and perused it, and I believe it was your favorite, Juanita, Maria and myself were singing. Mr Weaver enquired particularly after you. he is a very pleasant boarder, and we all like him very much, makes himself at home, which you know makes it more pleasant for us. the other night at the supper table he told me he expected I felt like eating, after reading a letter from you, but I believe it was more the other way that night, for being so glad that I had heard from you. Mother rec'd a letter from Amanda Thursday night. she was well, and she said that after the first day a great load was removed from her mind, but I believe the first day or two any one feels worse and more sad, she said she flattered herself that she had already gained the affection of all her scholars. I was amused at what she said about little Johnie Crosky. some of them asked him what he would do if the yankees got there? he said that he would try to save them all, but he would save miss Amanda first. I do wish it was near enough and that it was so that our children could go to Amanda, as I well know what a good idea of teaching she has, and what her qualifications are. If nothing prevents I expect to go home Thursday next. father is going to send me as far as the brick church and I wrote to sister Elizabeth to send for me there, and that if it was convenient I would be glad if we could send for Amanda Friday evening, as I do want to see her badly, and I know she will be anxious to hear from home. Oh! how I do wish my *own* *darling* you could be at home with us. when being up stairs late in the evening sometimes, I love to look at the setting sun, and behold also the beautiful evening star Venus and think of you *my dear Ruthvin*. but you could not imagine how much I want to see you, but I sincerely hope I may have this great pleasure soon. Daniel wrote to Lizzie he expected to be at Lynchburg Thursday or Friday. she went down there to meet him Thursday evening, so I hope they will be here to-day. I am very glad he is coming home while I am here, as I am anxious (torn) him. he said he could stay several days. Well dear Ruthvin I (torn) now draw this uninteresting letter to a close, and do write to me *very soon*. I wish I could get a letter from you Monday night, but if not I hope I may get one as soon as I get home. Mother cousin Charlotte Maria and all unite with me in sending you our *very very* best love, and many many kisses do I send you, and also give my love to dear brother Edgar and Isaac. did bro' E get my letter I wrote him? if so tell him he must answer it as I would be glad to receive a letter from him. I want to see sister E and the *dear* *children* *very* *much*, and hope I may find them all well when I get home. oh! that God may watch over and protect you and *soon* permit us to *meet* *again* in *health* is the prayer of your ever *loving* *and* *devoted* *wife* *Hattie*.

Bishopville 15 Feby 1862
Dear Ruthven

Your esteemed letter to Harriet & myself came to hand last Thursday and has cheered up the little girl very much for until then she was right uneasy for she expected a letter the Monday before. We were all very glad to hear that you were getting on as well as you are. Sorry to hear that your Bro. Edgar was unwell, and hope he is again up and getting well. A letter from Amanda Thursday. She was well at time of writing. Says she has good sweet children going to her and appeared in good spirits. Was at the Moods last Saturday when she finished her letter.

Mr. J. W. Ambrose goes down to Georgetown next week starting on Monday next and such being the case he can save you from some trouble about rice but you can give him information probably that will be of service to him.

Daniel has written to us that he expects to be home about this time, and Lizzie has gone down to meet him. We hope he will be up to day.

As you have the reading of the Charleston Courier it is not worth while to say anything about the war—Having written thus far I was called off till the evening, and this moment learn that Daniel has just passed on up to the house, and that he is well.

Henry Scarborough is now in the store and will go up with me later and so will see Daniel. Henry has been home several days and though not well when he left Virginia he has recovered (torn) is now looking very well. He has staid a night with us since he came home. Henry is a good fellow.

We shall be glad dear Ruthvin to hear from you often. Dear H. expects to return home next Thursday. Love from all Kind regards to your Brother.

Affectionately yours
William Rogers

Magnolia Hill February 15th 1862[120]
My Dear Brothers

I am permitted a privelege; which I could not have anticipated a few weeks since. for to all human appearance my appointed time of sojourn here on earth had well nigh come to a final close, when the earthly house of this tabernacle should return to its mother dust, and yet (thanks to His holy name) the last messenger was robed of all his terror, for I was made to experience and realise that truly God has said that the soul that trusts in Him shall never die, the promises of God ever sweet to me, for I felt that in His presence is feelings of joy and at His right hand are pleasures for evermore.

I was confined to bead seven weeks the greater part of the time unable to turn without assistance, and which I ackknowledge with much pleasure and gratitude was ever most readily afforded; for a devoted companion, and affectionate daughter, besides my dear friends, were ever at my bead side, but felt that creature comforts must long fail—that the Lord Jehovah was my strength and salvation. He givith power to the faint, and to them who have no might, he increaseth strength. His left hand was under my head; His right hand sustained me; and His banner over me was love. I desired to be released from my suffering (which in His mercy was not great) and prayed for patience to wait the good pleasure of the Lord; for I deserved nothing contrary to his holy will. It has been His good pleasure once more partially to restore me, and how great should be my debt of gratitude if I am to be an instrument of good to my dear family or fellow creatures but I fear and tremble lest, when things of earth engross too much of my time and talents, I strive to review His past dealings and dispensations of mercy, and stupendous display of revelation and divine power, which has been made to manifest to me, which I regret I am entirely incompetent to describe to you, on account of its exceeding magnificence and Heavenly splendor. Oh!

---

120 Though there is a "Magnolia Hill" in Pendleton, SC during this time period, it is impossible to determine the exact origination of this letter, as many homes of this period shared the same or similar names, and the letter is unsigned. Presumably written by one of Ruthvin and Edgar's sisters.

My Dear Brothers there is nothing worth living for on earth only in doing the will and pleasure of Our Heavenly Father. Oh what is this vain world with all its vain pleasures and honours to us should we fail to reach Heaven at last. Dear Brothers I have been recounting the dispensations of mercy I have received and enjoyed from the hand of our merciful Father but have not alluded to the chastening. my long and protracted illness I thank God for; I trust through divine grace to live a life of more entire consecration to His service, but there is a dispensation meeted out to me, in which the hand of the Lord seemeth to rest heavily on me for by day and night my mind ever turns to the bleak allegancies and rehearse the life and sayings of that most precious Boy entomed at their base who (torn) all in acts of kindness and affection that Parent Sister or Brothers could desire. Our Brave and Heroic Sons may fall in this unjust and unholy war, and many a parent will be lonely grieved but if God has so decreed we must lay them as sacrifices on the altar of our country and bow with unpining submission rejoicing that though "They may perish: Our cause is a just one and He will maintaint it." He alone is our refuge and strength: we should gird ourselves for the conflict feeling assured if we are worthy to take our place among the nations of the earth no human power can subdue us.

Dear Brothers, my hand has become nervous and weakness admonishes me to desist writing this page but my heart is full of love for you, and the more knowing your perilous situation and constant exposure to danger, but my Dear Brothers are the Yankies all that's to be dreaded in those days that try mens souls, when we apprehend so much spiritual declension and want of true (illegible) piety throughout the length and breadth of our land I can but anticipate that a fearful retribution awaits us and who of us shall be able to withstand the fireery ordeal which may be impending over us. Oh let us be more (illegible) than ever at a throne of grace. our blest mediator is still ready and waiting to intercede for us with our Father that He will lay aside his sword of vengeance and visit us in great mercy, that we may be his chosen people. How often am I made to meditate on the trials the temptations and the privations you are called to encounter: do you exercise patience, and forbearance towards those under your command. how much have I been pained to hear of the cruelty of some of our officers. I know they are often (illegible), and where my Brothers is your fortress amid all these temptations. I humbly pray that it is the great head and Capt of your Salvation who alone can shelter under His Banner of love and bring you off more than conquerers

(ends here–unsigned)

Plowdens Mills Feby 16, 1862
My Dear Friend & relative,

I receivd your kind and welcome letter last Saturday evening and I assure you I was truly glad to hear from you but was very sorry to hear that you had suffered so much with your throat since you went back. I hope and pray that you may get clean of that complaint for it must be a very painful one. I was also very sorry to hear that your brother Edgar was so bad off. I know he must have been bad of or he would not have taken his bed. but I do sincerely hope that he is well before this time. Well Ruthvin I have not seen a well day since I saw you. I mended up about a month ago considerably and flattered myself that I was going to get well right off but I took a back set and I have been taking medicine from the Dr for three weeks but I cant see that I get any better. I was so bad of last week that I had to send for Dr Ingram. There is a place in my side nearly as large as a goose egg and very much in the shape of one. it is as hard as a brick almost. The Dr says it is a very strange place. I dont think he knows what it is. he did not tell me but told Covert that he would not be surprised if it did not terminate in scrofula. I suffer a great deal with it. I can scarcely walk at times it is so painful but I do very little of that. I have not been a hundred yds from the house in three weeks untill a few days ago. we rode out to pa's and I had to laye down nearly all day. I tell you my friend it is the greatest affliction that has ever befallen me, but it is from the Lord and I must try to bear it patiently. I have been very anxious to get back to the company. it is no satisfaction to me to be at home. I am not able to see to my business—it is true that as I am sick and not at all able to be in camp I much prefer being at home where I can be <u>kindly</u> and <u>affectionately</u> <u>nursed</u>, but if I was only well enough I would be with you. Dr I proposed to me to write for a discharge for me. he said it would be a long time before I would be well enough to go back and he said if I went back my complaint might return on me at any time—but I do not wish a discharge yet. if do not get any better in 6 or 8 weeks I may then wish one—But I feel a deep interest in the co. and I wish to serve my country. I am glad to hear that the measles are through in the co. and that there was so little sickness. I hope you have all left

Camp Harlee before this. I think it is surely time to leave there. We have had the worst weather that I ever saw. it has been raining with very little intermission for 5 weeks and the coldest rain I ever saw. I often think of you all what you must suffer. well Ruthvin I suppose you heard of the fight at Roanoke Island. that was a sad business and it will be so as long as the government puts 1500 men on these little islands to contend against thousands. Well I must close as I have no news. give my best respects to R.J.W. Moultrie Dr D. Leuit Burgess Isaac Montgomery and all (illegible). Lizzie joins me in much Love to you & your Brother Edgar—

Your sincer frd
S. M. Plowden

P S

Give our love to Sam & Bro (illegible) and tell them how I am. and to write me—Pa's family all well. I have a very bad cough that troubles me a good deal at night. Do write soon and give me the news. I have not heard from your folks lately. Do ask your Brother Edgar to send me another furlow if he thinks it necessary—I don't like to be absent without permission if I am sick.

Camp Graham Feb. 23rd 1862[121]
Dear dear Hattie

Many many thanks for your sweet letter from Bishopville in answer to the one I wrote you there. I was so glad to receive your letter I see that you still enjoy good health. I could not help from shedding a few grateful tears for Gods watchful care & preservation of you all & humbly do I hope that this may find you all as it leaves me in perfect health. Brother E & Isaac also, & our comp. injoys nearly the same, nearly all able to eat their rations, & will here state for your especial benefit that the news I wrote in Haynsworth letter respecting the sudden deaths that had occurred in one of the companys. I am thankful to say abated no other attacks since their removal they are stationed several miles from us. We are now encamped on a high and beautiful sand ridge 5 miles from Georgetown & we have been quite busy since our arrival here cleaning up our street & fixing up generally. Please send my Rifle, Powder Horn, Bulet, moulds, Box caps, 6 Bars Lead, & the Flask ful of Powder as there is Deer Turkeys Ducks & Squirrels near our new camp Please Send my Rife Powder Horn & rifle wipers Charles can tell you which they are. I recd quite a mail this morn recd 5 Letters but as this chance presented itself for me to write you, have not read only part of yours. I think one is from Amanda as it is from Manning. Do write soon dear Hattie as I would like to hear from you all every day I would like to write you several pages but Mr. Johnson is waiting for me to stop. So dear Hattie & all Good bye & Gods blessing rest upon you all is the prayer of your devoted husband

Ruthvin Plowden

121 Unable to find information on "Camp Graham," but Ruthvin's return address on the outside of the folded letter is "21st Regt, SCV, Comp C.

Pine Forest Feb. 25th 1862
My ever dear, dear Ruthvin

Your most welcome letter, I re'cd last Sabbath morning, Mary Emily brought it to me, when she came to church, so you can just imagine how delighted I was to hear from you, and to hear that you were all well. I saw dear Amanda at church also, and was more than glad to meet her, I told her I did wish she could come home with us, for I could talk to her all day, but you may be assured our tongues kept pretty busy from the time we met until preaching commenced, as she wanted me to tell her all about home, she had a headache Sunday for which I was very sorry, but hope e're this she has entirely recovered. Next Friday the president has appointed as a day of fasting and prayer, for which I am truly thankful, and I trust that much good may result from that day, and Mr McDowell is to preach for us at Brewington in the afternoon; if nothing prevents Amanda will come home with us from church, and how I do wish dear Ruthvin you could be at home with us, for oh! what pleasure would it afford me. I do hope it may be so, that you and bro' Edgar can come home at the time you wrote of coming, if you cannot come before; do write to us in your next letter when we must send down for you, and when you come please give yourself more time and stay longer than you did before, but how I do wish wish this war would close, and that we could have peace so that you could all come home to stay with us all the time, and humbly do I pray and trust that ere long this may be the case, and could this prayer be granted oh! I do not think that my heart would ever cease to be grateful to our kind heavenly Father; I presume e're this you have rec'd the last letter I wrote you while at home, Mr. Ambrose thought of going down speculating on several things, but he sold out at Lynchburg so he had my letter mailed there, so it informed you that I had re'cd your letter, and I send you many many thanks for your very kind and affectionate letters, and you little know how much pleasure it always affords me to get them. I made quite a long visit at my dear home this time, and did not get back Thursday as I expected, I returned home Saturday, cousins Covert and Callie went up last Friday week, and they were anxious for her to stay until Saturday, so we prolonged our visit two days.

I was very glad to get home and see dear sister Elizabeth and the children. father sent me as far as the brick church, and Covert met us then with the carriage, before I got there I remarked to cousin Callie oh! what would I give if you could only be there with Covert to meet us, but my wish was in vain. The weather was very inclement most of the time while I was at home, but during some of the fair weather we had, Maria and myself paid several visits to some of my old friends, and we had a good deal of company also while I was at home; my dear mother came as far as aunt Peggy's with me to spend the day, on my way home, she told me to give you her best love when I wrote to you again, mother still has headache very often, she had one bad spell while I was there and was in bed all day, how I do wish she could be entirely cured of them, I told father and mother they must try and come down and see you when you come home, and I hope it may be so they can.

I am getting very anxious to see the latest news, that which we have been hearing recently is very bad is'nt it? but we must trust alone to God and look to Him to help us. It fills my heart with gratitude to our heavenly Father, my dear husband when I see from your letters that your trust is in Him, and that you are living near the Lord; were it not for the consolation of knowing that our trust is in Jesus, and that we try to live near Him, I know not what I would do, for in these perilous times and at all times the greatest comfort that we can have is to go to our Savior, and there lift up our voices to Him in prayer.

My dear brother came home while I was there, but he only stayed from Saturday until the next Friday. he left the day before I did, and indeed it was a hard trial for us to part with him, but I said that I had gone through with a greater in parting with my dear husband, but then dear Ruthvin how it fills each one of our hearts with comfort and consolation, when we know that your trust is in God, and that you have Him as your precious Friend to be with you wherever you are. Oh! how deeply did I sympathize, and how sorry did I feel too for my precious mother, but she said she knew he went wholly trusting in the Lord; and oh! that He may give us all more faith and strength to bear these trials in such a manner as would be pleasing in His sight is my prayer. In the last letter Daniel wrote to Lizzie before he came he told her how much he had enjoyed religion since he left, and said he did not know what he would do without this great blessing in this world. I am happy to inform you that we are all quite well, and I trust this may find you all enjoying perfect health, and you entirely cured of sorethroat and mouth. Sister E says you must let us know if you want another supply of provisions sent (torn) let us know when you write again. I saw Mr Haynsworth at Brewington last Sabbath, and he told me when I wrote to you, to inquire of you and brother Edgar, if you would both like for him to sell some of your cotton at eight (8) cents at Kingstree in order to pay the Confederate and State taxes, for he said they had to be paid and there was no money to borrow anywhere, and he said if you would both like to do this, let him know and he would attend to it for you. Sister E and myself spent yesterday at cousin Lizzie,s, Joe looks very badly, but was some better yesterday and is in bed; I do hope he may soon be restored to health again, I was very glad you wrote to him, for he told me some time ago to tell you to write to him, but I forgot it. In one of your letters to sister Elizabeth you said you had not re'cd a letter from me in a week, and for her to ask me if I was going to forget, you, it made me feel right sad, for I think it is one of my greatest pleasures, while you have to be absent from me, to be employed in writing to you, and I wrote to you three times while at home, but just here let me assure you dearest that never no! never never could I ever forget you, my ever dear beloved husband, and could you have only seen how anxious I was to hear from you, when I got home Tuesday and did not receive a letter from you until the next Thursday week, you would then be convinced of this, but after I found I was not coming home until Saturday I was very sorry I told you to direct your next here, for otherwise I could have re'cd it at Bishopville. You wrote to me by Jimmie B but I had left before it reached here. Lute says I must tell you howdye for him, Haynsworth has gone to school. Did you think the dogs would know me after I came home? but they did, and when going in the yard, sometimes they will rush upon me so I can hardly walk for them, they all look very well. My dear father told me he was very much obliged to me for the good long visit I made them this time. I re'cd a letter from Mary Dinkins the other day. she requested me to give you her best respects, and said she hoped when she visited

Brewington again she would find you and myself enjoying each others society again and this war at an end and I know I heartily agree with her here. The other day when I was coming down I met Bettie Sue & Cooper Muldrow, and bowed to them with a smile but they did not find me out until they had passed, when they stopped and we all got out of the carriages and went and embraced each other. We were all very glad to meet with each other again, for never can I forget the pleasant by gone days we all used to have at Orangeburg. Sue said she would be at Bessie McFaddin,s next Saturday, and that I must get Amanda and be certain to go and see her, but I do not know whether we will or not. Mr Weaver speaks of joining the army soon, but I doubt if he does, he was threatened with hemorrhage once while I was at home. I don't think he knows hardly (torn) to do, before I left home he made me a present of a nice little hymnbook which I prize very highly. has all kinds of hymns, one of which is (He died at his port) which you recollect I fell so much in love with when I heard Mr Hodges sing it. I think it so beautiful, Mother Maria and myself took pleasure in singing it while I was at home. I must now draw this uninteresting letter to a close, and do dear Ruthvin write to me very soon again, oh you can't imagine darling how glad I feel when I think of your coming home to see us, for I trust it may be the will of our kind heavenly Father to bring you all safely home to us. oh! what a happy meeting it will then be..Sister E joins me in our very best love to brother Edgar, Isaac, and accept the same dearest for your own dear self, and now praying that God may watch over and protect you and soon permit us to meet in health again. I remain as ever your devoted Hattie.

(single sheet–undated–presumably Feb. 1862) 4 clock P.M.

P. S.

Dear Hattie as a few more Liesure moments presents themselves, owing to the heavy rain that is now falling I will write you a few more Lines. The wind & rain has just run us in from Battallion Drill. Is not that good news? I wrote to Mr. Windham. I will tell you how it reached us. a Gentleman has just arrived here from Charleston & says the news was telegraphed there & it must be in Tennessee where the fight occurred as Beauregard had taken his position at Columbus not far from Nashville & (not in Missouri).[122] If this is correct a few more such blows will tell in this war & I am in hopes will bring our enemy to reflection & who knows but this is the result from the prayers that was offered in behalf of our country on Last Friday. There was great rejoicing in camp when the news was received & oh how each & every heart should be filled with gratitude to God for this great victory & dear Hattie I do believe if there was more ardent fervent & importunate Prayer at a Throne of Divine Grace there would be less fighting to do & that a permanent peace might be established & oh my dear wife if this sweet peace should be granted us & each & all of us should be spared to return to our dear family. our hearts ought to be filled to overflowing with gratitude to God for this great & condescending Blessing. Oh if I could only be with you all. if it was only for a few days I would like it very much for it appears like an age since I have seen you, but dear Hattie it is so pleasant (even here) to think of the many many happy hours we have spent in each other's society & the other night while on Guard, when all nature was wrapped in quiet repose my thoughts wandered to my dear ones at home (and as it were) watched over you when your eyes were closed in sleep & what room you were all asleep in & yesterday eve when the new moon made its appearance it reminded me of your namesake & that you might be looking at it at the same time.

122 The only two battles I could confirm for February 1862 were Battle of Fort Henry (Feb. 6) and Battle of Fort Donelson (Feb. 11-16), both Union victories in Tennessee.

I wrote to Spencer to try & plant all of the corn by the 15th but tell him he had better not plant more than half of it & not plant the balance before the 20th Do dear Hattie you & dear Sister write to me often & kiss the dear children for me & they kiss you & E for me Lots So now good night, pleasant dreams with the best Love to you all from your devoted

Ruthvin

Home March 8th 1862
My dear Sister Hattie,

We were so fortunate Thursday night to receive a letter from you, Amanda and brother William, and more than glad were we to learn that you were all well. Would that it were my happy privilege to report the same to you but am sorry to tell you that dear little Nora is sick. She and Sister Lizzie came down last Sunday to spend this week with us. Nora had a bad cold, but was very playful and seemed perfectly well all day Monday; that night however she awoke us, and seemed to have great difficulty in breathing. we sent for the Doctor, but he did not seem to think that there was much the matter with her, but gave her medicine which he thought would relieve her. We feared all the while that she had Pneumonia, but he did not think so, until Thursday, yesterday he blistered her, and since then she breathes much better, and oh! humbly do I pray that the precious one will soon be entirely well.[123] She is the best little thing you ever saw, stood the blister remarkably well. Sister Lizzie received a letter from Daniel Wednesday morning stating that he had to be in Camden on business for a day or two, and wished her and Nora to go up and stay with him until he returned. Nora's being sick prevented her doing so, but she sent the buggy and horses up, and wrote to him of the baby and told him to come down. he got here about ten oclock Wednesday night. He is looking very well; will stay with us until Nora gets better. You have heard I suppose that Daniel's company had disbanded. they could not succeed in making it up. he has not decided yet what he will do. He speaks of staying with Capt Green's Company until the boys come from Virginia and then go on with them. Mrs Durant's little Charlie has been quite ill this week with Pneumonia, but we have heard from him this morning and they think him some better. These severe colds are very prevalent about here now, but I sincerely hope there will not be any more Pneumonia.

---

123 "Blistering" was achieved by applying blistering agents to raise a blister on the skin. This was thought by doctors of that time to be an appropriate remedy for some medical problems. https://www.battlefields.org/learn/articles/civil-war-medicine

I received a short letter from Brother William last night, dated from Sumter, where he had gone to meet the presiding elder, so I suppose you are all at the Qtly meeting now together. I know you will have a very pleasant time. Mr Weaver went up last Saturday to attend the Qtly meeting up at New Salem. he says the next meeting is to be held at Bethlehem but not until sometime in June. I am glad of this for it has been some time since we had one here. Oh Hattie don't you think I had a lonely time here the day you left. You know I was here all alone as Mr. W. went over to Capt Dubose's. I did not allow myself to take the blues though as I had several culinary matters to attend to and besides I spent a great part of the time in answering some of those letters I received while you were here. Mr. Weaver said he missed "Sister Hattie" so much, and when I see you I will tell you something else. I was telling him this morning I wished Nora was well and I could be with you all at the meeting, he said for me to appoint a time and we would go down but this I never expect to do, no not with him. I declare I am so anxious to see you all, when is Sister coming up? I don't think I can stand it much longer without seeing my darling little Anna. Mr. Weaver has gone up to Mr. Barrett's to day, hope he may have a pleasant time. I know Pat will talk enough for him. Mother says to tell you she missed you a great deal after you left. I hope before very long you will favor us with another visit. Tell Miss (torn) sometimes when I am attacked with the blues I wish I could be with her, to hear her relate some anecdotes for I am confident (torn) could (torn) me. Kiss the children for me and tell Haynsworth, I expect before long to receive a letter from him written in his own hand. All (torn) a great deal of love to, Miss Elizabeth (torn) the children. Good by, accept a great deal of love from your Sister

Maria

Nora seems easy now.

Pine Forest March 10th 1862
My very dear Ruthvin,

As this is the anniversary of our wedding day, I feel that I cannot employ myself more pleasantly, than in spending a short time of the day in writing to you. have you thought of it? but little did I think then, that three years hence I would be writing to you under such circumstances, you seperated far from me, and gone forth in defence of our dear country, but oh! dear Ruthvin humbly do I hope and pray that if parsistent with God's will that there are many many more happy days and years in store for us all yet, here on earth, and I trust that He may enable us to live each one nearer and nearer to Him. I was indeed very much disappointed when you wrote to me that you could not come, for I had been looking forward with so much pleasure to your coming, but then I do hope it may be so that you can come when brother Edgar returns. if you cannot come with him, do try and do so if you possibly can, for you do not know how bad I want to see you. As I was going over to Sister Martha's Friday evening, I stopped at Sister Lillis' gate when she told me there was a letter there for me, so you can imagine my great eagerness to peruse its contents, but as I read that you were not coming, I could hardly tell you how I felt. I am living in hopes tho' that I may have the exquisite pleasure of seeing you soon. they are all well at bro' Edgars and we are all the same. I was sorry to see from your letter that you had cold again, but I hope e're this you have got entirely over it. We had a very good meeting at Zion, and Dr Boyd preached a very excellent sermon. Mr H's family attended on Saturday, and Amanda and myself went both days. there were three ladies that united themselves to the church yesterday, but I did not know who they were. I was very glad I had the opportunity of going, and it was with a great deal of pleasure I looked forward to the meeting. Mr. McDowell preached at Brewington Sunday also. Dr Boyd bro' Wm and Sister spent Saturday night with Mrs Coskrey, sister tho' took dinner at Sister Martha's, and went there in the afternoon. I had a very pleasant visit to sister Martha's, but oh dear Ruthvin how much much did I think of you, and you may be assured that dear Sister Martha and myself, spent some of our time in talking about your dear self.

and how many times I thought too of the first I was ever there, after we had been there awhile and dark began to make its appearance. I recollect so well about your coming, and how delighted I felt when I saw that it was you, for all seemed like strangers almost to me then, and when you came then I was perfectly at home and satisfied. oh you little know dear Ruthvin how much I think of you, and what my sad feelings are at the thought of our being separated, but oh that our heavenly Father may e'relong return you all in health and safety to us all is my fervent prayer. I came from sister M's yesterday evening, and sister let dear little Anna come home with me, for which I was very glad. She seems perfectly satisfied; is going to stay with us until Wednesday. I begged bro' Wm when he was here to tell sister to let her come home with me. Yesterday as we were coming home Anna said "well I do think uncle Ruthvin is the best man I ever saw in my life that did not preach." I suppose she thinks they (preachers) have to be the best; then just now she was in here and inquired who I was writing to, and she says "give uncle Ruthvin my love, and tell him I want to see him mighty bad, and whenever he comes home to be certain to come and see them in Manning. she thinks there is no one like aunt Elizabeth. I shall miss her very much when she goes home. Haynsworth has gone to school to day. the children are both growing very fast and are looking very well. dear little Lute says I must tell you howdye for him, and to give you his love. Sister Elizabeth says I must tell you that she has been looking for a letter from you ever since the 1st of March telling us about sending you down more provisions. do let us know when you want us to send. Sister E. says I must ask you if you are living in the wind? I guess bro E will come home when Mr Witherspoon goes back. I expect to send this letter by him, and I hope it will be convenient for him to carry you a basket for us. Did you have much snow with you? I thought of you lots I tell you and wished so much that you were here to join sister E & myself in eating it with cream and sugar. and I also thought of last year, when you took me up and laid me down in the snow. but we did not have the fun with this snow this time that we had last year, for your being away from me. I did not feel like it at all. Joe Plowden is still sick; I don't think that bro Wm has much hopes of his recovering, but sincerely hope that he may get well. I feel very sorry for cousin Lizzie. bro Wm and sister are coming to see him this week. Did you receive the letter I sent by Mr Johnson? it was in the bag with your articles. You must tell brother Edgar to come and see us very soon after he gets home, and do send me word by him if you do not think you can come home when he returns and please say yes and not no.

Dear Ruthvin it must be dreadful for you to see the wickedness that is carried on in camps, oh that they would cease from such, and give their hearts to God, it is indeed awful to think of the wickedness going on among our soldiers. you say it is hard to live the life of a Christian in camps, but only trust in the Lord my precious husband and look only to Him for help, for He alone is able to give you all the help and assistance you need, and we know that He is able to give us faith and strength to resist every sin and temptation and oh what comfort and consolation it is to me dear Ruthvin to know that it is in God you put your trust, and that you are one of His dear children and that you can feel that He is your friend wherever you are, and I know that could my weak petitions avail any good, your precious life dear Ruthvin would be a long and happy one. oh! how I wish you could be here with me. you cannot realize dear Ruthvin how greatly I miss you. You must be sure and tell me when you are coming by bro E if nothing prevents and write to me very soon. sister Elizabeth unites with me in sending you our very best and warmest love, also give much love to bro' E and Isaac. Oh! I almost forgot to tell you that in our last paper, it was stated that there had been a battle in Missouri, in which we gained the victory, killing one thousand yankees.[124] gen. Price was commander of our men. I don't suppose it is the one you referred to in your letter. I hope that (torn) I said that (torn) this victory was gained through the prayers of last

124 Confederate Gen. Sterling Price (1809-1867), with the Missouri State Guard, defeated the Federal Army at Wilson's Creek in MO in Aug. 1861, and he continued to occupy southwest MO until March 6-8 when he was defeated at Pea Ridge (Elkhorn Tavern) AK, about three miles south of Missouri. With this defeat, the Union controlled Missouri for the next two years. The Union's estimated casualties: 1,384, and the Confederacy's: 2,500. https://www.battlefields.org

Friday. And now praying dearest that Heaven's richest blessings may ever rest upon you, I remain as ever your own devoted

Hattie

(written on back of folded papers:)

If convenient do bring me some palmetto when you come.

March 12th 1862
Dear Ruthvin

I will send you a few lines to let you know how we are getting along. we will commence planting corn to day and will continue until we plant 225 acres. you said in your note I must try to get done by the 15th but that is sooner than I can get done but I will try to get done by the 22nd. I am not as far on as I would like to be. I have a great deal of hauling to do yet but I hope to get done in good time You must write to me soon as you can and let me know how much yellow corn you wish planted. you must come home soon as you can. I will be glad to see you and I will rush as hard as I can until you come. you must excuse a short letter.

Yours affectionately
T O Windham

Camp Mannigault Mch 12 (1862)
My dear Hattie,

Although a few days have elapsed since I wrote to you, I cannot resist the moments that I have of writing you a few lines I am Officer of the Guard to day & no time to spare, for I am looking every moment for the Officer of the day to call me out Tomorrow from 9 oclock untill 5 in the eve will be holliday with me, but then I could not get my letter off as I expect Brother Edgar will leave in the morn early. I am truly sorry my dear Hattie Sister & children that I cannot go home to see you all, but the Col will not allow two officers to leave the same camp at the same time I did my best with him this morn to get off. told him how punctual I had attended to business, but he would not consent for me to go. So dear Hattie you must not fret about it. It is God will for me to remain, therefore, we ought not to murmer & will come as soon as I can get off but cannot tell you when that will be. I am truly thankful to state my health is very good & humbly wish that this will find you all the same. The health of the camp is not as good as I thought it would be here, there is 3 men in the hospital, & 8 or 10 sick in their tents There is other companies in the Regt that there is more sickness in than there is in ours all pretty much with colds. I hope they will soon stop as spring is coming on although vegitation is very backward down here. We have no news of any consequence in camp. I see some in the Papers. I see the steel clad vessel Merrimac has played havoc with the enemys ships & Gunboats.[125] I only wish we had more of them & they would soon raise the Blockade just as it was done on the James River, but of those matters it is useless to write as you are posted. Well dear Hattie the anniversary of our marriage is past. Often often did I think of you on that day & how many happy happy days & those days have lengthend into years we have spent in each others society But God only knows if we will even see another, if not Let us try & serve Him hereafter Tell H & Lutie to be good Boys & learn fast so if their Lives is spared they will make good & useful men. Do dear Hattie you & dear E write to me

125 The Merrimack was rebuilt and recommissioned as the CSS Virginia Feb. 17, 1862.

soon & often I have been Looking for several days for a letter but expect you will write by James Witherspoon & I expect he will be here this eve. Tell Spencer to go ahead with his planting. I must now close dear Hattie to go on duty Goodbye darling May God watch over protect & bless you all is the prayer of your affect husband

Ruthvin

P.S. Kiss the children for me & E also & then you for me by the gross gross[126]

Ruth

126 Gross = 12 dozen, or 144

Bishopville 19 March 1862
Dear Ruthven,

I owe you an apology for not having written to you before this time, for I believe it has been several weeks since my last to you, though I think I wrote last. I can only say that if you will have the kindness to write us even a few lines as often as possible, we will answer each letter that we recieve.

I am happy to say that we are all tolerably well at home, and all of our family connections were well when we last heard from them.

Since my last to you I have been to Richmond Va. for the purpose of getting a settlement with the P. O. Department I sucseeded in doing so but had a tegeous[127] time in returning from want of commuting, and the failure of engines. I was gone from Tuesday until the Sunday night following–Richmond was crammed full of people, and mostly soldiers, on furlough, I found difficulty in finding a place to lay my head. There was a great deal of drinking and disapation when I was there but I think it is now much changed by martial law and closing the grog shops. It is now a time calculated to depress the spirits of our people, but we must hope for the tide to change and a kind Providence may still own and bless our cause and save us from subjection–for if it ever comes to that we are ruined indeed. But we can at present console ourselves with the fact that during the war of the Revolution everything looked as gloomy as at present and still all came out right in the end. but it was often a long and trying war.

Daniel has had much trouble of mind in regard to making satisfactory arrangements for enlisting the service. You are aware that Mr. Depliss and Daniel undertook to raise a company and almost sucseeded but the time of the late Ex(illegible) draft passed off. Strong influence was brought to bear against Depliss, and the men many of them drew off, and in consequence the company at length had to disband. Daniel has now attached himself to an artilery company at Charleston and I hear is a lieut and I trust he may be pleased with the company and find his position more pleasant than what it might have been in the first company. After the first commission fell through Daniel came home, and found

127 Tedious

his child very sick, but she has since recovered entirely. Daniel too was quite unwell after his return home, but is now tolerably well again. He left for Charleston on yesterday and may soon return again, and take a horse down with him for I believe the officers duty is on horseback. We have lately had a letter from Lucy and she reported all well including Harriet and Amanda. She says Amanda has secured the love of employers and pupil, at this I am not surprised and I trust you will agree with me that Amanda is herself a good dear child. Yes, they are all good children, if they are not ere found it out. Oh! if we could once more have peace, an honorable peace, does it not now seem that there might be much enjoyment even in this changing world?

It is indeed a trying time for those at home and how little do we feel it compared with you Soldiers? But so it is—we must hope for the best, pray the God of battles to bless us, and turn the arms and hearts of the Soldiers to the mighty struggle.

As there was some uncertainty of making a profitable trip to Georgetown, the road being represented as in very bad condition, we gave out making a trip of our wagon to Georgetown. By the bye, in case that the enemy appeared at Georgetown in force, will their landing be useless? It seems to be useless to attempt defending our coasts against their iron clad gun-boats. Let them land an attempt marching into the country and they can be met on more equal terms if we are provided with arms and ammunition.

Well my letter I cannot make interesting, and I must begin to close. I hope dear Ruthvin, you will try and find time at least to write even a few lines that we may know how things go with you.

You must give our kind regards to your Brother and all inquiring friends. May God bless and keep you all, and cover your heads in day of battle if it comes upon you as it probably will sometime. I hope we may soon hear from dear Harriet and your dear sister. Oh, how thankful I am that in that dear sister of yours H. has such a kind loving friend and sister.

May God bless and reward her for all her kindness. We all are happy too in the belief that Miss Elizabeth has kind regards for all our family. And now good-bye God bless and keep you is the prayer of your affectionate father in law

William Rogers

Columbia, April 5th 1862
My darling sister

Do you not think hard of me for not writing to you oftener? I could not blame you if you did, but I know your kind forgiving disposition so well that I know you will excuse me for my negligence. but the reason dear Hattie I do not write oftener is because Saturday is the day I generally write any letters and then I always have several to write, so it takes me a good while to get round. I had letters from home saying that brother Ruthvin had been at home. oh! were you not delighted to see him? I was so sorry though to hear that he was sick, but father wrote me that he was much better when he and mother left, so I sincerely hope that he has entirely recovered ere this. If he is still with you give a heart full of love to him for me, and if he has gone do it when you write. I know it goes very hard with you all to have to part with him and it isn't strange that it should for he is so dear kind and good to every one. there are few such men as he in this world. don't you agree with me in saying so? I know you do though for you could not help it. I received a letter from Amanda the other day saying that cousin Joe was no better. I do feel so sorry for him. oh! that it may yet please an all wise God to restore him to his afflicted family. poor cousin Lizzie. I know she takes it very hard. She said also that cousin Covert intended leaving very soon for the war. I do indeed pity cousin Callie for I know she will take it very much to heart. oh! how thankful would we be, if this cruel war could be brought to a close, and God grant that it may. The future looks dark indeed before us now. but oh! let us hope that the clouds that now hang so heavily over us may soon banish forever and that the remainder of our lives may be spent in sunshine.

I am sorry to say that two of the girls in school are quite sick. one of them a miss Agnes from Orangeburg has quite an attack of pneumonia. I sincerely hope though that she may soon recover. My dear sister I am very much obliged to you indeed for the nice bag of pinders[128] which you sent me and to miss Elizabeth too. no doubt you think I took a very long time to thank you, but the length of time

128 Peanuts

that has elapsed doesn't take away any of my gratitude at all. You ought just to have seen how we enjoyed them. Amanda told me that you were very much disappointed in not getting to send the box. I knew you would be, but you must not mind it. for I am just as much obliged to you as if I had gotten the box with all the nice things in it. Did you get any April fools I mean if any one April fooled you any way. I do not suppose you received any from young gentlemen for your day for that is past. You ought to have seen how we fooled one of the girls. two of the girls went in the parlor and sent one of the servants to tell this girl that a young gentleman had called on her. she did not once think of April and jumped up to change her dress and fix up a little, but we thought it would be most too much trouble for her to change her dress so we persuaded her to go as she was, and when she went down I tell you she was taken back when she saw these two girls sitting in there. but my sheet is full so I must close. Please excuse this paper for I am just out, and as I intended to send it to day I did not wait to get more. Give much love to all for me. Kiss Haynsworth and Lute for me. Goodby dear sister. I remain as ever your true and devoted sister.

Almira

April 15th 1862
My dear dear brother,

Words cannot express my sorrow when I heard you were to leave so soon and I would be deprived the great pleasure of seeing you again, and I still find myself hoping you will not go yet. I would have gone last Friday, but I thought if I did it might prevent all from here going, and as I had been to see you twice I thought I ought to stay, and besides I wanted to send for some things by sister when she went, and I was almost compelled to go. I feel so much for Hattie and Miss Elizabeth. I know their hearts are filled with sorrow this evening. Oh, that it may be the will of God to return you to your dear home in health and safety again. Many are the fervent prayers which will daily ascend to a throne of grace for you. I trust it may not be long before you can come home again. You must write me whenever you can. I hope you feel better than when I saw you. If you do not you really ought to return. I expect you were sorry when you heard you were not ordered to Charleston. I hope you may be placed in a more healthy situation. I recd letters from cousins David and Hu this week—they were well. Cousin D. said Capt. Frierson was very unpopular with his men. they had asked him to resign, but he had not done so. I do not know why he is so unpopular. Good bye my own dear brother. May God's richest blessings attend you through life, and a starry crown be yours in heaven, is the earnest prayer of your devoted sister,

Amanda Rogers

Monday night[129]
My own dear Hattie

Oh dear Hattie how very thankful I was to God for his watchful care of you all since I Left you, & all of us too. I am truly thankful that my health is still improving. This morning commenced Drilling & glad to say it has not tired me any more than before I Left. No one sick in the company except Moultrie Bagnal. he is not very sick yet but I think he has Typhoid Fever. I supose you have seen or heard of this Conscript act passed by Congress that all between the ages of 18 & 35 is to be mustered in for the war. I am very sorry dear Hattie for this as we will have to go in for another election for officers. & since we have been away Three men who I will not mention the names of now have perverted the minds of more than half of the company to cut Brother Edgar out of office. They are going to run Butler for Capt. I. Burgess for 1st (torn) Logan for 2nd & F Bro(torn) & myself for the same office I now hold. As yesterday was Sunday I did not do what a good many did (electioneer) but did to day & am glad to say if the men will do as they say I do not know that I will Loose 3 votes in the camp. Several told me no man in the comp could say ought against me & I humbly thank God for it as I told you He alone I put my trust in, & the greatest trial of my Life (except death) is to know what to do. If Brother is cut out of his office how can I bear to stay in a camp that has treated him in that way. For not one can say anything against him but cant vote for him as they are pledged to Butler. So you see the mean underhandedness that men will resort to. For you see Butler is sheriff there are judgments in the office against some of them & if they do not vote for him he can make them suffer for it. (But of this you must not mention (torn) anything Ive written about) until you hear from me again) I have been trying to get Brother to resign his office & return home as he is over age,

129 Though undated, this letter was probably written shortly after April 16, 1862, when the Conscription Act was passed. It required all able-bodied white men between the ages of 18 and 35 to serve at least three years in the Confederate military. Ruthvin would have been 38 at this time. https://civilwarmonths.com/2017/04/16/the-confederate-conscription-act/

but the Col & Lieut Col & nearly all the officers do not wish him to leave as they say he is the best Drilled officer in the Regt. The Col is very much put out about the way those men have acted & says he is going to tell Butler of his meanness as soon as he gets in camp. No other news dear Hattie & really my mind is so filled with what I have been writing about that I am misirable. So dear Hattie you & dear E write to me what to do, for if I was to resign my office & come home I could not be satisfied & our country invaded. & I might be drafted soon as I am afraid there will be a call for men from 35 to 45 & that would include myself. The first night I heard it I didnt sleep hardly any.

Many many thanks dear Hattie Elisabeth for the nice present you sent me for I tell you my appetite is keen as a razor. I do not know when we will Leave here we may be soon called away after going in for the war. So now dear Hattie & Elisabeth, Haynsworth Lutie & Henry Good night as it is late. Write immediately, kiss the dear children for me & try & train them up in the fear & admonition of the Lord. May God bless all of my dear family & permit us soon to meet again is the prayer of your devoted husband

Ruthvin

Pine Forest April 23, 1862
My <u>own</u> <u>dear</u> Ruthven,

I recd your dear kind letter today through Mr. Tindall, he and Mr. Hayes took dinner here, and left a short while ago. I was truly thankful to hear that you were well and that your health is still improving and in return I am happy to say that we too are all well. Well dear Ruthven from the contents of your letter I know your mind is considerably worried It has been on my mind ever since I read your letter and really it makes me feel very sorry to think that there are such men in the company, as would act in the manner that they did during the absence of brother Edgar, in trying to have him cut out of his office, but do not think they will ever gain anything by it, for I feel assured that they will not succeed in getting a captain who would be more kind to his men, and who would do more for them than brother Edgar. I know that no one can say anything against him, and that they could not give any reason if asked why they oppose him. How sorry I feel for this, for it seems to me dear Ruthvin that it will be so hard for me to think of your being away without dear brother E with you, and you request me and sister E to tell you what to do, but my <u>dear</u> <u>husband</u>, let me tell you just to pray <u>earnestly</u> to our kind heavenly Father, and ask him to direct you as to what you ought to do, for <u>He</u> <u>alone</u> can direct you aright, and Sister Elizabeth told me too to tell you what I have written and rest assured dear Ruthven that my weak prayers will be offerred up to God for you, and whatever course you pursue I trust my dearest that you may be enabled to feel that you are directed by God, and that it may all be for the best, therefore look to Him in faith, for by so doing we know that He is able and willing to give you all the help and assistance you need and oh that I could only feel directed by Him just what I ought to tell you. Dear Ruthven it makes me feel sad to think of your having to go in for the war, but oh! humbly do I pray and trust that God may ever shield and protect you <u>all</u> and at last return you in health and in safety to your dear homes. I hope you will write to me very soon again for I will be so anxious to hear from you, as to hear how you are, and further particulars about this matter, and as I have before told you my dear Ruthven, I trust that whatever you do you may feel that you are directed alone by the hand of a merciful God. Mr. T. told me that you looked very well, which I am so thankful to hear, and oh! that God may continue to bless you both temporally and spiritually is my prayer. Sister E and myself went up to see Covert yesterday but they were not at home and the house was all closed, so we came by the mill and got a nice plate of fish for supper, and I wish that you could have had them, was glad to hear you had a good appetite, is there anything particularly you would like for us to send you to eat, do let us know if there is, it is such a pleasure for us to have an opportunity of sending you anything. We went to prayer meeting yesterday but there was only four to recite the bible lesson so we had a small class. Mr. Haynsworth brought me a note from Amanda, and she seemed to be in a great ecstacy of delight at the idea of going home Friday next, she said that father and brother Wm made the arrangement while bro'. Wm was at home. Bro.Wm is to carry her part of the way, and then father will meet her, she expects to return Friday next. She gave me a very pressing invitation to meet her at sisters Thursday night, Amanda says they are going to have tableaux at Manning also, and the folks from there have asked her, Anna Haynsworth, and I think both Mary & Anna Coskrey to assist them, but I do not know when the concert is to take place, they were to meet there to-morrow evening for the first meeting. Have you heard that Fannie Burgess had another son, but it only lived a few days, died last night and was to be buried at Brewington half past 3 this afternoon, poor Fannie I expect she feels very sad this evening, but she ought to strive to be resigned, knowing that it is far better off. Have we not had some cold weather lately? and did you not need some of your winter clothing? there was some frost I believe this morning, but I don't suppose there was enough to hurt the fruit. Aunt Soukie (but I do not know exactly how to spell this name do you?) is still quite sick, and it is hard to get her to take any nourishment at all, she looks very badly, but I hope she may be better soon. I have not heard from home since you left, brother Wm and sister did not come by here on there way from Bishopville. I am sorry to tell you that one of the mules have died since you left the one named Kate, she was taken sick Saturday and died Monday morning Sister Elizabeth says she did every thing for her she ever heard of, and she thought that she was getting better. Oh! Ruthven you do not know how bad I want to see you and how much I think about you, last night when all was hushed in stillness, I was awake thinking of my dear and absent one; you must write me as soon as you receive this, and you must try dear Ruthven and not worry your mind so much about what you have written, but go to the Savior and pour out your whole heart to Him, and I pray that He may direct your mind aright. I must close as it is getting late, and dear Sister Elizabeth, Lute and Haynsworth join me in sending our best and warmest love to your own dear self and brother Edgar, and now asking you to remember us all very earnestly at a throne of grace. I remain as ever your own devoted

Hattie

Apral 25 (1862)
Dear Brother

Lillis sent for me this morning she had another chil at 7 oclock it did not go off till 10, she is quite sick now with her head & side but I trust she will be better she is sweating a little the Doc blistered her it drawed well if she gets any worse I will rite to you, every day I will stay hear till she gets better, Hatty is with Aunt Socky she is very low unless their is a change she will not last many days my Dear Brothers do put your hole dependance in god to direct you what to do & he will order all things for the best I have spent many sleepless our about that election I trust & pray that God will bless you both & soon bring you back to us

(unsigned; from Ruthvin & Edgar's sister, Susan Elisabeth)

April 25 1862
Dear Hattie & Elisabeth

I will only write you a few lines as I have been necessarily compelled to write nearly 8 pages with which I have just finished I am thankful to state I am quite well except my side which still continues to pain me more or less every day but not enough to keep me from duty I send this by Peter as we have sent him for the waggon & Buggy you will not have to send any mules to put in the wagon as Brother Edgar waggon & mules is coming to haul our things away. You must have the buggy greased & Peter is to get a horse from the Capt to put in with Slim. & tell George he must not Let him work any after you get this until he starts down here. I have concluded not to remain here that is if we can get off if we can get off. Flander with the waggon & Peter with the Buggy will start down next Wednesday morning & get here on Thursday evening & we will Leave on Friday morning (if we can get off) I do not see any more prospect of brother E being elected than when I last wrote. I have not heard of any one that is not going to vote for me, but brother E says he is not willing for me to stay with such men & several of my particular friends have advised me not to remain. I know a great many will talk about it, but I cannot help it. God knows my heart, & I know I want to do my duty. but how or where to go to do it is the thing that troubles me. But I know if I put my trust in God he will enable me to do what is right. Although my future course looks dark & gloomy yet I trust He will enable me to do his will & I care not for the opinion of men. Dear Hattie I must close. kiss them all for me. tell H. Lutie howdy for me May God watch over & protect you all is the prayer of your devoted husband & brother

Ruthvin

Pine Forest Apr. 26th 1862
My <u>ever</u> <u>beloved</u> <u>husband</u>

Only a few days have passed since I wrote to you, but having an opportunity of sending a letter to you to-morrow by Mr Witherspoon I can't refrain from taking up my pen again, just to let you know that we are all well, and I must tell you in the offstart to look for a short letter as it is now almost bedtime. I am sorry to tell you that Sister Lillis is again sick. how sorry I was to hear it, but I hope that ere'long she may again be restored to entire health, and that she may long be spared to her dear family, to train up her little children in the right way. Sister Elizabeth went over to bro' Edgar,s yesterday, and carried Lute with her. she has not sent me word as yet when to send for her, but I presume she will stay until sister Lillis gets better. I find it very lonely while sister E is away. I do not know when I was ever as glad to see Haynsworth come from school as I was yesterday evening, for you can just imagine dear Ruthvin how lonely I felt. directly after he came in we got to talking about you, and oh! could you only be here with us how happy I (torn) be, and humbly do I hope and pray, that ere'long, God may bring you in <u>safety</u> to us all, if consistent with His will. Aunt Soukie is still quite sick, but I think she is some better to-day than she has been. Mr Windham sent for Dr Dinkins to come and see her. he came this afternoon, and he thought her <u>quite</u> <u>sick</u>. he left some medicine for her to take which I hope may help her, and that she may soon be well again. Well Ruthvin from what Dr Dinkins was telling me about cousin Joe, I <u>fear</u> that he will not get well, but he says they think now that some of the food he eats passes through that place in his side, where it discharges. he told me that the other day he eat some peas, and upon examining he said that they seemed to be whole without having digested at all, and they passed through that place in his side. oh! is it not sad sad to think of it? I was so much in hopes that he was getting better that day we were there. but Dr Dinkins says that Joe has despaired of all hopes now of ever getting well, but if the will of the Lord I hope that his health may yet be restored to him, and that he may soon be well. I feel very sorry for cousin Lizzie, for I know it makes her feel sad enough. You recollect I told you in my letter before that Amanda had written me a pressing invitation to meet her at sisters Thursday night and as George said the horses were not busy the last of this week, I went, and I tell you they were glad to see me and I was equally as much so to see them, and sister went with me in the morning to see Mrs McDowell, but only made quite a fashionable call, but we spent our time very pleasantly while we did stay. Mr McDowell was at home also. while there we got to speaking about his going away but he says that he does not know yet what he will do, tho' he is willing to do either, to go or stay but does not like to choose for himself. he told me tho' if he did go off, that he had already told Mrs McD. that this was one place he wanted her to stay at a great deal. really I am very glad they think this much of us all, but they are pleasant folks, and I like them very much also. I do hope I may get a letter from you soon again. I am so anxious to hear from you dear Ruthvin, and to know if you still continue pretty well. I hope you will always tell me very particularly how you are, for you know how anxious I am to hear from you at all times.

Sam went fishing this evening and caught three very nice ones which he gave to me, so Haynsworth and I had them for our supper, but for a wonder I did not make out to eat a whole one this time, but if you had have only been here I guess I would have relished it a great deal more. H & myself, both wished that you had the largest one. he is now in bed fast asleep, and he learnt his lesson and recited it to me first rate. What would I give if you were here with me, but such a wish is now in vain. do write me very soon. I answered your letter the same evening I received it. Have you got it as yet? Amanda and bro' Wm made an early start yesterday morning and father was to meet her. she expects to return Tuesday. and now with my very best and warmest love I remain as ever your devoted wife.

Hattie Plowden

Pine Forest Apr. 29th 1862
My own dear husband,

Your letter came safely to hand and I was sorry to hear that you still had pain in your side, oh! how I wish that you could be entirely cured of that, and that your health could be entirely restored, and humbly do I pray and trust that ere' long it may be the case, if it is the will of our heavenly Father, and that your life may long be spared to earth to do much good and to be a bright and shining light in the church below. Mr. Tindall told me he expected to be here in the morning, so I will send this by him if nothing prevents. Dear Ruthvin I know that you have felt much worried as to bro' Edgars being cut out of his office, and I fear he has, too, but perhaps it has all happened for the best, therefore I would try and not allow it to worry me, and in the course you have pursued my dear husband I trust that you are directed by an allwise Providence, for He alone knows what is best for us. I know my prayer for you has been that you may be directed by God in whatever you did, and I trust that you have been, and if this is the way God has designed for you, I would strive to be perfectly resigned to His will, and so I felt that I had done what was right in His sight I would care not for the opinion of men; I know dear Ruthvin that it would have been hard for you to be with such men, who have not acted the right part towards your own dear brother. oh! sincerely do I pray and trust that whatever is done that it may all be for the best. Sister E. is still with sister Lillis, she sent me word that she would stay until brother Edgar came home, I was glad to hear this morning that she was better and I hope she may soon be entirely well again. I will look for you Friday night, and how glad my dearest Ruthvin we will all be to see you. I find it very lonely since sister E left, during these long days. I did not go out to church last Sunday, as aunt S was sick, and Bettie McFaddin and her husband children Eliza and Ned came by and took dinner with me, Bettie told me the Sunday before she was coming, so I had dinner prepared for them, but I was sorry they did not come some other day. Bettie told me to give her respects to you. Mr. Witherspoon stopped here on his way down, and he told me he was going to quit the company if they elected new officers.

I looked for him to come by in the morning, and I fixed up some things to send to you, and waited until I thought he was not coming, and I sent the basket to the church, but he said he could not carry it anyway, and I think he was in a sulky too so I presume it would have been in his way. I would have been glad if you could have got it, but you must take the will for the deed this time. Peter came for the buggy and went over to bro' Edgars with it since dinner, I hope you may get home safely and you must take good care of yourself. And now with my best and warmest love and praying that God,s richest blessings may ever rest upon you my dear husband, I remain as ever your loving and devoted wife.

Hattie

At Home, April 29th 1862
Dear Uncle Ruthvin

This will inform you that I saw Uncle Edgar this evening. he said I must send my musket, cartridge box, cap box, knapsack and haversack to you, and you must put them in his tent, and leave them there, without mention it to any one, I have a mattress tick, a pillow, two blankets, one pair of shoes, and a hat down there, the hat is in your tent. I have a confederate blanket, too but you better leave that with the rest of my things in your tent, I have mentioned all the things that I have down there, I am more than ten thousand times oblige to you and Uncle Edgar for sending me word not to return. Uncle I am thankful to my God that I am away from Georgetown, do contrive some way to get John off if you can, your family is well. Aunt Lillis is better than she was, I need not say any thing about the excitement as I hope to see you soon. Mother is unwell, the rest are all well.

I must colse, excuse the badly written letter, I hope this finds you better.

Your Affect. Nephew
Isaac Montgomery

May 1st 1862
My ever dear Sister,

I was truly happy to get your very welcome note. I want to see you all so much. have thought of you being alone. know you were indeed glad to have miss E come home. Father was waiting for me on Friday and after talking to bro Wm a little while we started for home. got there five minutes after two. All were well but Jane and she was better though she had been very ill indeed. dr. Dubose went to see her three times. She has milk leg now.[130] I was so happy to get home and enjoyed it so much. Went to the Meth church Sunday and said the Bible lesson. Father is teacher. Mr Weaver is better but very feeble yet. he sent his kindest regards to you, he told me he fell in love with you. I do not much think he will come to qulty meeting and if he does says he will not have time to come to see you. I can't tell you half as much as I want to, but will tell you when I come over. am very glad indeed you are going to send for me as I want to go frightful bad particularly as dear bro R will be there. I had heard of what you mentioned. Mr Y showed me a letter he got from bro R on the subject. I am so sorry it has happened but I trust that it is all for the best. Mother father Maria and Wm send you a great deal of love. I hope you (a page appears to be missing here, for the letter continues on the back:)

fear it will rain. Several of the girls have been quite sick with sore throat. Janie Rembert has it now but is much better and I hope she will be soon entirely well. I had my share of sorethroat last year. hope I will not have it now. Give my best love to cousin Hu when you write to him again. It is no use to ask him to write to me, for I asked him when he was here and then he talked like he would write me very soon but that is generally the last of it.

Amanda give my love to Mrs Haynsworth, and the rest of the family. tell her I am very much obliged to her for the box she fixed for me just as much so as if I had received it. it was really very kind in her. and I am also very much obliged to you both for the letters

130 Milk leg: a painful swelling of the leg caused by inflammation and clotting in the veins and affecting some postpartum women. https://www.merriam-webster.com/dictionary/milk leg

and palmetto. But I will have to close this now, as it will soon be dinner time. Tell Mary I intended writing her a letter to send in this although she has not answered my last letter but will not have time. give much very much love to her from me. And now dear sister goodbye. that Heaven's <u>richest</u> <u>blessings</u> may ever rest upon you is the sincere wish of your ever true and loving sister

Almira

I will send you the measure of my dress the next time I write which will be very soon.

Bishopville 6 May 1862
Dear Ruthvin

You have our kind thanks for your esteemed letter which came to hand a few days Since. I heard through it with deep regret of the difficulties that prevail in the company to which you belong and I feel very Sorry for it not only on your acct but also on your brother Edgars. If, as I suppose Edgar has failed to be elected–though you may have been–it Still leaves you in a very perilous situation. Whether or not you can consent to hold office after your brothers withdrawal or failure to be elected it will be for you to determine. If you cannot have friendly feelings toward the other officers, you would feel yourself in a very embarressed situation, and though you asked advice, it is not in my power to give it, and you can only be governed by your own judgement and feelings. If it were so that you found you could remain with any satisfaction to yourself–there is no knowing what time may bring about. The man who is on the popular side today may not be on the morrow–though I know that when a man is made Capt it is not easy to get clear of him when his men have no voice to make a change, though when they do have a voice they do not always use it to their own advantage. A man by the name of Absolom, was once made Captain, and for awhile deposed the older head, but all came right in the end, though Absolom lost Everything.

I went down and met Amanda in (illegible) last Friday and the following Tuesday carried her down to Scottsville and met WWM[131] who carried her back to Manning. From him I heard of Joe Plowden, that he was in a very dangerous situation, the abscess in his side having penetrated the bowels. I hope they may be mistaken about the case, but fear not, and I am now inclined to think that the bowels were penetrated before the abscess was lanced and that there was an accumulation of gas in the rising at the time it was opened, and that upon its escaping it became flatened as they informed me. I feel very sorry for Joe and his relatives on his account. You have probably heard that Jane has been very sick with pneumonia but I am glad to say she is better, though she improves very slowly. Heard

131 Rev. William Wynn Mood

from Daniel lately—He was well. Their company had reached to 170 men and they were discussing the propriety of making up another company—If you should leave your company I wonder if you will go to see theirs—and if you thought of doing so I wonder if you could carry some men with you?

Except Jane, all the rest of us are pretty well. I thank you again for your letter. hope we may soon hear from you again—If you come home do come and see us—we take a deep interest in your welfare—

Most affectionately yours -
William Rogers

Home May 18, 1862
My dear Sister Hattie

It really has been a long time since I have written to you, but I suppose you have heard from us through Amanda. I had the pleasure of receiving a letter form her this morning, she had spent last Friday night with you. I was so sorry to learn that my dear brother Ruthvin still suffered with pain in his side. I do wish he could be relieved of it. Tell I think if he would come and spend a few days up here he would improve, as I have no doubt this pure air of our little village would be beneficial to him. I really think you and he might for the last two weeks I have been telling mother perhaps you would come up the last of the week, but in this we have been disappointed. Next Saturday and Sunday our Qtly. meeting takes place. Can you not come up then? we would be so delighted to have you with us. Mother says you must come. I am looking for my friend Gertrude then or at least she wrote me she would come if she could possibly do so. I hope she can. I want to see her so much. Yesterday was observed as a day of humiliation and prayer. Oh! I trust the many fervent prayers offered up on that occasion may be answered and that God may shower down blessings upon us. Really the times are very dark now, but I hope that brighter days are in store for us. Cousin Hu has been up to see us this week. came up Tuesday and returned yesterday. he is looking very well. Daniel I know has been delighted this week as sister Lizzie has been to see him. She and father went down Tuesday, and have just gotten home. they left Daniel quite well. Little Nora stayed with me, she is so much company for me, and she gets prettier every day. I had Selena Jane and Elenora Durant to spend the day with me Thursday, and had quite a pleasant time. Cousin Hu and Mr. Weaver were both here so we had quite a crowd of us. Mr. Weaver and several of the girls went fishing this morning. I believe though they met with very poor success. I did not go but you know I never like going to such places much. And so you have attended the concert. Amanda writes they are have another in two weeks. Well Hattie you must really excuse this letter, as I have a very bad headache and can scarcely write at all. All unite with me in much love to you every one. Kiss my dear Brother Ruthvin for me and write soon to your sister

Maria

(written in pencil at bottom of letter:)

Dear Hattie,

As the named is changed I should think you would direct letters Lieut D M Rogers–Yeadon light Artillery, Capt Johnson's Co., Charleston SC I have been directing Palmetto Battalion but that might not be right now. Much obliged for the notes. wish you would go tomorrow night. Roper is better today. Do all of you come over soon. I forgot to tell you yesterday that Mr. John Hodges daughter joined the church at Qrty. meeting. She seemed powerfully (illegible) upon. Give my best love to all (illegible)

your affct sister

Camp Yeaden Near Charleston May 20th, 1862
Dear Ruthven,

I have been looking for a letter from you but have received none as yet, I sent word to you by William and also wrote to Harriet. I told William to tell you to come down. I heard that you declined being elected into Butlers company and you had not decided what to do. So I sent you word that if you would like to go into Artillery service that I would try and get you some position. We have divided our company and I have been waiting to hear from you. The position is 2 Master Sargeant. You have $22 pay and have a horse to ride and your duties would be light. I told William to tell you to try and get some men but if you can get no men you could help us out in making a company fund this will answer in place of the men if you cannot get them. If you would like to get the position let me hear from you I would be glad to have you with me I am 1st Lt. in the new company. I was much surprised on yesterday by meeting up with Samson on "Tar Island" he appeared quite lively he said there was some three or four that came down with him they are cutting wood to blockade Stono.[132] our camp is four miles from Charleston Hotel across big bridge. I have not time to write you a long letter Give much love to dear Hattie also Mrs. Eliz & the boys. Please write to me soon. I got my leg hurt by my horse falling on it but will be about in a day or two. Direct Lt D. M. Rogers Capt Johnsons Company Palmetto Battalian L. A. God bless and be with you all

Your Affect Brother
Daniel M Rogers

---

132 Stono River, southwest of Charleston

James Island May 15th 62
Dear Uncle,

According to promise, I now take my pen to write a few lines to you first mentioning our trip to the island. we left Kingstree Monday morning at 6 o ck. arrived at Charleston at half past ten o ck. and having no conveyance to take us on to the Island, were detained in Charleston until Tuesday at ten o ck, when we took the boat for James Island, we went quite near to Fort Johnson & Morris Island, but got a short view of those two places but got a better view of Sumter as the boat stopped there to leave provision, it is one of the most splendid and masterly looking places that I ever saw, I can not express the feeling that I had while passing before the guns, and at the same time seeing the blockading fleet some ten or fifteen miles off. we then moved off for the Island and reached it at one o ck, marched up to the tents, finding a number of acquaintances & relations present, we were gladly received by all, and fortunately were mustered in for the war by order of Col Simonton without hesitating one minute. we have not received the bounty yet, but will in a few days as the Capt. has it in hand. I have sad news to relate to you, the old planter with two ten inch Columbiads and a few rifle cannons, I don't know how many, were taken by one negro being a Pilot and some more and carried to the blockadeing fleet, the boat was in front of Gen. Riply's office.[133]

we are situated in a very pretty looking place but awful dusty. I will mention more about the Island and other things in general in my next, the mail leaves at 12 o ck. and having another letter to write I must close, this leaves us in health and hope it will find

133 Robert Smalls, 1839–1915, was an enslaved African American born in Beaufort, SC. He, along with his wife, two children and a few others, escaped to freedom in the "Planter," a Confederate supply ship loaded with guns, ammo, and important documents, by sailing past the forts of Charleston harbor and out to the Union blockade. He eventually became a Union sea captain, was a successful businessman, and and went on to serve in both houses of the SC legislature. https://www.biography.com/political-figure/robert-smalls

you and all the rest of the family enjoying the same. Give my love to all the family yourself included,

Your affect Nephew
Isaac Montgomery

Camp Pettigrew James Island June 13th 1862
Dear Uncle

This will inform you that we received your affectionate letter a few minutes ago, and was truly glad to hear that your health is improving, also that your arm is getting better, for you have not enjoyed what you might call good health so long, and hearing of the breaking out on your arm, I was fearful it would terminate very serious with you, but thank God, I hope you will be restored to perfect health again.

I would have written to you before now, but we have had so much picket duty to do, for the last ten days, that I have not had time to do any thing at all. we went out last Monday mor, and returned to camp Tuesday about twelve o ck. we wash off for breakfast, and after eating, lay down to take a little rest. by this time in came a courier riding pretty fast, and reported the enemy landing in force. the drum was beat, and off we had to go again, and did not get back to camp until next mor, as the report proved to be false. there is no more dependence to be put in these couriers here, than in the wind for they bring in so many false reports. I need not mention any thing to you about the battle that took place a few days ago, for you have seen the paper, and know as much about it as I do. this Regt. was held in readiness to reinforce them, if they needed us, but they succeeded in driving them back, without the loss of many lives.[134] You talk of flanking General Green, but we have a General here, that we will have a little more trouble to flank, than Genl Green. I wish I could of meet you and the rest of your family at home. what a pleasant time we could of had, riding over the crop, talking over the past, and enjoying the company of those who are so near and dear to us. it gives me so much pleasure to hear from you all, and things in general. I would like very much to see your crop, for I know you have a good one. We now have a chaplain, Mr. Porter. he preaches evry Sunday, and prayer meeting evry night. I hope he will do a great

134 In early June, 1862, several skirmishes took place as Confederate forces defended James Island from Union forces who were attempting to capture Charleston. (This was prior to the June 16, 1862, Battle of Secessionville.) https://www.battlefields.org/learn/civil-war/battles/secessionville

deal of good. whenever we (that is the Regt) go on picket he goes with us. I must close, excuse this badly written. both of us sends our love to your family and receive the same from your affect Nephew

Isaac Montgomery

P. S. Cousin Ebin Martin sends his love to you. we are both well. write as often as you can.

Home July 10th/62
My dearest Hattie,

Your very welcome letter was received, and gladly read on yesterday morning. It delighted me so to see such a nice, long letter; I hope you may be able to cheer me frequently with such lengthy epistles.

Manda wrote to me some time ago; it pained me to hear that she suffers from those distressing head aches. I fear she will always be troubled with them. I had one of the most severe colds last week, that I have had for a year. I felt little disposed to take interest in anything. am entirely free from it now.

The war is growing still more serious. The gunboats removed from James Is. must be to croperate with McLennan's army, the vessels near Charleston, I believe, are a mere feint. I expect to hear important news from Richmond. May God have mercy, and help our men. I have several relatives near Richmond–have not seen their names as yet–

Soon after the battle of the "Seven Pines" as I looked at the list of wounded and killed, the first name I saw was Capt. W. B. Lyles killed.[135] I recognized the name instantly to be Georgie (illegible)'s husband. Poor little Georgie, how much I feel for her! I have not heard anything of my darling friend since you wrote that she had a son. I know that I cannot enter deeply into her feelings, yet I sympathise to the best of my capacity with her. She was pious when I knew her–and I trust she is much nearer Jesus (torn) than she was six years ago, and will bow submissively to the will of her Creator.

Dear Ella Timmerman, who was she who did not love good Ella Timmerman This dear girl has married an inebriator. For many months I have been noticing for David Jamison's name in the Army, when suddenly (to me) I hear it announced by a stranger, that he is at home dancing while intoxicated etc. etc. They say he claps his hands over his partner's head, when the dance is over. How mortifying this must be to Ella's refined taste! Oh! may her affliction prove refining fire to her soul. We know that such afflictions have been blessings to

---

135 The Battle of Seven Pines, or the Battle of Fair Oaks, took place on May 31-June1, 1862, near Richmond, VA. Both sides claimed victory. https://www.battlefields.org/learn/civil-war/battles/seven-pines

many souls. I write this to you as you write to me, dear Hattie. You either misunderstood me, or else I was not particular in expressing my desires to visit Manda. I mean't when her school would close for the year, provided there would be no war. then I would visit her. You cannot imagine, my dear Hattie how much yours and Mr. Plowden's wishing me to visit you also, pleased me; it made me really happy to think I possessed a friend who would be so happy to see me. Let me assure you that there are no friends of mine that I would more willingly visit than your own dear self, and Manda, and if a kind Providence permit such a pleasure, I shall meet you at your homes— You must know how I have felt in regard to having you and Manda come to see me, and wonder if you will ever afford me such happiness. I think I would love your Father's family very much—I feel as great, or greater interest in them than I do for those whom I know, and then to see your mother with her children, and the children looking up to that dear mother would touch my tenderest feelings. —

You dream't of me, dear Hattie, and thought I had changed. I am twenty-three, almost twenty-four (1st of Nov.) and look true to my age. the white lock on the left of my head is still more visible than when I was at school. This is a true account of "Martha."

May the Lord bless you, and all with you.
Your sincerely attached friend
Martha

Camp Sept 26th 1862
My Dear Sister Harriet

Your kind letter and also two nice hams and potatoes came safely to hand. And now before going farther you can say to Ruthvin that I challenge him to meet me in combat at fifty paces with sand bags for not coming to see me while he was down here. He was in three hundred yards of our camp. our camp is just opposite the Eutaw Regt. in Wappoo County. he could have come over very easily in a boat. I am right provoked with him about it. Edgar B- brought over the letter and bag. I shall live well for a while. I got a keg of cider from Home and enjoy that very much. I send you and Miss Elizabeth many thanks for the provisions sent me. I was very much rejoiced a few days ago to hear that my dear Lizzie was the mother of a lovely boy and was doing well. How thankful I felt to my Heavenly Father for bringing her safely through. I received a letter to night from Jane saying she was still improving and doing well. May the child be spared to be useful and to be a child of God. I have been very well since I came from Home, and still feel very well. I saw Dr Mood in the City to day. he said Bro Wm thought of coming down Tuesday. Father also wrote me that Chas spoke of coming down Tuesday. I hope I may see both of them. I saw sister's piece in the Advocate[136] on dear Anna.[137] It was shown to me by Mr Witeman. it was very pretty. He (Mr Witeman) said he intended writing to Bro Wm to enlarge on it so as it may be put in pamphlet form for Sunday school. I am glad you are going to spend several days at home as Ruthvin goes on to Liberty Hill. I expect the dear folks at home are quite lonely too. Oh! about the scarf. you can make one for me. I have one but should we go to Virginia this winter two would not be in the way. My letters must generally be very short as I have to write

136 The Southern Christian Advocate, the official newspaper of the Methodist Episcopal Church, was begun in Charleston in 1837, and published weekly. https://digitalcommons.wofford.edu

137 Anna Elenora Mood, eldest child of Rev. W. W. and Lucy Mood, was born Nov. 3, 1856, and died Aug. 12, 1862. Information found on her tombstone at Bethlehem Methodist Cemetery, Bishopville, SC

fast and in short time. Do write to me again soon. Give much love to Ruthvin Miss Elizabeth & the boys and a good portion for yourself Good bye

Your affect Bro
Daniel

Sept 27th 1862

I am well this morning. have no news. the clouds are gathering as if we might have a rainy spell. I received a letter from William. the first one I ever received from the gentleman. he writes well and very correctly. also a good hand

Affect
Daniel

Bishopville 11th Oct. 1862
Dear Ruthven & Harriet,

I was from home some two days and arrived home the night before last. I hoped to find you at home with us but was disappointed, but hope it may not be long before we may have the pleasure of seeing you here. I found dear Harriet's good letter on reaching home. Sorry to hear that dear Ruthven was not well, but hope it may be nothing lasting. Since the last time I wrote you I have had a good deal of botheration on account of the movements made by the negroes of this section for you are aware that Ellick and Enoch were in it and so also was Bob whom I had hired. They are all in Darlington jail for 12 months. The three negroes Mitchel, Hiram and Alfred were Executed on yesterday at Sumter.

I do not allow myself to be disturbed about the matter now, there is nothing with which I can change myself and the fault was altogether their own.

I am sorry to say that Mr. Weaver is very low down—can barely walk about. He had a hemorrhage some three weeks ago and has never been as well since. Mr. and Mrs. Sifley are staying with us now and I am sorry to say that Mrs. Sifley has been very sick with fever for several days past. She is now a little better. I saw Almira on last Thursday. She was well. Lizzie had a letter from Daniel day before yesterday. He was well. Daniel regretted much that he did not see Ruthven. He was just on the oposite side of the river from where Ruthven saw Mr. Montgomery. I think all are well at Mr. Durants and our own family are well also. I have had some asthma along but I hope it may soon leave me as the weather becomes cool. Do on receipt of these lines write to us, and if you are up any time after the 25th of this month we shall have none but our family with us unless Mr. Weaver shall still remain with us.

Do let me before I close again beg you to come up and see us. Life is always uncertain—let us see each other as often as we well can while we live. and now dear children with love from all I will close remaining your affectionate father

William Rogers

One sack salt (Allum) is being kept for Ruthven

Columbia Nov. 15th 1862
My own precious sister,

I have just finished a letter home and as I have a few more leisure moments, I know of no other way in which I could more pleasantly employ them than to devote them in writing to my dear absent sister. But oh how much more pleasant would it be to be with and talk with you face to face. this cannot be though, so I will content myself in conversing with you in this way.

I had a letter from Amanda the other day in which she was telling me all about all of your visits home. I know you all had a nice time together. How much pleasure it would have afforded me to have formed one of the number. I cannot have this pleasure yet a while though but this only teaches me to prize it more, for had I always been with all the loved ones at home, I would never have learned what a blessing it was. But I can now fully realize and understand the import of these words, "the dearest spot on earth to me is home sweet home."

Amanda said that Monday afternoon you all with the exception of herself went to that little mound in the graveyard beneath which lies the little body of our loved Anna. How little those who were with her on her fith birthday thought as they imprinted a kiss of love upon her sweet lips, that ere her sixth birthday should roll around, they could not imprint that kiss upon her brow, but only carry wreaths of flowers and lay them upon her grave. Oh! how uncertain life is. still we are so negligent. ere the third of next November shall have come, we who are now in the enjoyment of health may be called to our last resting place. Solemn thought yet oh! how true. Oh that we could so live on earth that we should be ready, ere the summon comes, to meet all the loved ones who have gone before, on the right hand of Him who reigns eternal in the Heavens.

Mr. Haynswort called to see Mary Coskrey and myself the other night. I assure you I was not a little glad to see him, particularly as I could hear directly from you all. Amanda asked me in her letter if the fare was very bad this year. tell her I am happy to say that it is not, but that Mr Black still does his best to give us nice fare, and a plenty. I can truly say that we have no cause to complain. Tell brother William and sister that Mr Moods family are all quite well except the baby who is still sick, but is better. Mr Moods little son Preston reminds me some of dear little Anna. his hair is very much like hers was when it curled. his forehead too is like hers. His niece Carrie Hill came the other day. But I will now have to close. Give a heartfull of love to Brother Ruthvin, Miss Elisabeth and kiss Haynsworth and Lute for me. also give my best love to William sister and Amanda tell brother Liam and Amanda that I will answer their letter very soon and you and sister both must write very soon to me. I would beg brother Ruthvin to write but I am afraid it would be no use. Goodbye my dear sister. remember me as ever your devoted sister,

Almira

Jane and Ellen are quite well and send love.

Bishopville So Ca Nov 19th 1862
My dear Sister

As Maria is going to write to Mammie and I have not written to you in a good while I will write you a few lines and send it in Maria's letter. We are all quite well except Mr. Weaver he says he feels better to day than yesterday. Cousin Caroline got a letter from the girls last night they said they were all better. The call from 35 to 50 took mighty near all of the men from about here even Mr Vaughn had to go they left yesterday and last night Mr Wm and Mr Drafus Dixon left last night. Sister Hattie did you know that Miss Salina Carnes and David Durant were married they got married last Thursday morning at 11 oclock. Sister Lizzie got a letter from Bro Daniel last week and he said they did not get anything to eat but bread so Mother and sister Lizzie made up a box and sent it up to Camden by Jim and it went off yesterday morning and I expect he got it to day as sister L wrote to him where to get it. But I must close all join me in love to all I remain your affct Brother

W. A. Rogers

I will write you very soon my precious Sister

Maria

Bishopville Dec. 24th 1862
My darling Sister

Wm's and your kind letters were recd last mail and we were more than happy to hear from you that all were well. I suppose ere this dear bro Ruthvin has got home. I do hope he is well, that his throat is better. wish so much we could hear from him now whether he has gone or not. if he does go in that company don't feel bad about it, dear sister, it may be for the best that he should. I do wish he would apply for exemption. You must write us all about it. I have no doubt but it will all work together for good yet, only let our trust in our Saviour who doeth all things well. and if we do trust him he has promised to be with us until the end. I know you have been anxiously looking for Daniel. Lizzie has quite sick she came here on Sat. morning and was confined to her bed until yesterday, when she got up, and she was well enough this morning to go up to her father's. Daniel though still speaks of going to see you next week. his cough troubles him very much. wish so much he could get rid of it. The rest of us are quite well, but Mr. Weaver. he keeps pretty much the same. Dr. Dubose was to see him Thursday and I think he has gotten better under his treatment. His niece got here last Friday night. she is a sweet girl, we all like her very much. she looks so much like him. he is delighted to have her with him. Dr. Dubose said he would see him again last Sunday or Monday, but he has not come yet owing to the extreme illness of Mrs Manning Brown. the Dr. has no hopes of her recovery. poor Mr. B. I feel so much for him. he has been so much afflicted. I presume you have heard ere this bro Wm's appt. he was elected president of Davenport F. College, and he did not give them a decided answer at Conference, but has concluded not to accept it but will return to Manning. Jane and Ellen Durant have got home. they left Almira quite well. she is now with her friends the misses Hulle. this is Christmas eve. though it seems little like it. A merry Christmas to you all dear sister and many happy returns. we will have a very quiet but happy one I trust here—but oh much happier would we be could you dear bro R and Wm and Almira be with us and oh dear Sister how we miss our darling little angel Anna. how happy she was last Christmas when she and little Mary were here together. but thrice happy is she now with her blessed Saviour. we know not who of us will have passed away ere another year has gone. may it find us ready to meet the summons. tell dear little Wm we miss him sadly, and often speak of him. tell him we hope he has kept well and enjoyed himself finely and as (illegible) do want to see him very much. Nothing new (illegible) since you left. Sister and I have been (illegible). We have just got back. Cousin David came over yesterday. he has just left for Mr. Crosswell's. his mother and sister have given up the idea of breaking up, they will still stay in Sumter. There is to be a Tableaux performance in Lynchburg New Years night. if nothing prevents I expect I will go with Lizzie. Mother says to tell you not to look certain for Daniel next week. he will come if he can. Lizzie and her mother are to have their babies baptized tomorrow. Daniel has named him Eliazer. I do not know what other name they will give him. they are dear sweet children. Nora has been sleeping with me and seems to love me more than she used to. Father sent Vermeille Wm and Ada to Manning this week. Jim carried them. got back last night. Cousin David says tell you he is thousand times obliged for the scarf. Father intended writing you about Wm's staying longer, but thinking Daniel would go he did not do it. We will look for him when he comes. You must let Henry and Haynsworth come with him. do hope they may. All send their best love to you bro R Miss E the children and Wm give much love to Mr H's family for me. tell Lizzie she must write to me—I will try and write her soon. You must excuse this awful written letter but I have written in great haste with a poor (illegible). I hope dear sister you have kept well. How much I wish we could be together now. kiss bro R for me and dear little Wm. I will be so glad when he comes. I almost forgot to tell you that Mr Thomas Fraser is dead. Bro Wm and sister send their best love to all. We could have made no difference about Wm's staying until Monday but if he comes before that it will make no difference. sorry we could not get you word. do write us soon all about bro R. we are so anxious to hear. I will write you again soon and try and write a better letter. May God richly bless you all is the constant prayer of your devoted sister

Amanda Rogers

Columbia Jan 27th 1863
My own precious Sister,

Had I followed my own inclinations I would have written you as soon as I got here for I longed for your sympathizing heart, and I thought you knew my feelings so well. Well I will go back to when we parted. You know not how much I felt it to be separated from you. more than five months seemed so long, you know it is longer than we have ever been from each other. I thought of you and bro Wm very often and was afraid you would suffer with cold. I was busy getting ready until Sat evening. I got through and Ellen and I went to call on Mrs Holleyman and while we were their Vermielle came. Sunday evening father and I left and oh! Hattie it was so hard for me to part from all the dear ones. sometimes I think no one ever felt as bad as I do, but I try to control my feelings and not let it be known much. this world would be too happy for us if we never had to endure partings. we staid at cousin E. S. Sunday night, expecting to take the cars before day Monday but we were deceived as to the time they left and just as we were leaving Cousin E. we heard the whistle blow. Mr. Walker who was to go on too did not get to the depot until after we did. so we all went back to Lynchburg and staid until next morning, when we got off in good time. got to Kingsville and as there were a number of passengers they got the conductor to put on a passenger car to a freight train and we got here between eleven and twelve. Mr. Weatherly was on board with his three daughters and Colin, who was taking them on to Salem to school. there were a good many representatives came on with us. We found Almira looking very well indeed. I got acquainted with all the teachers directly after I got here. I like Mr. Mood and all the teachers very much indeed. Miss Jones and Miss Backus are both young ladies. Miss B is not much older than I am. they have both been remarkably kind and sociable and I feel already as if they are old acquaintances. A stranger knows how to appreciate kind acts and I know I will never forget them. We have a nice sett of girls and I think when I get accustomed to my new life I will like it very much. I did not feel homesick much until after father left and then oh how I felt—last quarter was not a circumstance to it. Do you remember how we felt when we first got to

O—particularly early in the morning? well strive as I would against it those same disagreeable feelings would come and many bitter tears have I shed thinking of you all and how I wished I could see your dear faces if only for a few fleeting moments. I was telling Almira the other day how happy I would feel now at the thought of seeing sister or yourself one every week and of visiting you. Last year was such a pleasant one to me but this cup was not unmixed with bitter for in that year we saw our almost idolized darling pass away, but oh to a home infinitely brighter and happier than ours. but it will not be long before we too must bid adieu to this earth. then may we all greet each other on the eternal shore.

I entered upon my duties Thursday. have one soph, one intermediate, one Junior, one Senior, and the primary classes, and give writing lessons. I took miss Backus place, as there are so many music scholars she devotes her time entirely to music. she is a niece of Mrs McIntosh. she often talks of her relatives to me. her mother is teaching now with Mrs Mc. she says Lizzie is grown says she is a nice girl and plays splendidly and is quite intelligent. she graduated last Summer. I saw her likeness this evening. she has changed a good deal I think since I saw her. Mr. Mood has not been well to day but is better this evening. we all miss him very much. Mr. Mood is quite sociable. they have a very interesting family. I rec-d a letter from Lizzie and was glad to hear she still thought of coming. I will be so glad to see her for I love Lizzie very much. Mr. Mood is perfectly willing to take her only for drawing, painting and music as she wishes. I went with Miss Jones and Mr. Wannamaker to the state house Sat. Col Bradley made a speech, but a short one and I could not hear what he said. saw your representatives from Clarendon also and some others that I knew but did not have an opportunity of speaking to any of them but Mr. Kennedy. his daughter was with him. went into the Senate chamber and heard Col Moses make a speech. Cousin Charles and Cousin Elisha have been to see us since I have been here. I wish bro Ruthvin would come to Columbia sometime soon. Give my best love to him and tell him I will judge of how much he thinks of me now by the number of times he writes to me. Do please both of you write often. Give dear Miss Eliz- much love, tell her I often think of her and wish to see her. kiss Haynsworth and

Lute for me tell H he must be smart and improve lots by the time I see him again. Give much love to Henry. tell him I am looking for a letter from him. hope he will not disappoint me. I was very glad to hear Mary Jane would come. Glad they will get so good a teacher. Give my love to Mr E Plowden and family and Mr M- family to Cousin Callie, children and Cousins Joe and Lizzie. I do hope he is better. Almira has been cooking sausages and burnt them terribly and has been cooking at a dreadful rate. the fare is very good indeed for these hard times. Almira says give her best love to all and tell you she will write you soon. Mary C is quite well and seems very contented now. she is very studious. stands first in her classes. Mag Murchison is here too. she is a right nice girl. I have seen Annie Crook since I have been here. she is as lively as ever. they are living now in columbia. Well dear Hattie I will again beg you to write to me very soon and then close. How I wish I was with you tonight and we could have one of our long talks but I trust the time will pass pleasantly away and we be permitted to see each other again. Mrs. Durant wrote to Ellen and Jane that Daniel's cough was no better. I was so sorry to hear it. wish so much he could get well. May Heaven bless you and may your life be a useful and happy one. Good bye darling Ever remember in your prayers,

Your devoted sister
Amanda M. R.

Bishopville 6 Feby, 1863
Dear Ruthvin

Yours and dear Harriets letter of the 29 came to hand and I made arrangements to send wagon down for the pork to leave here on Thursday (yesterday) but the day was so bad I could not send. and now there is no chance until next week. I hope to hear from you again, and will still send if not too late. But even if it is killed and salted, I am perfectly willing to allow you full price for salt and salting and still take the pork. Will pay you cash for it and as much more in price as you think proper. I mean in difference between pork in the hog and pork cut up and salted. Still if you prefer not to sell now, it will be all right. I wrote you last Wednesday to send by Mr. Holmes, who was going down for me, but it is now to late for that you know.

I am happy to say we are all pretty well except Mr. Weaver who is getting worse. and dear Lucy had a Daughter born last Wednesday morning. She is doing very well. The negroes that were in Darlington jail I got a pardon for and they came out last Monday morning. I believe I will try them on the place and hardly think there will be any excitement among the people on the subject. Perhaps you will have written to me before this reaches you, but if not please write me by mail to Lynchburg. I have not time to write but few lines as I have just now a chance to send to Lynchburg.

I hope this will find you all well. May God bless you all. Love to all the family.

Yours affectionately
William Rogers

Feby 15th 1863
My Dear Sister Harriet

For so long a time to have elapsed before writing to you I am really ashamed. You must not think that I have not thought of you by no means. You, Ruthvin and dear Miss Elizabeth have been in my mind often very often. I have felt so badly most of the time and then company business to attend to that I have neglected writing until now. and then I always write to Lizzie once a week. You must not think hard of me for not writing before. My health is about the same as when I was at your house. my cough still troubles me. I hope I may improve towards spring. I was glad to hear that our dear Sister Lucy was the mother of another girl and was getting on well. May it live to be a comfort and blessing to them. Mr. Durant has been very sick but is up again. I suppose dear Amanda is getting used to her new home by this time. I saw Aunt Nancy & Hugh yesterday. he had just got back from Wilmington—was looking very well indeed. I saw Edgar Montgomery the day after he got back. he also was looking very well. The excitement about the attacke on Charleston seems to be getting much less. they seem to think Savanna may be the first place. It is hard to tell. I received a letter from Lizzie & Bro Wm. they said Mr. Weaver was sinking rapidly and would not live long. poor man he has suffered so much. but he is ready for the change. I was thinking of getting Lizzie to come down and stay a while with me. I have procured a house near camp where she could stay very pleasantly. I wish so much I had stayed longer. I hated to leave you all so bad. I would have enjoyed myself so much if I could have stayed. You all are so kind to a body

(Here the letter ends; no page 2 was found. Presumably written by Daniel Rogers, Hattie's brother.)

Columbia Feb 19th 1863
My dear brother & sister

Your letter dearest Hattie was joyfully welcomed and it did me so much good to hear from you all that you were well. I will write you both at once. We have all been anxiously looking for Lizzie all this week and she has not yet come. but I do hope she will, it will disappoint us dreadfully if she does not. I have my heart set upon it. I wrote to her telling her about the room. I am sorry she cannot room with me. there is no one except dear Almira I would rather have with me here, but I will try and make her stay most of her time with me. I have engaged a place opposite my room, just three or four steps so we will be very near. Since I wrote you we have had to move on the 4th floor (illegible). Jane Ellison Mary M. Mary C. and Lilly Ragin came with me so we are all up here together and I assure you we have right pleasant times. The school is increasing so rapidly that soon every room will be filled. there are now nearly a hundred boarders. Alice and Mary, or Babe Henegan (as cousin Mary always called her) came Tues. they are very sweet girls and Mary is beautiful I think. she has such beautiful black eyes. They also room up here. so I have no bad girls on my floor which relieves me of great trouble. We heard from home Sunday, and oh how it grieved me to hear that dear Mr. Weaver was so much worse. how I pity dear Ellen. I fear it will almost kill her and her situation will indeed be an afflicting one. she will lose her best earthly Friend. Well dear Hattie I had written thus far when I had to quit to hear my recitations and little did I think that ere I took up my pen again I would see my darling brother Ruthvin. the girls all went out walking this evening and soon after they left Mrs. Gist sent up to know if I would not go and walk with her so I soon got ready and went and did not get back until right late. imagine then my delight on getting to the college, when Mary C. called to me and said here is Lizzie and Mr. Plowden. they took tea with us and have not long been gone. We begged them to come and see us again and I do hope they will. How provoking that they could not come right on. oh Hattie it has done me so much good to see bro Ruthvin, so unexpected too, and oh I am so glad to hear from you, dear miss Elizabeth and the children. A <u>thousand</u> <u>thanks</u> to you and

Miss E for the very nice box you sent us. It was acceptable I assure you. Almira has just made way into it with the tongs and I have finished eating a large slice of the nice ham and biscuit. everything is so nice and reminds me so much of the dear hands that fixed them and I can imagine I saw you both while fixing it with so much thoughtful care of us. We are so delighted to have Lizzie with us. she and Mary have just gone to bed. I do hope Lizzie will be pleased here. I know she will be loved. I had many questions to ask after you all, but didn't get half through. wish I could go home with him and be with you all. You dont know half how bad I want to see you. How do Haynsworth and Lute come on? Tell them not to forget "Aunt Mandie" for she thinks often of them. Mary is quite put out at her mother's having twins. Lizzie has been teasing her a great deal about her little sisters. Bro Ruthvin says he thinks they will name sister's little babe Lucy. I hope they will. I thought perhaps they would name her for sister. O how sorry I am to hear how bad poor Mr. Weaver is. it is so dreadful his losing his eyesight. truly he has been sorely afflicted but there is a joyful rest awaiting him beyond this "vale of tears" Mysterious are the ways of divine Providence and past our feeble comprehension, but God will one day make it plain to our weak discerning eyes. Lizzie has not given me your letter yet as it was in her trunk, but I will get it in the morning. The retiring bell has long since rung—and all have retired I expect, but A. and myself. she is busy now eating some of the nice pindars you sent us. how good you and miss Elizabeth are. hope we can one day repay you both. I am afraid I will have the blues after bro R leaves but I will try not. wish you could come to see us. how happy I would be. I am fast getting accustomed to my life here and I am much pleased. Every thing (illegible) on very smoothly. Mr. Mood is one of the best of Presidents and is a favorite with all. You would laugh to see me with a long train of girls. we have to take turns taking them to walk and shopping, and when Mr. Mood is gone I take them to church. I hated it badly at first but am getting used to it. I am afraid you can hardly read this but the paper is bad. you must excuse it. Almira says give you, miss E and the children her best love and says to tell you, you sent her favorites, potatoes. we will feast now for a while. Give my best love to Henry and tell him dont forget his promise to write to me. So my precious sister write me again soon. I prize your letters so highly. Give my heart full of love to dear miss Elizabeth, Haynsworth, Lute and accept the same your own dear self. Tell Jeremia uncle George and all the negroes howdye for me. May God bless and keep you all ever more. Good bye -

Your ever devoted sister,
Amanda

Please give the enclosed to bro Wm

Bishopville 22 April 1863
My own dear Harriet

I am about to write you here a few lines and am happy to say that all are pretty well except your dear Brother Daniel. He is still very unwell and this week he has been blistering his chest. He staid at our house the last two nights and rested very well, but in the day time his cough has been troublesome.

To day he has gone up to Mr Durants. He has been intending to go down to see you all this week but I have advised him to put it off awhile longer, and as our meeting carries on next week you may not look for him until that is over. I sincerely hope and pray that he may by that time be able to make the trek without danger of its doing him injury, and beside I wish to go the last of this week to your Aunt Nancys and I shall need one of his horses to drive. Erwin came up from Charleston with the horse he had there, last week, and She is in fine order. I know you will not blame me for his not going now to see you, though it deprives you of pleasure for the time. But I know it is against him to do much talking at present. He staid too long in camp with such a cough as he had, and I know it is now best that he should do all in his power to be relieved, and he ought to be very careful of himself. Well dear Harriet you certainly have a live Uncle McCallum. We have received a letter from him. He being near Blairsville Union County Ga. He wrote that he had written repeatedly to S. C. and to Tennessee and heard nothing from either place, and so quit writing. He at length was heard from by your cousin James, and then his sister Ann wrote to him and he received the letter, and has now written to us. I hope and trust he may visit us before long. It would rejoice the heart of your dear mother in particular to see him and so it would all the rest—And So I am is Mrs Carter and So I am uncle Powell will be. Dont give us out about visiting you. If all are well we will try to come the latter part of next month. Tell Mary Jane we will send what books we have, but we have no Websters Spellings no Davis Arithmetic but I have put up Smileys and C—locke Phylosophy—no Taceck! I don't know of any chance to send the books until Daniel goes down. I suppose you have heard that I saw the girls in Columbia week before last. Amanda looked well and Almira fat.

We hope soon to hear from you all again. Tell our dear Ruthven to write to us and now I will close. Give love from all of us to all the dear family and tell my good friend Miss Elizabeth that the next time we meet I hope their will be no blunder made. God bless and protect you all.

Your affectionate father
William Rogers

Tell Ruthven we have done very well with some cotton that was sold two weeks since to the Gov. Cotton is much lower now.

C. F. College, May 18th 1863[138]
My darling Sister,

Your long looked for letter came at last and was none the less welcome for its tardy appearance. But I hope that you and bro Ruthvin will treat me a little better in future, tell him he ought to write to me more than once in six months. We are all very well and truly hope this may find you all well. You have recently had Daniel, Lizzie and Maria to see you so sister wrote me. O that I could see our dear brother. I feel so sad sad when I think of him and I fear I do not know how bad he is. Most earnestly do I pray that God may speedily restore him to health if consistent with His holy will. I hope traveling may do him much good. I expect you felt rather lonely after they all left you. We had the pleasure of seeing Mrs. McDowell while she was here, but were only with her a few moments. It was quite a treat to see her. Made me almost think I was at Brewington or Manning. She looks very well. Lizzie has been quite uneasy recently about her father. hearing he has been sick, she said this morning she intended writing to ask them to let her come home, but I do not know whether she did or not. hope that she may soon hear that he is entirely well. 19th May—I began this yesterday, but did not have time to finish it so I will try and do so today. What a bright beautiful day it is. would that I could spend it with you. And it is pleasant indeed to think that only a few more weeks and the privilege of seeing you all will be mine, should nothing prevent. You and bro Ruthvin must be sure and meet us at home, the last of June. Wish you would both come to commencement. Can't you come? Wish so much that you, mother, sister and Maria would all come. I got a letter last night from dear Maria. All were well but dear Daniel, and she thought he had improved some. Maria was just going to Lynchburg. It will not be long I guess before mother and father come down to see you, so you will be fortunate seeing "home folks" Almira and I were

138 Columbia Female College, founded in 1854, is one of the oldest women's colleges in the United States. It was established by representatives of the S.C. Methodist Conference. The college president from 1861-1865 was Henry M. Mood, Rev.W.W. Mood's brother. In 1905 the name was changed to Columbia College. https://www.columbiasc.edu/about/history-mission

to see cousin Joe yesterday. He still thinks he is improving some. Hu, cousin Lizzie and Mary J. all told me to give their love to each one of you, and cousin J. says to tell bro R. that he would write to him but he does not feel strong enough yet. They think so much of you all. I trust that the good Lord may restore him. he has been sorely afflicted, but I know it is for some wise purpose. Cousin L. & M.J. are both quite well. They gave me a letter to read, which they had just rec'd from Mr. McDowell. It was such a good, comforting letter. I expect Mrs. McD. has reached home now if she went on after leaving here. Hattie I wish you and Miss E. could come here now. Columbia looks so beautifully with its flower gardens and shady walks. Have you had any strawberries this Spring? Mrs. Black has given me some once or twice. Lizzie and I took a very pleasant walk with Mr. Calvin Nelson and Lieut. Richbourg. Is he the one to whom Amarinthea was engaged? I think his name is Rufus. Edwina is really married. They are partial to their brother in laws. Mrs. Tora Bagnal must find it lonely there now, but I almost forgot that miss Margaret was there. Have you ever been to see her? There was a very old lady here last week who married quite a young gentleman. he is pretty far gone with consumption too. The Gen Assembly adjourned last week. Mr. Wilson came to see me a short time one day, saw Mr. Cousar too. he spoke to me and called me Mrs. Plowden, I think. Father saw Ellen Thomas while in Spartanburg and I was rejoiced to hear that she would get her uncle,s property. I wish so much she would come here to school next session. A protracted meeting begins at Washington St. church next Thursday. Mr. Kestler and Mr. Moore are both expected I hear. I trust that this meeting may be blessed to some of the precious souls here. Tell bro Ruthvin that he has never gratified my curiosity about that letter he wrote me yet, and to please do so very soon. Give my very best love to dear Miss Elizabeth. Tell her I want to see her so much. I want to write to Henry and Haynsworth so I will close this. Almira sends much love to all. Kiss Lute for me, and remember me to Mr. Edgar P's family. Please write <u>very</u> <u>soon</u>. Our best love too to bro Ruthvin. I remain as ever

Your devoted sister
A. M. Rogers

Bishopville July 22, 1863
My own dear Sister,

Gladly do I avail myself of a short time this morning to write to you, as I feel assured that a letter will be welcomed by you. I know too that you will be glad to hear that we are all well, and am glad too to tell you that when we last heard from our dear brother he was as well as usual. We hear from him very often now. he writes us every day or two as he knows how very anxious we feel about him. We received a letter from him yesterday. Oh! how thankful I was to see from the last paper that God had blessed us with another glorious victory. I trust he will still interpose in our behalf, that ere long we may hear that our insolent Joe have left our beloved State. We have received letters from cousins Hu and Jim this week. Cousin Hu said they had just passed through the battle of Gettysburg, and that it was one of the hardest fought battles of the war.[139] He says our troops fought splendidly. I am so sorry to see from the paper that one of Cousin Mary Jane McLucas brothers was killed. poor creature. I feel so much for her. may grace be given her to bear this affliction with christian resignation. Has she returned from Marlboro yet? Do give our love to her and tell her we deeply sympathize with her in her trouble. Anna Della Dixon spent the day with us last Monday. she says she tried to get here to see you while you were up, but could not possibly etc. do so. There has been another call for men and Cousin Charles thinks he will have to go. I do hope brother Ruthvin will not have to go. I really think he cant stand it. Have you seen Sister since you got home? I hope you got to attend the meeting. I am so anxious to see the precious little baby. I hope you found Miss Elizabeth and the children quite well when you got home. do give them all a great deal of love for us. Amanda says to tell you she will try to come to see you the last of next month. She wrote to Lizzie Haynsworth the other day and said she would go down the last of

---

139 The Battle of Gettysburg was fought in Pennsylvania July 1-3, 1863. Union forces were commanded by Maj. Gen. George M. Meade, and Confederate forces by Gen. Robert E. Lee. Union losses were 23,049, with Confederate losses at 28,062. https://www.history.com/topics/american-civil-war/battle-of-gettysburg

this month, but she says to tell Lizzie she made a mistake, she meant next month. Tell Lizzie she and Mary must be sure to come to see us, we will be so glad to have them come. Miss Clelia is up now. She stays at Cousin Charles. Cousin Charlotte has gone to stay with Cousin Albert awhile. If you see Sister anytime soon tell her to tell Ann her child is some better now, and hopes she may yet get well. Do Hattie write soon and tell us what you all think of the war. Mother says do write to us often. All send a great deal of love to every one of you. And now my dear Sister praying God's blessing upon you I remain as ever your devoted Sister

Maria

Bishopville 25 Augt. 1863
Dear Ruthven & Harriet

As Amanda expects to go to Manning this week I will write a few lines which she no doubt will have opportunity to send you soon.

I feel thankful that I can say this morning that I feel much better and one of my ears improved a good deal last night and I very much hope that I may soon hear well again, and I hope also that my health may soon be restored.

As you will see Amanda or hear from her soon after she gets to Clarendon she will tell you all the news so it is needless that I should say anything on that head.

Since our dear Harriet left here Daniel and my self have been to Columbia and I am sorry to say the physicians think his disease very serious, still we hope that a visit to the Springs and change of climate may benefit him. God in mercy grant that he may again be restored to perfect health.

Since we last saw dear Ruthvin we have all passed through deep affliction. God has seen proper in His Holy and Wise Providence to take the dear little Lucy to Himself and she is now where the wicked cease to trouble and the weary are at rest.[140]

Dear William and Lucy they have waded through deep waters. Once again and again has death snached from their loved embrace those sweet flowers that He lent them to bloom a little while. but they are gone where they will ever bloom on the shores of the Celestial River which breaks forth from the Throne of God and the Lamb.

May God comfort and console their sorrowing hearts until they shall meet their loved ones—meet them to part no more. How thankful I feel that you dear Harriet with dear good Miss Elizabeth were with Wm & Lucy at that trying hour when the little Lucy went to heaven. Dear Miss Elizabeth—we can only love her more and more. May she meet her reward at last for she can never be rewarded here.

---

140 Lucy Rogers Mood, born February 4, 1863, died August 9, 1863, at six months old. She was Rev. W. W. and Lucy Mood's third daughter to die young. Information from her tombstone.

We expect to leave home for the Springs so as to reach Augusta Thursday evening—and after we reach the Springs I will try and write to you and at that time I can probably let you know how to direct letters to us and we shall hope for letters from dear Ruthvin.

Yours affectionately
William Rogers

Warm Springs, Merriwether County GA 2nd Sept. 1863
Dear Ruthven & Harriet

We arrived here much fatigued yesterday two o'clock pm. 28 miles from (illegible) Depot above Columbus over a rough hilly road. To day Daniel is much rested and appears much as when he left home. We expected to have stop 8 miles nearer the rail road at Chalybeate Springs, but they were <u>full</u>. but we like things better here. The warm springs here are mineral, and are drunk to great advantage by many persons here beside them are here Chalybeate and Sulphur Springs. This place is very full of people and they seem clever. It is a very hilly country and fine dry climate though farther south than our home nearly as far south as Charleston. I pray that our Heavenly father may bless this trip to your dear Brother and grant that he may be greatly benefitted and I beg that you will send up your prayers to Almighty God in his behalf that if consistent with His Holy Will He will restore him yet to health.

Lizzie left home with the mumps but is now about well and has not complained at all though her jaw swelled very much. I can write you but a few lines now. Do write to me to this office as at head this poor letter. It is now just night. God bless you.

Ever your affectionate father
William Rogers

Warm Springs, GA 12 Sept. 1863
My own beloved wife,

It will be two weeks tomorrow since we came to this place and I am sorry to say that to this time we have not a word from home. I have no doubt you had some of you written forwarded you had rec'd letters from us, or rather my letters for I believe all Lizzie's letters were directed to her fathers house.

I am sorry to say that I dont think Daniel has improved any since we left home. He has this week suffered from disordered stomach and pain of the stomach but of that he is now better. He kept pretty comfortable until he was thus troubled. We expect to leave here next week. making some calls at other places and will write again and possibly may then say at what time we may be expected home. I wrote to Charles asking him to send me some money. If he has not done it when this reaches you, he need not send it at all for I don't now think I shall need it. Please see to this.

I hope my dear that you have got well since we left and that all the rest are well. Lizzie and myself are well. I have had no symptoms of asthma since I have been here and am about as strong as before I was sick last June and my hearing restored. The warm water here appears to act like a charm with me. The first time I bathed I found on the next day that my cough was half cured. Expectorations became much less and is now almost entirely stoped. Oh how I wish I could say as much for our dear Daniel. But God can restore him to health in his own way if it be consistent with His Holy Will. How little we think of the comforts of our own dear home when we are all quietly there, but dear does it seem when away from it as we now are. among strangers who are but little interested in our welfare, but ere long we hope again to see the dear place and may God in mercy grant that nothing shall prevent its being a happy meeting. May He bless you all with health and may it be well with us also when we get back to you.

Paper, envelopes etc. are all scarce so suppose you first send this to Lucy and she will send it to Ruthvin and wherever it goes oh how much love from all of us goes with it. It is for all all though directed to your own dear self.

Gen. Bragg's wife is at this place[141]—so is Gen. French—Dr. Wightman has been here but I think has left.[142] A Gen Barrow is here from Nashville. He was a Tenn senator—was arrested for treason—imprisoned exiled and has not seen his family for 16 months. Heaven bless and keep you all—love to all.

Your affectionate husband
William Rogers

141 Gen. Braxton Bragg, 1817-1876, served in the Confederacy, and Fort Bragg, NC, is named for him. https://abc11.com/fort-bragg-renaming-braxton-confederate-leaders/6243153

142 Dr. William May Wightman, 1808-1882, a leading Methodist minister in SC, was editor of the Southern Christian Advocate, and later served as the first president of Wofford College. https://www.wofford.edu/academics/library/archives-specia-collections

Warm Springs Ga 15 Sept. 1863
Dear William, Lucy, Ruthvin & Harriet
Dear Children all -

The esteemed letters of Wm & Lucy came safely to hand this morning and I will now write a few lines to Manning and William will send them after he has read them to R & H.

Before Daniel started for Georgia he had been to Columbia and was considerably tired down and his stomach and bowels had gotten out of order consequently the trip was harder for him than it would otherwise have been and last week he suffered a good deal with his stomach. I am happy to say that he is now (illegible) so that he now walks about when he chooses and feels much better. It is now our calculation to leave here probably tomorrow to go down to Houston County as Lizzie wishes to stay a few days with some of her cousins and some of her aunts. The distance will be about seven miles from Fort Valley on the railroad to Macon. Dear Lizzie is quite well and so am I. I have been relieved from my cough and expectoration for several days and my strength is very good now so that if nothing happens I may hope to return home in very good health. We can't say yet at what time we may be expected home but must write again to let you know.

You are doubtless very anxious to know whether Daniel is better or worse than when he left home, and it is hard for me to say whether he is better or not. Had he not been kept back by his stomach for some time I think he would have been improved, and now as he is relieved in that particular. I hope he will improve still. It will not be worth while for any of you to direct any more letters to Georgia for after this we should fail to get them and we shall probably hear from you next at our dear home, dear I say for so it now seems to us -

May our Heavenly Father grant that ere long we may have a happy meeting around our own fire side or those of our dear children. We have gotten along here as well as we could, but here there are none to love us, and what is worth so much as love?

I am sorry to send you a letter so uninteresting but accomodations for writing are poor and it makes it more of a task to write, but still you will hear from us and that you most desire. Daniel and

Lizzie with me send you much love and may God bless and keep you all my dearly loved ones.

Most affectionatly your father and friend
William Rogers

I believe my writing is a little worse than usual, but you must excuse it. I am more than usual out of practice.

Bishopville Sep. 17th 1863
My darling Sister,

We got home safely yesterday evening. Stopped awhile at Dr. Rembert,s and Aunt Peggy,s. I found all well at home. Mother coughs but very little now but she is so much troubled about Daniel. They got a letter from Father on Monday and he said that Daniel seemed very much the same, and he was sorry he could not say he had improved any yet. Ellen got one from Lizzie at the same time written three days later, and she said our darling brother was worse, that he was troubled with his bowels and if he did not soon get better they would start home, this week or next. Oh I cannot tell you my feelings when yesterday before I got home I met Mr. Walker and he told me how he was. It seems as if this our only hope seems cut off, but God is all powerful and can yet restore him to us. His dear little children are here, both well. Nora is such a dear little creature. she is so good. Elwyn is rather cross, poor little fellow. I know he misses his mother. We are so anxious to hear again from our precious brother. Father says he himself has improved very much, that he coughs but little, and his hearing is as good as before he lost it. How thankful I feel for this. Father says we must let you all know how Daniel is as he did not know when he could write you again. We will write as soon as we hear. They only have a mail once a week so their chance for writing is rather bad. Oh that God in His mercy may yet bless dearest Daniel with health if consistent with his will. I fear it would almost kill our darling mother, should he be taken from us, but she seems right cheerful to day. I found cousin Hu here. he came last Friday, is looking very well. He started home to see his mother but could not get there. His brigade is to be moved soon, he does not know where yet. Daniel Crosswell lost his right hand at Battery Wagner. he is the only person I know who has been wounded. Charlie Bartlett is now at home. It was with <u>pecularluarly sad feelings</u> that I parted with you, my dear brother and sister in that home, around which are clustered so many <u>sad</u> but pleasant associations. It is a dear & sacred spot to me and doubly so must it be to you. I feel very grateful for the many hours I have been permitted to spend with you there, and I hope they have not been without benefit to me. I love to review them in memory. Very grateful do I feel too for your many kindnesses to me. It was hard too to part from all at dear bro Ruthvin,s and I shed many tears in thinking of you all. We had a pleasant ride home. Alice, Emma & Gertrude had a great deal to say about their enjoyment, said they loved you all down there better than ever before. We were in a right hard rain but kept dry. Have you seen the advertisement of the college in the Advocate. Board & tuition are 700$. I guess it will prevent some from going. I am afraid mr C will not send Anna. Salina Durant has a son, born last Sat. I found a long affectionate letter from Almira awaiting me. Col. Green and Lottie have lost their youngest child, died of sore throat. The people generally are well now. Old Mrs. English just from Marlboro says that Mary Jane,s brother is sinking rapidly. he is just like Robt. Bradley was. is a perfect skeleton. Oh how I feel for her. Cousin Charlotte is here now, she is as well as usual. Mother sends you both a great deal of love. She thanks you very much for the apron, says it is a very acceptable present. Wm too sends thanks for the cake. Tell bro Wm that they have not yet rec-d the letters he & I wrote, the first week I was at your house. Perhaps Mrs. Stuart forgot to send it. They got your letter written afterwards. Maria, Almira, Wm & cousin Hu join me in much love to you both. Give our best love to all at bro Ruthvin,s and please let them hear from us. I will write to Hattie in a day or two. Hope she will stay with you while bro Wm is away. that is, if you stay at home. Remember me to all enquiring friends. With much love.

Your devoted Sister
Amanda M. Rogers

William will get word to Pompey about the lasts as soon as possible.[143]

---

143 Last—a wooden or metal form in the shape of the human foot on which boots or shoes are shaped or repaired https://www.dictionary.com/browse/lasts

Bishopville Sep 21st 1863
My precious sister

We have recd another letter from our dear father, which we will send to sister & yourself, so I will write a few lines to send with them. I know your hearts will be pained indeed to know that our precious brother is still getting no better. We are expecting them home this week. O Hattie we could better bear it were it not for our dear dear mother. Sometimes it seems as if it is more than she could bear, but we all try to be as cheerful as possible where she is. O that it may be the will of God yet to spare him to us. Dear Mr. Reid was here yesterday and talked so sweetly to her. told her that he knew it was hard indeed to give up such a son. Said he had been to Camden and heard him spoken of so highly as a citizen, a professional man and above all as a Christian, a bright light in the church. I can't think that he will never get well, but most earnestly should we pray to God in his behalf and oh may He give us submission to His will. I hope they may call at White Sulpher Springs on their way home. perhaps they might help him. You will see from father's letter that we do not know when exactly to expect him, but I expect the last of this week. How thankful we should feel that our dear father is so well. I long to see them all home again. It is only two weeks now before I return to Columbia. I have this morning begun to get ready. I feel very sad when I think of it, but if I can leave Daniel better I will go with a happy heart. Mother is very well, has got over her cold & cough. The rest too are all well. You see from my last letter to sister that I found cousin Hu here. He is now preaching at one of the upper churches where they have a protracted meeting. He preached at the Pres. church Sat afternoon, has improved very much I think. The meeting closed yesterday afternoon. Little Sallie Bradley joined the church. I thought David D. would but he did not. Alice D- has been giving glorious accounts of her visit to you all. E. & G. too enjoyed themselves so much and long long will I remember it. You were all so kind and good to us—each visit draws me nearer and I cannot express the deep love I feel for you all. I do hope you can come up to see us before I leave. Emma and Gertrude and Alice are going back to Laurens Wednesday. They did not expect to go until next month, but have to go now in order to get board. Poor Emma cannot speak of it without crying. I do not know whether we will go to the L. Camp M- or not. It depends on Daniel entirely. If we do we will not go before Monday as Mr Walker preaches Sunday. Preaches Hamilton Husbands' funeral sermon. May Scott spent Sat night with Almira. She is a nice girl. Mother Anna Almira Wm cousins Hu & Charlotte all join me in their best love to all. Give my love to dear Miss E- the children and bro R. Tell him perhaps I will forgive him for not writing in my album provided he visits often in Columbia. I hope Lizzie can come to see me before I leave. If you cannot come do write soon. and now dear sister good bye. May God bless you and may He in mercy permit us all to meet again in this our dear home in happiness and peace.

Your devoted sister
Amanda

P. S. Tell bro R. that father left the hogshead for him and it is here waiting. Mother says let her know when he can send for it and she will send to meet him half way with it. She was very sorry I did not think to ask him but I hope 'tis not too late yet. Write immediately and let us know when to send. It is wholesome and will help him very much.

Home Oct 21st 1863
My very dear Sister

I am up bright and early this morning, in order to send you a few lines by James. We had just received your letter sent by mail, and I was reading it to mother when James stopped at the gate and gave us your letter, and all the nice things you sent to mother. She says she thinks you and Miss Elizabeth are too good. She thanks you many many times for all you sent. She will send you the thread you wanted herself. This I am glad to say leaves us all quite well. Daniel has been pretty well most of the time since you were up here, but had something like Colic a few nights ago, which was caused from his eating something which disagreed with him. I believe he has gotten over that though now He has been staying with us since Saturday, but went up to Mr. Durants yesterday afternoon. He expects to go to Columbia tomorrow, and either father or Mr. Durant will go with him. (torn) Amanda will be delighted to see him. he received a good long letter from her yesterday. She seems quite happy now, and says everything is moving on smoothly at the College now. They have ninety seven boarders, but she has written to you and told you all about this I guess. oh! Hattie you cannot tell how rejoiced we were on reading a note from dear brother William to learn that our dear sister Almira had given her heart to the precious Saviour. God has indeed been good to us. Mother says it seemed to her all the while that Almira would be converted at that meeting. we were glad that Sister was able to attend the meeting too. I was glad to hear that dear Miss Elizabeth was so much better. trust she will soon be entirely well. Hope too that my dear brother has sufferred no more from pain in his shoulder. Do give much love to every one for us, also to sister, brother William and Almira when you see them. I believe James is waiting so I will close. Father I think is going to write to brother Ruthvin. Good bye my dear good Sister. may Heaven bless and keep you. Tell brother Wm we are glad we are going to have (torn) with us Sunday. Write soon, and (torn)

from your affct Sister
Maria

Bishopville 21 Oct 1863
Dear Ruthven & Harriet

Jimmy arrived here in good time yesterday evening. He brought the valuable presents of blueberry from dear H. and eggs from good dear Miss Elizabeth. Many thanks for them. They will be of much service to dear Daniel for here such things are very scarce.

Daniel is much as when you saw him last. I don't think he is hardly any better but I think no worse. Tomorrow he expects to go to Columbia to see the proper officer, as his furlough is nearly expired. If he cannot get some light appointment up here, he will resign.

All the rest of us are pretty well. We will try and be down after awhile and until then you will have Almira between you and the other dear children.

Probably they (W & L) are now with you; much love for them.

Tell Wm. that we rec- his note. I was in Sumter when it was handed to me. There will probably be a few hours to hear Rev. Mr. Ware.

Letter from Amanda yesterday—was 97 scholars boarding. good news, that tell Wm from Almira indeed our Heavenly Father greatly eases among our afflictions. to Him be all the glory.

Thanks to Ruthven for his trouble in processing tallow for us—Dont know the cost. I send $15.00 and will pay any balance when I see him. Tell Wm if he has not bought any he need not now as we can get along but if he has it is all right. I send this 50 lbs. sugar. wish it was better, but the last time I was at Columbia it was very scarce indeed and high, but this was bought before then.

I send the thread. No charge for it.

Hope the dear family with you will soon be all well and the same with Wm & Lucy.

Hope soon to hear from you all again.

I am in haste for Jimmy is waiting and so I will close. God bless you all.

Your affectionate father
William Rogers

Columbia Oct 30th 1863
My darling Sister Hattie,

Your <u>long</u> <u>looked for</u> letter came at last. Yesterday I rec-d it with one from Lizzie and many thanks to you both for them. I wish you would write often to me, it give me so much pleasure to hear from you all. This morning I was much rejoiced to get a letter from Fannie, and a sweet letter it was. I prize her friendship so much. She said they were all well, but a brother of her mothers who was there quite sick. Has Miss Elizabeth got entirely well? father told me she was suffering very much with her head. I hope very much she is well, together with all the rest of your dear ones. I wish too my dear sister I could have made one of your number when Almira and Lizzie were there. I know they had a pleasant time. Has Almira gone home yet? I got such a sweet letter from her after camp meeting, and oh it was indeed joyous news that she had found her Savior. precious is the salvation of her soul. What can we render unto Him for His merciful goodness and kindness to us? It should indeed draw our hearts nearer Him and I do pray that we may all grow in grace, that our lamps may burn brightly and peace and joy fill our soul. Nothing new has transpired here. We are moving on at the usual rate. The school is almost full, only three rooms unoccupied. Mary, Anna H., Anna C. are well. not Mary either, she is suffering some from (illegible), but I think she has promised Mr. Mood to go with him tomorrow to have it taken out. I have only had one severe headache since I came back, so you see I am improving. it was on Monday too and I had to miss school which I regretted very much. I went last Sabbath night to the Baptist church to see a young lady immersed as I had never seen the rite performed in church before. I imagined it would be very solemn, but she spoiled it all by looking over the congregation and up into the gallery, and coughing, just before she was put under the water. The minister was very rabid on the subject of baptism, which is the first sermon I have ever heard on the subject.

You wished to know what you could get your dress dyed for. it will be five dollars. You had better wait until you see the silk I had dyed for sister, which I sent home last week. Where I had that done, is the best dying establishment I know. If you like it, I will have it done with pleasure, though it seems like a pity to have that pretty dress dyed. Of course I'll say nothing about it. Am glad the articles I got pleased you. I believe I have not written you since my dear father and brother were here. I do not think he looked much better. it was a great disappointment that I could not be with them more. Maria wrote me a few lines by Mr. Walker who was over this week, and told me that all were well, that our dear brother was no worse from his trip here. Maria wrote me she liked her bonnet very much, which I was glad to hear. I did not see it after it was done at all. I found some Lilly White in town the other day sent sister and yourself some, thought Maria would have an opportunity of sending it to you soon. Tell bro R. I still want his "old bride" to show off. Johnny Hughson is boarding here at Mr. Crook's. he has been quite sick. sent me word the other day that he was coming to see me as soon as he got well. Mrs. Eugenia Hodge came to see us yesterday evening, she left for home this morning. she has been staying with her husband who is sick in the hospital here. I have begun taking music lessons again, so I hope I can play a little better for you when I go home, though I won't promise, for I haven't much time to practice. Fannie says she enjoyed the camp meeting very much which she attended soon after her return. Has Mrs. Plowden got well? Give my love to her, Henry and all the children. I hope Mr. P. has kept well since he has been in Camp. Does bro Ruthvin suffer with his side yet? Tell him it <u>might help</u> <u>him</u> to <u>write to</u> me occaisionally. The bell will soon ring for dinner so I must close, though I know I have written you a very uninteresting epistle. Remember me to E. & A Nelson when you see them. Give my heart full of love to dear Miss Elizabeth, bro Ruthvin, Haynsworth and Lute, to cousin Callie and Lizzie and Mr. Y Plowden's family. Tell cousin L. I went to see Mrs Howell the other afternoon. She asked many questions about her and M. J. and sent much love to them. Please my darling sister write to me very soon. I will send you the money in the hope you may get it safely. May Heaven's blessings ever abide with you all. With warmest love

Your devoted sister
Amanda Rogers

Bishopville Nov 23rd 1863
My darling Sister

Gladly will I devote a short while this morning in writing you, as I know you are at all times anxious to hear from home. I am happy to say that we are all well this morning, and Daniel for the last several days has seemed better. Dr Dubose has been over to see him recently and he thought him improving. Oh I do trust he may yet be restored to health in answer to our many prayers. I suppose you will have dear Sister and brother Wm with you this week and next week we hope to welcome them home again. oh! <u>how precious</u> are these visits to us. I know you will feel sad to see them leave. Can you not come up again soon? Amanda says in her next letter she will tell us whether she will come home Christmas or not. I do hope she will come though she will have a very short time to stay. You and brother Ruthvin will of course come up <u>then</u> to see her. Has Miss Martha Roberts paid you the visit she expected? I hope so, for I know you and her enjoyed yourselves a great deal together. You will hear through Sister of the death of Mrs Carnes. Though she leaves a distressed family, yet their loss is her eternal gain, for hers was a very triumphant death. Poor Dr Holleyman's family. they are indeed sorely afflicted. Yesterday they lost their youngest child, little Mary. She is to be buried this afternoon. Mother was there a short while after she died and she says it really seems like Vermeille will go crazy, she takes it so hard. Poor girl I pity her. Her cup of sorrow is indeed full. Mary died of typhoid fever. she had gotten better of the scarlet fever and then it assumed a typhoid form. Eugene is still very sick. They think he too is going into typhoid fever. I do trust he may be spared to them. Ada is getting well again. No other new cases of scarlet fever that I know of. Mrs John Dixon has been quite sick for sometime, and is not much better yet. We heard Mr Walker preach his last sermon at Bethlehem yesterday. He has been right sick with sore throat and is looking badly. The ladies are to have the parsonage cleaned up next Thursday and wonder who will occupy it next year? I sent the nice present you gave me to Amanda soon after I got home, and she wrote me the other day that it <u>should</u> soon be done. Hattie I can never thank you enough for your kindness to me, but can only pray that you may be rewarded for it. But it is time for this to be sent to the office. All send much love to <u>you</u> <u>all</u>. Tell dear brother Ruthvin he must <u>please</u> come up and spend Christmas with us so that we may all be together once more if consistent with our Fathers will. Good by my dear Sister. kiss the children for me and accept much love for your own self from your affct Sister

Maria

Bishopville Dec. 10th 1863
My beloved Sister

It is "Fast Day," & I have just returned form the Presbyterian church where we had services. God grant that the prayers offered this day in behalf of our distracted country, may be heard & blessed from on High. God is our only hope, & if we trust Him aright, we need not fear what man can do unto us.

Well Hattie I am here again, surrounded by the endearments of home, & waiting patiently the issue of the Conference now in session, not knowing what is to befall us after that. I feel more like trusting our case entirely to the Lord than ever before. The past two years though they have brought heavy trials to us, have been laden rich with blessings, not the least of which dear sister, was giving us a home near to you, and the other loved ones of your home. I thought I loved you all well enough before, for dear brother Ruthvin & Miss Elizabeth have ever felt like an own brother & sister to me, but now I feel that I am bound to you, & to them, by new ties never to be broken, on earth, or in Heaven, where at last I trust we shall all dwell together, never more to be separated. It shall ever be our prayer that God may richly bless & abundantly reward you <u>all</u>, for the affection you have shown us. It was with <u>sad</u> <u>sad</u> heart, that I left your pleasant happy home, long may it continue what it now is, & your household band unbroken for many long years to come. I suppose you have recd the few lines Wm wrote on our arrival, & he told you that mother met us on the way. It was indeed a pleasant surprise. We found dear Daniel not quite so well as when Maria wrote us, but he looked better that I expected to see him. He rides out every day & stays down stairs with us a part of almost every day. Still dear Sister I must tell you he is <u>very</u> <u>feeble</u>. Let us continue earnestly to urge our petitions at a throne of grace in his behalf; for in God's hand is <u>all</u> power. He can yet restore him if it be His will. I feel very grateful tho; that he seems perfectly willing to leave his case in the hands of his Heavenly Father. He told Wm he was perfectly resigned either way, that he had never doubted his acceptance with God, that one of the greatest pleasures he hoped to have on earth was to do what he could for the advancement of the cause of God. Is it not this a great consolation? Who can doubt that so good a God will do what is best for him & for us. The rest are all in usual health & dear mother seems cheerful. I have been helping Maria make up the nice dress you gave her, & it looks very nicely I assure you. I know you will like it She has also made up a new home form this week, and is now about ready I believe to go to Conference. I expect she will leave tomorrow, hope she'll have a pleasant time. Wm left on Tuesday. I hardly think I'll go over at all. Father thinks of going either on Sat- or Sun. Mother & I called to see Eugene Holleyman a short time since. He is improving & I hope will get well. They all seem very sad. How deeply I feel for them! There is no other sickness now in the neighborhood except Mrs John Dixon, & she is better again.

Dear brother Ruthvine's good letter has just come to hand, many thanks to him for it. We are all so glad to hear Miss Elizabeth is better. I do hope she will have no return of the pain. Give a heart full of love to her from us all. We are very much in hopes brother Ruthvin's State exemption will serve him still; but if otherwise like him, we will bow to the will of his divine Captain, who is able to shield him from all danger.

Amanda's last letter tells us she hopes to be with us on Thursday the 24th. And now won't you both come up the same time, she will only be at home one week. Do come if it is possible we all say. I am very anxious to hear from all our Manning friends again, Give our love to any and all of them when you see them. I will send bro. R's letter over to Wm by Maria. I must not forget to tell you how much obliged Daniel was for the nice custard you sent him. His appetite is pretty good most of the time. Tell Callie & Lizzie all are well at their mothers. Mary is going over to Conf. Give my very best love to my dear brother R & to Miss Elizabeth & to Lute, Haynesworth & Henry, and tell the negroes all howdy. Write soon as you get this dear sister and tell us when to look for you. And now good bye may God ever bless you & yours.

Your devoted sister
L. J. Mood

P. S. I have omitted to tell you that my own health has been steadily improving. I now feel quite well. Hope this may find you all so.

Dec. 12th '63
Dear Ruthven -

Dear Maria handed me your kind letter last night. I am sure it was pleasant indeed to read it & know you loved me sincere. Your many kindnesses to us has endeared you all to us more than ever before. May the Lord reward you in Eternity. The (the 4) have been all together at Mr. Hawks & have enjoyed ourselves together most pleasantly (illegible) the sickness of his little Sally caused him to leave yesterday for Columbia. And may I say too that Bro. John has been very sick all night (now early Sunday morning). We have just sent for Dr. Witherspoon trust he'l come directly. Asbury is quite well has been very busy since conf. opened. Heard from B yesterday through Father all were pretty well no change in Daniel that is perceptible. He is feeble. Oh, how disturbed my heart gets when I think of him. But "His" ways are past finding out. Let us pray for resignation to "His" will. we are getting on pretty well I believe in conf business Asbury tells me that the appts are made and he thinks we may hear them Monday night but I don't know. The Puckett case may consume much of Monday if it does we'l not hear them Monday. It is fully understood that all who have been two years at any point will be moved. The Bish will not hear to anything else. I have no idea where in the Providence of God I am to labor the coming year. Asbury significantly asked me, "Billy how far can you move?" He may have intimated by this that I would not be moved far. All I want Ruthven is grace enough to go cheerfully wherever it may be. If my Master goes with me I ought not to be troubled about where this point may be. Dr. Boyce has asked my opinion about the one to take my place. As far as I know the one he indicates to me will suit Manning. I have made inquiries of his other Presiding Elders & they say everything in his favor. So I hope you and the family will like him and his family. The case of Dr. Briggs Puckett has been given to a committee of 5 of the most precious elderly ministers of body. They have not made a report yet. They may not like or be satisfied with his report if not we'l have to take time & investigate it. Maria got here yesterday so did Father. Maria came with Capt. Stuckey's wife. Father came after. Maria has met at Capt. Lorings an old friend of hers from Jim Wadeboro Farm Beverly. she was a little girl when I saw her last. She was so glad to see her. I met several others here from Wadesboro. I have not seen them since '54. There are great crowds here. I have our Miss Henrugan at Mr. McCallum's. May is there too. While I think of it Ruthven I want to speak of my shoes and I yet I am in fear it may bother you. I am sorry but they are too short the left shoe particularly. The truth is if you can take them for Lute and have Nero to make me another pair I will be fixed. Will be too much trouble They ought to be a little longer than they are. They might be a quarter of an inch or more longer. I will see you all as soon as I can after Conf will bring those I have with me. I am glad you wrote to me about your furlough. I will greatly concerned when you have to leave but trust that things may so turn out that you can yet remain at home. I want you to give my kindest love to Harriet Miss E. and tell H. & Lute be good boys. Remember me to Uncle George and the dear aunts—I'll finish this when I get my appt -

Most Affect
W W Mood

Tuesday—I presume dear Ruthven that you will hear my appt before you get this—Sam Pit Mission is attached to Georgetown. this is my work. I will preach in Georgetown in the morning & on Sampit in the evening. wonder how you all like it? I want you all to pray for us. The will and all the grace the good one may be willing to give in standing up to the work. I would have desired Lucy sent to other parts. her health & the exposed position etc. don't make it desirable but will by the assistance of God do our best. What my plans will be it is now out of my power to say. I'll come down I think next week on my way to Georgetown. I am told the house is very comfortable & it is furnished. I'll take as little as possible down. the trouble will be to get that little carried. but I trust my way will be opened before me. It is hard to get any thing there (they all tell me) to eat but I trust I'll not starve. There is a nice Gentleman sent to Manning brother Stoll. I go to B with Maria today. good bye

Affecty
William

C. F. College Jan 14th 1864
My ever dear Sister,

Again it is my pleasant privilege for a few moments to hold pleasant converse with you whom so short a time ago I had the pleasure of seeing though now I can scarcely realize it. Would that we were all again together at our dear home, but I fear that happiness will never again be ours. It was so hard for me to leave them all, particularly our dear dear brother, and when I bade him farewell, my heart almost failed me. oh that it were consistent with the will of our heavenly Father to spare him and raise him up. He doeth what is best and I pray to be submissive to His righteous will. I know it was a hard trial for sister to leave them all. I thought so much of her. I suppose you have parted from them too. May the blessing of God go with them and abide upon them, making our dear brother Wm instrumental in the salvation of many precious souls. They have had such cold disagreeable weather for travelling. Did you ever experience such intense cold. Tell bro Ruthvin I think even he must have been satisfied. he is so fond of cold weather. I hope miss Elizabeth has not suffered any more with her head. What would I not give to see you all. You are seldom absent from my thoughts though and many moments are spent in thinking of the loved ones from whom I am separated. I rec-d a letter from Fannie since my return which did me much good. I have to write to Fannie. She is such a punctual correspondent. Scholars are coming in very rapidly and we will soon be full. Every thing bids fair for us to have a pleasant year and I hope we may not be disappointed. Anna H. and the other girls are quite well and getting on well. I have not heard a word from home since I left and you may imagine my anxiety to do so. You and my dear brother must take pity on me and write often. I felt very lonely after bro Wm left. He stayed until Wednesday.

Ellen Durant rec-d a letter form Jane telling her that Aunt Molsey was very ill. I was so sorry to hear it. but earnestly hope she may soon be better. I suppose cousin Jim has left ere this to return to camps. I know they will all miss him at home. Cousin J. from Vicksburg only staid a very short while here. he came to see me but had to hurry home to be in time for the train. oh Hattie it seems like a long long time when I think of not seeing you all for six months. I had such a sweet dream last night: thought I was at home, that we were all there together and that our dear brother was almost well. I saw him so plainly and was sorry indeed to awaken and find it all a dream. The new year has fairly begun and I trust my dear sister that we may all spend it more profitably. I do hope that I may more glorify my Father in Heaven, consecrate myself entirely to His service and by the grace of God make my way to Heaven. Remember me dear sister in your prayers. I am really afraid you can't make out to read this letter and the paper is so bad I can't write any better. I send a little primer to Lute in which our little angel Anna is mentioned. Mrs. Miller happened to buy one for her little daughter and found it, so I went and bought some of them. I do not know the author but she must have known Anna. Please my dear sister write often to me, and tell bro R. to do the same. Give him, Miss Elizabeth, Haynsworth and Lute much love for me. to Henry too and remember me to all my relatives and friends down there. I will send you your pin and ring the first opportunity I have after they are finished. Good bye my dear sister. May God ever watch over and bless you all is the earnest prayer of

Your affct. sister
Amanda M. Rogers

Georgetown Jan 18th 1864

Well my beloved sister, I have just written home, & I feel that you, dear Miss Elizabeth & Bro. Ruthvine are justly entitled to the next letter, so I'll try and write to you, but I have fears as to whether you'll be able to read it as I am writing with a bad goose quill pen.

After our sad parting on Thursday morning we rode slowly along (the roads being in such a condition we could not travel fast) neither of us felt like talking, for as we separated from you all, we felt that we had indeed bid adieu to Home with all its endearments. Then too the oft-repeated and disinterested kindnesses which each and all of you from dear little Lute up to the oldest of your family had shown us so continually while we were near you, came upon us in all its reality, and our hearts were too full for words and again we could only pray—"Almghty Father, keep them all in thine arms of love and mercy, and bless and reward them every one. It was after dark when we arrived at Mrs Wilsons, and we found her quite sick with pneumonia, but they took us in and treated us very kindly indeed. She was very glad to hear from Miss Elizabeth and from her other friends about Manning. On Friday we found the roads in a dreadful condition, so that altho we only had twenty-five miles to come, it was near five o-clock when we reached Georgetown. I felt quite encouraged as we neared the town at seeing the heavy pine forest still standing on either side of the road, and to see the few cattle which were grazing by the roadside for this I thought a happy omen that everything wasn't quite destroyed, and I made up my mind I wouldn't freeze while all those pine trees stood there. We found the Parsonage closed when we arrived but a servant man of Mr. Kirton's was here with an invitation from them that we should go there and spend the night before going home. we did so and received every attention from the two old people & their two children that their comfortable and abundant home could furnish. Saturday morning we came home, our servant had arrived in good time so we made up a fire and set about getting ourselves accustomed to our new home. But oh dear sister with what overpowering force then came over my mind. the day we first went to our dear little home in Manning, of all the trouble that had befallen us since then, & of our being so far separated now from all were such a comfort to us in our afflictions, then above all the thought of having had to part from my poor sick brother, with no hope of seeing him again. My heart seemed almost ready to burst and I had to give vent to my feelings in a flood of tears. Dear Wm was scarcely better off than I was, but after this we both soon felt better and entered cheerfully upon the duties before us. We believe God has directed our steps, and He is as able to take care of us here, and of our dear ones we have left behind, as tho' we were with them.

Our home is a snug house of six rooms furnished with everything we need, in fact far more so than any we have ever had before. We found a nice lot of wood cut up ready for us & Dr. Foster has assured Wm that we shall not want in that particular, and I tell you I have felt much better since I found that out. The things sent by the wagon turned up all right, and so don't be anxious about us now, for from our present prospect, I have no idea we will lack for anything we need. God has seemed specially to open up our way before us in every respect. We have a good sized garden where we hope soon to make a beginning. Wm preached here yesterday, and I was really surprised to see as many persons as were there, altho' there was also service at the Episcopal church. We find that some of the first people of the place are here, all have been away, but have returned. Several very nice ladies have already called on us. I have been thus particular dear sister in speaking of everything for I felt that it would interest you. To day it is raining quite hard. We have been busy all the morning getting things to rights in our room. And now as I sit in front of the fire writing to you, when I look around and see how cozy it looks I cant realize I am in Georgetown. But come and see it for yourself. Oh how glad I'd be to see you all down here. For it seems already an age since we parted. I want you dear Hattie, if you can send the box by the wagon when it comes, please also to send the lounge bed as I think I'll need it. You'll find the lounge bed with the other bedding Wm thinks. Do write us very soon and tell my dear, good brother Ruthvine also to write us whenever he can. William joins me in warmest love to you, dear Miss Elizabeth, to Bro Ruthvine, to the little boys & to Henry. Remember us too very kindly to all your brothers & sisters and their families when you see them especially

Capt. H'h. I do hope Mr. Edgar Plowden can come to see us. Do remember us all of you when you pray, and that God may ever richly bless you all will ever be the prayer of your ever devoted sister

L J Mood

P. S. Give our love to Mr. & Mrs. McDowell when you see them. Love to Callie & Lizzie and their families.

Jan. 18th 1864
My dear Manda,

Your kind letter was received some time ago. I have been wishing to reply for weeks, but have had so many duties that I thought it best to delay. I hope you had nothing to mar your happiness during your vacation. I thought a great deal of you at that time. Do you know I came very near spending Christmas with you and Hattie? I would have gone but for Beaureguard's order for the people of this District to move all that was valuable. That distressed me so much, with our other trouble that I concluded to wait. Now I see no opportunity that will ever take me to the friends I so dearly love, unless I can prevail on a very busy Johysicia to accompany me. I did think I would not tell you anything about my "most dearly beloved," but take you on a surprise. After reflection I thought it would be unjust, as it might be more pleasant to you to have me confide in you. It is true my dear Manda that I have engaged myself for life to one of the dearest little men. oh! he is such a nice, refined and good man. Let me describe him. He is your brother's height, with broad shoulders, fair complexion, light hair and eyes. He is a practising physician (may have to join the army soon) and a steward in the M. E. Church, my own dear church. Makes an humble, sweet prayer. I wish you could see him. I know you would like him. He shall love you, that is certain. I am in great haste, dear Manda. Do excuse a short letter. I shall enclose one to Hattie, which you will please enclose in yours. My poor dear brother Tampee had his knee (illegible) while leading the 50th Ga. Regt. up to the fort at Knoxville. His leg was amputated above the knee. Read Hattie's letter.

Your friend
Martha

My dear Hattie,

I am just about to leave for the Pope's and will write a few lines to leave at the office in that neighborhood. I would have written to you in Dec. but thought each day I would find out what day I could leave for your house. Pa wrote to me from Columbia that I could go, but Providence seemed to order otherwise. Yes, it is certainly a Providence, for I was ever anxious to go. Pa disappointed me first, and then when he gave his full consent the orders of our Gen. prevented. I know not if I can ever have the pleasure. I shall trust for a meeting. May be I can prevail upon Mr. Plowden to bring his little darling to my poor country home. I shall promise you a pleasant time if the means are in my power. Julie Pope's father died about a week ago. I am now to leave to visit them in their sorrow. We too have had much to distress us. Our elder brother is now a prisoner at Knoxville with but <u>one</u> <u>leg</u>. oh! it is distressing. Poor fellow! We have not heard a word from him since the first day of his affliction. That was 29th Nov. He is a professor of religion. Thank God for this. Write to me soon dear Hattie. Write before I become Mrs. Smith.

Your ever dear
Martha

Georgetown Jan 27th/64
My beloved Sister

Wm is writing to dear bro. Ruthvine and I cant resist the temptation to write you at least a few lines. Your dear letters were both rec-d today and I was never more glad to hear from you all. The waggon rolled up yesterday bringing all things safely, again many, many thanks to all. The wheel is indeed a very nice one and I think I feel almost as proud of it as I did of the old piano when it was first put up in the old house.[144] Mr. Evans came with the wagon, and he told me Bro R- was going into service in ten days. Oh! Hattie I could scarcely control my voice to speak to him after that, and I spent by far the saddest evening yesterday that I've done since I came to G-n. But I see from your letters there is hope still that he may not have to go, and I assure you my dear sister I did not need your request to pray God if in his wisdom He may see best, to avert the necessity of his going, for apart from my sympathy for you and dear Miss E- I feel that it would be severe affliction to my own heart, for Bro. R- feels as near and dear to me, as my own brother. But dear Hattie if the trial should come, bear it bravely for his sake. It will be a sore trial to him at best, but if he sees you bearing it cheerfully, it will strengthen him more than anything else could. Have strong faith in God. We are but poor Christians, remember, if we are only willing to trust Him in the sunshine and not in the storm. He sets you a noble example himself of faith & resignation to God's will; try dear sister to imitate so worthy an example. I beg of you do write soon again, and if dear Bro- R- should have to leave, tell me where he is, so we will know where to write to him. We have not seen Mr. Edgar Plowden yet but I still hope he may come to see us before he leaves. Wm has been speaking of going out to camp to see him. I heard from home a day or two since. Our dear brother keeps much the same. was glad to hear that aunt M- was so much better. Amanda was kind enough to send us one of the little Primers also. It was like a sun beam to our hearts. We cant imagine who Mrs. Moore is. I was sorry to hear of your uncle Hamptons death, but for him to die, was

144 Spinning wheel

doubtless life eternal. I can never forget his countinance at communion seasons there in Manning. I am glad Mr. & Mrs. McDowell got to see you. Is he still at home? Did they have a good time at the sacramental meeting in Manning? I hope they did. I have nothing new to tell you of our life in Georgetown. We have not had time to be lonely yet, between work & visitors together. I like our servant very much; you will be glad to know this.

Three very nice young ladies called to see me this morning. Two miss Coachman's & Miss Wilson. But my paper has given out- Give my warmest to my dear brother Ruthvine & to Miss Elizabeth & to the dear good little boys. And now praying Gods blessing upon you & all yours, & begging you like wise to remember us. I remain as ever

Your devoted Sister
L. J. Mood

Bishopville 29 Jan. 1864
Dear Ruthvin and Harriet

We have recd your Esteemed letter and are again happy to hear that are pretty well.

It pains me deeply to have to say to you that dear Daniel is no better—in fact that he is not so well as when I last wrote you. His throat is now very painful, and it is very difficult and painful for him to swallow anything, and when he coughs his throat causes great suffering. Poor fellow Our hearts bleed for him, but all that we can do is to try and alleviate his sufferings and trust him in the hands of his Heavenly Father. Oh may God help him and save him from pain and suffering How gladly would we see you, but you know that in Daniels present situation we cannot leave him long enough to go to you. I know he has your sincere prayers in his behalf and oh, may they be heard and answered. Would to God that I could write to you more favorably—that I could write without giving you pain. But so at present it cannot be, but even now God can raise him up and restore him. Your dear mother is deeply exercised about him—how can it be otherwise? We this week have had letters from your Uncle Arch and two of his Daughters. They were tolerably well. Their country has been mostly over run by fires our men retreating and then by the Federals but they have not been at your uncles. This change of affairs prevented your uncle from being here last Christmas which he deeply regrets. We have letters too from Lucy, Wm & Amanda. All tolerably well. I thank dear Ruthvin very much for his letter. It is all plain. and dear H. your letter is highly valued.

Dear Ruthvin has always been so good and kind. We can never repay him. And dear Miss Elizabeth—we love her as a near and dear relative. May God reward her for all her goodness to our family. We never can.

We heard with sorrow of the death of your Uncle H. A most shocking accident happened on the Rail Road on Wednesday evening Mr Nichols—Mr Powell Carters Son in law—fell between the cars in passing to the baggage car and was torn all to pieces He was a clever man.

I send you the stamps as requested. Let us hear from you as often as you can. I do hope Dear Ruthvin will not be called off. He can do as much good in serving in his own neighborhood

Your affectionate father
William Rogers

How glad we would be to see you up here.

Bishopville Feb. 29th 1864
My darling sister

As to day is mail day, I gladly take my pen, to write you, but dear sister though it affords such great pleasure to write yet much more would it afford to have you with us now. It is so lonely. Amanda left last night, so you may imagine how we feel this morning. I am glad she had a good deal of company on the way. Sister Lizzie, Mr. Durant, and Mrs. McCorquodale all went to Columbia. I truly hope they may succeed in getting all the things they wish. Dear Amanda she hated to leave so much, but she can only pray that the blessed Savior may give her grace sufficient for her and that He may live in sacred nearness to her and all of us, and then though her heart is very sad, yet at the same time, she will feel happy in His love. We have not heard from our dear sister and brother since we heard of our precious brother's death.[145] Oh may God give them strength from on high to enable them to bear the sad blow, and may they from the depths of their hearts exclaim, "Thy will be done." We heard a few days since that old Mr. Mood, brother Williams father, was at the point of death. I feel so much for brother Wm wish so much he was so situated that we might get to see them. This is indeed a sad time to them. We are looking for a letter from them to day. Maria no doubt wrote you of the death of Billie Muldrow. Is it not sad to think of? It seems dear Hattie that we should not shed a tear for our dear brother, when we think of their affliction, for thank God we have the happy assurance of knowing that he is now in glory. Singing praises to God and the Lamb. Mrs Muldrow's two little girls have been very ill but are now, I am glad to say, getting better. Mrs Muldrow too has been quite sick, but she too is getting better I believe. Oh that God may now see fit to stay His afflicting hand upon our bereaved neighborhood. Truly He has indeed called us to mourn. We were taken by quite a surprise the other night. Just as we were getting ready for bed, some one drove up and who should it be but Cousin Hu. We were all you know very glad to see him. He has a thirty days furlough. Wish he could stay longer. Mother

145 Daniel Rogers died February 15, 1864.

received a beautiful letter from Cousin (& Miss) Jim. He was there in Brownsville. I expect he has ere this gone to Cousin Drucilla's. Amanda received a letter from Miss Fannie Plowden a few days before she left. She was quite well. She wrote that a brother of her Mothers was dead. I expect though Miss Elizabeth has heard since then. Mr. Walker has been very sick indeed, but is now improving very happily. Nora and Elwyn are both with us. I do not know what we would do without them. Dear little Nora has sore eyes very badly. As my sheet is nearly filled I will have to close. All join me in much love to brother Ruthvin, Miss Elizabeth, Haynsworth, Lute, and your own little self. And now dear sister praying that God may ever bless and keep you, under his own wings of love, I remain your devoted sister.

Almira

Has dear brother Ruthvin heard whether he can remain at home or not? Truly hope he has, and that the answer is as we all so much hope.

Columbia March 3rd 1864
My dear dear Sister,

As I take my pen to write, this my first letter since my return to this place, sad memories fill my mind. Yes thoughts of the irreparable loss we have sustained, of the bitter cup of anguish we have been called to drink overwhelms my poor heart with grief, and the only comfort I feel is when bowed before my heavenly Father. I lift my voice in earnest prayer to God. His hand indeed. "To suffer and be strong." Oh Hattie . I feel the loss of our precious brother more since I have been here if possible, than at home, for there I was with those who knew and loved him as I did, and we could spend hours together in talking of him, for you know what a comfort it is when we have one whom we can freely tell the thoughts of our hearts. And though I have many dear sympathizing friends here, yet 'tis not like "home sweet Home." Yet my precious sister how much we have to be grateful for, how much of sweet has been mingled with the bitter. Together we stood around his dying bed and saw our noble, pure-hearted brother pass calmly, joyfully away to that rest prepared for the people of God. Oh my precious brother 'twas hard to give thee up, but we would not have thee back, but in those mansions of bliss we will be contented for thee to dwell. There we will, by the grace of God, meet thee. meet to part no more. As you say my sister–we must submit with patient resignation to the will of our heavenly Father. Not much longer must we journey here below ere we too will be called to pass o'er Jordan's stream. If then we can meet death as did our loved brother what joy, what happiness will we enjoy forever with the Lord. Oh that we may all so live as to meet an unbroken family in our Father's house. where there are many mansions. where too our blessed Savior has prepared a place for us. My darling mother, how often I think of her. she seems to feel our dear brother's death more every day. May God help her bear all that in His Providence he has afflicted her. It was so hard for me to leave home and sometimes I feel as if I cannot stay away. I pray God to bless each one of us and permit us to meet again. But dear Hattie we will miss the smile of welcome from our Sainted brother. I went to his grave the day I left and oh how hard it was to leave him sleeping there. I thought of my sad parting with him in Jan, of the sweet words of hope and comfort he whispered to me. Never will I forget them. They seemed dear to me then, but how much dearer now—Lizzie came over with me, so did Mr. Durant and Mrs. McCorquodale. They left Weds evening. I cannot tell you how much surprised I was to see Lizzie—nor can I thank you and dear miss Elizabeth enough for the very nice things you sent me. Such an abundance too. Would that I could do something to repay you all for your goodness and kindness to me but I never can. I only pray that I may be more worthy of the love and affection you have ever shown me. I have been so disappointed about not having your bonnet ready to send. It will be done tomorrow but Lizzie leaves at four o'clock in the morning. There is no alpacca except what is very inferior at an enormous price. I got mother Maria and Almira a dress apiece for eight dollars a yard but it is all gone. There will be a new stock opened the first of April, and the clerks and every one thinks goods will be much cheaper. So I thought I had better wait as I cannot get alpacca now for less than 10 or 12 dollars a yard. I send you a collar. it was ten dollars. there are no gloves at all—and stockings are so high I did not get them. I do not think I would get black stockings unless you needed them anyway but of course you know best. I have not got a black dress for myself either except a calico which I got before I left home and I intend wearing that and my black silk until April. But please my dear sister if you had rather I would get the things now let me know immediately. tell bro. R. to tell you which I had better do. I will send your money to you and if you want me to get them now you can easily send it back. I hope the hat will please you, though it is not done as nicely as I wanted it. It cost eight dollars. I trimmed it as I thought you would like it. They ask so high for trimming bonnets now that I bought the materials and will trim it myself if you are not afraid to trust me—the trimming cost $6.60. I could send it now as I have just got the bonnet but am afraid it would be hard for you to get any one to trim it for you. I did not know whether to keep the trunk until I get the things or send it now but thought perhaps I had better keep it until I do get them. You must be sure and let me know immediately which I had better do. You reccollet you gave me ten dollars 75 cents. last winter. I will send it too and will send in this a list of what the things cost. I send the money because I thought you would rather have it now. I will send your bonnet by the first opportunity and you can return my box whenever any one comes over. It is very late at night and I must close—though I feel like I could write you all night. I send Martha's letter to you. Give very much love to my dear brother, Miss E, dear little Haynsworth and Lute—to Henry and Sammie too. Please my precious sister write often to me, and let us remember each other at a throne of grace. Have you heard that Mr. Mood—bro Wm's father was dead—died day before yesterday—his death was so triumphant. Good bye. May God ever bless and keep you.

Your ever devoted sister
Amanda M. Rogers

If you have any old black silk scraps it will help. You had to line it inside. wish I had something to do it for you.

Hattie I would just wear my black silk with your collar and hat until you get your other things. I think I can send your bonnet in a few days.

Yours affectly,
Amanda

Columbia 10th March 1864
My darling sister,

Not knowing when Lizzie may have to leave, I will write you this morning in order to have it ready for her in time. I am much afraid you will need your things before you get them. Lizzie has been much disappointed about not getting off. She has not been well either, has sufferred so much with asthma. it distresses me to hear her breathe, but she has been better for the last two days. Hattie I send two dresses. the purple for Miss Elizabeth, the black for you, a present from bro Wm and sister. They sent me the money to get them for you and I got the prettiest I could find. hope you will both be pleased with them. I tried again for your alpacca and found some at eight dollars a yard–but very course and I did not know whether to get it or not–if you want me to do so though let me know immediately and I'll get it. I send a black lawn. it too was eight dollars and I thought I had better get it–it is so nice and wide and you would soon need something then to wear in summer. I got Maria and Almira one too. hope I did not do wrong in getting this for you. I scarcely knew which bonnet to send you and Maria–but thought perhaps you would like this one best and so concluded to send it. I thought too you would soon see each other and if either wanted to change you could do it then. they are trimmed just the same, and I do not know which I like best. they are both pretty. The bonnet cost thirty dollars. I did not think it would be quite so much. They are both the same price. It took more crape than I thought it would. I hope so much you may be pleased with all the things I send. You must write soon and let me know. I concluded after I wrote you (which letter I hope you have rec-d) that I had better spend your money now as I sense it would be some time before I could get the money to brother Ruthvin. I'll send you a list of the things with their prices so that you'll see what they all come to. Cousin Hu has been to see you 'ere this I suppose. Maria wrote me he expected to go. I guess he'll be disappointed in not seeing Lizzie. He is coming to see me next week and I am looking forward to it. I feel so anxious to see some one from home–for dear Hattie I have felt very lonely very desolate since I have been here. I had such a sweet dream about my darling brother last night. I have never dreamed of him—although I so constantly thought of him, until two nights ago. Oh how hard it seems that never again will we see him—oh we must not say never. In Heaven with the glorified and blest we'll meet him—meet to part no more. This is a joyful thought, and cheers us as we journey here below. not long will we be separated, but soon we'll join them on the heavenly shores.

March 11th

I could not finish yesterday. This morning much to my surprise cousin Hu came. William who was going with him to see you was not well so he thought he would come to see me first. I feel so uneasy about Wm. cousin Hu says he had sorethroat and I am so afraid he will have scarlet fever. Oh Hattie, it would almost kill me to have my darling only brother taken from us. I am afraid I love him too much that it is sinful. May God spare him and make him a bright and shining light. Dear Maria too has not been well—and her cough is not well yet but she is much better other wise. The rest of the dear ones were all well. Melissa Spencer was married last night. Father and cousin Hu came down to the wedding. did not have many there. Emma was one of the bridesmaids. Cousin Hu says Melissa looked very pretty. he is going down to see you soon. Lizzie says she was never so glad to see Ned in her life. I am so sorry she is going. I'll miss her so much. Lizzie is a sweet girl. I only send you one collar as I thought that would do. Wish I was with you to help make your dresses. I would make a frill of the same for your calico and make the lawn-frill front and back—and you'll have enough for a cape too if you want it. There are ten yds. I thought I had better send you that many, though it may be too much but you can make some use of it. You recollect I had $10.75 of your money before which with what Anna had made $110.75. Trimming for your bonnet was $30.00 Fixing your hat was $8.00 Lawn dress $80.00 Black silk thread $5.00 Which makes $123.00. I had some black silk and some crape one of the girls gave me and made strings for your bonnet as ribbon is $25 a yard. It is not very good silk, but I hope it will do. Please my dear sister if there is anything else that any of you want let me know and I'll get it for you with pleasure. Will you please accept the collar from me, wish I had something more to give you. I made a small bone for you to wear with it. It is late and I must close. Give the truest love of my heart to my dear bro Ruthvin Miss Elizabeth and the children. Oh I would give any thing to be with you to-night. Lizzie said she did not think she could take two trunks, so as cousin <u>Hu</u> leaves tomorrow I will let him take it home and carry it to you when he goes down. Write to me soon my precious sister—I love your letters so much—The nice things you sent me are not all gone yet. Do not be in a hurry to send my box. I will not need it—I will take good care of your box and take it when I go home. If I cannot send it before. Good bye my sister. May God bless you all evermore. Remember at a throne of grace your loving sister

Amanda M. R.

Georgetown March 12th 1864
My beloved Sister,

Your good, kind letter would have been replied to ere this, but I knew Wm had written and I thought best to wait a few days longer. I write you dear Hattie under circumstances different from what I've ever done before. Our family band has again been broken, but glory ever be to God, we are assured that another of our number has been safely housed in Heaven, forever secure from all the sorrows of this poor mortal life. Oh! I can never tell you the overwhelming sorrow which filled my poor heart, when I felt that my precious brother was indeed gone from us. I thought I was prepared for the blow, for I knew it must come, but for a time, it almost crushed me, but I thank God that <u>dark hour</u> has passed, and my faith now enables me to look beyond the sufferings his dear body endured in this life & to see him as he now is among that happy throng in bright array, of whom it was said to St. John "These are they which came out of great tribulation and have washed their robes, and made them white in the blood of the Lamb." Yes I feel that his crown is all the more bright for what he suffered here. And oh! what a triumph of grace was his departure. I feel that our Heavenly Father has now a higher claim upon our love than ever before. Oh dear Hattie let us seek more & more to cast the world behind us, and to live for eternity; for <u>we must not miss Heaven</u>. If it is hard to be separated the short while we stay on earth, what would an eternity be. May God help us to live that we may meet death fearlessly, as did our angel brother. I try to be resigned to my separation from him in his last days, but dear Sister, be grateful that this satisfaction was yours.

Yes, like you when I think of him in Heaven my little angel band are ever near him, and often have I seemed to see my precious Anna, her face lit up with rapturous joy, as she shows him the glories & beauties of her Heavenly Home. And now "grand-pa Mood" has joined the happy company, Now her joys in Heaven are increasing. Oh Hattie will it be mine too one day to meet that joyous welcome? God grant that it may. How sweet the rest of Heaven must be to dear brother, after his long life of toil & care! I feel that his is a high seat there. I cannot grieve that he has gone home, but it is hard to think we shall see him no more. Things move on with us here much as usual, indeed our life for the past several weeks seem more like a fearful dream than reality. Yet we have much for which to be grateful, for we have kind sympathizing friends. We were surprised yesterday by a visit from Mr. Robt. English. He with several others have joined an artillery company several miles from here. He brought me good long letters from home, and you dont know how I prize letters now, all that any of you tell me of our dear brother is treasured in my heart of hearts. Mr. John Dixon's son Wm & Mr. Reese Durant's son David are also down here. Wm met them in the street & he said they looked so sad & forlorn. I have thought of them ever since. it grieves me so to see young lads have to enter the army, especially those whose elder brothers have fallen. A letter from Amanda tells us that Lizzie H was on a visit at the College, I know the girls were glad to have her with them. dear Amanda seems very sad, but can we feel other wise? however resigned we may be. Wm asks if you & dear Miss E- have recd a bundle. he directed it—to send you from Columbia, & if so begs you to accept it from him. wish it was something better. Dear Father tells us the glad news in his last letter, that he & dear mother may come to see us next month. I need not tell you my feelings when I heard it. I pray nothing may prevent them & that the trip may do our poor mother good. Tell my dear Miss E- nothing save going <u>home</u> would give me more pleasure than to go and see you all, but I must wait till toward the close of the year, to think of it. It looks like a long time, & much may happen before then, but may God bring us to see each others faces again. I trust my good bro- R- is fixed at home now, do tell me if he is & where has Mr E- Plowden gone? Give a heart full of love to Bro R- Miss E- and the dear boys. Write soon to your devoted sister

L J Mood

The ten cents is due at Kingstree, sorry it had to be added to the postage. Give much love to all our relatives & friends, near you.

Bishopville Mar 23rd, 1864
My darling sister,

I now have a few leisure moments at my command, and knowing of no other way in which I could more pleasantly spend it than in writing to you dear sister, I will endeavor to do so. Brother William and myself are all alone in the sitting room. How much pleasure dear sister would it afford us were you with the other precious ones here with us. How happy, how surpassingly happy it makes us dear sister, after so long a separation to be again clasped in each other's arms, to sit around the cheerful fireside and listen to those voices which are so sweet, so dear to us. But my sister should God in His mercy spare <u>us</u> all to many many happy meetings on earth, which I earnestly and fervently pray that He may. There will be one vacant seat, one sweet voice we will miss as around the family altar we raise our voices to sing praises to that God who ever reigns on high. But though we miss him so sadly here dear sister, how sweet it will be to have him welcome us in that bright home above. That welcome will not be less sweet in heaven than those by which he greeted us here. How very precious this to bind us to Heaven. God grant we may all meet those loved ones there. Maria with Cousin Hu went this evening to carry Cousin Mag home, who has been staying with us since Sunday evening. Maria will write you from Aunt Peggie's but I thought as Jim was going down I would write also, as I did not think you would mind getting two letters. Father, Maria and myself went Sunday evening to attend the funeral service of Mr. E Durant. He died Saturday evening with disease of the heart. He had been very low for about a week. St. Luke's church has lost one of its brightest members in his death. Mr. H. D. Green preached his funeral service. He said in conversing with Mr. Durant on any subject connected with the world, his mind would be wandering all the time. But as soon as the subject of religion or pertaining to heavenly things were brought up, his mind would be perfectly clear. He expressed a perfect willingness to die. Amanda sent your trunk by cousin Hu. Jim will take it to you tomorrow. I am glad that you can get it as I know you must need it. Have you made up any of your black dresses yet? How do you like your bonnet? I hope it suits you. I have to stop now, as I wish to leave a space for father to write a few lines. All join me in much much love to all the dear ones at home. Good bye darling sister with a heart full of love I remain

Your devoted sister,
Almira

Bishopville 23 March 1864
Dear Ruthvin

I will try and send down tomorrow for a load of corn as I am now out at home, and I feel sorry that I have not been able, (as I expected to be) to send long ago.

For thus disappointing you in regard to the time of Sunday you must pardon me if possible. I have to send by the way of Lynchburg and Jim will not get to your place until Friday.

We are all tolerably well to day—I hope this may find you in good health.

Hugh and Maria expect to go down to see you next week and I hope nothing will prevent their doing so.

So far as I know you have not been written to by any of our folks since the death of Mr. Elins Durant. He died after a short illness last Saturday night. Maria, Almira and my self attended the funeral Sunday evening. Mr. Wilsons man Frederick died also last Saturday of Tiphoid fever.

I send you a bottle of whiskey thinking in may be of service in case of sickness—and please say to my friend—your good sister that she will find a piece of homespun in Harriet's trunk which we have got her from Columbia (the trunk) The whiskey is in the homespun—

Thursday 24 March

We are all very well this morning and Jim will start soon.

I intended to have given you notice when I would send for the load of corn but was not able to determine until yesterday. I would be glad that Jim should leave Saturday morning by day break. The moon will give him light enough to start off by.

As H & M are to leave shortly to see you I need not write more. Love to <u>all</u>

Affectionately yours
William Rogers

Columbia F. College April 1st 1864
My dear dear Sister,

Your sweet good letter was rec-d yesterday and I will try and express a part of my pleasure at least, in answering right away. I had been looking for a letter from you for some time. I am so sorry to hear that dear miss Elizabeth was again suffering with her ears but I do hope she is better now and will not be troubled with them again. I am always so sorry to hear of her suffering. Oh Hattie my thoughts have been with you all very very often to day. Dear Maria and cousin Hu are with you now. Lizzie and Jennie too I guess. I have seen you all in imagination getting ready and starting to Midway and I would not object to sitting down to Miss E's nice dinner. I don't think she would complain of my not doing it justice. I do wish I could be with you all to hear some of the good sermons. I guess the girls will try to captivate some of the young ministers if you have any. When you write you must tell me everything about it as Ned will scarcely give you the light of his countenance after treating Lizzie so nicely I should not think. I trust you may have a good time, that the good Lord may pour out his spirit abundantly, that your souls may be richly blessed. How pleasant it is for Christians thus to meet and how precious the hours spent in serving God. I hope dear Maria's visit may do her good. she needed change of this kind. I have felt very uneasy about her—and oh Hattie at times I would feel so miserable fearing that our dear little brother might take scarlet fever. I heard once he had sore throat and oh the anguish of soul I felt no mortal knew but I thank God he has preserved him, that he has not had it. I cannot feel grateful enough. Oh that he may spare him, permit him to live a long happy and useful life, but oh above all things I desire him to be a true christian. Tis for this I pray—that he may now be brought to the knowledge of the truth as it is in Christ Jesus. I trust that all those so dear to us may be bright and shining lights in our Master's service.

I am so glad dear Hattie you were pleased with the things I sent you and that Miss E. liked her dress. They were the prettiest I could find. You need not have troubled to send me the money, as I did not need it. I am much obliged to you. We have just to day gotten through with our examination. we did not have many visitors. the weather too was very inclement. What sudden changes we have had in the weather. I am afraid it will cause sickness. Did you eat any snow? Miss Jones had a little sugar so we had some. right nice. She is now quite sick has not been able to attend the examinations, but I trust she may soon be well. I am writing you in her room with the blinds all closed which will account for my pretty writing. Anna Haynsworth has had measles but is getting well fast now. She was broken out very thickly. Anna C. will have them too I expect. Dear William wrote to me last week—a sweet letter. The first I have had from him since I have been here. He said they were drawing the Seine so I suppose they have had fish. Mag had been staying with them and had just gone home. It made me feel like wishing to be with them so much, but never mind June will soon be here, then I hope to see you all again. But oh my sister how that pleasure is marred by the thought that there will be one who will not be with us. whose sweet voice will never again be heard around our home fireside. no, no, he is gone forever gone from our mortal sight. Sometimes I can scarcely endure the thought. Oh that I could this evening look into those loving eyes—clasp that dear hand. but oh my Father, this I can never never do. but thank God for the hope of being welcomed by him on the eternal shores. I want to write to Lizzie which I will get you to give her. Isabella Stephens sends much love to you. Give much love to dear bro Ruthvin, Miss Elizabeth, Haynsworth, Lute and Henry. To cousins Lizzie and Callie when you see them to Mr. E. Plowden and family. And all my Clarendon friends. Good bye dear sister. May God bless you all. write very very soon to your loving sister—

Amanda M. Rogers

April 3rd 1864

Dear Harriet—a friend of mine is going to King's Tree in the morning and I'll get him to put this into the Post for me. It strikes me that I wrote some time ago to Ruthvin and that no reply has yet come to hand. I may be mistaken however, perhaps I am in his debt, if so please let me know—Lucy wrote to you just before the reception of your last—which we were glad to receive—Hope you recv'd Lucy's—The contents of yours have been well discussed by us and talked over repeatedly—it is certainly a great pleasure to receive letters these times especially—Hope you receive a great many—We have nothing Harriet specially to communicate to you. We are trying to get along the best we can. The weather has been very rough and cold. And last evening we had quite a storm of wind and rain and this morning the sun wants to try to shine but I fear it is a failure. The unusually cold spring so backward too must certainly affect the planting interests—What does R have to say in these matters? Last Sunday was a pretty day and I felt rejoiced to see the sun look so bright and it (illegible) that the season was settled. I went out & harnessed my horse as usual preparatory to my afternoon's work—having to go off just after dinner. but I was taken with a very severe cholic and did not get relieved till about noon so I missed all my appts—Sunday school and all—I have got to feeling quite right yet. The cold has kept back our garden very much. Our peas are however doing very well and our irish pot are now showing themselves. Hope they'l do well for they will be a great help in the general scarcity of every thing to eat. I have fixed a large spot in the garden for my millet for my horse—what is the conclusion with you all about the fruit. We think our peaches are gone. The apple and pear trees however had not bloomed before the last cold spell. The figs we are looking forward to with much satisfaction. We have a very large scuppernong grape vine in our garden—but alas—the arbor has rotted down—it now lies upon the ground. It is a very fine vine indeed from all we can learn—but it will do us no good. I feel to regret its being upon the ground every time I see it. How are you all getting along at home. I suppose Miss E keeps as busy as usual about all matters at home. You must give much love to her and tell her it appears like a long time since we have seen her.

I recv'd a letter from bro James on yesterday. He has been fixing up Father's papers and letters which have accumulated now for a number of years. He says he has a great many very interesting letters among them and he wished more than once that I was with him to share in the pleasure of reading them. He has sold some of the odds & ends of the old furniture and is trying to settle the (illegible) up as well as the times will allow—Dear me how sad this makes me feel. How rejoiced I am however that I did go to Columbia before I came down here and that I was privileged to be with Father at least a short time before he passed away to his reward. I'll always feel glad that I paid this visit. I feel now so sorry that I was never able to ask him the many questions relative to his early christian experience which I always intended doing. When of late years I have been with him the circumstances never appeared propitious and now the opportunity is past. And then I have so often of late years desired to hear him preach; but this has not been allowed me—The last time I heard him was in '43. I remember his subject but the text I dont. He urged faithfully upon the congregation the importance of family prayer—My earliest recollections of him are associated with him and the church and I'll always recall these lessons with pleasure. But dear Father is gone. I ought to feel very grateful that I had such a Father and that he was so good and kind to me. His prayers were constant and faithfully offered up and his children were near his heart. God has been graciously pleased to hear their prayers and through his dear mothers faithfulness they were blessed with children who never committed any (illegible) and who as they grew up became religious & I love Harriet to think of them in Heaven, safe from all the storms and anxieties of this fleeting earth. Associated with them are their children who died in infancy and my angel band are with them too. And thus we pass away, not all at a time, but one drops off and our end too must come. Let us be ready—prepared—what attachments how strong they are to that good world. The mail has just brought a letter from Dr. Burgess telling us of the death of his youngest son James—He is sorely afflicted. But I must close do give just as much love to Miss L R- and the boys for us. What company has Mr Edgar

P formed—and what Hodge is it that we have heard was killed near Manning by certain deserters? We have heard something about it but none of the particulars—Do write very soon—

Affectly
William

Columbia May 2nd 1864
My much loved sister

Your thrice welcome letter was most gladly perused and would have been answered ere this but I knew you were in Georgetown and thought you would appreciate it more after your return. I know you had a pleasant time with our dear brother and sister though I know feelings of sadness would start o'er your hearts and thoughts of our precious sainted brother fill your minds, but I know 'twas a small pleasure for dear sister to hear you talk of him and tell her of his last days on earth. Sometimes I feel so much better when thinking of his being taken from us then at others, most while writing of him, my heart seems well nigh bursting. I know it was hard for dear sister to have you all leave her again, but I pray she may ever be under the care of our watchful Father, that no harm and anger may come near them and may He permit us in safety to meet again. Did bro. Ruthin go to Georgetown too? I hope he did as I know he would be warmly welcomed. Maria, Almira and Wm all wrote me while father & mother were away. They missed them so much but cousin David staid most of the time with them. I wished often to be with them and to be with you all too at dear sister's. but it will not be long 'ere I will see you all again—a kind Providence permitting. It is only seven weeks now I think before school closes. I can scarcely realize that May is here.

May 3rd

I began this yesterday but did not have time to finish it. Yesterday evening Whitfield came to see me and I was glad to see him. he was very pleasant and talked a good deal. I know his family hated to see him leave again but I trust he may be spared to them. he told me of miss E Nelson's marriage, did any of you attend? I suppose Mary Emilie was one of the bridesmaids. Was Lizzie H. there? They are all stepping off fast. Amarinthea will be very lonely now I should think but I suppose she will soon follow their example. Wallie Witherspoon has been to see us often since his company has been here. Sat. though he went over to Bishopville but I guess he will be back to-day or to-morrow, when I hope to hear from home. I sent your ring and a pillow case of yours by him and thought you would get it from there sooner than here. Mr. Dennis came from home last Friday. he told me all about them. I wish he would go oftener. he is a good hand to tell you all the news. said cousin Hu's Jim had gotten back from Marlboro and expected to go to the army again soon. he does not think his wound is any better at all. I fear it will be a long time before it is well again. I heard that dear little Lute had measles, but hope he is well ere this. was he sick much? I hope they may have them very lightly. I was glad to hear that Capt. Haynsworth was better. do they still think of going to the springs? I read a letter from Fannie not many days ago. She had been to (illegible) to attend (illegible). I think said they had a very good meeting indeed. But I suppose you have heard from her since then. Has Mr. Still been to see you yet? Whitfield says he has been giving it to his servants about drinking and surprise parties. I think he ought. People were never more gay than now, when their hearts should be constantly lifted up in humble supplication to Almighty God. I had an invitation to a military ball given here last Friday night. Willie sent it. Do you think of going up home soon? You must write and tell me all about your visit. every thing will be interesting to me. and ask my good brother if he never intends to honor his sister with another letter He must not forget that I am still in the land of the living and still love him and his letters as much as ever. Give a heart full of love to him and dear Miss Elizabeth what would I not give to see her this morning. I do love her so much and look forward with as much pleasure to seeing her as my dear sisters. Give much love to Henry Fannie & Haynsworth. tell them to study hard and improve fast. Tell them they must all write to me soon. Kiss Lute for me. and now dear sister I must tell you good bye. God bless thee with all blessings both temporal and spiritual. Remember me to Mr. E. Plowdens family. much love to cousins Lizzie & Callie. Write very soon to your loving sister

Amanda M. Rogers

Columbia May 17th 1864
My dear sister Hattie,

I believe you are owing me a letter but I have time this morning and will gladly spend it in conversing with you. I trust this may find you all well and Lute entirely over the measles. I guess it will be some time before they go through the family. We have had several cases of sickness among the girls but only two have been seriously ill. one of the teachers, too, Miss Jones has been ill. but she too is getting well. I have done little else than nurse her since she was taken so that I have got behind answering all my letters. Cousin Albert came from Bishopville, the first I have heard from there. says he left all well. I am looking for my dear father this week and truly hope he may come. He is coming over by private conveyance. if it were only a little faster I could so easily return with him. Cousin A. came again to see me last Sunday. he says he thinks of bringing his family over and living here in about three months. It is only five weeks now before our last examination. it is hard for me to realize that so soon I shall again see all at home. You must come up then too dear Hattie. I want to see you all so much. I attended a fair last week given in behalf of the sick and wounded soldiers held at the Park. I think they must have made quite a sum. there was a crowd. I had the pleasure of meeting Mr. Banks there whom you reccollect taught in Bishopville. Cousin Albert says Cousin Charles is looking dreadfully again. I wish so much his health could be entirely restored. Almira wrote me in her last of Col. Green's death. I did not think he was long for this world. I feel so much for his family—his brothers and sisters. He has been so much like a father to them, and how much will they miss him, but he, I trust, he is now in that world freed from sin, enjoying the love and presence of God. There is to be a three days meeting at home next week. Oh that God may bless them with an outpouring of his holy spirit. and let us earnestly pray dear sister that it may be blessed to the good of our dear little brother. Oh that he may now give his heart to God and taste of the sweets of a redeeming love. I had letters from cousins Hu and Jim a few days ago. they were both well. Cousin Hu was having a revival in his regt- and much good was being done. I trust his labors may be blessed and that he may be instrumental in winning many souls to Christ. I hope Miss

Elizabeth has not been troubled with her head any more. Has cousin Covert gone to Va? I know it will almost kill cousin Callie if he has. May God spare his life to his dear family. I suppose that cousin David too is now in Va. though I have never heard whether he had relisted or not. Oh I dread the many hard battles which I know must still be fought there. Col. Jenkins remains got here on Sat. how much I feel for his young and lovely wife. you remember he married miss Carrie Jamison of Orangeburg. I have thought of Lydia and Abbie too. it will be a sad stroke for them. I had a letter from dear Lizzie a short time ago. she says dear little Elwyn is beginning to talk. I want to see the dear little creatures so much. I had some nice straw berries sent me last night. wish you could enjoy them with me. do you think the fruit is killed entirely. Hattie wont you and bro R come to our commencement? Dr. Palmer is to deliver the address before the Literary Society on Monday. the (illegible) of (illegible) and Bishop (illegible) the address to the graduating class on Monday night. I do wish you would come and if you can't come here, please go to Bishopville as soon as I get home. Give my best love to dear brother Ruthvin, Miss Elizabeth, Henry, Haynsworth, Lute, to cousins Lizzie, Callie and all my friends. I forgot to tell you before that cousin Jim sent a great deal of love to you all and said he would write you soon. Please dear Hattie write me soon and a long letter. May God bless you all evermore.

With warmest love
Your ever affct sister
Amanda M. R.

I expect I have seen the letters of our precious brother you spoke of. oh what comfort it is now to read those words penned by his loved hand. Oh that we may prove faithful and meet him where never more we will have to say farewell but the time seems so long long since we have seen his face. And not long will we be separated. A happy reunion in Heaven together again. well sister again I must tell you good bye

Your sister Amanda

Geo-Town May 20th '64
Dear Ruthven—

Your kind letter came safely to us today and I write now so that I may mail this afternoon. and who I ask is more prompt in replying to your letters than —We have been waiting for a long time a letter from you but we have not thought your not writing grew out of any indifference. We know your hands are busy in many matters. but still let us hear from you sometimes and in the meantime let Harriet show her hand. I asked Lucy if I must direct this to you or Miss E? and she says <u>direct</u> it to you but let it be to <u>all</u>. What she means I suppose is that Haynesworth and Lute and you and Harriet and Miss Elizabeth and George and Serener, Chloe, Charlotte and <u>Lane</u> and Dick and <u>all</u> the rest. I wish very much I had something to write of interest to you all but really this is impossible. You mentioned that all the W family were well.[146] This indicates that Miss E's trouble with the ear is better. I hope so that the servant now sick may soon be perfectly well. I suppose you are not anymore behind in farming than are <u>all</u> the rest. Hope your rice will make a good showing yet and that you may be yet able to give us a Hellow when we drive up. And now with reference to our visiting you. You must really not write so earnestly on this matter. You cant form an idea how delighted we'd be to do this. Yes it would give us real pleasure to be with you a week or more—but it will not be possible to leave our home 'till we have to leave it. This may be a disappointment to you. but it is also on us but so it is and we'l have to be patient under this deprivation. Harriet asked in her last after my horse. He has been very lame and I have not had him in harness for a long time. He has been under the treatment of a farrier here. I am rejoiced to say that he is better now. and though not yet himself hope he soon will be. He goes out to the grass now with Mr. Mckusky's horses. This is a great help to him and to me also. How are all the neighbors and friends? You had not turn to mention any of them. I suppose Covert and your sisters sons are all about Petersburg Va. Trust the good Lord may spare them. Did M.

146 W family = white family

Witherspoon come to see you. He and Miss Easterling Rebecca are engaged to be married. She is (illegible) of it. We learn this from a lady friend of Miss E's to whom Miss E. wrote. Better not mention it as coming from me. Though it is no secret I have my opinion about that match. What is yours and Harriet, Miss Elizabeth's. You all know better of him than I do. when I hear yours then I will tell you mine. A letter from Manning indicated that there had been great doings in the line of dancing there. I have had no names mentioned to me however. wish I could be with you on your trip to (illegible) Saturday there to meet Brother Simmons. Hope that Harriet will not fail to introduce you to him. He is a great friend of mine. I think you will like his preaching. Do tell us all about your trip over there & of the meeting also. Lucy says if Miss E's ear troubles her anymore that she & Harriet must go to Bishopville and let Dr. DuBose prescribe. I hope she will not have any more trouble with it however. Hope you can read this. I am trying to write plainly. my pen is so poor—but if you can't read it send it back and I'll rewrite it—we have no news here but what you also see. I trust our grand sweep in the Trans Mifissippi (illegible) will be followed with still greater success about Dalton Va. We have lost a great many fine officers and some choice soldiers. Oh! when will this awful carnage end. Trust Grant will be driven away from Richmond and put to shame before the eyes of Yankeedom. Don't you think things look like it is his (illegible)? From what you tell us I don't suppose there will be any trouble about your papers being passed and also E's. Hope it (illegible) this will of itself keep you busy to keep up with what the Gov. requires of you. But I must close. Tell Harriet that the next time I get as pretty rose bud as I had when Lucy forbid me sending it to her that I will send it to her in spite of all her forbiddings and the consequences and they may be great upon my poor head. Hope H. is getting on well at school. Tell him and Lute howdy and Henry also. Write when you can to us. Have not heard from Charleston very lately. Asbury wrote sometime that he was about taking his folks to the city from Summerville. Just as he got his plans (illegible) & about executing them an enormous shell burst just at the gate—so he was at sea-[147] Have not heard since . Lucy sends much love to you Harriet & Miss E & to the boys—Old McLeod is quite sick.

Affectly—W W Mood

147 "at sea" = confused, or unable to decide what to do https://idioms.thefreedictionary.com/at+sea

Bishopville June 20th 1864
My darling Sister

If you will please excuse this paper upon which I write I will endeavor to hold a few moments conversation with you. Like yourself we are out of paper, so I have to write on any thing I can find. We received your dear letter by last mail and were truly thankful to hear that you were all quite well. I am glad too to tell you that this leaves us all very well, though our family just at this time is quite small, being composed of mother, Almira and myself. Father and dear little William left Friday evening for Columbia, and tomorrow afternoon we hope to welcome them all back again, with our dear sister Amanda. I do hope no accident will happen to them but I really feel uneasy now when my friends are travelling on the cars. Mr. Durant and James also went over at the same time. Father too had Miss Roupe to travel with him. She has been wanting to go over to Columbia for some time now. he offered to take charge of her over there. She was very glad of the chance and seems quite grateful to us all. Father will find her quite a talkative companion. I am glad father and William can stay at the College. Amanda spoke for a room for them. they furnish their own provisions. I hope dear little William will have a vey pleasant time. I know the girls will make a great deal of him. If nothing prevents, Almira, Mary Bradley and myself want to go down to the depot tomorrow evening to meet them, so that we can see some of the girls as they pass on. Sister Lizzie spent last week and a part of this with us. She is up at Mr. Durant's now. The children grow prettier every day I believe. Wish so much you could see them. Sister Lizzie is anxious to go to see you all, but dont know now when she will be able (illegible) Nora goes to Sunday school now up here. Hattie you will <u>surely</u> come home shortly now to see Amanda, will you not? You and my dear Brother must certainly come, ask him to let you stay up sometime with us, then Amanda can take you home I expect and stay with you some. Please come <u>soon</u>—we wish to see you all <u>so</u> <u>much</u>. Glad to hear that Mr. Isaac Montgomery has gotten home, hope Mr. W will get well. I know his dear mother is rejoiced to have him with her again. Always give my love to Mary Emily, you know she and I are good friends. Ask Tommie if he ever thinks of me those times. wish he, Henry and Haynsworth could come up to see us all this summer. Hattie when you come up again try to persuade Lute to come with you, we would all be so glad if he would. I entirely forgot to send your scarfs by Almira, so I will put them in this letter. Tell brother Ruthvin father says he has no pipe lead at all now. I suppose Almira told you all about our meeting, and of what great friends Mr. Cricles and I got to be while he was here. He begged mother to let Almira and I go down to a meeting he is to have commencing next Friday week. A few days ago I received a very pretty note from Mrs. Cricles telling me that we must not disappoint him, but be sure to come. wasn't that clever? I am acquainted with her and like her so much. Cousin Charles is still improving and I trust will soon be well again. Cousin Mag has family over in Marlboro now, tell Cousin Callie all are well at her mothers. I feel so sorry for Cousin Callie. I know she feels anxious all the time. But really Hattie I am afraid you cant read this but the paper is so bad, you must excuse and try to make it out if possible. Write to us whenever you can. Mother will get the (illegible) and send it down the first chance she gets. Mrs. Elizabeth is too good to us. Mother prizes her dress and stockings very highly. I can assure you they are beautiful. Remember me to Mrs. McDowell when you see her. Love to dear Brother Ruthvin, Miss Elizabeth and kisses to the children. May God's protecting care ever be with you my darling Sister is the prayer of your affct. Sister

Maria

Georgetown June 24th 1864
My very dear Sister

Your good letter so full of interest to us was rec'd a few days since, and I take this the first chance I have had of replying. I am sorry a longer time than usual should have elapsed without your hearing from us, but I hope the letter I wrote to dear Miss E came to hand soon after you wrote to me, and your anxieties about me relieved. I ought to be very grateful that I have so many dear ones who feel such an interest in my welfare. I trust I am so and may God bless & reward them for it all. We are all well to-day, tho' we are both rather jaded from a long, hot ride we took yesterday out to visit Mr. Rognie's family. It is nine miles and tho' we had so pleasant a time after we got there, I felt we had fully earned it, we had such a warm, disagreeable time getting there. Last Friday afternoon we were both delighted to see Mr. Robt English who has been home on a visit lately. How pleasant it is to see any familiar face when we are far from home! He brought us letters from home and a bundle dear Mother sent me. They said that Father & Almira had recently been to see you all. Almira was in great extacies that she had caught so many fish. I wonder if I were to try again if I would'nt have better luck? You know thanks to Haynsworth I did pull one out of the water. I was sorry to hear dear Hattie that they did not leave you quite well. Hope it was nothing serious, that long since you have become yourself again. I have been quite busy this week doing my first in the art of dyeing, but I have not succeeded up to my expectations. I am afraid it would be more than even Miss Elizabeth could do to learn me how. However it was for a coarse piece of cloth, & I hope it will do somehow. Next week I hope to get some dyed for myself, but I fear that pretty <u>black</u> will never come out of the pot for me. Last Tuesday we had old Mrs Beatty to spend the day with us, you remember her, dont you? I think she can talk better, and has more use of herself than when you saw her. Poor old lady, she enjoys a visit so much. I was so glad to have her with us. Old Mrs. Wright and her daughter-in-law Mrs Gurdon Wright were also here that day, and we had a nice time. Had quite a nice treat sent us this morning in a piece of fresh veal. something we have'nt had before in a long time. We hope tho' after a while to be able to get beef, at least often enough to make soup occasionally. the tomatoes and okra are backward here. We have'nt had any yet. We were so glad to hear that Isaac Montgomery had got home, and Edgar with him. I do hope he will rapidly recover under his kind mother's treatment. How has J. M. Pendergrass got? Glad to hear Mrs. McDowell & Miss Hort got to see you. I would like to have enjoyed their company with you. I suppose dear Amanda is at home now. I know she was glad to get there. I expect Wm enjoyed the sight-seeing in Columbia very much. I am anxious to know how the Commencement came off. I am so dissapointed that Wm's sister can not come to see us this summer. She was afraid to come on account of health & has gone to visit bro. John instead. I am so anxious to see her and her little Clara. Well dear sister I am like you short of paper, and must close. I doubt if you can read what I've written. Tell dear bro. Ruthvin we are getting anxious to see one of his letters again. Won't he favor us with one soon? And you write dear Hattie when you can. Wm joins me in warmest love to you to bro. Ruthvine, Miss Elizabeth and to the dear boys all of them. Remember us too very kindly to all our relatives and friends. Tell Callie to try and keep a good heart & trust in God that all will yet be well. And now dearest Sister good-bye May God ever bless & keep you & yours, I am as ever your very devoted Sister

L J Mood

P. S. Tell all the servants howdye for me.

Bishopville 15 July 1864
Dear Ruthvin

On yesterday we rec'd our dear Harriets letter and were pained to hear of your illness. and we do hope you may now be fast recovering. It is sad beside all the rest that you have so much trouble with your throat. We do hope it may not continue thus to affect you. We are so sorry to hear that your illness will probably deprive us of a visit as soon as we had expected it. If you should soon feel better would it not be well to make the trip anyhow? You know that people travil for health. Would you try it? Perhaps it would be the best you could do. I am happy to say that we are all tolerably well. We have at this time us a visitor—Mary Jane She will be here a few days. Mary J. McCallum is in the neighborhood but we have not yet seen her. People are generally well except for Mrs H(illegible)- She is terribly sick with fever -

Since Harriets letter came I have seen Mr. Durant. He asks me to say that "the hunt" is postponed a week to suit the (illegible) of Mr. Plowden and perhaps others- He begs that you and Edgar come if possible—and others are much interested that you shall come—We all hope you may be able by the time now set the 2nd day of August—(Tuesday) is the day to start—well Ruthvin—what think you? I had concluded to go if you should come. As I have not been right well I concluded to try a change of climate and water and if you come I shall try and go—who knows but what we both might be benefited? and we want to see your Bro. Edgar up here very much. W. A. (illegible) will not go satisfied if he dont come. If you improve handsomely we shall still venture to look for you at the proper time and Harriet with you—what do you think about it? Do let me hear from you soon as possible, and I will inform Durant and the others.

C. Spencer is still improving slowly. He has called for a letter while at the store this morning for the first time.

We will wait to hear from you before we say much about the visit from here to you.

Tell dear Harriet we thank her very much for all her good letters, and that our good friend your dear Sister for all her kindness not forgetting wool and dyeing cot. yarn. ask her how it was that the wool got heavier in coloring? God bless you all. & <u>much</u> love from all.

Most affectionately
William Rogers

Bishopville 18 July 1864
Dear Ruthvin,

I wrote you last week and forwarded the letter on Saturday by N K Dixon, in order that it might leave Sumter this morning, but fearing he may have forgotten to leave the letter I write a few lines this morning. I hope and pray that you may soon be well again and we were all as sorry as you could wish us to be on hearing that you were sick. I mentioned in my letter that the hunt was postponed until Tuesday the 2nd of Augt. and all hope that ere that time, you may be so well as to come up with Edgar and join the affair. There are several that will be very much disappointed if you and Edgar fail to come.

If you do come, I intend going with you in the hope that a change of air and water may benefit me and I hope you may be much improved if you can come.

Tell Harriet that Maria and myself went over to Qtly meeting at Cypress on yesterday. I saw P M Hames the preacher. I am sorry to say that the Federals have overrun that portion of Ark. where J. B. McDaniel lives, and his negroes, horses, (illegible), and furniture have been carried off. His family are with his Son in law.

I mentioned that my dear Lucy was with us. She is well. I suffered a good deal with asthma last night but am a little better now.

Dear Harriet asked me about the crop in her letter and I forgot to answer. I am sorry to say my prospect is very poor. Rain is greatly needed and unless we get rain soon it will be a bad chance with us. Hope yours is doing well and that you have fine seasonable rains.

Just while I am writing there are indications of rain and I do hope it may come to day.

I have been pained by hearing that Capt. Haynsworth is not improved by his visit to the springs.

I esteem Capt H. very highly and do hope that his health may yet be restored. But all of Earth is uncertain—"There is nothing true but heaven."

I hope dear Ruthvin soon to hear from you again by letter—write us soon as possible and let me know whether you may be expected for the Hunt. I hope you and dear H may come yet.

Affectionately yours
William Rogers
love to all from all

Bishopville July 26th 1864
Mr Ruthven Plowden
Dear Sir

We anticipate to having a camp hunt in Chesterfield our old hunting ground considering on the 7th of next month. If you can we would like for you and your brother to join us. I expect Mr. Bradford and our Sumter friends up on Tuesday the 6 so as to go up on Wednesday the 7th—I spoke to Mr Wm Rogers sometime back to notify you but he has been quite sick and informs me that he has neglected to do so but I hope you will receive this in good time—This leaves me and my family well and all of your wifes relatives Mr Rogers up again. our crops are tolerable good especially corn but I fear it not the case in the greater portion of the district—hope you have a good crop and are all well

Truly yours
John O. Durant

Bishopville Oct 6th 1864
My own dear Sister,

Amanda received your last kind letter by Thursday's mail and as she had not time to reply before she left, I will gladly devote a short while this morning before the mail leaves in writing to you. We were glad indeed to learn that you were all well and that dear brother Ruthvin and Henry were still with you. Oh! I do trust that they may never have to leave you all, though the times do indeed seem dark now, but I trust a brighter day may soon dawn upon our beloved land. Dear Amanda left us Tuesday night for Columbia. I believe I never regretted to see her leave so much before. She is such a dear good sister—I always miss her sadly when she leaves. Matilda Durant went over with her. Ellen does not return this session. William went down to the depot with them, and saw them off. Father was afraid to go with Amanda as it generally makes him sick riding on the cars. Cousin David had to go over soon anyway, so he concluded to go this week, as the girls wished company. Does Anna H. return this year? or Anna Coskrey? I hope they will have a pleasant year at the College this year. Amanda hopes that school will not be so large, as the prices have been raised to such an extent. We are all quite well. Sister is still going about though she does not feel very well this morning. Dear little Nora is much better now, she had a severe rising on her neck, but it was lanced and is now nearly well again. If the children keep right well Sister Lizzie wants to go down to see you next week, in order to come back with you and brother Ruthvin as you come up to Synod.[148] She will go down I expect on Thursday, and you will come up Monday, will you not? I hope so at least. She wants William to go down with her and he is glad of the chance I can assure you. Sister says to tell you she is looking forward with a great of pleasure to the time when you and brother Ruthvin will be with us, so are we all. It has been such a long time since brother R- has been to see us, I suppose though it is not his fault. Brother William is still with us, though he expects to leave next week if he possibly can.

148 synod: a council or an assembly of church officials or churches, https://www.wordnik.com/words/synod

I am sorry he cannot be here when you come up. The young ladies about here have had another concert. it came off last Friday night, it was not so good as some of the others they have had. I really think it is time to give them up. I fear the girls have them more for their own amusement than any thing else. Jeana Rivers managed it for them. She has been up some (illegible), and I guess she will remain up with them until after Synod. Cousin Charles is still very feeble. He really looks badly indeed. I fear he will never be well again. I cannot imagine how the girls can be so lively as they are. I don't think they can be conscious of his situation. We spent the day with him one day last week, he suffers so much with his back, he is stooped very badly. Mother thanks you very kindly for the preserves you say you have made her. I tried my hand at making some out of figs and (illegible) since they all say they are very nice. We are glad the boys were so much pleased with their caps, were they not too large? We heard from Cousin Jim last week, he was on Morris Island under fire of the Confederate guard. But my sheet is filled, Give very much love from us all to every member of the family. You must bring the boys with you when you come. Accept much love from your affct. Sister

Maria

Bishopville Nov 10, 64
My very dear sister,

Once more I take my pen to employ a few moments in writing to an absent sister. When brother Wm wrote you a few days since, Jim and Jessie were both very sick, Jim extremely so. I am glad to tell you though, they are both able to be up now, and I hope may soon be entirely well. Our family is quite small just now, brother Wm and Maria both being away. Brother William left Tuesday evening for conference. he left several days early as he wished to spend some time in Columbia with his brother and family. Maria accompanied him as far as Columbia, where she intended staying two or three days, at which time two of her school mates, the misses Muller will meet her there and take her home with them. She will spend some-time with them, and then return to Columbia in time to return home with brother William. I do hope she may have a delightful time, as I have no doubt she will, if nothing serious happens to mar her pleasure. We attended the funeral of Hartwell Alexander yesterday at Bethlehem. Mr. Abra Alexander's son was buried. His death was a great shock to his poor family. When they last heard from him he was quite well. They were entirely ignorant of his sickness when a messinger came to them bearing the sad intelligence of his death, and telling them that his body would soon be home. It is almost more than his poor mother can bear. she fainted away when she first heard it. All the family take it very hard. May the Lord comfort their poor bereaved hearts, and give them grace to bow submissively to His divine will. You have no doubt heard ere this of Gertrude's illness. She too has had typhoid fever. I was to see her yesterday morning. she was a good deal better, is clear of fever now. Cousin Charles is no better. Continues to suffer with his back. Oh that he might be restored to health again. We had a letter from dear Amanda Monday. She was quite well. I know she will be delighted to see Maria with brother Wm. How is Mr. Plowden now? I fear from what we last heard that he has ere this breathed his last. If so, no doubt he is now in that bright world above. When the wicked cease from troubling and the weary are at rest. Has cousin Mag been to see you since she has been in Clarendon? William wrote to Henry a few days since which I suppose he has received ere this. Father will write a few lines and put in this, so I will close. All join me in <u>much</u> love to brother Ruthvin Miss Elisabeth and the children. How is brother Ruthvin now? Tell him he must write us soon. Good bye dear sister. Write soon to your loving sister

Almira

Bishopville 10 Nov 1864
Dear Ruthvin

I am very glad in commencing to write you a few lines to be able to say that all our white family are pretty well, and that Jess and Jim are steadily improving. I felt rather sad when you and dear Harriet were with us, that Jess was down with that Severe Scourge of humanity "Typhoid Fever." but when Jim got back from NC almost speechless I found that matters are never so bad but what they may be worse. Jessie having been down toward the coast I presume then took his sickness which broke out upon him while he was up the country. He suffered much. had chills and fever for six days before he got home every day or two, and finally reached home with a fever chill upon him. We got him to bed, and he never raised himself up any more without help I think for about nine days except when out of his head. He took a chill on last Sunday week which nearly finished him, but fortunately that was the last. It did not appear that he could have survived another. Both of them can now walk about a little. On night before last we were shocked to hear that Hartwell Alexander was dead—had not heard he was ill. He was sick but a short time and died with a congestive attack at or near Harleeville. They took his death very hardly. His poor old mother—it seems to me it must nearly kill her.

John H. Dixon left here yesterday for Georgetown in the hope that he may get William home. Wm. has been sick some time and has been spitting blood. If they refuse him a furlough I fear his case may indeed be a hard one.

I don't think I have any news to write to you. unless what I have already written is news. Matters and things are going on much as usual. Some boys have gone forward to the camps and others who have been deferred are now required to report. WWM & Maria have gone to Columbia but no doubt Almira mentions this to you. Your Nephew is coming on fairly well and your Sister & his mother also.[149]

---

149 Your Nephew: William Reader Mood, Rev. W. W. and Lucy Mood's fourth child and first son, was born October 7, 1864, at Lucy's childhood home in Bishopville, SC. https://www.findagrave.com/memorial/68248608/william-wynn-mood

I want to go and see you (as Aunt Peggy says) I do. and hope ere long to do so. if possible soon after they get back from conference and Columbia. In the mean time let us hear from you as often as possible. You are all very dear to us—I rejoice that is the case. Give very much love from all our family to all of yours. May God bless you and keep you as Ever—I remain most truly and affectionately yours,

William Rogers

April 12th 1865
My dear Sister,

I have time to write you only a few lines by William Holleyman who will take brother Williams horse and buggy to Sumter tomorrow and from thence to Manning. It is needless for me to attempt to tell you of our great suspense for the last few days knowing that the enemy were in your midst.[150] But we have been rejoiced to hear that you escaped them, you cannot imagine how thankful we were to hear this. We were sorry to hear that Mrs. Montgomery had been burned out, and that Mr. Haynsworth had suffered so much in having his provisions taken from him besides having his furniture Lizzie's Jim's etc. destroyed. Hattie I know not when I ever felt so sad and troubled as I did Sunday night after learning that fighting had been going on in Sumter. We knew that in all probability dear brother Ruthvin was there and we could not rest until we could learn of his safety. But thank God his precious life is still preserved, oh! may he ever be sheilded by an almighty arm. I felt so much too for you and Miss Elizabeth for I knew it would be so hard for you to part with him. We feel so anxious to hear from Manning. We have heard that the people there fared very well but know not how true it is, trust it may be so. Dear father who was quite sick when brother William left, is now able to be though he is still sick. hope he will soon be strong again. Cousin David has been with us since Monday. he left for Sumter again to day. Cousin Hugh wrote us a short note yesterday, so he is safe. I would be so glad if he could come over and give us all the news. Hope Hattie you will write us by the first chance, tell us all about brother Ruthvin, where he is etc. I suppose in all probability he is at home, if he is give him a kiss for me. Dr. Huggins was here awhile on yesterday. he told us of having been at your house, that Henry had just gotten home. I know you were all delighted to see him, much love to him from us all. Saw Willie Witherspoon a short time to day. he spoke of going on to Manning and said that

150 Gen. Edward E. Potter's raid into lowcountry and central South Carolina (including Manning, on April 8, 1865), to gain supplies and destroy railroads, was one of the last operations of the war. https://www.scencyclopedia.org/sce/entries/potter%C2%92s-raid/

he would return next week. if so we can hear from our loved ones there. So sorry that dear brother William is sick, he was feeling very badly when he left us Thursday, hope it may be nothing serious with him. Mr. Higgins who has been sick for a long time died yesterday. Mary is now living with her mother again. Has Mr. Edgar and Isaac Montgomery or Cousin Covert gotten home yet? We all feel very much for Mrs. Montgomery in her great loss. Was she at home? We have heard that she stood it until she saw the yankees approaching and left. But I can not write more now. All send much love to every one of you. Do my dear sister write when you can and tell us all the particular you can learn of the yankee raid. I forgot to thank you dear Hattie for the very nice present you sent me by mother. It was a very acceptable one I assure you and I prize it very highly indeed. May God bless you my dear sister is the prayer of your affct. sister

Maria

Bishopville April 22nd 1865
My own dear sister,

Mr. McFaddin has just called for a few minutes on his way down, and as he will take breakfast with us, I will embrace the opportunity of writing you a few lines. I know dear sister you were delighted to see dear brother Ruthvin. You were, I know, very very anxious about him. We were so surprised and delighted to see him the other morning, was very sorry he could stay no longer, but of course were reconciled to his leaving as we knew how anxious the dear ones at home felt about him. We were so sorry he was so unwell. Father heard from some one that he was compelled to stop that night. I hope he reached home safely the next morning, and that now he is himself again. I can not tell you how very glad we were that the enemy did not reach you. God grant that they may never get to your sweet home to disturb or molest. We received letters from dear sister and brother William a few days since. The dangers that they have passed through, Oh my God I thank thee that their precious lives are still spared. How awful I felt when I heard how they did our brother. To sister the moments that passed while they were in his room must have seemed like hours.[151] How anxious we are to see you all and to hear sister and brother Wm tell all about their enemy's visit to them. Please thank them for their letters, they were so interesting to us. Tell brother Mr Judge Dixon left before we received the letters was why we did not send his things, and we knew nothing of Dr Holleyman's going. We will send them as soon as we can. What awful times these are. General Lee who is not only respected but honored and loved by all has had to surrender his army to the

151 Rev. William Mood was sick in bed at the parsonage in Manning on April 22, 1865, when men from Potter's Raid came into the room, demanding gold and silver from him. They left the area the next day, after taking almost everything from the Mood's larder. Thigpen, Allan D., *Recollections of Potter's Raid*, 1997, Gamecock City Printing, Inc.

enemy, sad sad news.[152] But you have not yet given up have you? May He who is "too wise to err, too good to be unkind" still do (illegible) forever the power of our calling. Mr. McFaddin is about ready to leave so I am compelled to stop. Have you heard of Mr. Higgins' death. He died about two weeks since. Mag's mother has taken her back. poor creature, I feel truly sorry for her. Mr. Muldrow's little son Fulton is also dead. You know he was very subject to spasm it was in one of these he died. his poor mother she took his death so hard. Poor Mrs Mary Shaw has lost her little infant. She has only one child left. May God sanctify these afflictions to the eternal good of the bereaved.

All all join me in much love to the dear ones. also to sister and brother Wm when you see them. Kisses to the dear little boys. Cousin Charlotte sends love to all. Please say howdey to all. And now dear sister with much love I am

Your devoted sister
Almira

---

152 Gen. Lee surrendered on April 9, 1865, at Appomattox Court House, VA, https://www.history.com/this-day-in-history/robert-e-lee-surrenders

Bishopville 7th Oct. 1865
My dear dear Sister,

It is late at night yet I feel as if I cannot rest until I have written you at least a few lines to send by Mrs. McDowell. I did not have time to write you by Charlie. Many thanks for your kind letter. We were so glad to hear from you once more, and that all were well and dear brother Ruthvin improving. We have felt so uneasy about him. Mr. Haynsworth told Henry that both he and dear Miss Elizabeth had been sick again. I do hope they are well ere this. Tell them they had both better pay Bishopville a visit and perhaps they will get better. We are all pretty well. father has had asthma a good deal lately though. I was so much in hopes that the improvement in him would be permanent. How much I wish he could be relieved entirely.

William, Almira and I went over to Presbytery to day and Mr. and Mrs. McDowell returned with us. We have had a pleasant time. I do love them both so much—hope they will enjoy their visit. Emma and Hollie were married Thursday night. had a quiet party but very pleasant. Only their relatives in the place were there and cousin Elisha's family. Emma looked beautiful. We all like Mr. Wilson Scarborough very much. he and Gertrude spent one day with us since they were married. Emma had four waiters. Maggie James and John McDonald, Lucy and William Scarborough, Mr. Henry Scarborough and Mary Holmes, Maria and Lh DeLorme. had a very nice supper. Mr. Dennis' school closes next Friday night, with an exhibition. Do some of you come up to see how Henry requits himself, if nothing else. We will all miss him so much when he goes home. He is a sweet boy. and oh Hattie he now trusts and believes that he is a child of God. perhaps he has told you of this. I told him I knew that it would rejoice the heart of his dear Auntie, for I knew she had offered many fervent prayers in his behalf and they have not been in vain. He says his first serious impressions were caused by the sudden death of Dr. Wilson. Those such deaths have I trust not been in vain sent to the hearts of this people. Mr. Wilson began a meeting the week afterwards which continued for several days. Robert Muldrow, Willie Barrette, Bobbie Carnes, Jim Dennis and May Higgins and Bettie Bartlette all joined the church. Henry did not join, said he preferred waiting until he got home. Mr. Wilson begins another meeting next Sat. and our qtly meeting embraces the 4th Sabbath in Oct. commencing the day before. May got here just in time to see Johnnie McEnnis, he got there the same evening I think and spent two nights and a day. Soon dear bro. Wm and sister will leave Manning again. I do hope they may be returned. I know it will be hard for you to see them leave. But Hattie it is late and I must close. Good bye. We will write you by Henry when he goes home. All write with me in warmest love to you all.

Ever your affct. sister
Amanda M. Rogers

Hattie dont trouble to put much work on what I send. I had rather you would not.

Bishopville Oct. 14, 65
My dear kind Friend -

I cannot let Henry go, with out writing to tell you how well he did last night. I know you would have felt proud of him, and I wished many times you could be there. He was tremendously applauded, and you must get him to show you the pretty boquet he got. Mr. Dennis came to me after the exhibition and said, "Miss Amanda you were so anxious for Henry to do well, and he has done well" said he had considerable of the orator about him. We are sorry to part with him. he has been a good boy, and oh we rejoice with you that he returned to you with that greatest of blessings—"that peace which passeth all understanding. We are troubled that dear bro Ruthven has been worse again. Oh that he could be entirely relieved. We can only lift up our prayers to Him who "doeth all things well" feeling that what He doth is best. You may imagine with what pleasure we are looking forward, to the coming of bro Wm sister and the precious little boy. May God direct their homes for another year. You have got in the notion of paying us <u>that</u> <u>visit</u> I begged you so for, haven't you? If you have not yet you must if it is a possible thing.

Henry and Haynsworth will soon be ready so I must stop writing. Give our warmest love to br R Hattie, to Sister Bro Wm for us all and accept the same for your dear self. Kiss Lute and Wm Reader for us. Praying the kindest blessings of Heaven upon you all. I remain yours afftly—

Amanda h Rogers

Bishopville Oct 20th 1865
My precious Sister

We were so glad to hear through the boys that you were all well, and that dear brother Ruthvin seemed now to be improving. We have felt anxious about him for sometime but I trust that now the worst is over and he will soon be himself again. This leaves us all pretty well. I imagine that you are now having a very nice time with Sister brother Wm and with precious little William (torn) did not mention when they would be (torn) but we will look for them on Monday (torn) and that seems like a very <u>long</u> time to us. it has been so long since I have seen my dear Sister and the babe. We are all anticipating a great deal of pleasure in having them with us. How much I miss my precious Sister–oh–if you two were to be with us so soon, but we hope to have you up before long. I think a trip to our very healthy little town would be very beneficial to your husband's health. We have all missed dear Henry very much since he left, was glad to hear that he was pleased with his stay up here. Henry is a dear good boy and he feels very near to all of us. Tell him that he has been very much complimented since the exhibition, a great many have spoken in his praise. He was a very great favorite (torn) Mr. Dennis. Tell him his Tutor left on yesterday for the "Old Dominion" where he hopes soon to claim his Pauline for his own. He is <u>very</u> happy in the anticipation. Last night Mr Charles Barrett and Mary Stukey launched forth upon the matrimonial sea. They only had a few relatives besides the sisters. Willie Witherspoon was one of the groomsmen. The red hill is getting famous for marriages, that is the third within the last few weeks. I hope Mr. Kistler realized a good fee last night. Our <u>Qtly</u> meeting begins tomorrow. the Presiding Elder will not be here. Mr Hill and Uncle Mac I believe are to appt Mr Kistler. Hope very much we will have an interesting meeting. It is hard to realise that another conference year has closed. They will certainly return Mr Kistler here, if they should not it will be a great disappointment. He and father are such good friends I regret to see them separated. He will leave on Thursday for Conference. Hattie mother says she dont know how to thank you and dear miss Elizabeth for the nice present sent us, also Sister for the hams she sent. You are all too good to us. Wish we could in some degree repay your many kindnesses. Amanda will write you a note in this, so she will send miss Elizabeth her thanks for her nice present. We have had dear little Nora with us this week. She left us yesterday and we do miss her so much. She is such a smart child. Do give much love to all, and accept very much for your precious self.

Your affct sister
Maria

Dearest Hattie,

I first write a note to ask you please to give Miss Elizabeth a thousand thanks for the nice present she has sent me. She does so much for (torn) that I could repay her the same measure for her many kindnesses. I forgot entirely to tell you in my letter about the floss, and I regret it so much. Father bought floss, but when the goods came it was all silk floss and no linen or cotton. it was a mistake on the part of the merchants. If you have any more I will return it to you when I can get any. But if not dont trouble about it. I can make it some other way. I am so glad bro R. is better. Give our hearts best love to him dear Miss Elizabeth bro Wm sister the children and Henry and accept the same from your affectionate sister

Amanda

Bishopville 14 Nov 1865
Dear Ruthvin

I reached home from Columbia yesterday evening where I had been on acct. of Seizure of 30 bales of our cotton which we were notified would be taken of last week but which was not sent for until yesterday. I went to C. to see Gov. Perry and Col. Moses but before I reached Sumter in going, I heard that Gen. Richardson had succeeded Gen. Beale at Darlington and that he was favorably spoken of—I sent word immediately to Charles advising to send to the new Gen. He issued an order to stop forwarding of taking cotton until investigation should be made. All we want is justice. We have not a bale of Gov. cotton nor have we ever had a bale in our charge. Is it not awful!

Well I must stop. I have no time to write as James is waiting. love to all.

Yours affectionately
William Rogers

If they call upon you for cotton dont yield an inch—nor deliver a bale—If any is taken let it be done under protest and leave all the burden upon them.

Poplar Bay, SC Novem 17th 1865
My very dear friend

Your very kind & sympathizing letter deserved a more prompt notice, but I know you will pardon the delay. I have felt so little like writing lately that it has become almost like a task, rather than a pleasure. We have suffered & sorrowed much, dear Hattie, since I last saw you. but oh I humbly trust our Heavenly Father has, and will ever, sanctify all our sad afflictions to our spiritual good. He has given grace & strength to endure with much submission many hard dispensations of his just & all wise providence and I know He will sustain to the last, all who trust Him. It is hard, oh how hard! to bear this temporary separation, from those we love so tenderly, but what a priceless consolation to know, it is only for a time, and that eternity will give them all back again, perfected in all that is holy & enduring.

Dear Hattie, you have no idea how anxious I am to hear from my Clarendon friends, and particularly the children, or pupils rather, as some were rather than children. I think some of them might have written to me before this. Have they employed a teacher yet? I regret exceedingly that I was not able to complete the term for which I engaged, as I know it has been a serious disappointment. I wrote to Mrs. Haynsworth long since, but have recd no reply. Do you remember Mrs. Alan Edens? formerly Martha Purnell? she died a few days since leaving eight children—most of them quite small. I scarcely ever knew a more sad circumstance—her husband was in the army when she died—they telegraphed to him, and he reached home a few days after her death—his arrival was followed by one of the most piteous scenes imaginable—she was not buried until after he got home. How truly I compassionate her poor little children and I ca'nt conceive what will be done with them, as their Father cannot remain with them. How much sorrow & suffering there is in the world!—enough at all times, but oh how miserably aggravated by this unholy war; and no prospect of a speedy dawn of the long prayed for Peace.

I have not seen cousin Nancy's family since several weeks, but heard a few days ago—all were well. Hugh has very good health, is now in Ten. near Chatanooga. Cousins (illegible) & A.J. are getting on very nicely. There has been more fever in our section this summer & fall than I ever knew, and other diseases too, which have proven more fatal than fever generally. Has Miss Fannie Plowden gone home? I am sorry I did not see her before leaving Clarendon. Hattie give much love to all the school children from me when you see them, and give Haynsworth that kiss he refused me when he bid me good bye. Tell him he must write me a little letter and let me see how much he has improved in writing, as he was so much opposed to it in school. Are Henry and Fannie in school? I greatly fear they may yet have to fill the places of soldiers before this war is ended. My love & respects to Miss Elizabeth & Mr Ruthvin, and accept the warmest love & kindest wishes for yourself from your affectionate friend

M J Lucas

Hattie please write very soon and tell me all about the neighbors etc. Ask Henry if he cant find it in his heart to write me a good long letter. I would take great pleasure in replying to him. Give much love to Lucy when you see her. I remember her as one of the loveliest women I ever knew, and deeply sympathize in her sorrows.

THE LATER YEARS
1866–1868

Bishopville Jan. 29th 1866
My own dear Sister,

I got here just two hours ago and regretted so much when I heard you had been home and I had not seen you. I came to-day with cousin Charles who got up from Charleston last night and expect I will stay this week at our dear home. I missed seeing cousins Hen and Lizzie too, and I am so anxious to see them. I feel so sorry that Henry could not stay and I reckon Sammie will go with Henry. I know Mr Dennis regrets not having H- for he thinks so much of him. Hattie I have been wanting to write you a long long time, but did not have an opportunity suitable. I wrote to sister and wanted to write to you at the same time but could not. But I think you might have written me for you know I have nearly always written you oftener than you did to me. But I will never be ceremonious, for 'tis too great a pleasure to me to write you. I hope you found dear Miss E, brother R and Lute all well on your return. How I would like to see them all. and I hope that pleasure will be mine before very long. William was just wishing the other day he could go and said he was going to try very hard to get off next month which is almost here now. Wish I could tell you positively what time but I cannot. Tell Miss E. I am going to bring down my handsome grey headed old gentleman to show her. But I ought not to talk about him that way, for he is a right clever fellow any way.[153] Tell Almira I miss her but I know she will have a nice time. She will have to take my place in giving you visitations, though I feel loth to give it up and do not know that I can. We are going to house-keeping next week sometime, and I assure you I dread it! Twill not be like having mother to go to about everything. We will have house room enough if we do not have much to put in it. When we get fixed you must all pay me a long visit, for I expect I will get very lonely sometimes not being accustomed to stay by myself. Tell Almira I saw Jesse Layton the other day and she asked many questions about her, and is so anxious to see her. says I must make her stay a great deal with me. I am sorry you took her for I

153 Amanda married William J. McLeod https://www.geni.com/people/Amanda-McLeod/6000000019856492787

was going to try and get her to go with me next week. I promised Jesse to bring her up to see Almira sometime. She is going to begin teaching next Thursday for Mr. William Smith. I guess some body will be disappointed when they come and find their bright particular star gone.

I was glad to hear that Serenia had not left Miss Elizabeth. I did not much think she would. Cousin Charles says the negroes are doing nothing in the Low Country. Cousin C. has improved very much indeed. Give my best love to my dear precious brother, Miss Elizabeth, Almira, Henry Haynsworth and Lute. and give much much love to dear bro Wm and sister for me when you see them, and kiss the dear little boy for me. If I have an opportunity I will send you word what time we can come down or Maria will. All send much love to you all. God bless and keep you all my precious sister. Write to me when ever you can. With much love -

Your affcts sister
Amanda

Lynchburg Feb. 14th 1866
My dear Sisters Lucy & Hattie,

Not having time to write you separately to day I will write both at once, as William is going over to Sumter to night and may be able to get a letter to you. I presume you rec-d- Maria's letter telling you we expected last week to be able to visit you, but we were again disappointed. a day or two before we expected to start, William's horse was taken sick, has been very bad, and is just now beginning to get some better. I told Maria and Henry they had better not wait for us but I do hope we may be able to go soon. Perhaps we may be able to go next week. if we are we will go next Wednesday, if we do not you may know the cause but I hope the horse will be well by that time. We heard from home yesterday, all were well.

We are at last domesticated in our new home, came last Friday. You do not know how much I dreaded coming, dreaded housekeeping especially as Jimmie D. was here, but he soon made me feel at home, took me about the yard, went with me when I went to give out dinner, and helped me about the house, so we became friends right away. He had brought me before I came a nice lot of sausages and had been out to try and kill some birds. last night he gave me a beautiful pair of salt cellars.

My dear parents were so kind and sent me so many nice things, more than they ought to have done, I am afraid. I can never repay them for all their kindness. they have the warmest gratitude of a loving heart. I hope it will not be long before you can all come to see us now. I do wish so often for you. I get very lonely here sometimes, all day alone. tell Almira I have wished for her dear little self a hundred times. Miss Lizzie and Eliza G. were here the other afternoon and asked after you both. They are very much put out with Mr. Walker and his lovely wife. They, that is, Dr. Green, had hired Clarissa their servant, who lived last year with Mr. C. Durant when Mr W and his wife came. Before going up to Bishopville, they sent and tried to get Clarissa to go back with them, but she concluded not to do so. When they came here again, just before leaving they paid Miss Lizzie a visit, were very pleasant and said nothing about Clarissa at all. but when they went back to Mr.

Wrightman Durant's they saw her again and laid out every inducement for her to go with them, and to meet them at Sumter. She concluded then to go but again gave it out. Miss Lizzie says she was sick in bed at the time and has no other servant but a nurse. Dr. G. was outraged about their underhandedness in the affair. Mrs. W. and her bosom friend Mrs Barrette had a falling out the last time she was there so I hope their visits there will cease though the Stuckeys are still fine I guess.

Mrs. Patrick, a schoolmate of Almira's was to see me yesterday. She told me they expected Louis McCants up this week. He is a relative of Mrs. McCants.

I was grieved yesterday to hear of the death of Miss Ollie Coachman. I suppose she has never been well since her illness last fall. Mr. McIntosh oldest son (William) died last night of Typhoid fever. they have two other children with it now. Poor fellow. I fear he was unprepared too, he was rather wild and I have never heard that he spoke of dying during his illness. I heard Mr. Parker preach Sunday for the first time. he took up a collection to defray the expenses of the delegate to Conference. he seems very zealous on behalf of the "Weekly Record." Spoke of Mr Mood in the highest terms. he and William together have been right successful in getting subscribers. How does Henry like his new teacher Hattie? I hope he may make a good teacher.

Have cousins Hu and Lizzie been down since you saw them in B? Mrs. Esther has another little daughter so Maria wrote me. I hope Maggie Belle will not be spoilt quite so much now.

Tell Almira I expect she is getting right anxious to see some of the M. D.'s above Bishopville. I was at home when he came there last. he told Maria he had the blues, not seeing her. that she must be sure and go after her last week. I spent a night, Lizzie and I, with Mrs Carnes while I was at home. had a very pleasant visit. she seems as much at home as ever Mrs Carnes did. he says the boys love her dearly and that she has done them good already.

But it is time for William to start nearly and I must close. Give much, very much love to my dear brother Ruthvin and bro William, kiss dear little William for me, Haynsworth and Lute. my best love to dear Almira and Miss Elizabeth and Henry.

William sends much love to all. Hoping soon to see you. I bid you good bye.

Ever your loving sister
Amanda

William says now he is pretty sure he can go next week so we will leave here either Wednesday or Thursday, cannot positively say which.

Lynchburg SC Feb 15th 1866
Rev W W Mood
Dear Brother

As I expect to go to Sumter tomorrow I write you a few lines hoping I may have an opportunity to forward it from there. We are quite well & getting on pretty well considering the hard times. we moved home last week. I assure you I felt pretty awkward at first, but begin to feel like I was at home and my little wife[154] moved around like it was no new business for her to keep house, but as we hope soon to visit you she can tell you all about housekeeping. We made arrangements to visit you last week but my horse was taken sick which broke up the arrangements. he has farcy[155] and though I have it somewhat arrested I fear he will never entirely recover. I have secured another horse for the trip & if not disappointed again, will get down next week (Wednesday or Thursday. Business has been very good but rather dull now & I fear will be worse. not much news of interest to write—hope you will not think by my not writing you sooner that your kind favor of Jany,, was not appreciated; rest assurred that it was & ever will be. I was very busy at that time & have been since then. Amanda wrote you sometime since which I hope reached you; we very seldom have an opportunity of sending a letter. Mr. Parker & myself have succeeded in raising a club for the weekly Record. We have some sickness in the neighborhood, some cases of typhoid fever in Mr. McIntosh's family. he lost his oldest Son William last night. he was about 19 years old. he will be buried this evening at the Presbyterian Church. I am fearful it will go through the neighborhood—I heard from Bishopville a few days since, they were all well. Hope you, Sister Lucy & William jr. are enjoying good health & all other blessings of life. We are quite well. Amanda joins me in much love to you all. If nothing happens will be down next week.

Affectionately
W. J. McLeod

---

154 *Amanda*
155 a bacterial infection

Bishopville—April 1866
Dear Ruthvin
Dear Harriet

Once more at home and all pretty well. I have the pleasure of addressing you but first must apologise in that I did not write to you while in New York. This I fully intended to do and to send my letter to Manning to be forwarded.

At the end of one week after I reached New York I was taken sick, and was quite sick. I had Doctors for six days. After I got about again, I had to use all the time and strength I had to go forward with my business, and at night would be very tired, and so very often days passed away and you were not written to. and so I put it off until I could reach home, and then waited for the present opportunity to send the letter by Bro. Kistler. and now beg you to forgive me for seeming remiss and I know you will do it for you know I do love you both—oh, how much! Yes dear Ruthvin, no one connected with my family by marriage can ever have a warmer place in my poor heart than you, and my own dear Harriet—what a blessed child has she ever been to her parents. Yes I do love you both, and rejoice that I have a dear Daughter who is the wife of Ruthvin Plowden, and then I never forget that dear good Miss Elizabeth. God bless her—and I know she too has kind regard for me, and the dear children they too I believe love me and so I say <u>God</u> <u>bless</u> <u>you</u> <u>all</u>—How I do want to see you, and when Charles comes up I must, I <u>must</u> see you. I was a long time in N. York 22 days and I wanted to see home badly enough but could not neglect my business, and I had a great deal to do for all old business in both Phil—Boston and New York was to be settled and stock of goods to buy. You must help me to be thankful to the Good Lord for his great mercy in sparing me and permitting me to return home in comparatively good health, and I know you will in your thanksgiving to Him. Many New York friends called, and called to see me while I was sick, and to Mr. Harral of the firm of Harral Risby & Tompkins I can never be sufficiently thankful for assistance in helping me in settling off old business and for his visits to me while sick—but I am filling up my sheet, and still have not written any thing hardly, but then what I write is with a warm heart and all else you can pardon if there is no want of that.

We are now getting up a nice stock of goods, and who knows but what we can be of mutual service to each other—and if you want goods will make it a point to sell them very low, and they can be settled for at such time as will probably sell very well.

Bro. Kistler expects to leave here tomorrow morning, and I hope this will soon reach you. I wonder if I dare to inquire if you can come up soon to see us? I believe I will. Will you?

Well now I will close—all send love of course—a good deal of love. Hugh and his Lizzie staid with us Sunday night to Tuesday morning last. both well. And now good bye good bye—and I remain your affectionate father

William Rogers

Bishopville 27 July 1866
My dear Ruthvin

We had the very great pleasure on yesterday evening to once more welcome our dear Harriet to the old home and withal find her looking very well. Our pleasure would have been still further enhanced if her "worser half" could have come up with her. However we are thankful for any favor. Glad to say that we are all pretty well, and any news Harriet will convey to you. Glad to see Henry up again. We will do as well for him as we are able. Muldrow too is glad to see Henry back again. Harriet says that Mrs. Montgomery wishes to know whether or not we can board Samuel in case she should conclude to send him up here. in reply I will say that notwithstanding we had no idea of taking any on except from your family. We will try and take care of Samuel if desired. In regard to price of boarding Fifteen dollars—is what is usualy charged for board and washing, but should Sammy come we will make it $13.50 per month. As usual we are found with but little money. I send you sixty dollars and it leaves us still in debt to you about forty.

I think I have gotten a clever man on my place this year and hope to pay expenses at least. Chas. J has been in Charleston ever since before Christmas but is expected up to night. If he stays long enough to allow my doing so, I will try to see you all. Much love to my good friend Miss E. and all the rest. I remain most affectionately yours,

William Rogers

Bishopville 1st Augt 1866
My dear Ruthvin

I want to see you. I recd your letter—it dont answer the purpose of a visit, but I thank you for the letter, and I thank my beloved Harriet for hers a few days before. John O. says, he does want you at "that hunt" the 13th of this inst. I dont see how I can wait longer than that time, unless you send up that dear good sister of yours, in which case I will allow you a short further credit.

Look here! if you dont come oftener I feel like making a fuss! But stop old fellow! Ruthin in that case might get mulish, and not come at all. Thats a fact. Well then, I'll hush up. I've hushed.

Sorry to hear that your crop is poor. Better luck next time. The drought has cut short my corn, but late soaking rains still help. I want to see my darling Harriet.

Who says he has beat me at raising good girls? Who speaks? Nobody? Well there is sense there is some good sense in the world yet. You say I am disposed to brag? Cant help it—on that subject and will at this time—I,d just as soon do it as not—I,ll only promise mot to make a practice of it. So now if you are satisfied with that promise I,ll drop the case—(till I begin again)

You say I,m determined to have the last word do you? Well, come up and let,s try it.

Have you had plenty of rain? Last Saturday we had a pouring rain, another last Monday. I am sorry of the delay about your carriage. Cant you borrow?

I enclose a few lines for Edgar. they will speak for themselves. It would be pretty if Harriet should bring you both up here—and she so small.

All pretty well—all send love to all. I must close. Dear Ruthvin Dear Harriet I want to see you. God bless and keep you.

Your affectionate father
William Rogers

Home Sept 9th 1866
My beloved Brother[156]

Your highly appreciated letter received some two weeks since has never yet been answered though it certainly merited a more speedy response. But I know my dear brother will excuse what might seem negligence in me, when I tell him that I can not write without pain. Yes! that pain in my side still continues to give me much trouble, and I am scarcely free from it many moments at a time. I hope ere this you have recovered from those dreadful risings on your leg, and that you may have no return of them. I have felt so much for you, for I know your sufferings have indeed been severe. Glad you could enjoy the apple preserve (not quince) mother sent you. She did include (illegible) in making them, for like you we thought them very nice. I wish you had some of the water melon rhine preserves I made for her a while back, but by the by if you dont love the melon, I doubt if you do the preserve either. But they are certainly very nice, if I did make them, you will say Maria has to be her own trumpeter, but others have pronounced them good too. I suppose you heard through Hattie that father would soon leave for New York. He and Mr. Carnes went on together last Friday week. It was very hard for us to part with him, but I think he takes great delight in going. Oh! that he may have his health while away and be returned to us in safety is my prayer day by day. Tis sweet thought to commit him into the hands of a merciful God, who is able to preserve him though far away from home and those he loves. We had a letter from him last Thursday, written while in Baltimore. He was quite well then and said he would promise to be very prudent with himself while away. He mentioned that there was no cholera of any consequence in the city though there had been a good deal of Cholera morbus. He intended buying a part of their goods in Baltimore. Mr Frank Kennedy, his oldest daughter, Mr. David Finn and his wife were also in Balt. We heard a day or two since Mrs. Kennedy was very ill. This is bad and her husband so far from her. Father expected to be gone about four weeks when he left, he will write to you though no doubt—and give you all particulars.

---

156 Rev. W. W. Mood

mother went down to see Amanda last Friday. got back last night. all were well down there. She went down in the carriage and expected Amanda to come home with her, but she has put off her visit for a week or two longer, as some of Brother Williams relations from Cheraw are visiting him now. The Craigs I believe; there are five of them along. Mother says she has a great deal of company. Mother has been a good deal better lately. The mint Miss Elizabeth sent her by Hattie she thinks did her good. she felt much better while taking it. since that gave out she has had another one of those attacks, but

(next page is torn; partially legible)

...could get more. ...she had a supply of...is certainly good where...are affected. ...I hope dear...right strong again, she too was not very well when you wrote. We hope to hear from you by the mail tomorrow as we have not heard in two weeks now. I know you and sister were shocked to hear of Mr. Gibson's death. Almira though has written you since then and given you the particulars 'Tis sad sad indeed. His family though seem to bear it with a great deal of fortitude. ...know they feel it keenly in...It is so hard to realize...He has not been...the last time he preached...about three weeks before his...made me feel sad to...his voice was so very...he looked badly too. ...his last message to his...here, but oh! little did they dream it. Lina Dennis has been right sick for a week or two past, her heart seems to be very much affected. She is some better I believe but she has to be kept very quiet. I know her mother feels anxious...it is soon just one year since Mr. (illegible) died. I hope the trimming sent by Hattie suited Sister. it...the very best that could be...here. Henry is over home...he says he wants to write by next mail, that is he ...so yesterday. I miss him so much...he leaves home. How is dear...as happy and lively as ever I hope. Tell...you a cork shoe in New York, so I ...to ask the next time he sees him. You...of this that I have written on the Sabbath—...like very much to do, but no one else had written...you would be anxious to hear. Love to Sister—and...to Willie for all of us and last but not... your good self. Always remember in your p...devoted Sister

Maria

Palm Mass. 17 Sept 1866
Dear Ruthvin
Dear Harriet

I will just write you a few lines this morning to let you know of my whereabouts etc. As you are aware we left Lynchburg on the last day of Aug. went right on to Baltimore—staid thru Sunday, bought goods there on Monday—went to New York Monday night. bought goods for ourselves and W H Smith Co. until last Friday Evening, then went to Boston, bought shares thru Saturday last, left for Conn at half past 3 p.m. Came here and have to wait for cars for Wilsons (illegible) until this morning. I soon start for that place. Must go to N.Y. on Tuesday night—to Phil- Wednesday night, when I am to meet George M. Rogers and he will go home with me and visit. The Lord of all the Earth has been very kind to me since I left home and has blessed me with health, blessed me in my business, and now I hope soon to be at home—Say on next Sunday morning I hope to be at Lynchburg. One great object with me in coming North this time was to open the way, so that we might carry on business thru former channels. I have met with no disappointment in business most times since I left home.

I find that a credit is now established for us from Baltimore to Boston, and hope it may avail us something. We are (illegible) to try and make a living—I am satisfied that so far, since the war, I have managed our wealth with but few mistakes.

But I must close and in haste. The cars soon leave. I have been greatly disappointed that I was compelled to stay <u>here</u> two nights. But in the mean time I have procured some medicine from an Indian Doctor for headache—your mother and my self. He is 1/4 Indian and strange to say his name is Manning—2nd cousin to your ex Gov. Manning. I hope soon to see you. Heaven bless you all. Much love to Miss E. and the children.

Most affectionately your father & friend -
William Rogers

(addressed to: E. R. Plowden Esq, Care of Rev W W Mood Manning South Carolina)

(printed return address in upper left corner: Antique House, Palmer, Mass., By E. B. Shaw, A good livery stable attached to the House)

(written in pencil on reverse of envelope: Dear Ruthvin I have taken the liberty of reading this- W W M)

Home July 11th 1867
My dear, dear sister

Home again, home again. and this great pleasure being mine and owing you, my dear sister a letter, I will on this account, because it is a pleasant task, and also at the request of dear mother write you. I got home on last friday week, so have now been here almost two weeks. Had quite a pleasant, and unpleasant journey: pleasant, in having traveling companions most of the way; unpleasant, in having to lay over at many places; though did not miss connection. I took a different route to Petersburg, from the one I did last January when going out, coming by way of Lynchburg Va., instead of Richmond. The places I had to lay over at were these one night at Lynchburg; leaving there the next morning arrived at Petersburg on the evening of the same day; where I again spent the night; had the pleasure of seeing here Mrs. J. N. Dennis's brother; next morning, just before leaving this burg, I had the pleasure of meeting Isek Inglis, a fellow student from Cheraw, who had left Lexington the day after I did, but coming via Richmond, overtook me and I, having seen no one, with whom I was personally acquainted, since I left Lynchburg Va., was indeed glad to see him. Leaving here after, or about 7 o clock we entered the notorious town of Weldon before 12 o clock (about 10) and it being Sunday, the trains were not running as usual. Leaving there after midnight, we, going very slowly, (for the rains had been great) did not get to Wilmington untill about 11 o clock next day! and now came the "most unkindest cut of all", for we had to lay over from that morning (Monday) untill Thursday morning: on the night of which day, at between one and two, I found myself safely housed at Capt. Mc's. The next day I arrived at my dear home, finding all well, or as well as usual. Cousin David came up from Sumter on same day, intending to go back last Thursday, but on the Tuesday night preceding, was violently attacked with pain in his side, which, I think they say was colic. for several days he was very ill. on last Thursday, I went down, intending to bring Cousin Mary J. and Aunt Mabry, but met the former, already on the way but went on and the next morning took Aunt M. up. He is now doing tollerably well, out of danger. I have the sad intelligence of the death Mrs. Bartlett to communicate. she was buried yesterday morning. Mrs. Hammett is now very sick and some others in the neighbourhood. Mannie gives vacation this or next week, and is coming up to spend some time, and I think they are expecting you too, at any rate be sure and come, and bring as many of your dear family as you can. It is about time for the mail to be made up, and I must go down to the store. I have written this very hurridly. Thankful to Almighty God that I am again at home and hoping soon to see you. I am

Your Affct bro,
Wm.

Love to all

"Cabin Home" July 12th 67
My Beloved Sister,

Your long looked-for letters have reached us at last—came both together by our last mail, more than one month after the first one was written. That was slow business certainly. I had become really anxious about you all, thought some of you must be sick. We were truly glad that such was not the case but that yours left you all in usual health. I am thankful to say this leaves us likewise. We are just from dinner, and all were able to eat heartily of the nice mutton roast a kind friend sent in to us. You inquire after the health of my two Wms—The elder one has'nt had any return of the feebleness which troubled him when you saw him, but is quite well & able to meet his appts punctually, besides lending a helping hand toward the garden now & then. Master Willie just now has some cold, tho' he is playing about lively as usual. Before he took this he had been very hearty ever since the little sick turn he had soon after his return home. He often talks about his visit to you, of how much he loves you & "Uncle Ruthvine" & "Aunt Lizabeth." Says he loves "Aunt Hattie" the best of all his aunties. When asked who he loves will say "Ma first, then pa, then Aunt Hattie." He wants you to know that he has a pair of pants & jacket. I wish you could see him with them on. I made them of the white Marseilles Amanda gave him, & trimmed them with green lawn & white buttons. He looks mighty sweet in them, but reminds me much of Tom Thumb. We heard of poor Bro. Hemmingway's death thro' Mr. Barron who came down with Alice Witherspoon, the week before I got your letter. He must have passed off suddenly at last. I do sympathize deeply with his poor wife & fatherless children. His younger brother went up to see her last Saturday, but I have'nt heard from him since his return so I cannot tell what she intends doing. I expect tho' will go to the city with her parents. We had a wedding in our neighborhood here the same day he died. Miss May Wilson & Capt. Anderson. Wm married them & I also attended the wedding. had a pleasant time notwithstanding the bad weather. I find you have all shared with us in the floods of rain we've had, but I sincerely hope the crops are not as much injured as they are down here. We scarcely know of any one who have not had to throw away part of their crops, & some have replanted. The prospect is fully as bad, if not worse than last year, the farmers say. This is truly discouraging. Let us pray a merciful Providence, yet to grant us an abundant harvest, that none may lack for bread the coming year. Our garden I believe has stood rain better than any I've seen & it still furnishes us with plenty of vegetables, tho' our tomatoes are almost a failure which I regret very much. I have just got thro' making a lot of pickles, which are pronounced to be good. Had I the jars I'd make more, but have filled all I've got. Wm has a two days meeting beginning at our church here tomorrow. Hope we'll have a good time. You have doubtless heard before this of our dear brothers safe arrival home. I was so rejoiced to hear of it. Hope his company may so cheer dear Mother & Maria, that we may hear much better news of them soon. When Maria wrote me last she said she began to feel like herself once more, & that the <u>nervousness</u> had left her entirely. What has taken Hugh to Fla—recently I heard he had gone there. Glad to hear Wm H's examination passed off well. Ask Haynsworth if he won't write his aunt Lucy one letter in the course of the next session Tell him I'd prize it very highly. Wm joins me in a heart full of love to you my dear Sister, also to dear bro. Ruthvine & Miss Elizabeth. Do come & see us if possible & let us know before hand so we can tell you when we have preaching here, you know Wm is away every other Sunday. Love to each of the dear boys for us. Do write again very soon to your devoted sister

L J Mood

Give our love to all your Sister M's family, your Sister Ann's & Bro. Edgar's also to Mr. & Mrs. McDowell & Miss. Tell Mrs. McDo to write to me, I want to write to her very soon. I forgot to allude before to the things I forgot. Do don't feel at all concerned about them. It don't make the least difference. The Doyly was nearly worn out and one handkerchief won't break us up entirely. So again I say don't mind it at all.

Your Sister L.

Home July 24th 1867
My own beloved Sister,

Your L—me received sometime since has not yet been replied to, but you have heard from us through William and Almira both of whom have written you which letters I hope you received. I am glad to tell you that we are all well, with the exception of father who has been suffering from asthma, but is now better, having been at the store all the forenoon. I suppose you heard of cousin David's extreme illness while visiting us. He was very ill and suffered most awfully but God in mercy has raised him up again. He left us last Tuesday with his mother and sister for Sumter. William took them down and said he stood the trip pretty well. We heard from him a few days since and he was still improving. William saw Cousin Hu while in Sumter and he told him of brother Ruthvin's great misfortune with his horses. I was so sorry to hear that he had lost Rena. We so much hoped to have had you with us during the Qtly- meeting, which came off last week. Mr Pritchard our P. E. preached some excellent sermons. There was a good deal of feeling manifested. Many were at the altar for prayer. There have been only two accessions to the church. Mrs Dr Green and David Dixon. The meeting is still going on though we only have service at night as Mr Kistler has no assistance since Mr. Pritchard left. oh! I trust that much good may be done in the name of our Heavenly Father. Amanda and dear little Melvine are with us this week which makes it very pleasant for us. Melvine is a large boy I tell you. Little Annie is very affectionate and fond of kissing all babies. When Melvine came she seemed delighted and threw her little arms around and tried to kiss him, but he treated her—as father says "with utter disgust pushing her away from him intently. Annie is growing very fast now. I suppose it is because my health is so much better, and my milk is more nourishing to her. She is a good little eater, loves to eat almost anything we will give her. Sister Lizzie and the children are with us too this week. Nora and Elwyn grow very fast, and it is surprizing to see how fast he can get about, and he never seems to get tired either. There are two new babies in our little town now. Mrs Dr Dennis, and Paulie both have little girls. They were born the same morning, there being only one hour between them, and they both weighed exactly the same 7 1/2 pounds. Paulie has named hers Virginia Carolina after Jennie. They are both pretty. Paulie thinks hers looks like Annie some. Gertrude Brown came over last Friday with her cousin Mr Flowers who by the way is the gentleman to whom Matilda Durant is engaged. She stayed until Monday morning. Gertrude is now engaged to Mr Moultrie Wilson, and she talks about him so much, that it almost tiresome to listen to her though perhaps I might not to say this. I do hope Hattie it will not be long before you and dear brother Ruthvin can come to see us. Mother says that she feels about as well now as she ever did. Hope dear Miss Elizabeth is well with all the children. excuse this very poor letter for I can scarcely write having written two more letters this evening. With much love to all I am your affct sister

Maria

Bishopville 24 July 1867
Dear Ruthvin,

We are pretty well–except myself–I have had a hard time with asthma. I would be glad to write a long letter but am not able, but must write and trust will get all right.

Well I had the four bales cotton sent down to Charleston and soon after their arrival two bales were sold at 23c but one of them was afterwards rejected and thrown back and had to be sold at 20c The other two bales are still unsold. They say they have not had as much as 20c offered for them. Shall I direct them sold at the best price they will bring, or have them held? I expect to do anyway with you in regard to the cotton that you may ask–but still I know that you will have regard to the quality of the cotton and know at which it sells to some extent. I am so sorry both on your and my acc that there is any trouble with it. I would be glad to hear from you soon as to what you think best for the unsold bales.

I feel very sorry dear Ruthven to hear of your great misfortunes with your horses. it does appear that many troubles are ours. I paid $165- cash for a good mule last winter–but it died a month ago. We had a prospect of a heavy crop of corn–but the rains cut us short probably one half.

But we must not murmur–for we profess to believe that everything is ordered for the best.

Accept a great deal of love for yourself and also all the dear blessed family. How glad we would be to see you all–I hoped to have done so by this time. But I am poorly. Yesterday weighed 108 lbs. in health about 125. but I hope soon to improve fast

Most affectionately your Father & friend
William Rogers

Bishopville 27 July 1867
My dear Ruthven

A few days since I wrote you rather a forlorn letter for I have long been in a suffering condition, but since then I have rapidly improved and I am now feeling very well and the rest are all tolerably well also and so with the people of the neighborhood. Since I last wrote we have had two light rains and they will prove of great service and who knows but what they may improve my poor corn.

Early in the season I thought I might have a crop of corn this season that I shall be glad to show to Ruthven, but am disappointed, but I tell you I do want to see Ruthven. Have I ever confessed it , & if not I will now, You are indeed <u>very</u> <u>dear</u> to <u>me</u>. Your high toned principles, truthfulness and liberal mindedness, long since made deep impression upon my heart, and I thank God that <u>our</u> dear Harriet is <u>yours</u>—and though troubles many and sore are have been apportioned to us all, yet I hope if our lives are spared, we may yet see many pleasant days. I do hope this may find you all well and that our dear beloved Miss Elizabeth may not suffer more with her head.

Well dear Ruthven that hour is near, and Mr. Durant is very anxious, for you and your family to be and appear at the time appointed which is to meet at Bishopville on <u>Monday</u> <u>the 6th</u> <u>of</u> <u>August</u> to go to the scene of action on the following day. I do hope you will come—and if so may not H. come with you? Before I got sick Mr. D. asked me to write you, and when I got better the other day I forgot it—Tell my dear H. I will write to her <u>next</u>—Love to <u>all</u>

Your most affectionate
William Rogers

Bishopville Sept. 13th 1867
My own beloved Ruthvin,

In haste I write these few lines, as it will not be long before William will have to go. I am sorry to tell you dear Ruthvin that our precious mother has been very sick indeed, has been a great deal worse since you were here. had a very bad night of it last night. She has suffered terribly from sick stomach. The Dr has been attending her. I hope the medicine she has taken may have the desired effect, and join your prayers all of you with ours dear husband, that she may be speedily restored to health if consistent with the will of our kind heavenly Father. I expect you will be disappointed at my not going home, but if I were to go now I expect I would be very anxious about mother, and on acc't of mothers sickness I expect I ought to stay longer; so I hope you will not think hard of me, oh! how rejoiced would I be to see our darling mother enjoying the blessing of health, and I pray God that this blessing may ere'long be hers if His will. If you can't come up beforehand I would be glad if you would send to meet me at the same place next Thursday, and father can send me part of the way if you can't come up. I truly hope dear Ruthvin this may find you dear sister Elizabeth and the children all well, if you are not well tho' or if you get sick please send for me right away. If you have an opportunity to write to me too how all are, and ask sister Elizabeth what she does for sick stomach that is to be so bad off with it as mother has been. She has also had high fever, but at times it would seem to cool off. Remember us all at a throne of Grace. With my best love to dear Ruthvin, and also with love from all (torn) all the loved ones of home, and praying if God's will that He may permit us all to meet in health. I remain your devoted wife

Hattie C. Plowden

Written on the death of my beloved sister Hattie, who left this world for realms of heavenly bliss, on the 19th of Sept 1867 and presented to Bro. Ruthvin, who tho' now, if possible, e'en more afflicted than I, yet has this great consolation, that tho' we cannot call our loved ones back; yet, we can go to them.

One by one we're gathered home
Gathered to the Saviour, God:
And with loved ones gone before
Shout salvation, thro' his blood.
For another, still another
Has preceded us to God.

Sudden was the blow that took
From our view my sister dear;
Yet, tho' sudden, she was ready;
She had nought, from death, to fear.
And another, still another,
Went prepared for judgement there.

Happy christian she was called.
Oh! How well she served her God!
Morning, noon and nights Yes midnight

She has asked his promised word.
Thus another, still another
To her Saviour's bosom soared.

Round her dying bedside stood
Husband, parent, loved ones dear:
And, tho' we no aid could give
Precious truth! her God was near.
And another, still another
Angels bore beyond despair.

Just before her spirit fled,
Brightly glanced those dying eyes;
And methinks she saw the Lord

And the loved ones of the skies.
As they took, yet, still another,
To her home in Paradise.

Now she sings in glory there,
Jesus' dying love, the theme.
At his feet they cast their crowns
Giving glory to his name.

That another, still another,
Has been ransomed thro' the Lamb.

Could we but behold her now
In that O'er enraptured band
Would we not then wish to flee
This poor world for that fair land?
That we all might join together
In God's praise? before him stand?

Here we leave thee, Hattie dear:
Sweetly sister, sweetly rest,
Till the last, long trump shall sound
Mid the glories of the blest.
Where we'll meet, no more to sever,
At the lamb's eternal feast.

Saviour send thy spirit down
To sustain the husband dear.
Oh! how saddened is his heart!
Often drops the briny tear.
As he thinks their lives all over,
Now in pleasure, now at prayer.
To the parents, loved ones all
Thy soul-strengthening grace impart
On that sister, (more to her;)
On the children of her heart.
How they miss that absent mother!
To her memory revert!

Let thy favour and thy smile
Ever Savior with us be.
May we shun destruction's path,
Keep us in thy care we pray
That of thee, we may together
Sing, to all eternity.
Affectly
Wm A. R.[157]

157 William Anson Rogers

Home Sept 27th 1867
My own beloved brother.

The astounding intelligence has reached me! and the terrible blow has fallen upon me, well-nigh crushing me to the earth!! Many sorrows have beset my pathway thro' life, but there have been none like this. I cheerfully resigned my first-born darling child into the hands of Him who gave her, but oh! this seems too much to endure. Were it not that I still know, & feel, that God's word is true, and His promises sure, I feel that it would crush me entirely. But tho' my heart seems almost breaking, I remember my dear brother, that the awful blow falls with more than double force upon you, and if possible I grieve more for you, than for myself. I feel scarcely able to write, and yet I feel that it will be a sort of comfort to pour out (in a measure) my full heart to you, who now seem doubly dear to me, as being all that we have left, of our precious loved one "gone before." Oh! how gladly would I comfort your bereaved heart were it in my power! but this I know I cannot do. no other Hand, save the Almighty one that has dealt the blow can do this; and my dear brother He can, not only comfort your heart but make this affliction, severe as it is, a blessing to you, and to us all. It is a blessed thought that God did it. God, your father & hers, whom together you tried faithfully to serve thro' so many years. Him whose love you have together felt shed abroad in your hearts, and who gave you His blessed Spirit to witness that you were His own dear children. His providences are dark, and mysterious, but we must not on this account doubt His goodness or His mercy, or least of all, His love to us. He promises, "What I do, thou knowest not now but thou shalt know hereafter." And oh! brother Ruthvin I feel, I know that when the veil of eternity is drawn aside, and we view all things by its enduring light, we shall exclaim with joyful surprise "He hath done all things well." "Praises be to His Holy name, that He heeded not our cries, but did His own Almighty, gracious will." I need not speak of what our Angel Hattie was to you, for you knew her better than I did. You knew the purity and sincerity of her Christian character, and how insignificant to her were all things of a worldly nature, compared with the importance of having her soul pure & spotless thro the atoning blood of Jesus.

But I would bring to your mind (and it ought to be a comfort to you) the thought of how happy you made her, by your devoted love, and attentions, by your guidance, and support, during the years of her married life. Yes dear brother, there was nothing withheld by you, that could add to her happiness, and she knew and appreciated it. You know how freely she would open her heart to me, I have so often heard her express so much thankfulness, that God had blessed her with such a devoted, affectionate Christian husband. She often told me too, of what a help, and support you were to her spiritually, and how grateful she felt in hearing you say that you felt that she had been the same to you. Nor would I omit to notice here the affection and obedience shown her by your dear children and how much they conduced to her earthly happiness; and least of all would I omit the love, the tenderness, the watchful, motherly care ever extended over her by your dear dear sister. Yes! so faithful, so devoted; so entirely like our own mother has she ever been to our precious Hattie, that she seems to us almost superhuman. Again, I say may God richly bless and reward her, as we never can, tho' our hearts will ever burn with love and gratitude to her. Yes! I rejoice that she had so large a share of earthly happiness granted to her during her short life, that her peculiarly sensitive, dependent & affectionate disposition was never crushed, seldom wounded, and ever found objects worthy upon which to lavish its wealth of affection. She was a precious, precious Sister to me, so thoughtful, so careful for my happiness & well-being. She was, I might almost say, my best Christian friend. I cannot, or at least never have, even with either of my other dear Sisters opened my heart so entirely, or have them do the same, as was the case with my precious Hattie & I. Then how much have my dear husband, and my precious child lost, in her!! Oh! she was but too dear to us all. But my dear brother, our separation will not be long, at most. Let us then, by God's help, endeavor to bear it cheerfully; to go forward in the discharge of our duties to our God, and to all around us, never murmuring, or repining, and in due season we shall reap, if we faint not. I do not forget dear brother Ruthvine that this is the second dear one, you have had so suddenly snatched away from you, & this causes my heart the more to bleed for you. I can only cry to God, to comfort you by the power of His grace, and give you strength according to your need.

We will always love you dear brother Ruthvin as an own dear brother, and dear Miss Elizabeth and your precious children like-wise, as we have ever done while dear Hattie was with you.

I am glad dear Wm will be able to get to see you. Wish he could stay longer with you. He will tell you that Willie and I are doing well as could be expected. Much much love to each of the dear boys, tell them we will always love and pray for them for their dear mother's sake, as well as their own. To dear miss Elizabeth give our warmest love, yes my heart overflows with love and sympathy for her. I know how keenly she will miss, and feel the loss of our now sainted Hattie. And now my own dear brother, with the warmest love a sister's heart can send, and praying earnestly, God's richest blessings, and the comfort of His grace upon you all, I remain as ever

Your devoted Sister L. J. Mood

Excuse my many errors, I fear you may not be able to make out what I've tried to write. Tell each of the dear boys for me that tho' they may fail in all things else, not to fail in meeting our loved ones "gone before us, in that bright world of bliss, where there is no more death, no more sorrow, because there is no sin. My dear brother you have now another guardian angel ever near you. I imagine you almost felt her presence with you, on that long, desolate ride home, after seeing her body consigned to the dust. Oh! such love as she bore to you here, will still follow you till you are reunited on the happy shore, where there is no more parting.

L.

Biography

Jean Lowery Wilson grew up in a family of voracious readers, and has long shared their passion for the written word. She and her husband live on their family farm with their hens, roosters, cats, and a dog. When not immersed in a book, she enjoys spending time with their three married children and their spouses, and seven wonderful grandchildren. Traveling, history, and outdoor activities are some of her favorite things. A member of New Harmony Presbyterian Church (PCA) in Clarendon County, Jean prays that with this publication, all glory will be given to her Lord and Savior, Jesus Christ.

CPSIA information can be obtained
at www.ICGtesting.com
Printed in the USA
BVHW051656100523
663941BV00012B/102/J